W9-AGU-333

"**Battle Angel Alita** is as twistedly ultraviolent as **Preacher**, although the bizarre technological ways in which flesh gets mangled, combined with this black-humored future, also bring to mind **The Road Warrior** and **RoboCop**. People don't just get their brains stuck to the wall; they get stuck to the wall *by* their brains."

Wizard Magazine

"**Yukito Kishiro's** story is much more than a science-fiction adventure. Woven into the violent, roller-coaster plot is a strand of philosophical speculation. **Battle Angel Alita** takes us to a world where technology blurs the boundaries between human and machine, begging the question 'What makes us who we are?'

Amazon.com

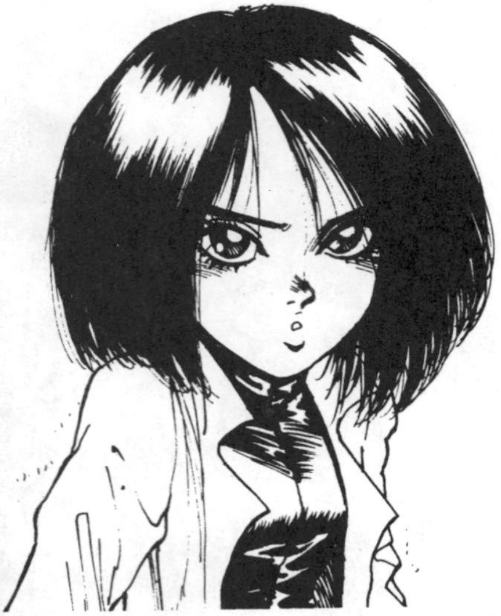

VIZ GRAPHIC NOVEL

TEARS OF AN ANGEL

A BATTLE ANGEL ALITA GRAPHIC NOVEL

STORY AND ART BY
YUKITO KISHIRO

CONTENTS

OUT OF BLUE SKY

IRON MAIDEN

RAINY DAYS

BITTER DREAMS

BEYOND THE CLOUDS

STORY AND ART BY YUKITO KISHIRO

Translation/Fred Burke & Sterling Bell and Matt Thorn
Touch-Up Art & Lettering/Wayne Truman
Cover Design/Viz Graphics
Editors/Satoru Fujii & Trish Ledoux
V.P. of Sales & Marketing/Rick Bauer
Assistant Editor/Toshifumi Yoshida
Publisher/Seiji Horibuchi
Editor-in-Chief/Hyoe Narita

First published as *Gunnm* by Shueisha Inc. in Japan

Printed in Canada
Nineth printing, June 2001
Tenth printing, April 2002

741.5
952
Kish

• get your own vizmail.net email account
• register for the weekly email newsletter
• sign up for your free catalog
• voice 1-800-394-3042 fax 415-384-8936
www.viz.com

Get your free Viz Shop-By-Mail catalog! (800) 394-3042 or fax (415) 546-7086

Published by Viz Communications Inc.
P.O. Box 77010 • San Francisco, CA 94107

YUKITO KISHIRO'S GRAPHIC NOVELS TO DATE:

BATTLE ANGEL ALITA   ANGEL OF REDEMPTION   FALLEN ANGEL
TEARS OF AN ANGEL   ANGEL OF DEATH   ANGEL'S ASCENSION
KILLING ANGEL   ANGEL OF CHAOS   ASHEN VICTOR
ANGEL OF VICTORY

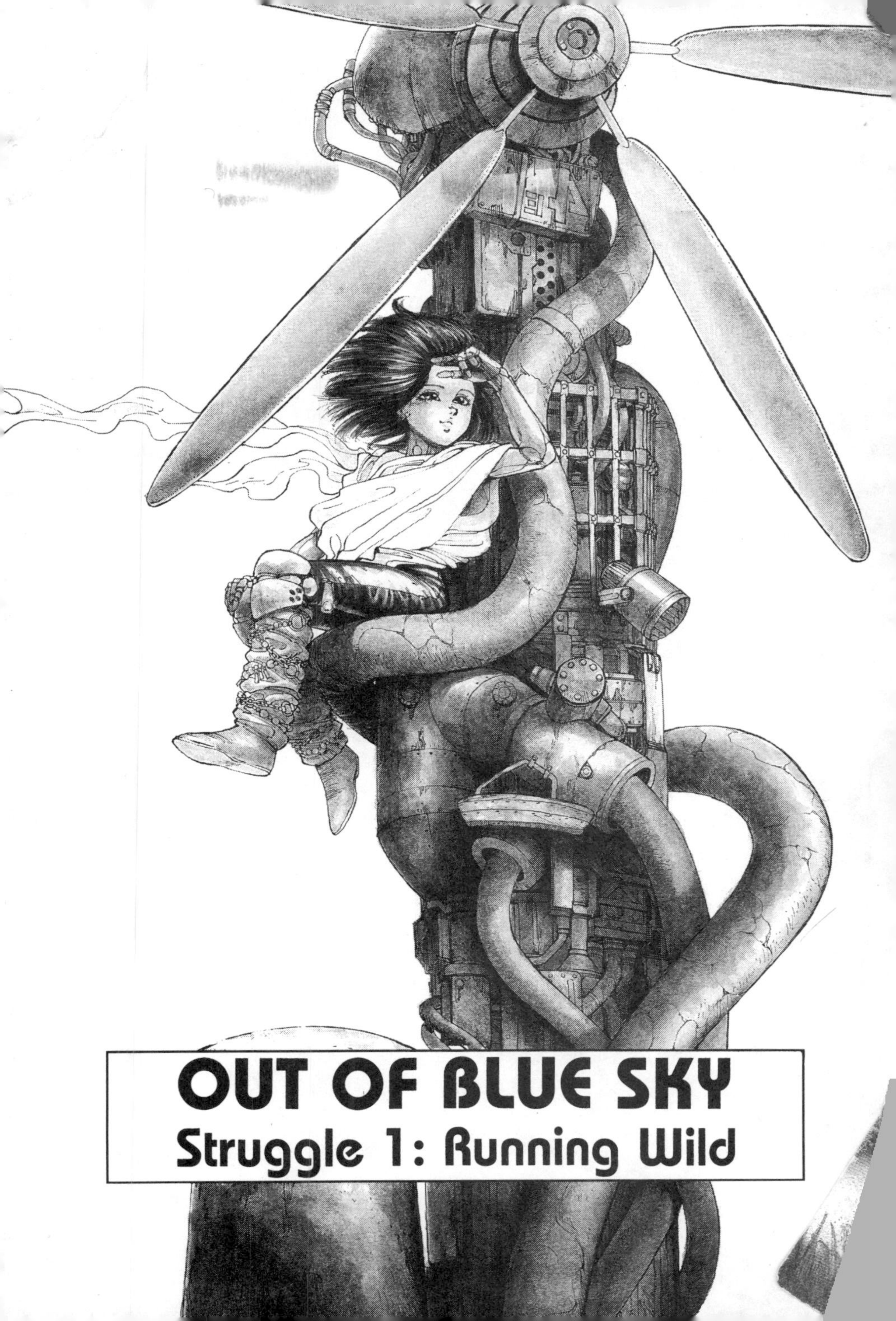

OUT OF BLUE SKY

Struggle 1: Running Wild

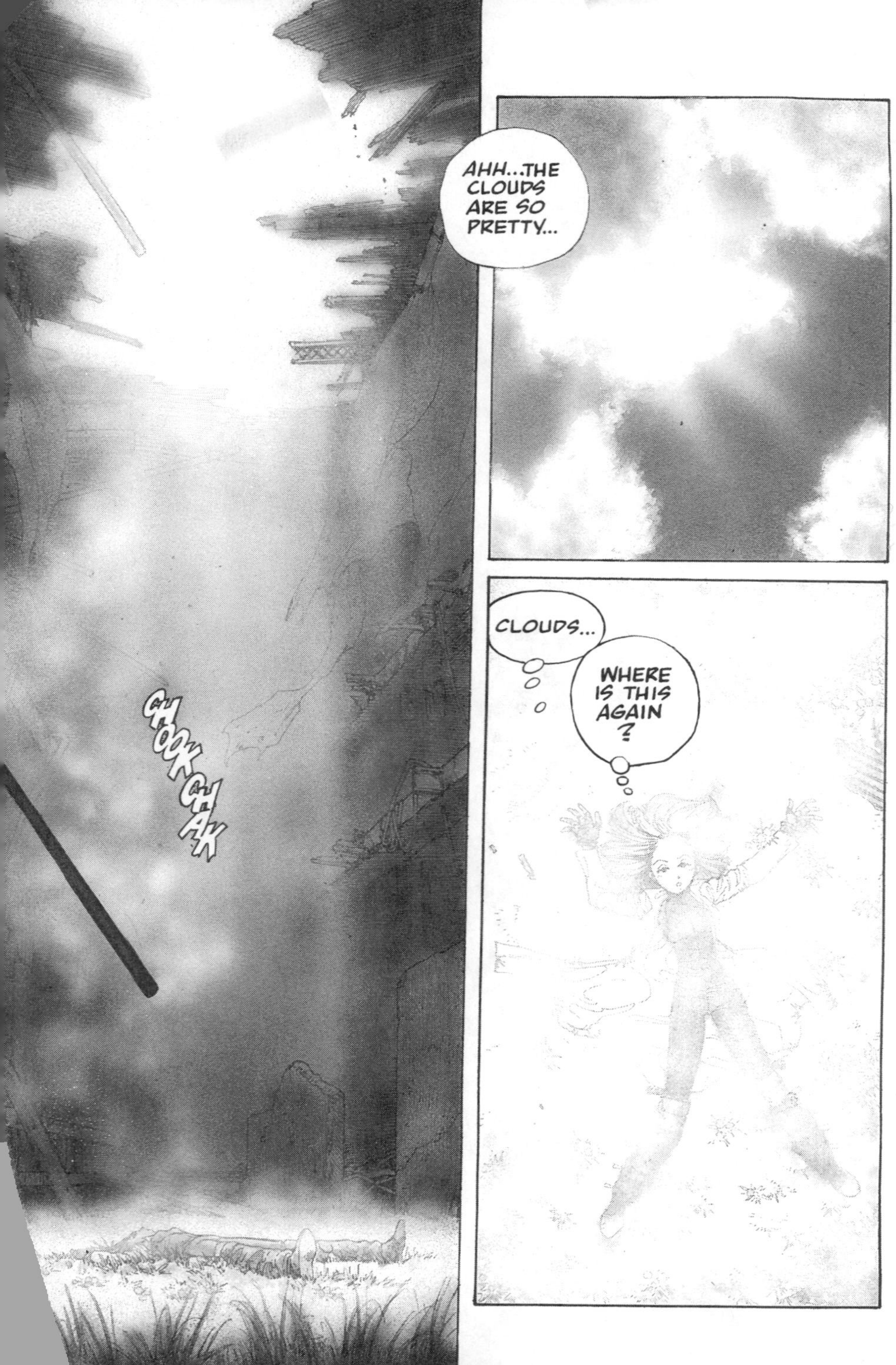
CHOOK CHAK
AHH...THE CLOUDS ARE SO PRETTY...
CLOUDS...
WHERE IS THIS AGAIN?

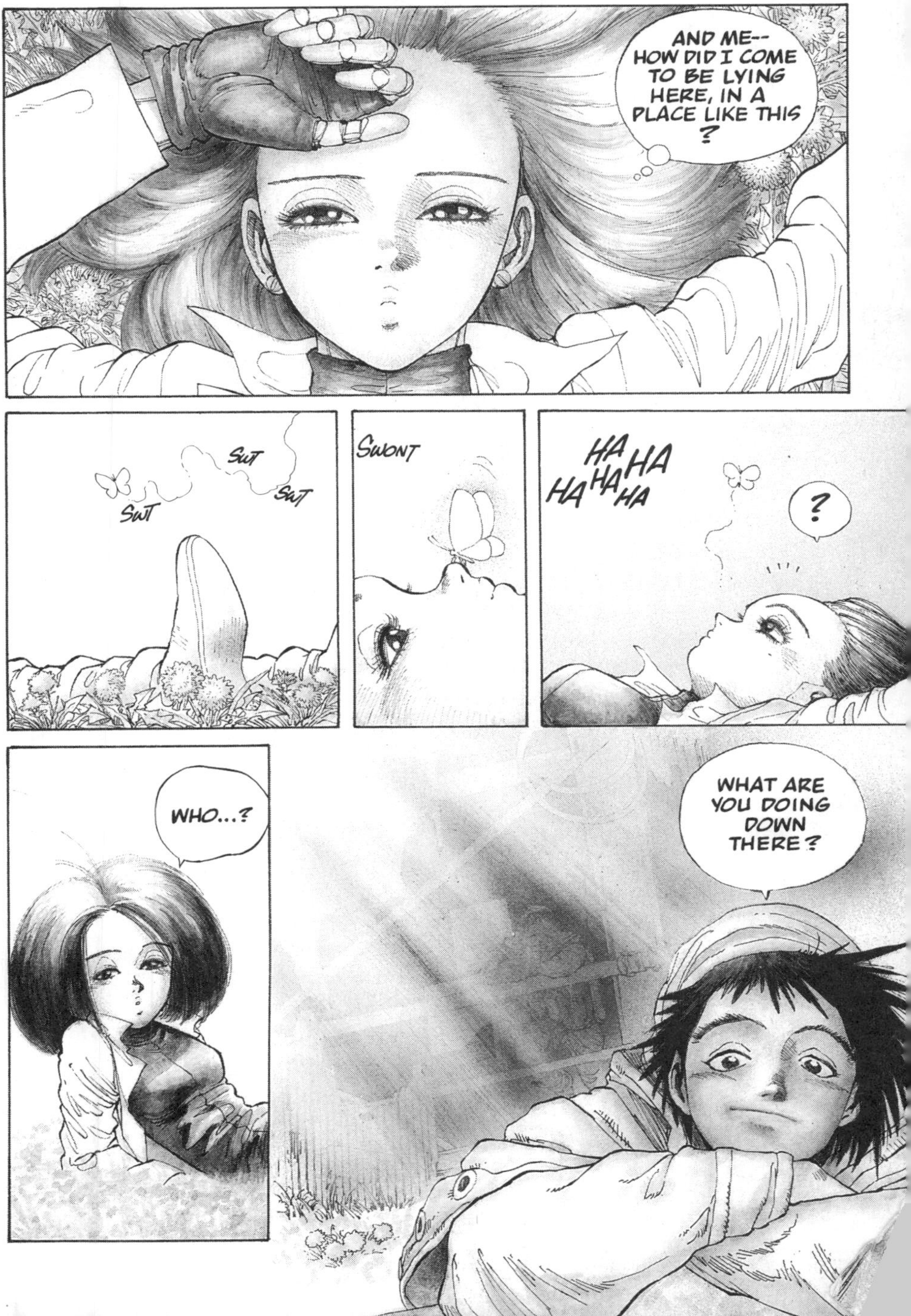
AND ME--
HOW DID I COME TO BE LYING HERE, IN A PLACE LIKE THIS ?
SWT
SWT
SWT
SWONT
HA HA HA HA HA HA
?
WHO...?
WHAT ARE YOU DOING DOWN THERE?

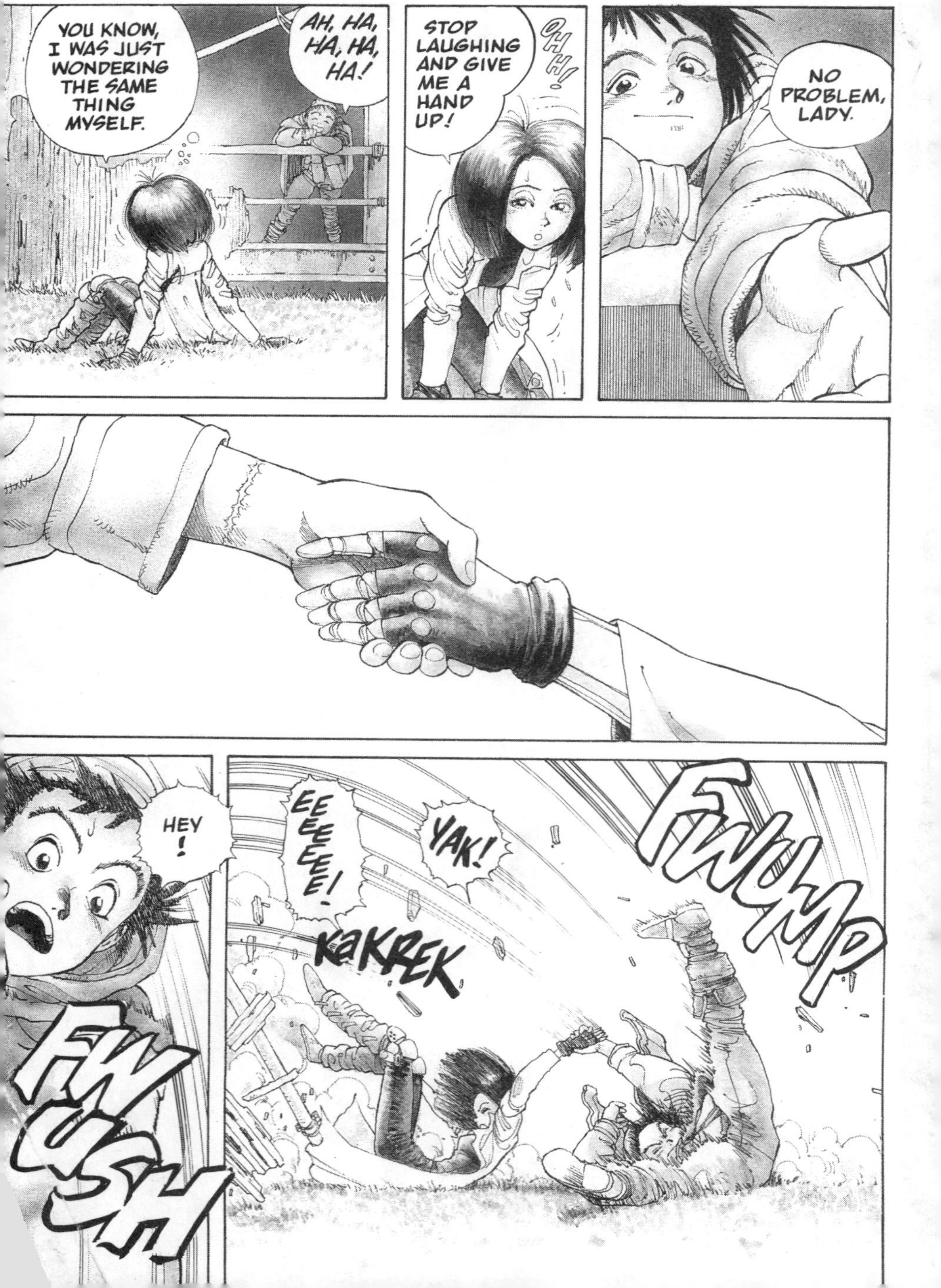
YOU KNOW, I WAS JUST WONDERING THE SAME THING MYSELF.
AH, HA, HA, HA, HA!
STOP LAUGHING AND GIVE ME A HAND UP!
OHH!
NO PROBLEM, LADY.
HEY!
FWUSH
EEEEEEE!
YAK!
KaKREK
FWUMP

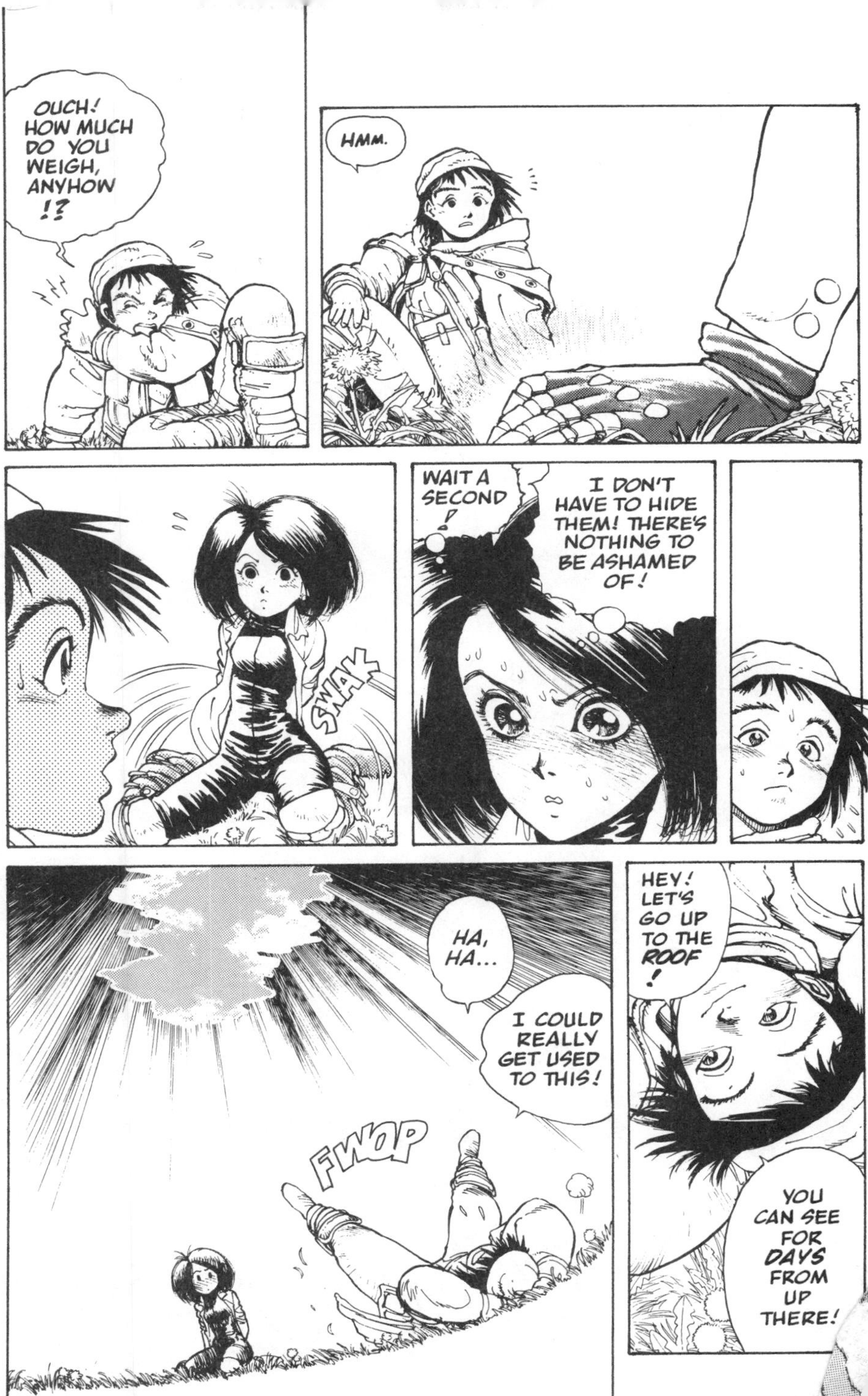
OUCH! HOW MUCH DO YOU WEIGH, ANYHOW !?
HMM.
SWAK
WAIT A SECOND !
I DON'T HAVE TO HIDE THEM! THERE'S NOTHING TO BE ASHAMED OF!
HA, HA...
I COULD REALLY GET USED TO THIS!
FWOP
HEY! LET'S GO UP TO THE ROOF !
YOU CAN SEE FOR DAYS FROM UP THERE!

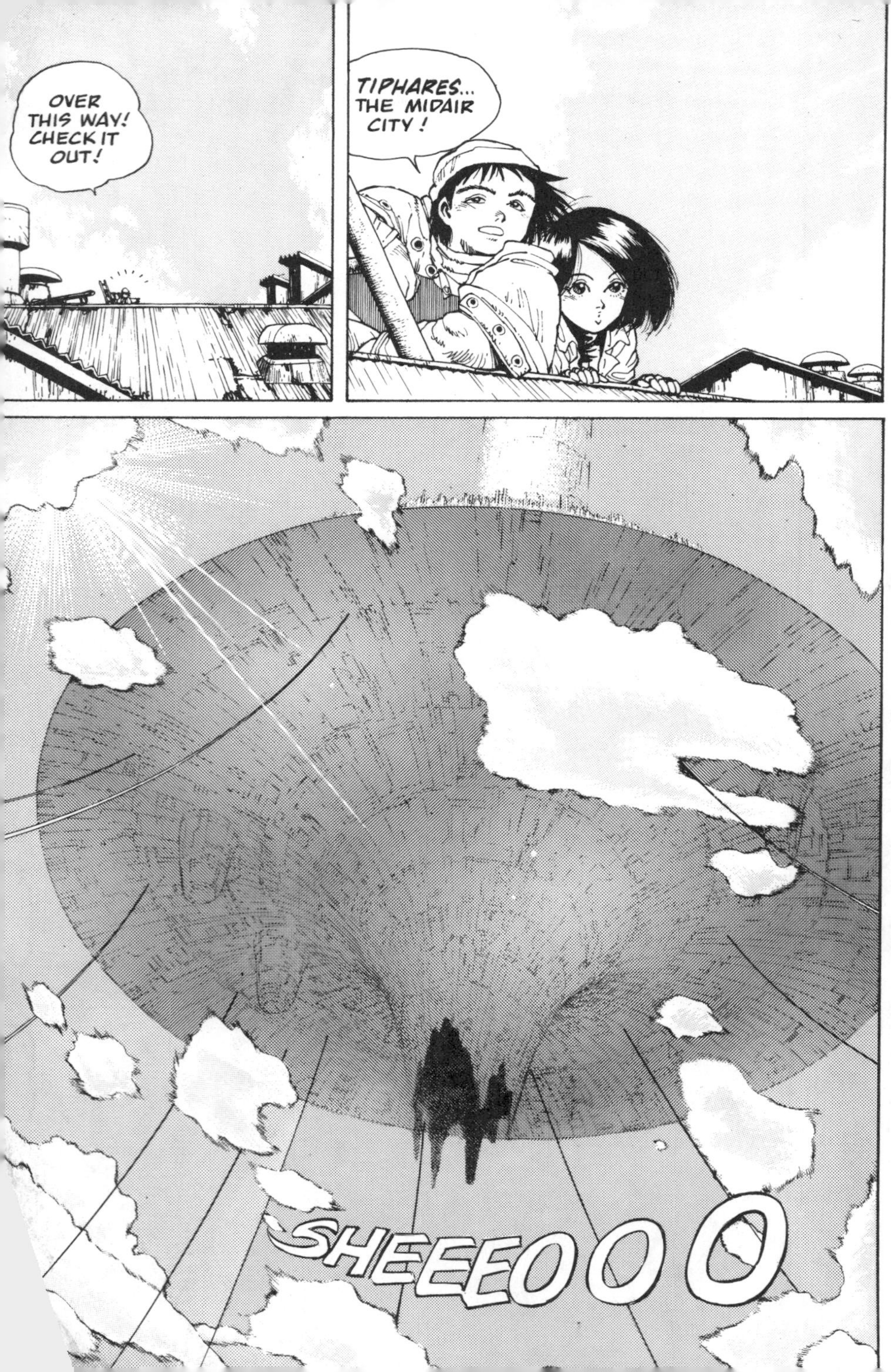
OVER THIS WAY! CHECK IT OUT!
TIPHARES... THE MIDAIR CITY!
SHEEEOOO

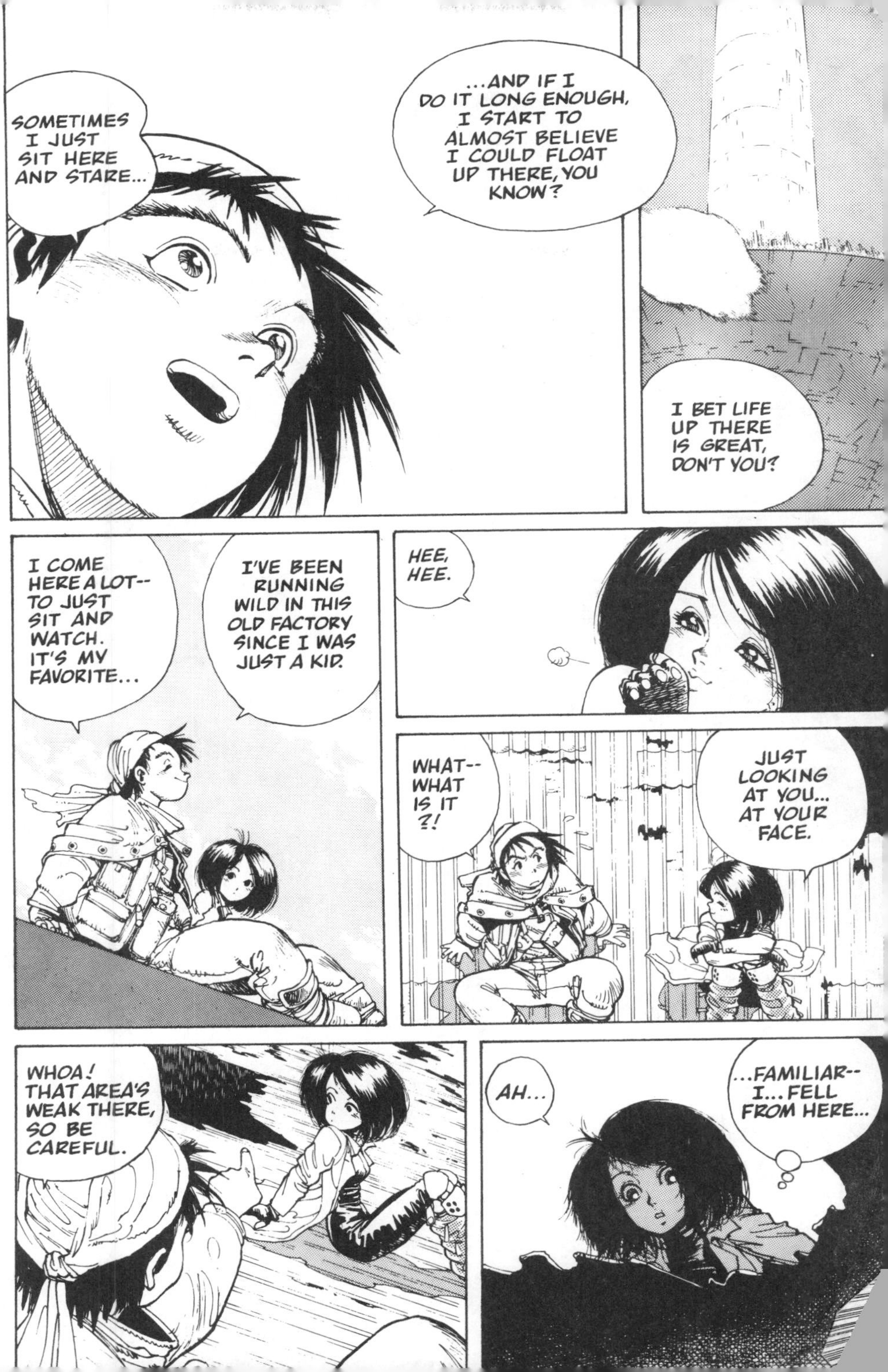
SOMETIMES I JUST SIT HERE AND STARE...
...AND IF I DO IT LONG ENOUGH, I START TO ALMOST BELIEVE I COULD FLOAT UP THERE, YOU KNOW?
I BET LIFE UP THERE IS GREAT, DON'T YOU?
I COME HERE A LOT-- TO JUST SIT AND WATCH. IT'S MY FAVORITE...
I'VE BEEN RUNNING WILD IN THIS OLD FACTORY SINCE I WAS JUST A KID.
HEE, HEE.
WHAT-- WHAT IS IT ?!
JUST LOOKING AT YOU... AT YOUR FACE.
WHOA! THAT AREA'S WEAK THERE, SO BE CAREFUL.
AH...
...FAMILIAR-- I...FELL FROM HERE...

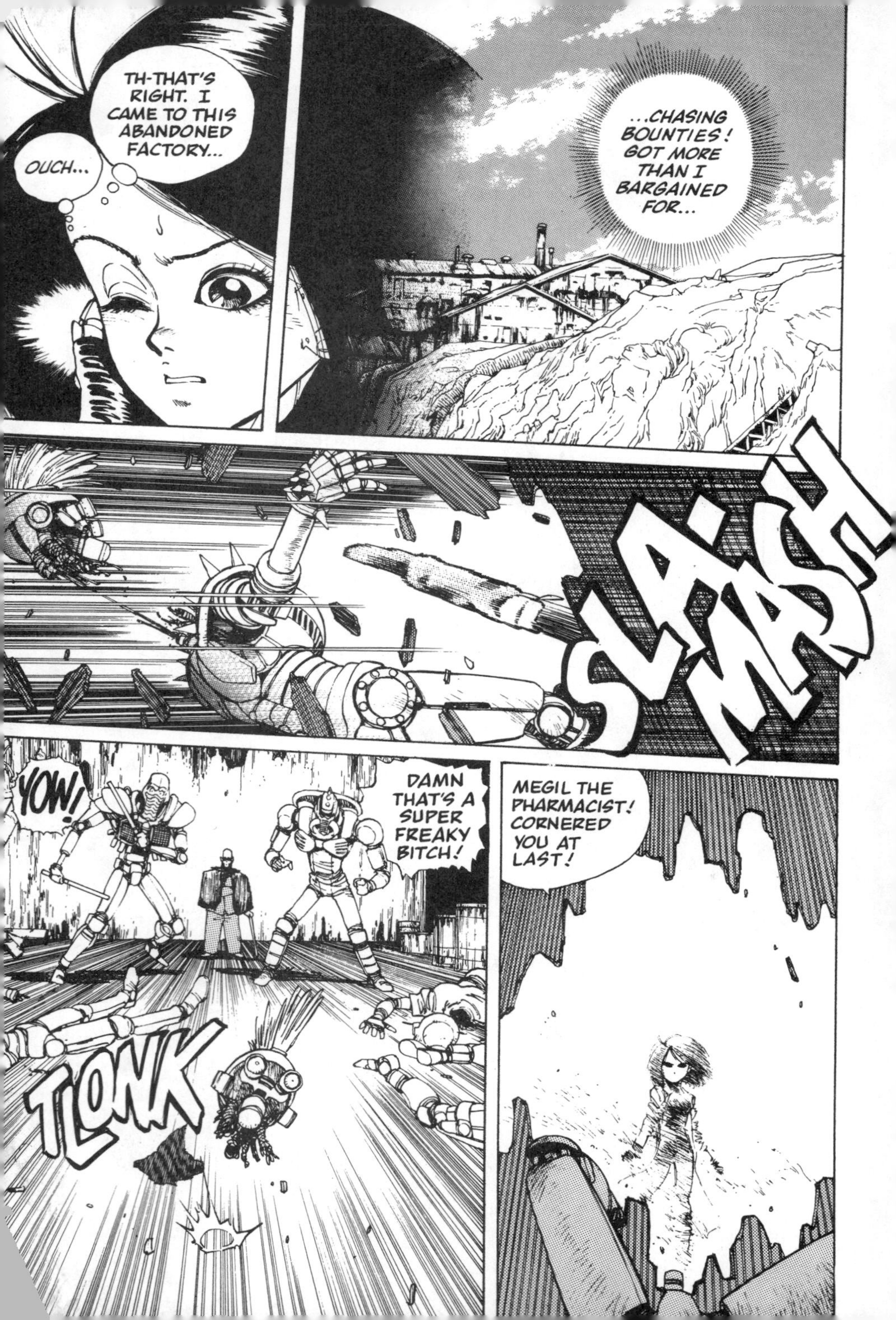

TH-THAT'S RIGHT. I CAME TO THIS ABANDONED FACTORY...
OUCH...
...CHASING BOUNTIES! GOT MORE THAN I BARGAINED FOR...
SMASH
YOW!
DAMN THAT'S A SUPER FREAKY BITCH!
TLONK
MEGIL THE PHARMACIST! CORNERED YOU AT LAST!

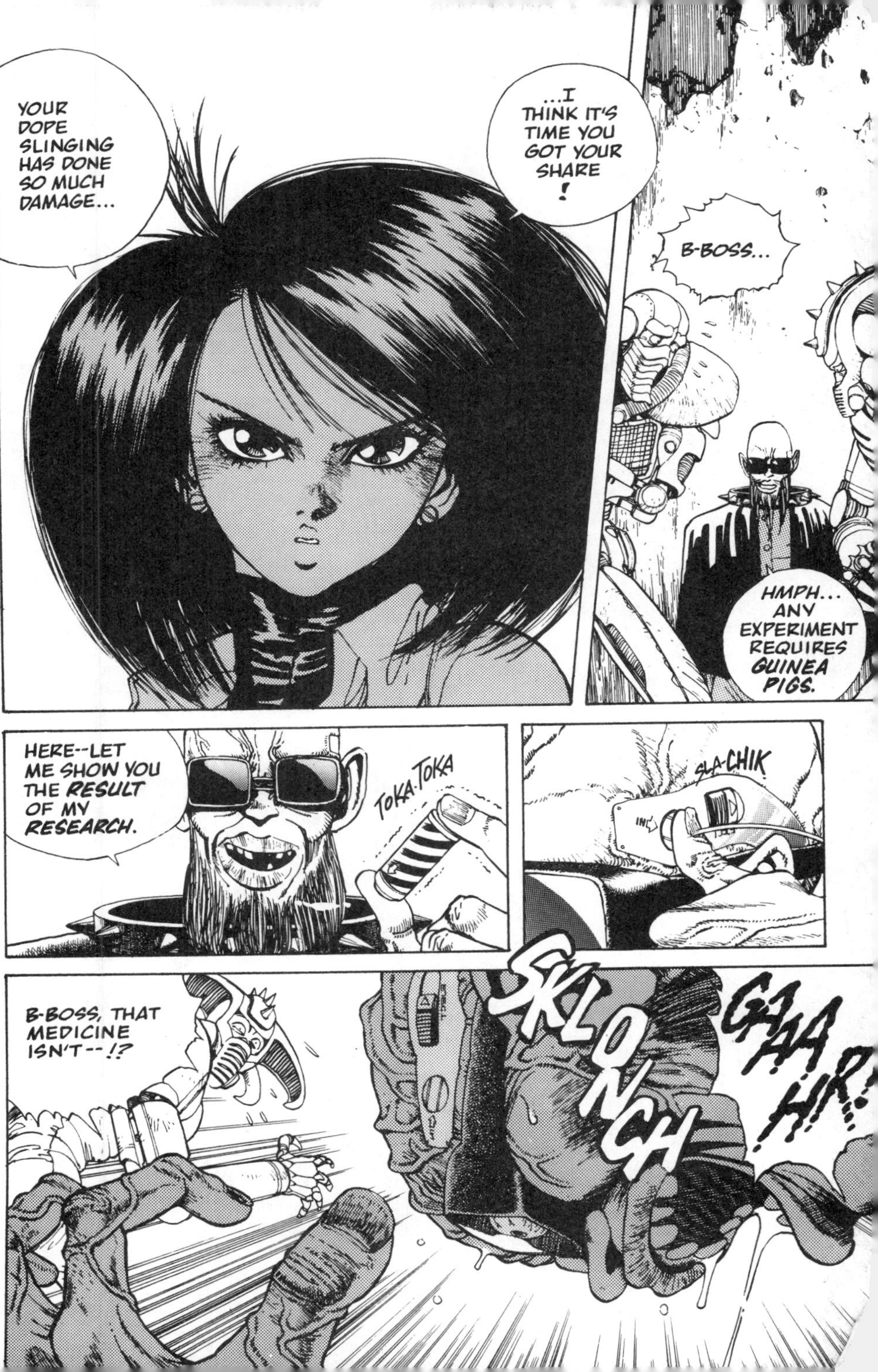
YOUR DOPE SLINGING HAS DONE SO MUCH DAMAGE...
...I THINK IT'S TIME YOU GOT YOUR SHARE!
B-BOSS...
HMPH... ANY EXPERIMENT REQUIRES GUINEA PIGS.
HERE--LET ME SHOW YOU THE RESULT OF MY RESEARCH.
TOKA TOKA
SLA-CHIK
IN
B-BOSS, THAT MEDICINE ISN'T--!?
SKLONCH
GAAAHR!!

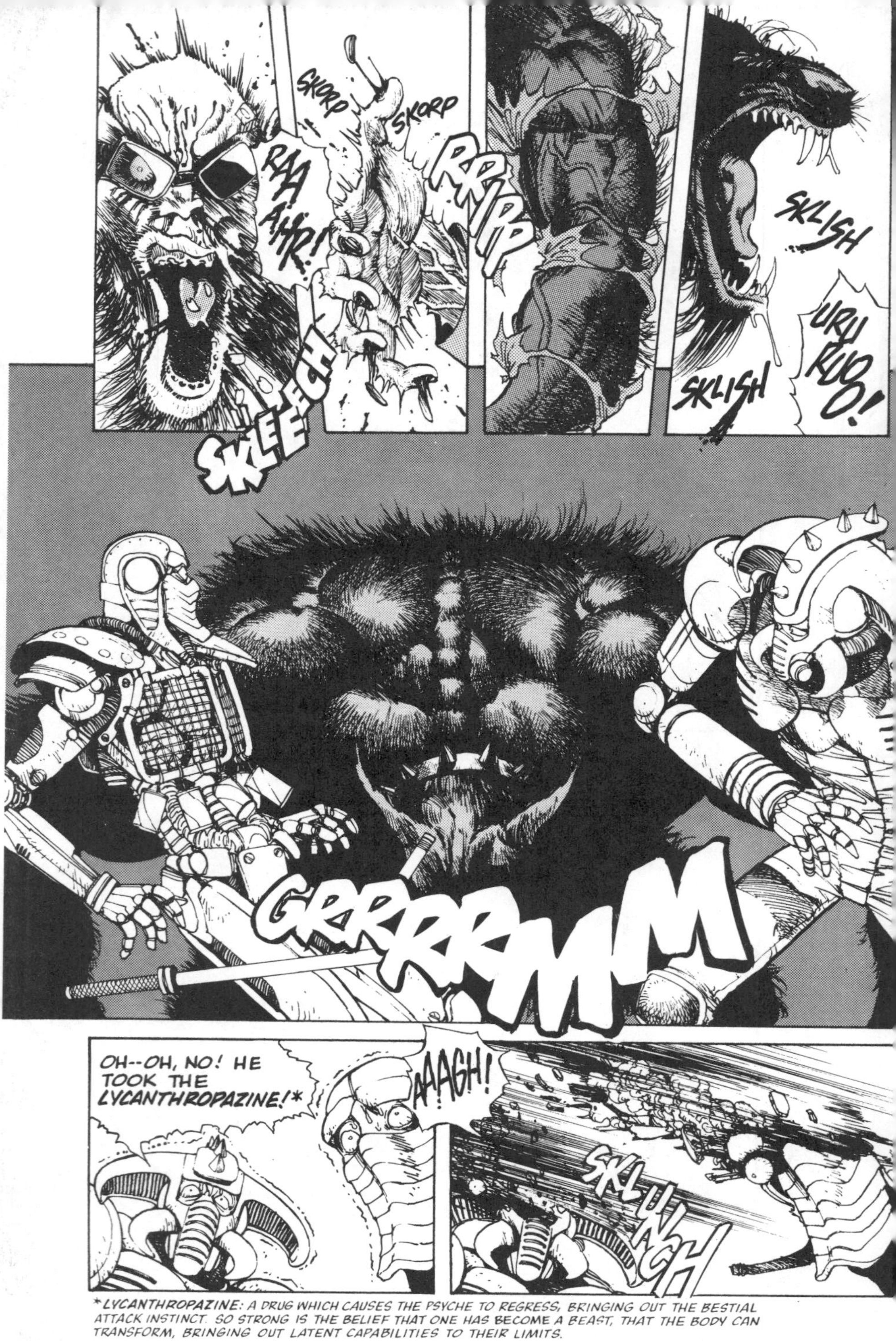
RAAAARR!
SKLEEECH
SKORP
SKORP
RRRIPP
SKLISH
URU RUOO!
SKLISH
GRRRRMM
OH--OH, NO! HE TOOK THE *LYCANTHROPAZINE!**
AAAGH!
SKLUNCH

**LYCANTHROPAZINE:* A DRUG WHICH CAUSES THE PSYCHE TO REGRESS, BRINGING OUT THE BESTIAL ATTACK INSTINCT. SO STRONG IS THE BELIEF THAT ONE HAS BECOME A BEAST, THAT THE BODY CAN TRANSFORM, BRINGING OUT LATENT CAPABILITIES TO THEIR LIMITS.

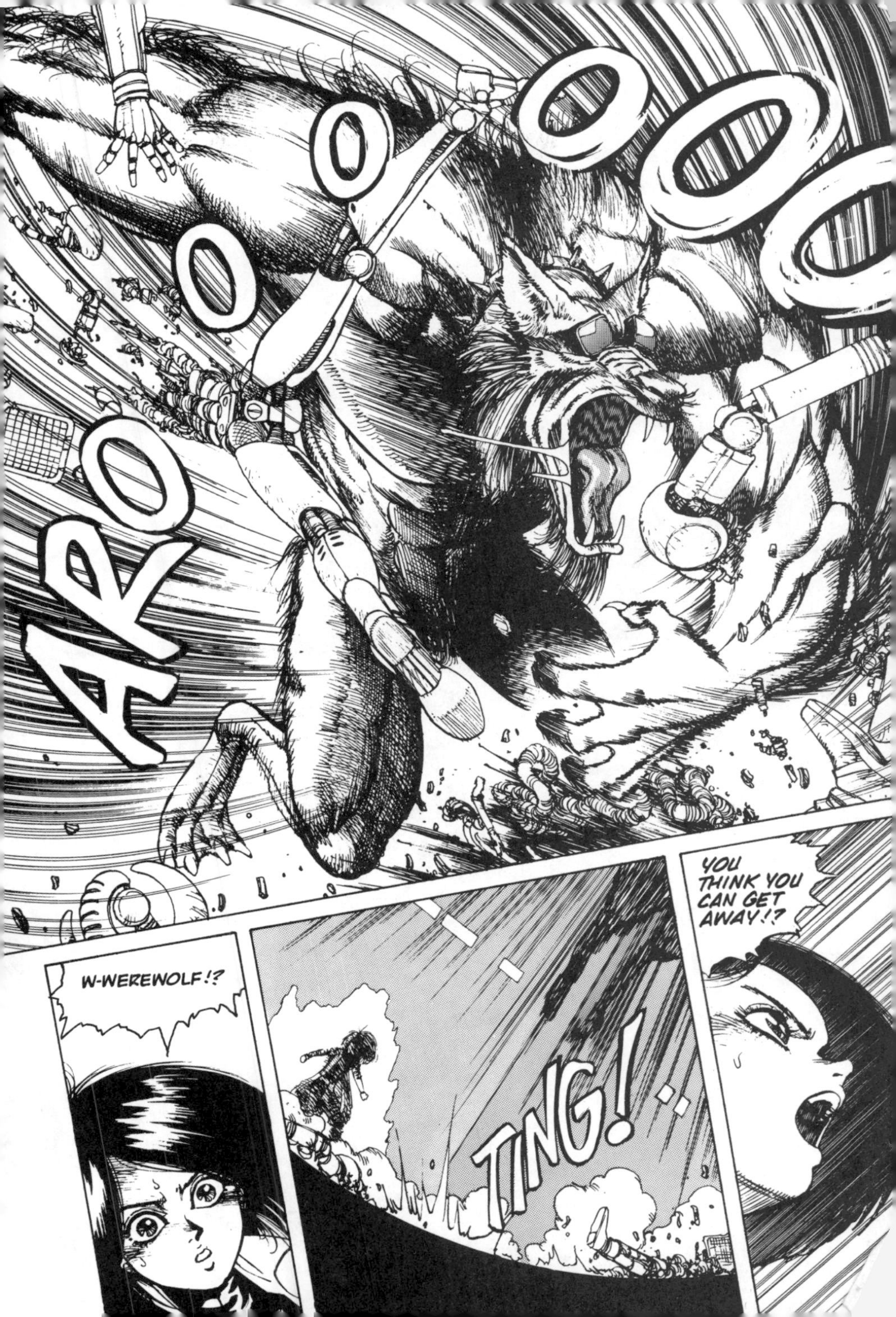
AROOOOOO
W-WEREWOLF!?
TING!
YOU THINK YOU CAN GET AWAY!?

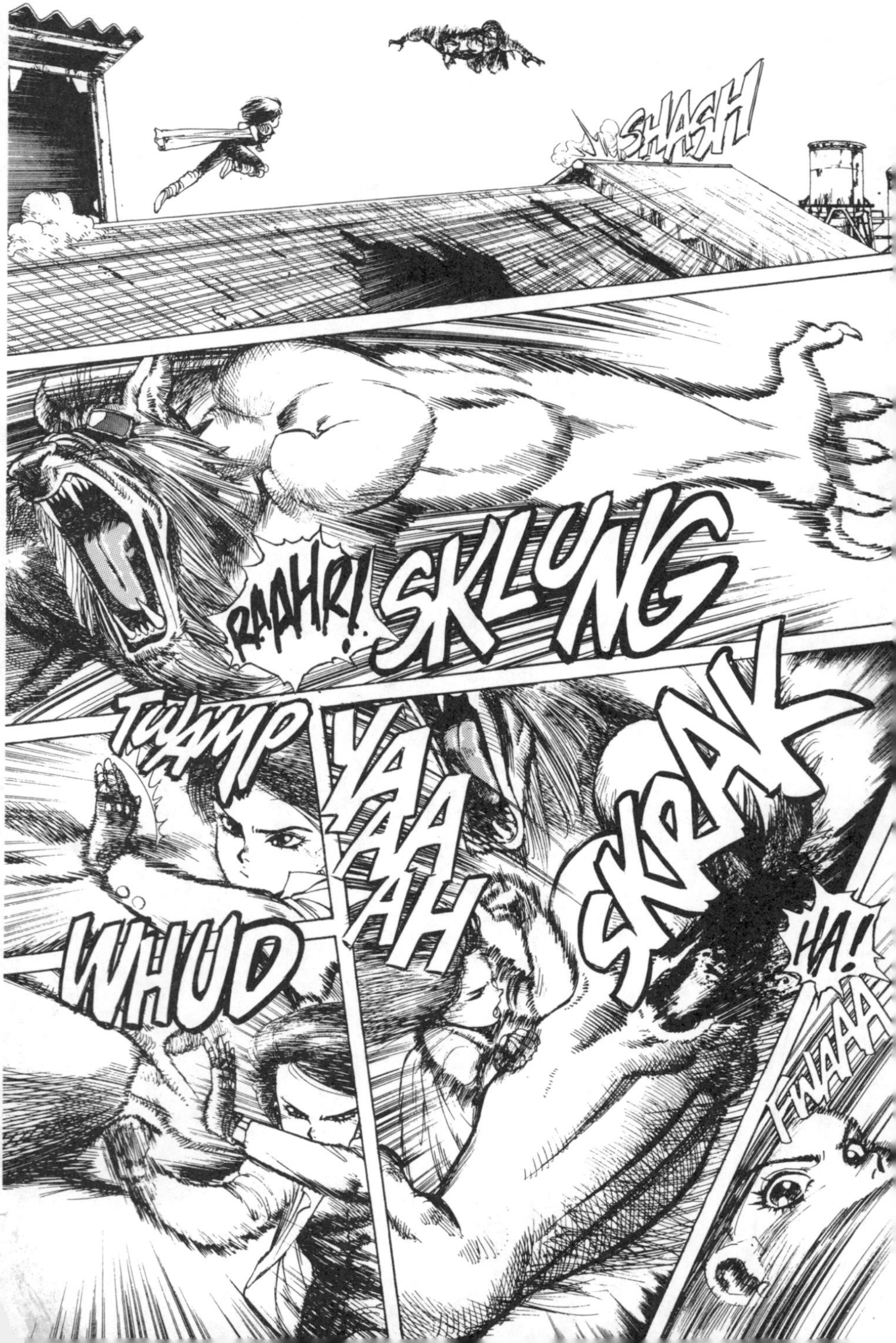
SHASH
RAAHR!
SKLUNG
THAMP
YAAAAH
SKRAK
WHUD
HA!
FWAAA

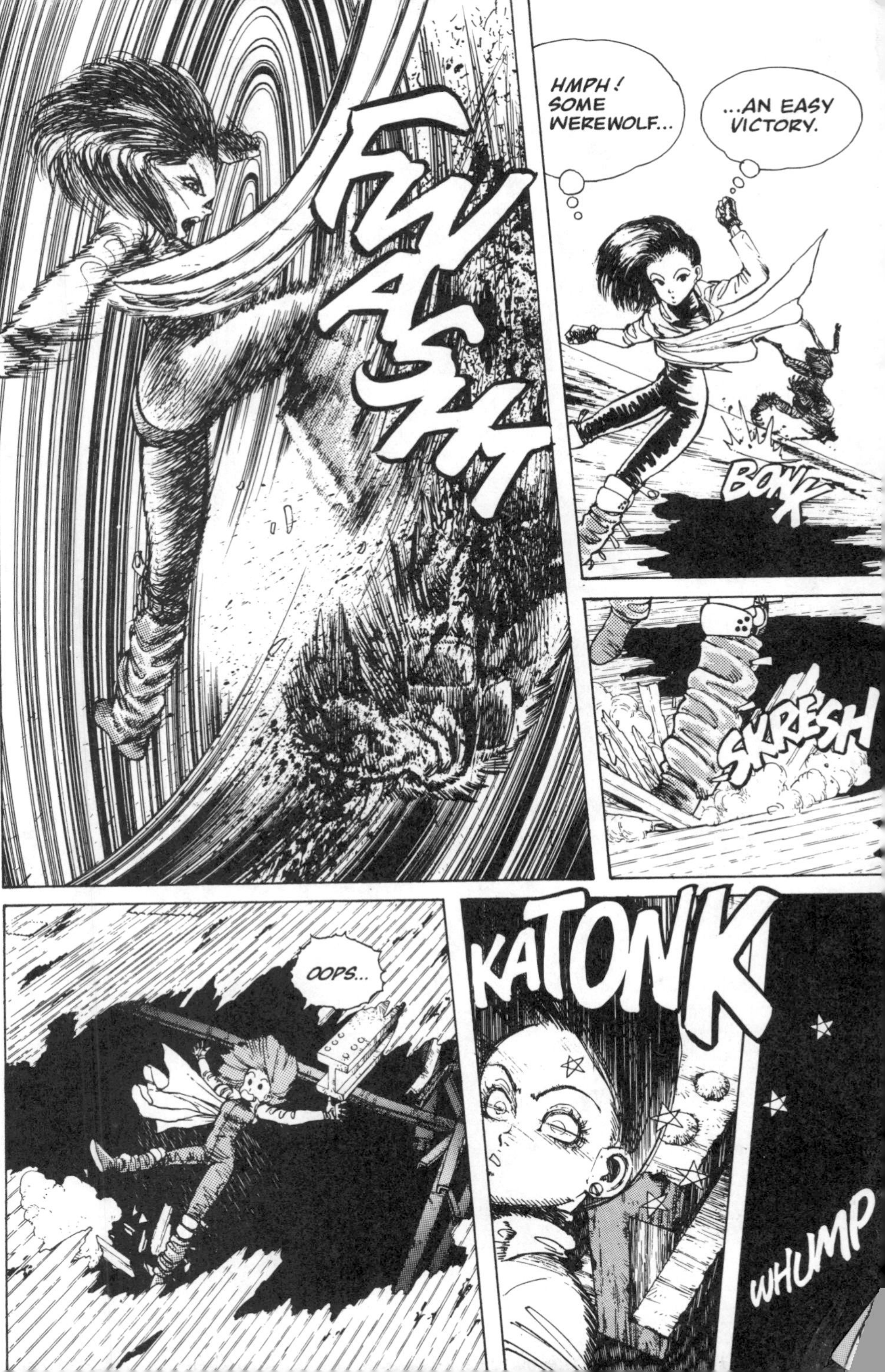
FWASHT
HMPH! SOME WEREWOLF...
...AN EASY VICTORY.
BONK
SKRESH
OOPS...
KATONK
WHUMP

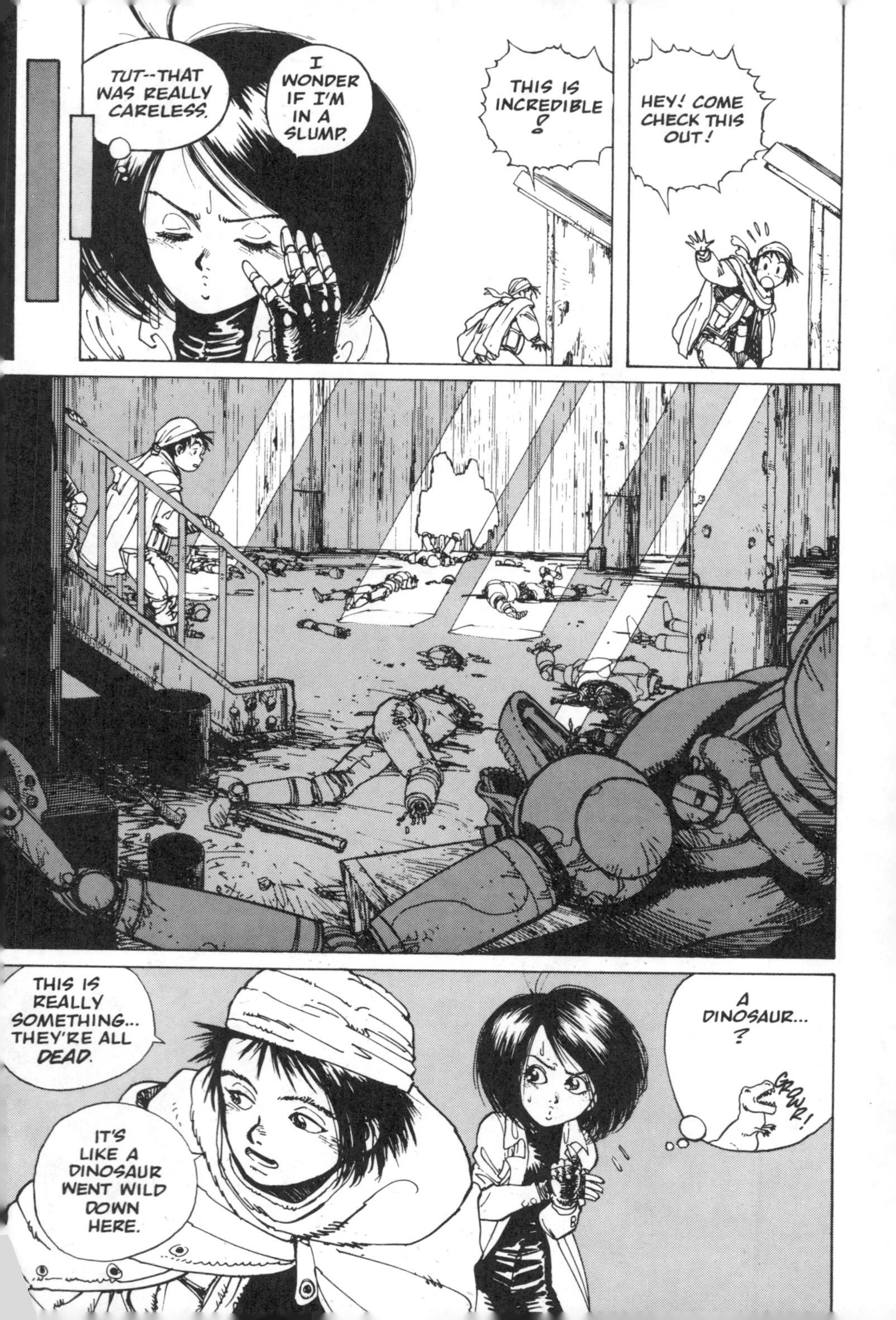
TUT--THAT WAS REALLY CARELESS.
I WONDER IF I'M IN A SLUMP.
THIS IS INCREDIBLE!
HEY! COME CHECK THIS OUT!
THIS IS REALLY SOMETHING... THEY'RE ALL DEAD.
IT'S LIKE A DINOSAUR WENT WILD DOWN HERE.
A DINOSAUR...?
GROWR!

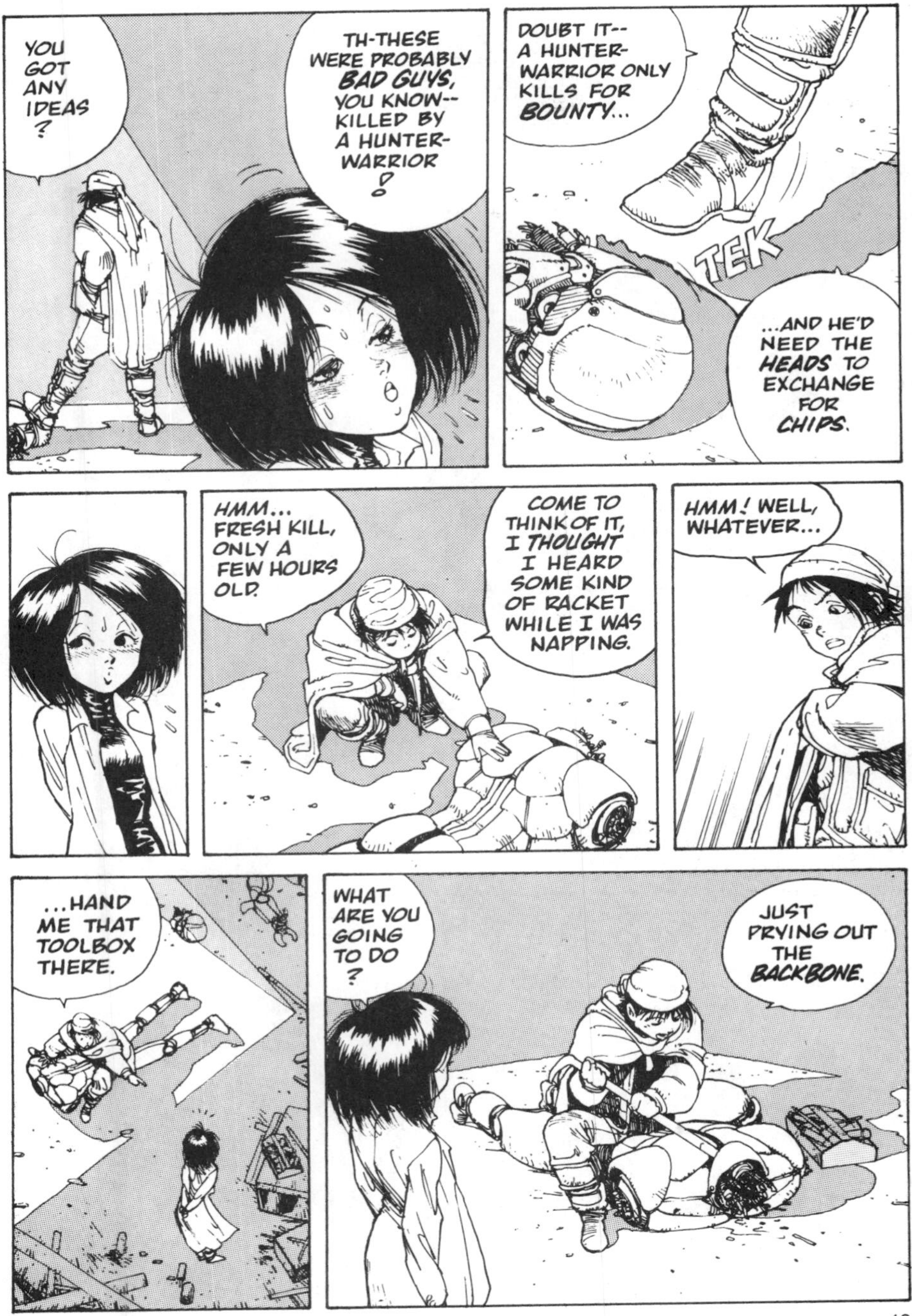
YOU GOT ANY IDEAS ?
TH-THESE WERE PROBABLY BAD GUYS, YOU KNOW-- KILLED BY A HUNTER-WARRIOR !?
DOUBT IT-- A HUNTER-WARRIOR ONLY KILLS FOR BOUNTY...
TEK
...AND HE'D NEED THE HEADS TO EXCHANGE FOR CHIPS.
HMM... FRESH KILL, ONLY A FEW HOURS OLD.
COME TO THINK OF IT, I THOUGHT I HEARD SOME KIND OF RACKET WHILE I WAS NAPPING.
HMM! WELL, WHATEVER...
...HAND ME THAT TOOLBOX THERE.
WHAT ARE YOU GOING TO DO ?
JUST PRYING OUT THE BACKBONE.

BACKBONE
!?

THAT'S RIGHT. IT'LL BRING IN A GOOD PRICE AT THE PARTS MARKET.

OUCH-- TIGHT FIT!

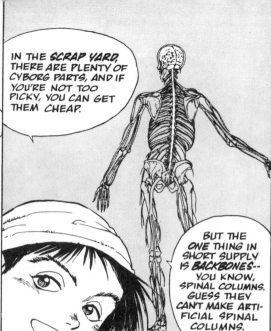

IN THE *SCRAP YARD*, THERE ARE PLENTY OF CYBORG PARTS, AND IF YOU'RE NOT TOO PICKY, YOU CAN GET THEM CHEAP.

BUT THE ONE THING IN SHORT SUPPLY IS *BACKBONES*-- YOU KNOW, SPINAL COLUMNS. GUESS THEY CAN'T MAKE ARTI- FICIAL SPINAL COLUMNS.

YOU CAN'T DO THAT! IT'S LIKE STEALING!

WH-WHAT DO YOU MEAN-- CAN'T !?

IT'S JUST LYING HERE, RIGHT? SAME AS ONE THAT'S BEEN THROWN AWAY! NO SIN.

I'VE GOT TO MAKE MY WAY-- YOU THINK I CAN WORRY ABOUT APPEARANCES !?

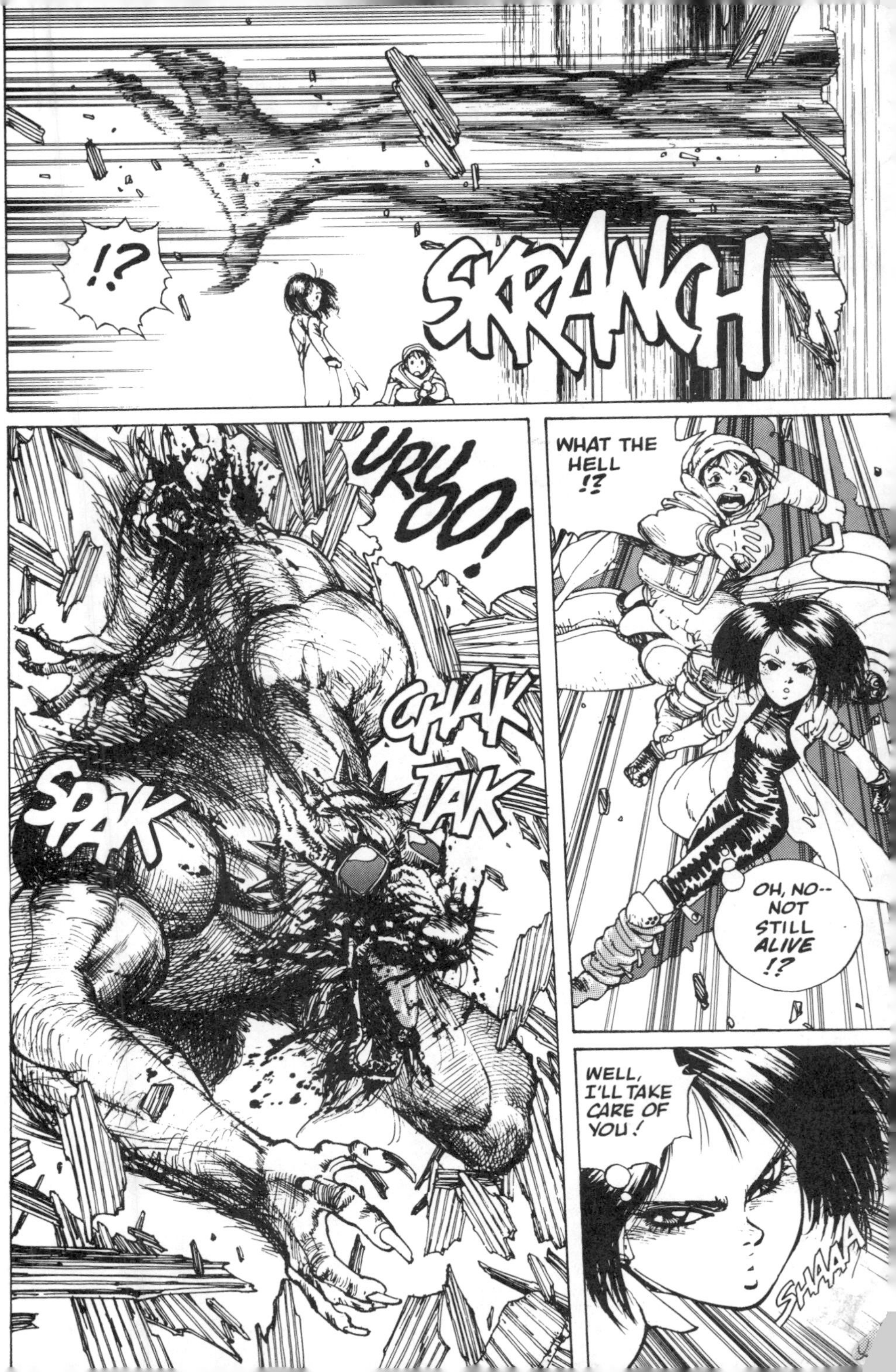
!?
SKRANCH
URUOO!
SPAK
CHAK TAK
WHAT THE HELL !?
OH, NO-- NOT STILL ALIVE !?
WELL, I'LL TAKE CARE OF YOU !
SHAAA

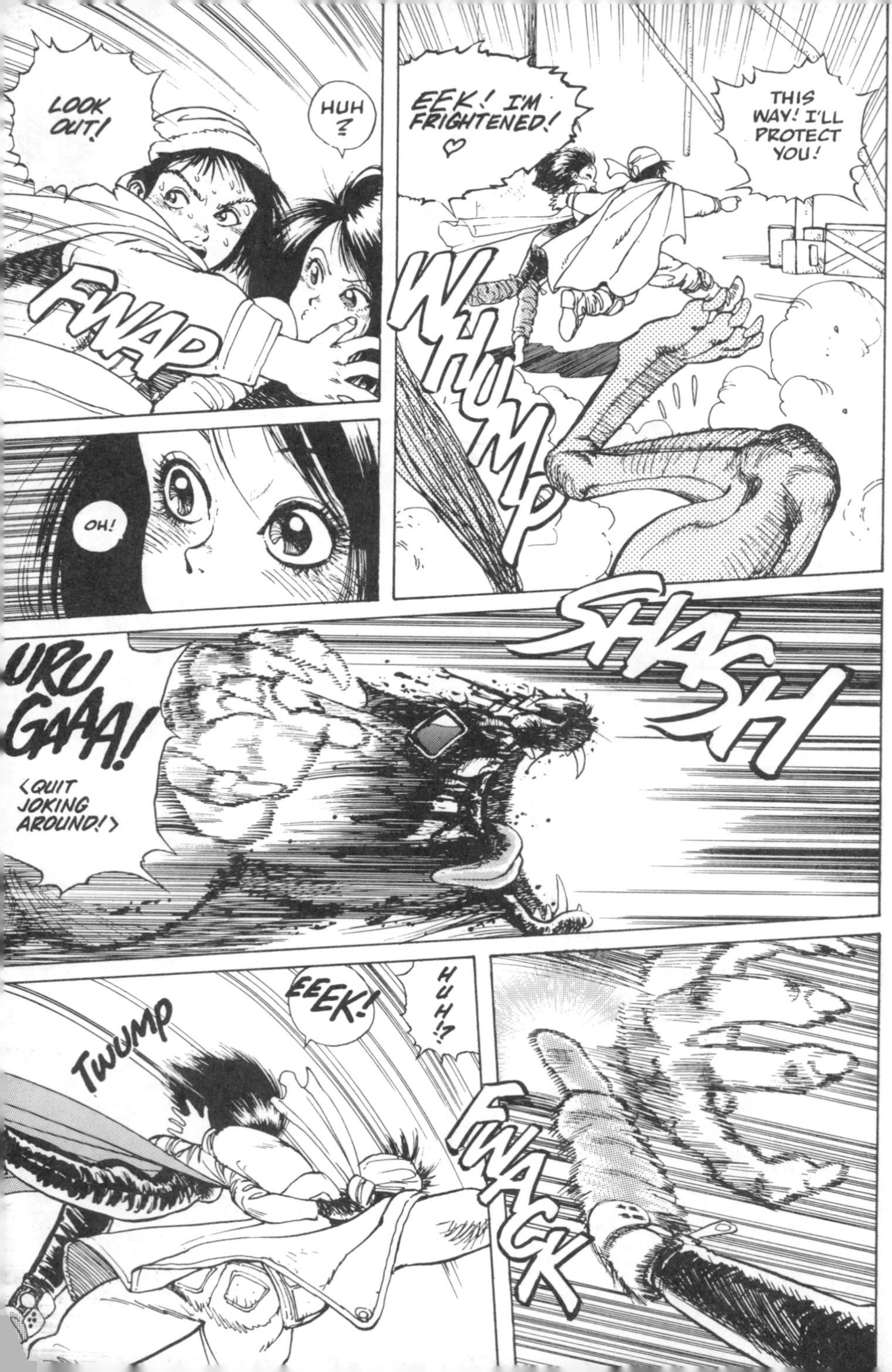
LOOK OUT!
HUH ?
FWAP
EEK! I'M FRIGHTENED! ♡
THIS WAY! I'LL PROTECT YOU!
WHUMP
OH!
SHASH
URU GAAA!
<QUIT JOKING AROUND!>
TWUMP
EEEK!
HUH!?
FWACK

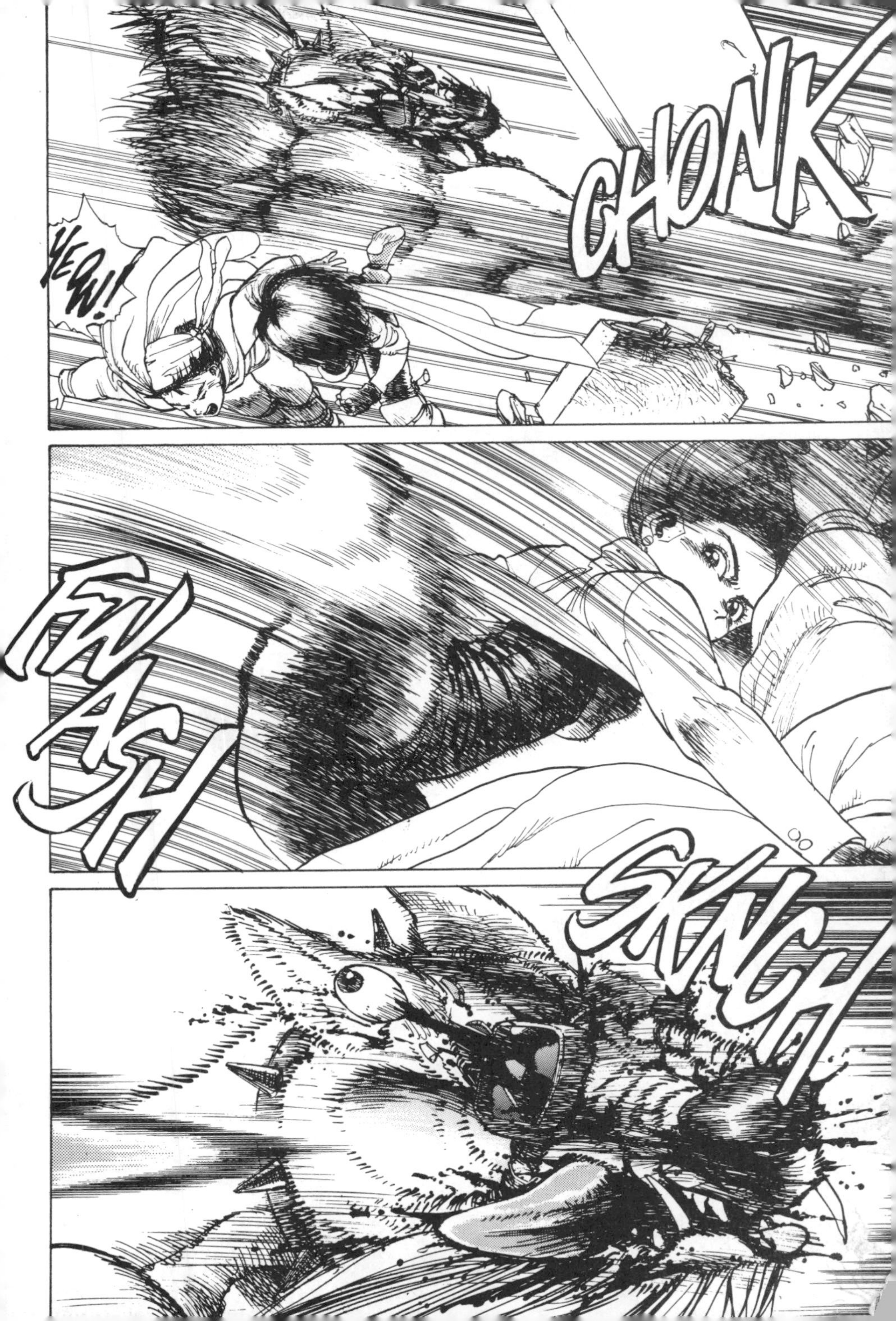
YEOW!
CHONK
FWASH
SKNCH

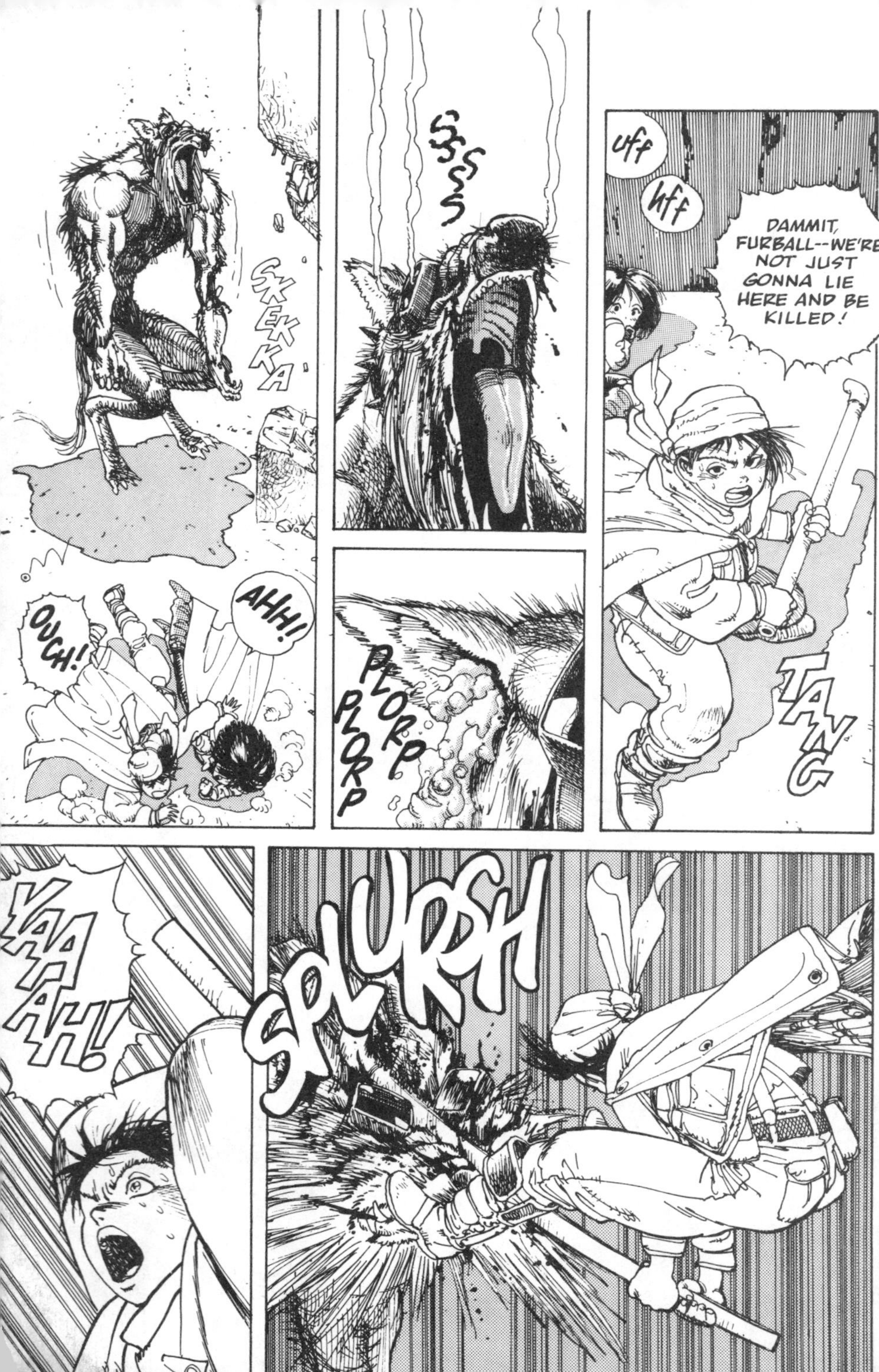

SKEKKA
SSSSSS
uff
hff
DAMMIT, FURBALL--WE'RE NOT JUST GONNA LIE HERE AND BE KILLED!
OUCH!
AHH!
PLORP PLORP PLORP
TANG
YAAAAH!
SPLURSH

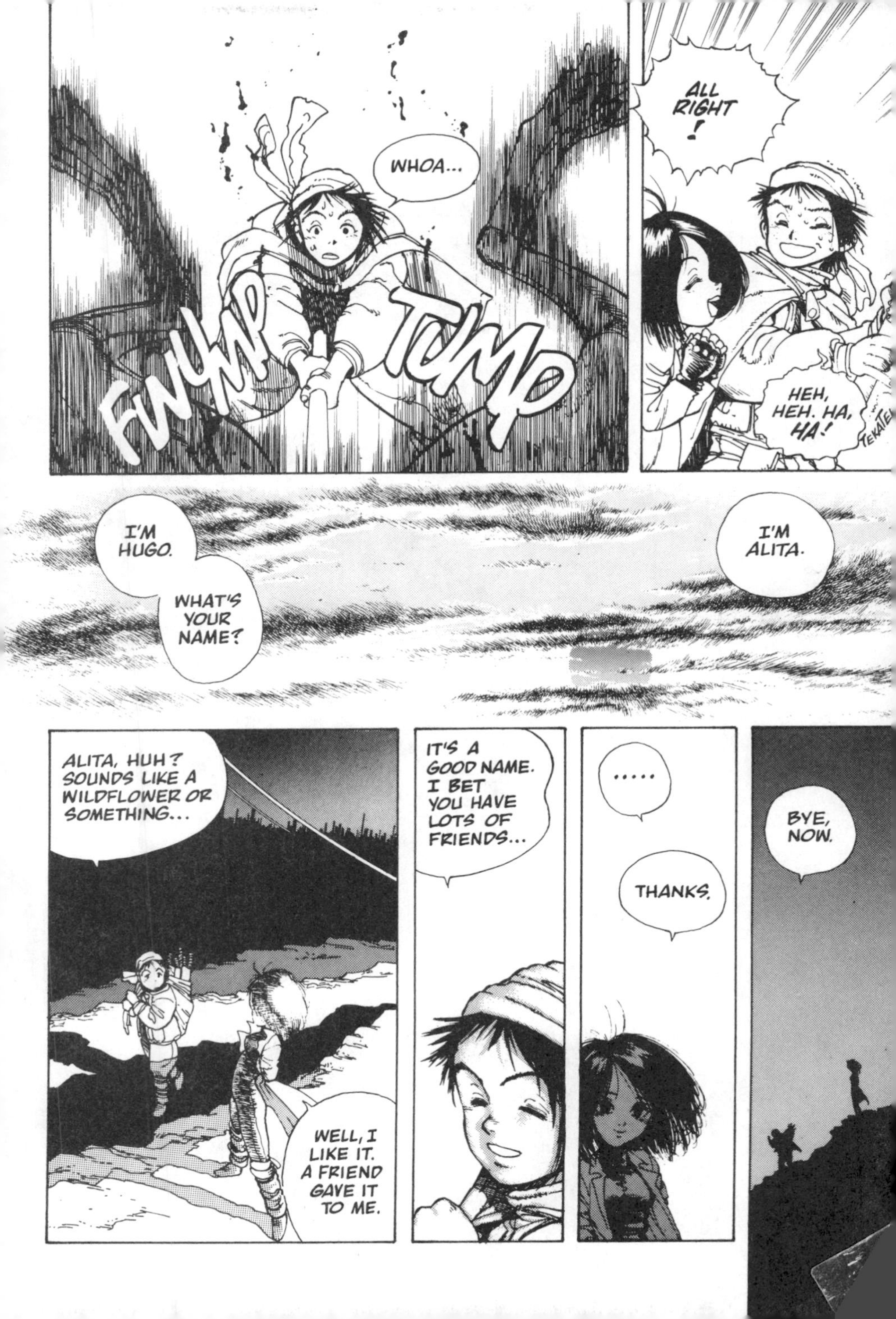
WHOA...
FWUMP
TUMP
ALL RIGHT!
HEH, HEH. HA, HA!
I'M HUGO.
WHAT'S YOUR NAME?
I'M ALITA.
ALITA, HUH? SOUNDS LIKE A WILDFLOWER OR SOMETHING...
WELL, I LIKE IT. A FRIEND GAVE IT TO ME.
IT'S A GOOD NAME. I BET YOU HAVE LOTS OF FRIENDS...
.....
THANKS.
BYE, NOW.

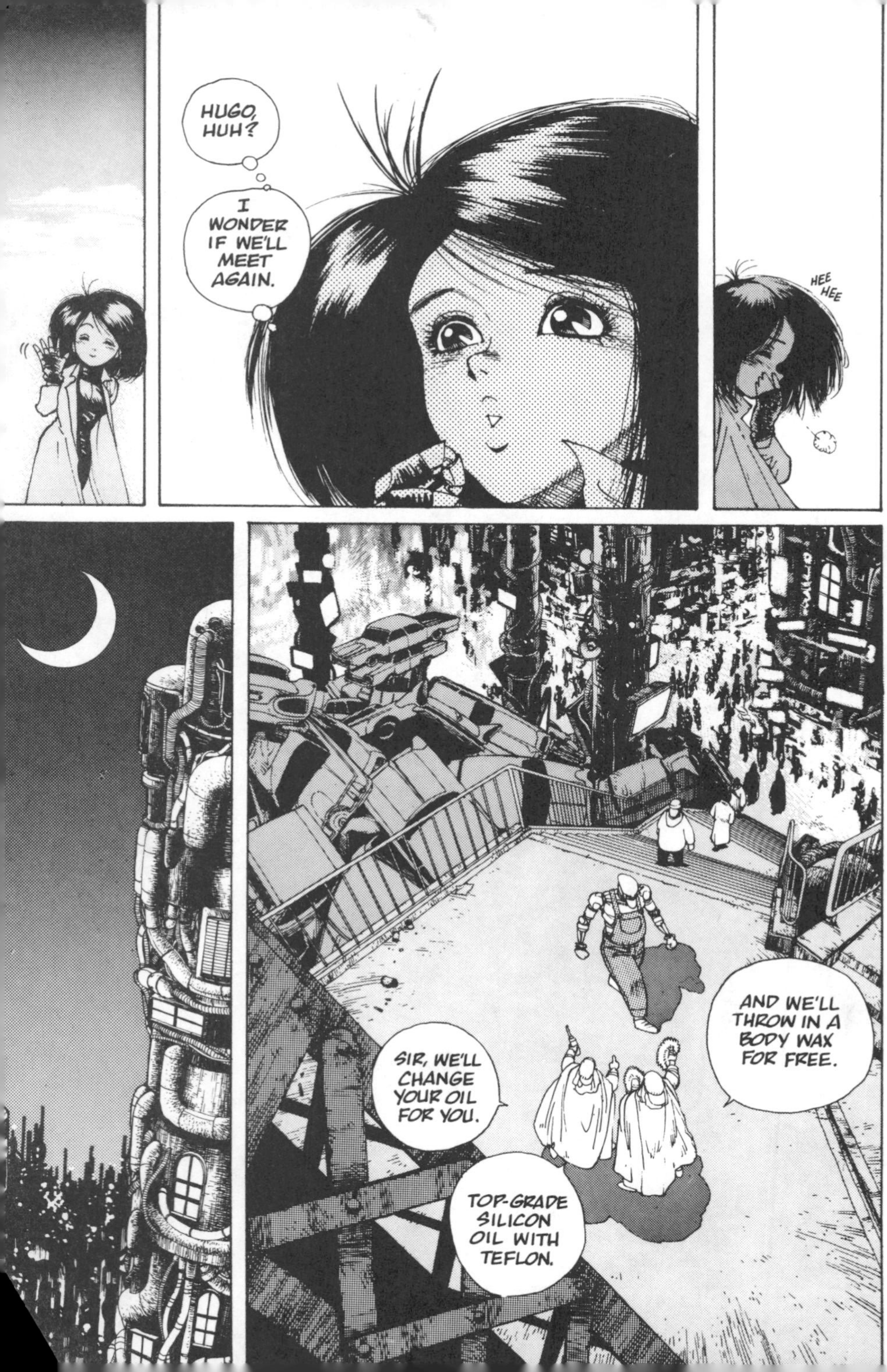
HUGO, HUH?
I WONDER IF WE'LL MEET AGAIN.
HEE HEE
SIR, WE'LL CHANGE YOUR OIL FOR YOU.
TOP-GRADE SILICON OIL WITH TEFLON.
AND WE'LL THROW IN A BODY WAX FOR FREE.

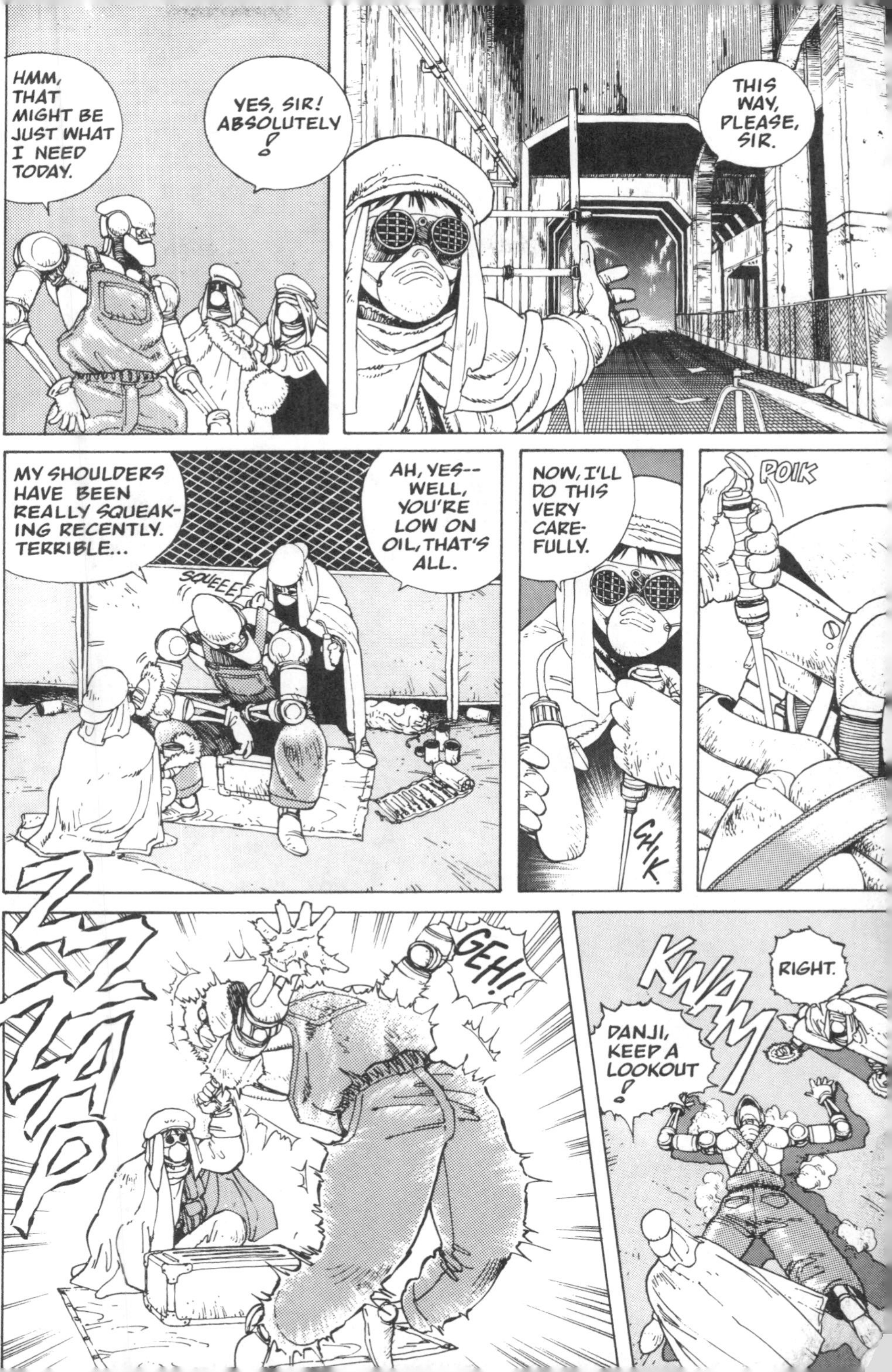
HMM, THAT MIGHT BE JUST WHAT I NEED TODAY.
YES, SIR! ABSOLUTELY!
THIS WAY, PLEASE, SIR.
MY SHOULDERS HAVE BEEN REALLY SQUEAKING RECENTLY. TERRIBLE...
AH, YES-- WELL, YOU'RE LOW ON OIL, THAT'S ALL.
SQUEEEE
NOW, I'LL DO THIS VERY CAREFULLY.
CHIK.
POIK
ZZAPP
GEH!
KWAM
RIGHT.
DANJI, KEEP A LOOKOUT!

WH-WHAT ARE YOU--!?

TAK

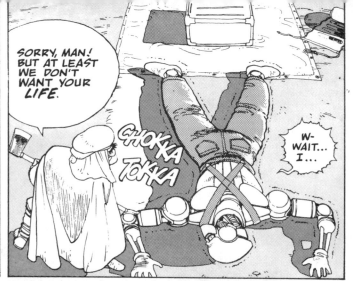

SORRY, MAN! BUT AT LEAST WE DON'T WANT YOUR LIFE.

CHOKKA TOKKA

W-WAIT... I...

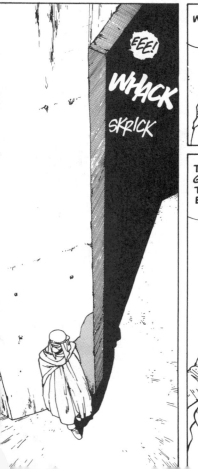

EEE!

WHACK

SKRICK

WELL?

htf uff htf

NO SWEAT.

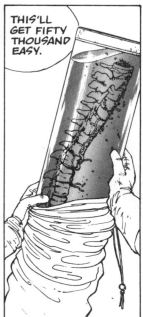

THIS'LL GET FIFTY THOUSAND EASY.

THIE-E-E-E-F! GIVE BACK MY BACKBO-O-O-NE!

TETCH TETCH

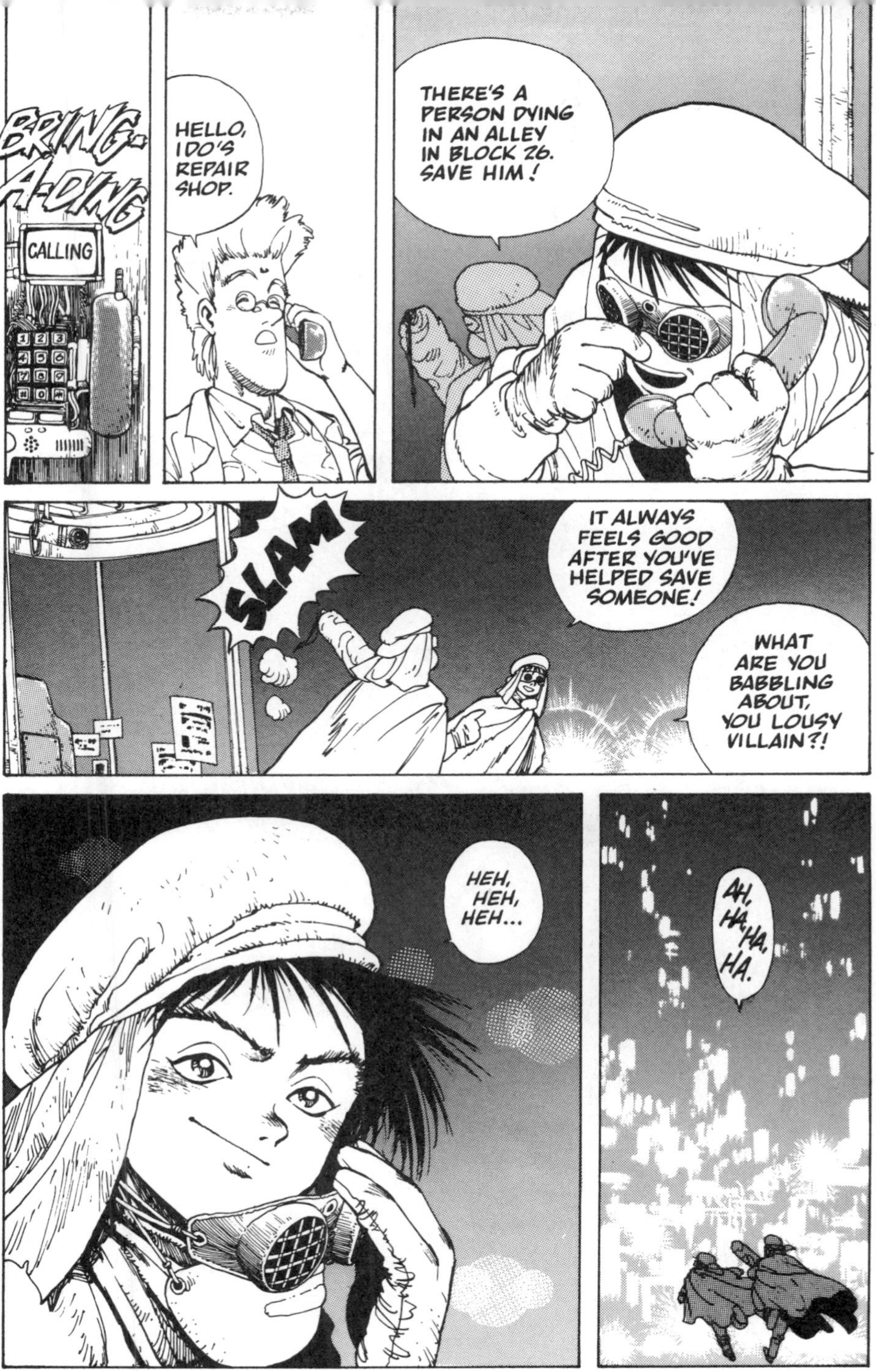
BRING-A-DING
CALLING
HELLO, IDO'S REPAIR SHOP.
THERE'S A PERSON DYING IN AN ALLEY IN BLOCK 26. SAVE HIM!
SLAM
IT ALWAYS FEELS GOOD AFTER YOU'VE HELPED SAVE SOMEONE!
WHAT ARE YOU BABBLING ABOUT, YOU LOUSY VILLAIN?!
HEH, HEH, HEH...
AH, HA, HA, HA.

IRON MAIDEN

Struggle 2: Awakening Heart

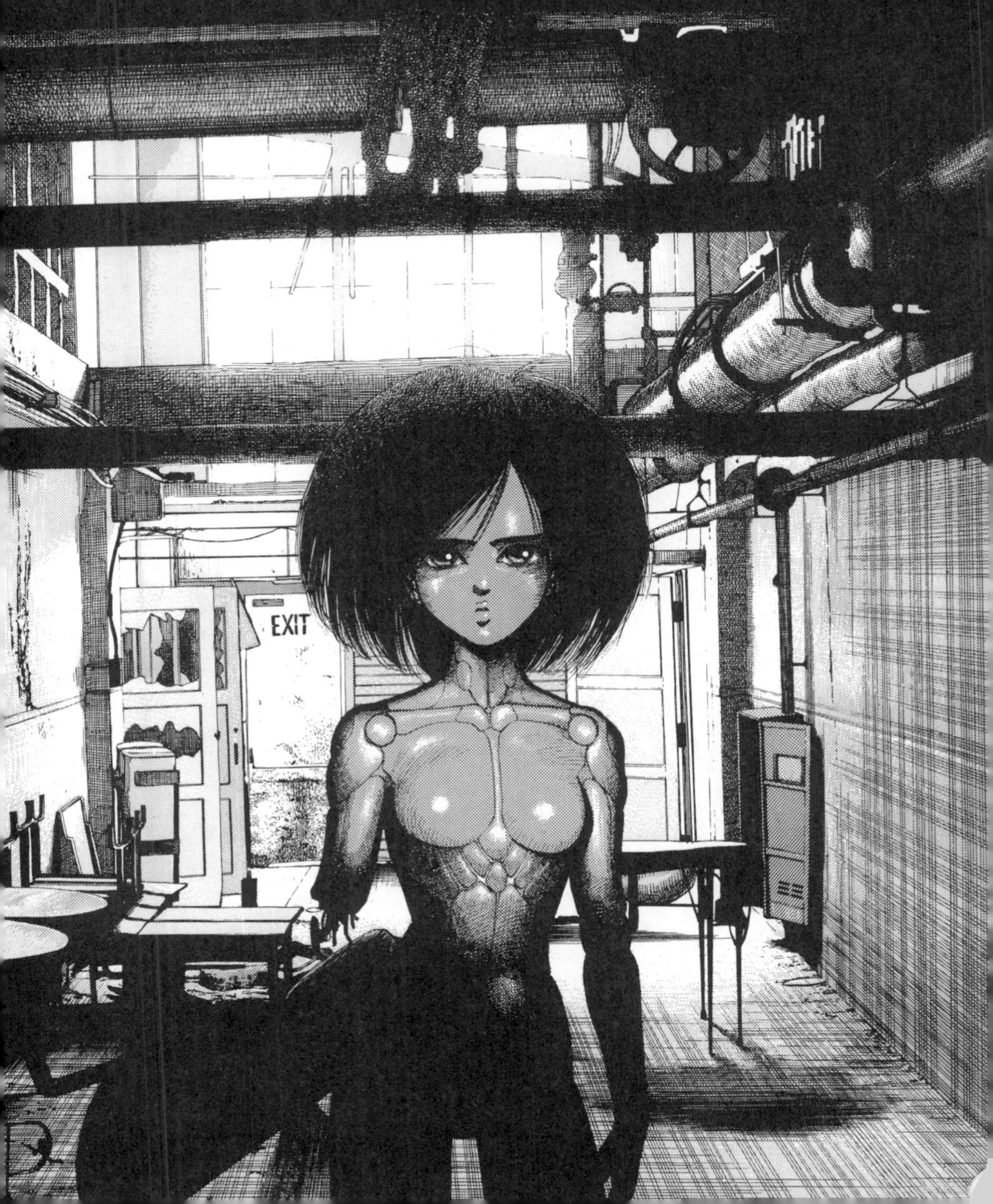
EXIT

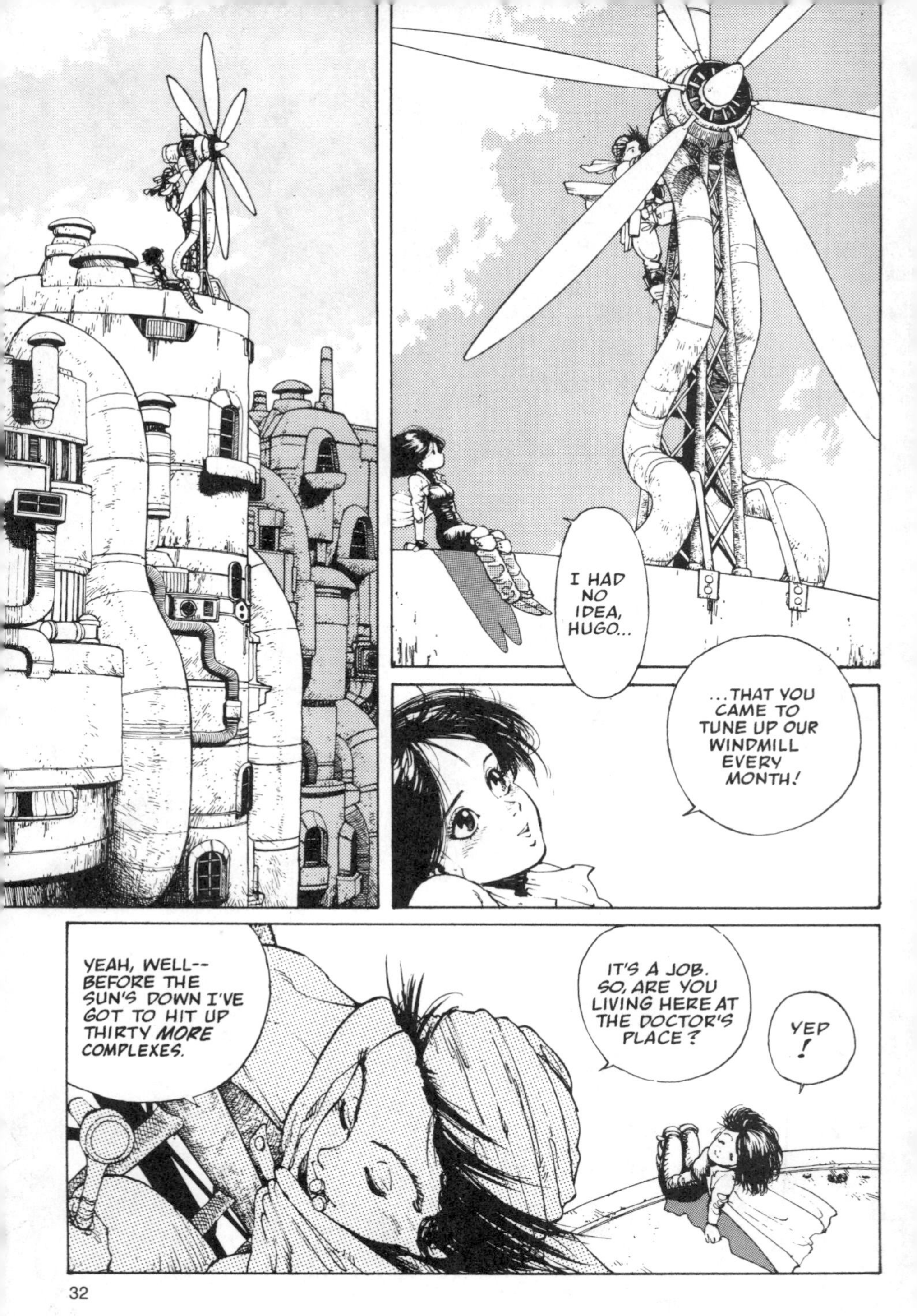
I HAD NO IDEA, HUGO...
...THAT YOU CAME TO TUNE UP OUR WINDMILL EVERY MONTH!
YEAH, WELL-- BEFORE THE SUN'S DOWN I'VE GOT TO HIT UP THIRTY *MORE* COMPLEXES.
IT'S A JOB. SO, ARE YOU LIVING HERE AT THE DOCTOR'S PLACE?
YEP!

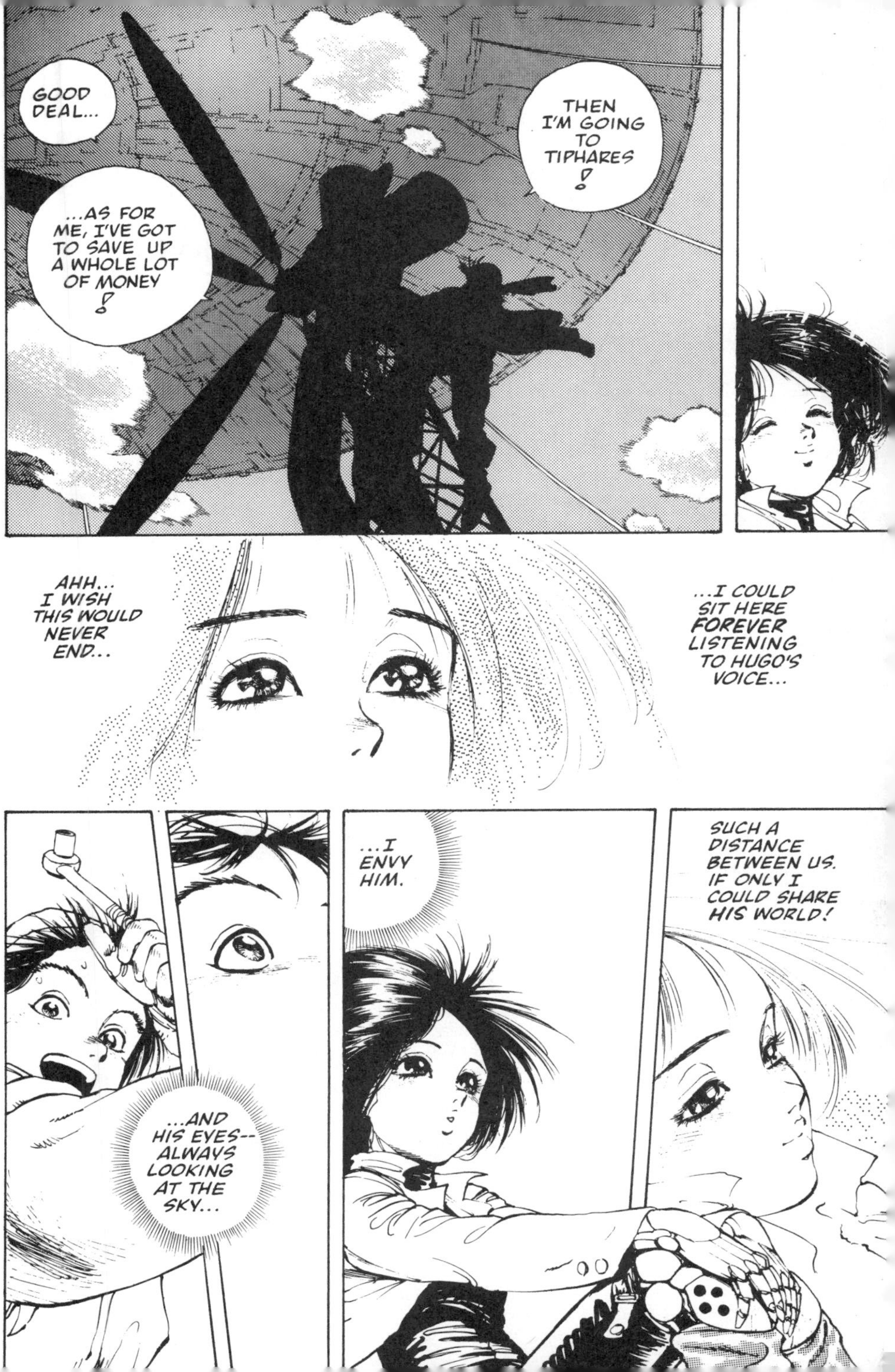
GOOD DEAL...
...AS FOR ME, I'VE GOT TO SAVE UP A WHOLE LOT OF MONEY!
THEN I'M GOING TO TIPHARES!
AHH... I WISH THIS WOULD NEVER END...
...I COULD SIT HERE FOREVER LISTENING TO HUGO'S VOICE...
...AND HIS EYES-- ALWAYS LOOKING AT THE SKY...
...I ENVY HIM.
SUCH A DISTANCE BETWEEN US. IF ONLY I COULD SHARE HIS WORLD!

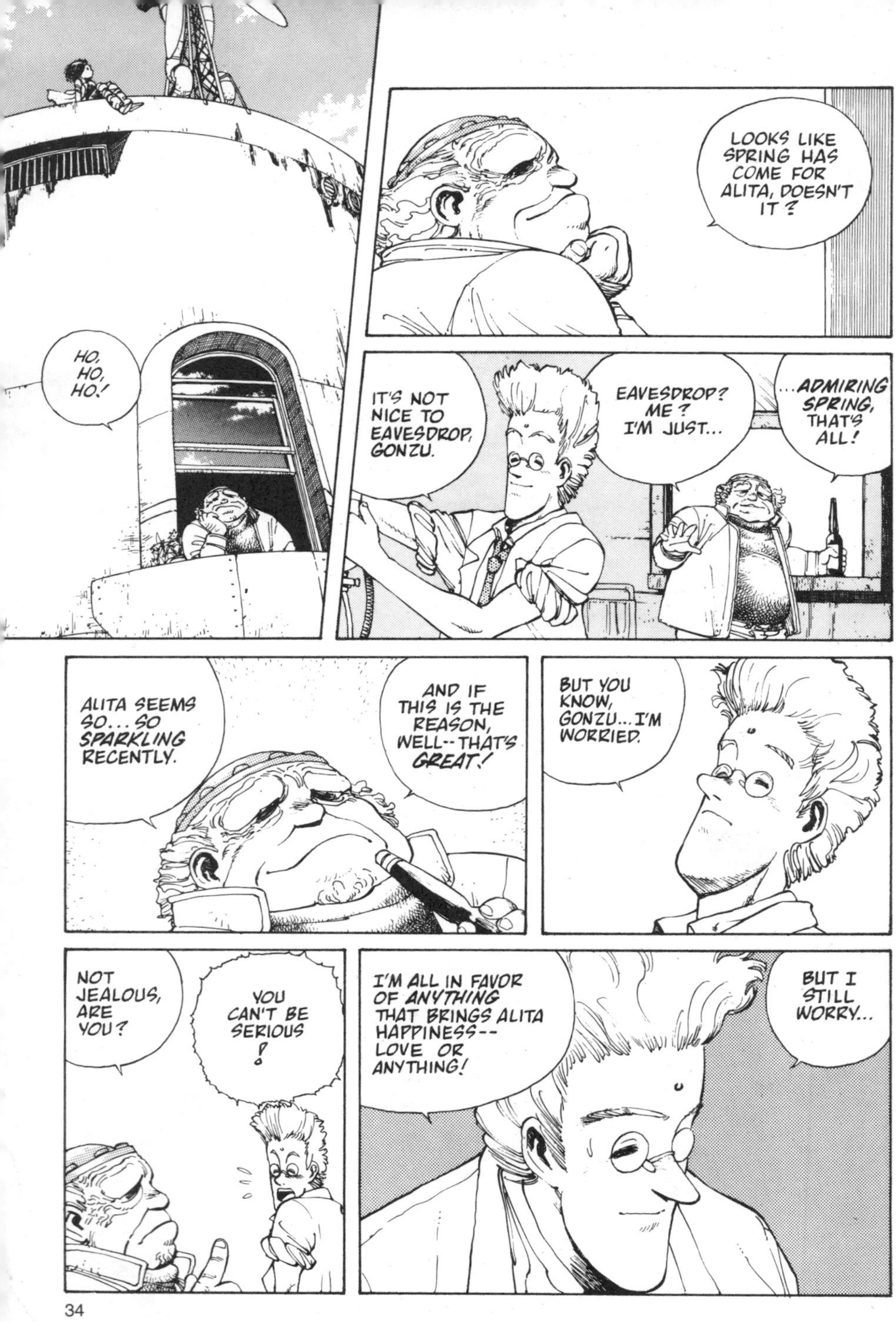
HO, HO, HO!
LOOKS LIKE SPRING HAS COME FOR ALITA, DOESN'T IT?
IT'S NOT NICE TO EAVESDROP, GONZU.
EAVESDROP? ME? I'M JUST...
...ADMIRING SPRING, THAT'S ALL!
ALITA SEEMS SO... SO SPARKLING RECENTLY.
AND IF THIS IS THE REASON, WELL--THAT'S GREAT!
BUT YOU KNOW, GONZU... I'M WORRIED.
NOT JEALOUS, ARE YOU?
YOU CAN'T BE SERIOUS!
I'M ALL IN FAVOR OF ANYTHING THAT BRINGS ALITA HAPPINESS--LOVE OR ANYTHING!
BUT I STILL WORRY...

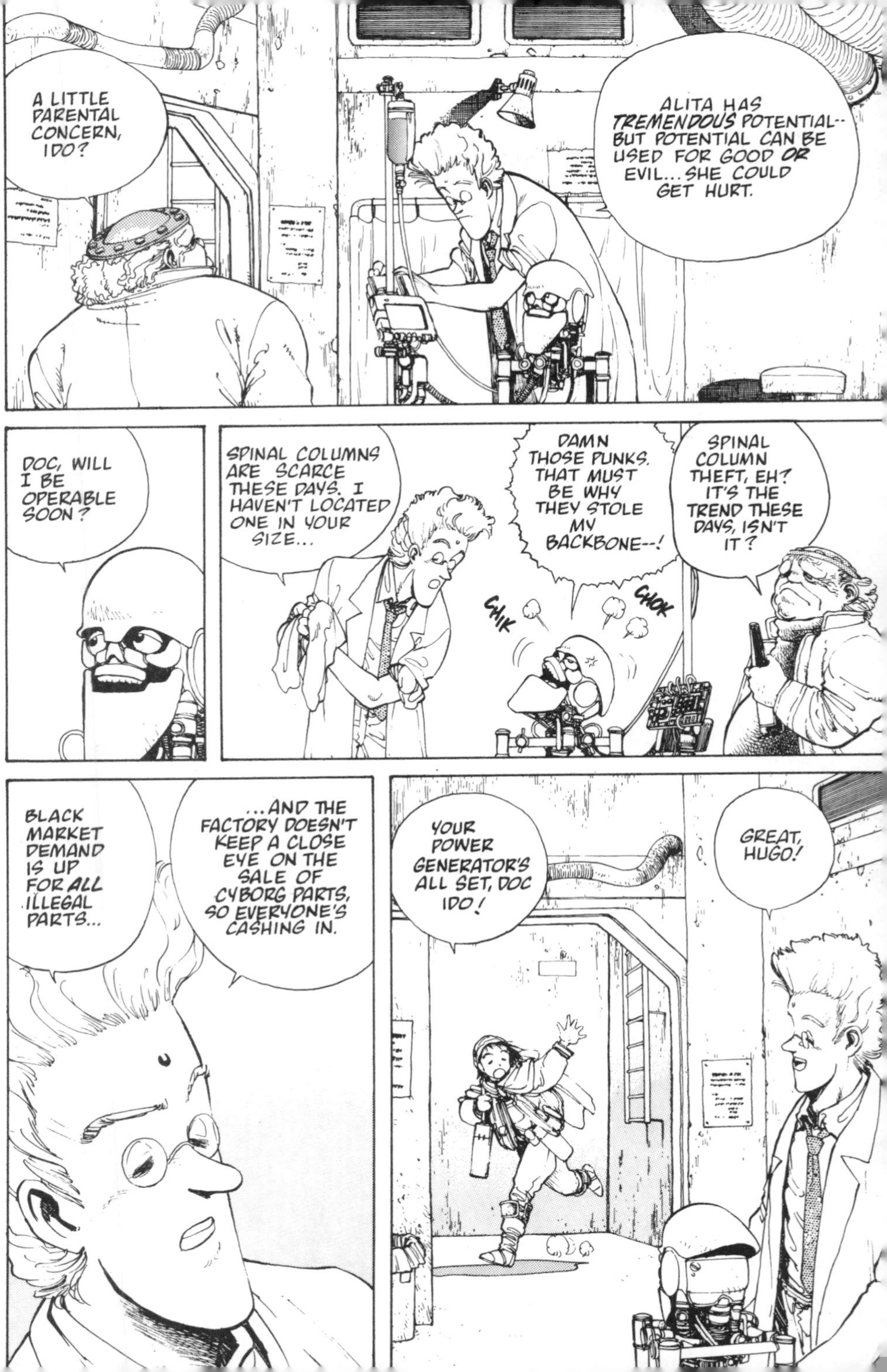
A LITTLE PARENTAL CONCERN, IDO?
ALITA HAS TREMENDOUS POTENTIAL-- BUT POTENTIAL CAN BE USED FOR GOOD OR EVIL... SHE COULD GET HURT.
DOC, WILL I BE OPERABLE SOON?
SPINAL COLUMNS ARE SCARCE THESE DAYS. I HAVEN'T LOCATED ONE IN YOUR SIZE...
DAMN THOSE PUNKS. THAT MUST BE WHY THEY STOLE MY BACKBONE--!
CHIK
CHOK
SPINAL COLUMN THEFT, EH? IT'S THE TREND THESE DAYS, ISN'T IT?
BLACK MARKET DEMAND IS UP FOR ALL ILLEGAL PARTS...
...AND THE FACTORY DOESN'T KEEP A CLOSE EYE ON THE SALE OF CYBORG PARTS, SO EVERYONE'S CASHING IN.
YOUR POWER GENERATOR'S ALL SET, DOC IDO!
GREAT, HUGO!

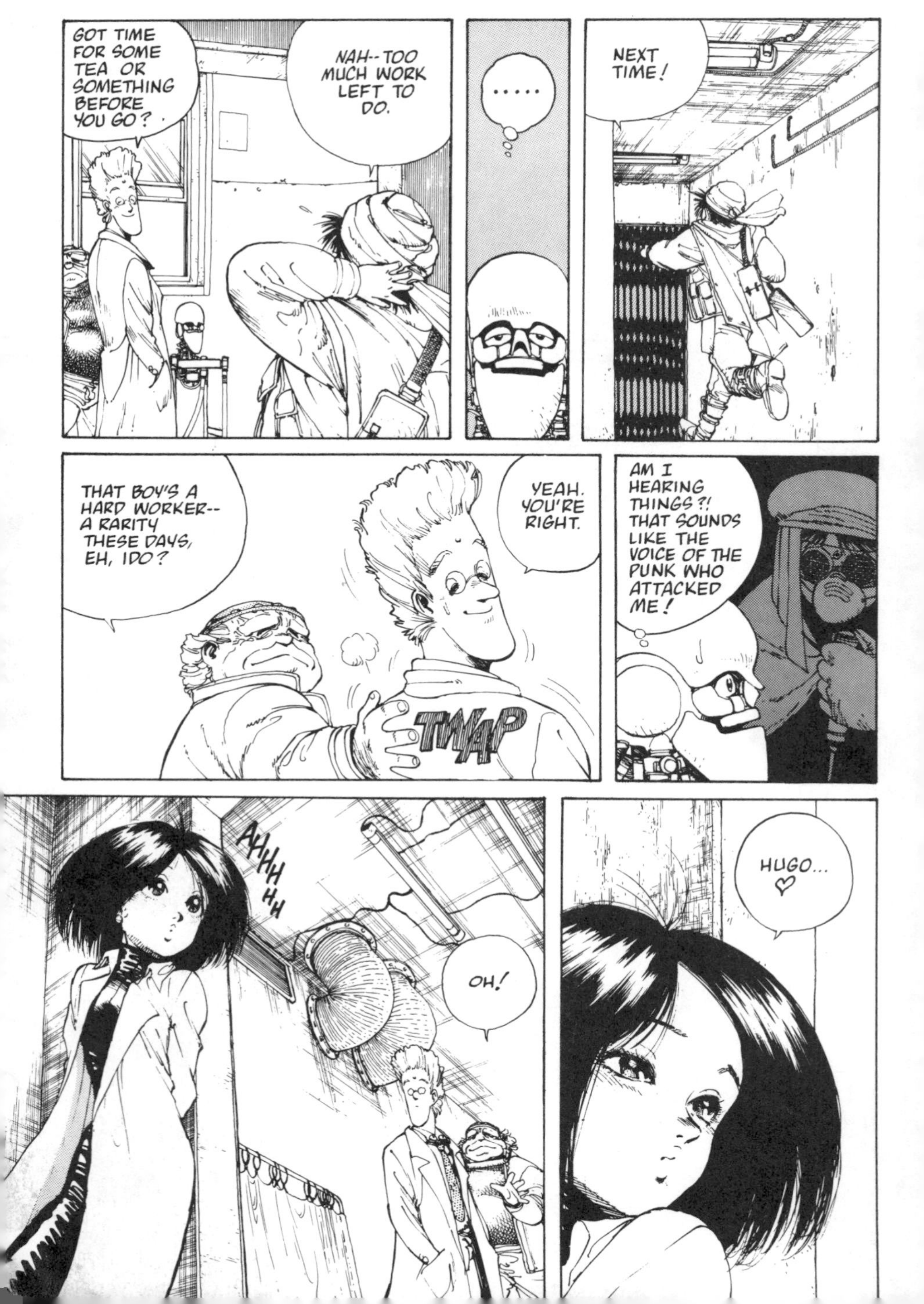
GOT TIME FOR SOME TEA OR SOMETHING BEFORE YOU GO?
NAH--TOO MUCH WORK LEFT TO DO.
.....
NEXT TIME!
THAT BOY'S A HARD WORKER-- A RARITY THESE DAYS, EH, IDO?
YEAH. YOU'RE RIGHT.
TWAP
AM I HEARING THINGS?! THAT SOUNDS LIKE THE VOICE OF THE PUNK WHO ATTACKED ME!
AHHHHH
OH!
HUGO... ♡

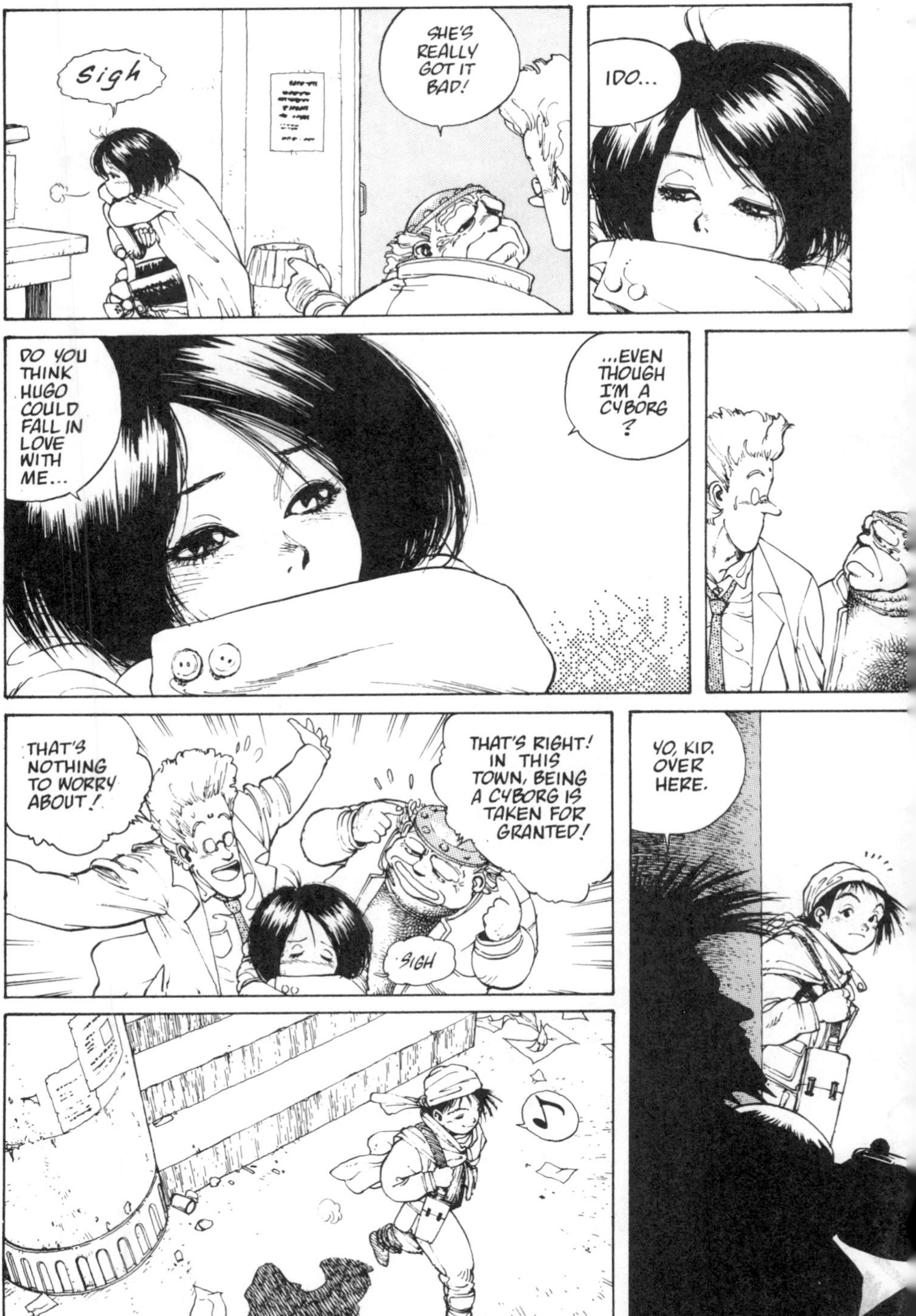
Sigh
SHE'S REALLY GOT IT BAD!
IDO...
DO YOU THINK HUGO COULD FALL IN LOVE WITH ME...
...EVEN THOUGH I'M A CYBORG?
THAT'S NOTHING TO WORRY ABOUT!
THAT'S RIGHT! IN THIS TOWN, BEING A CYBORG IS TAKEN FOR GRANTED!
SIGH
♪
YO, KID. OVER HERE.

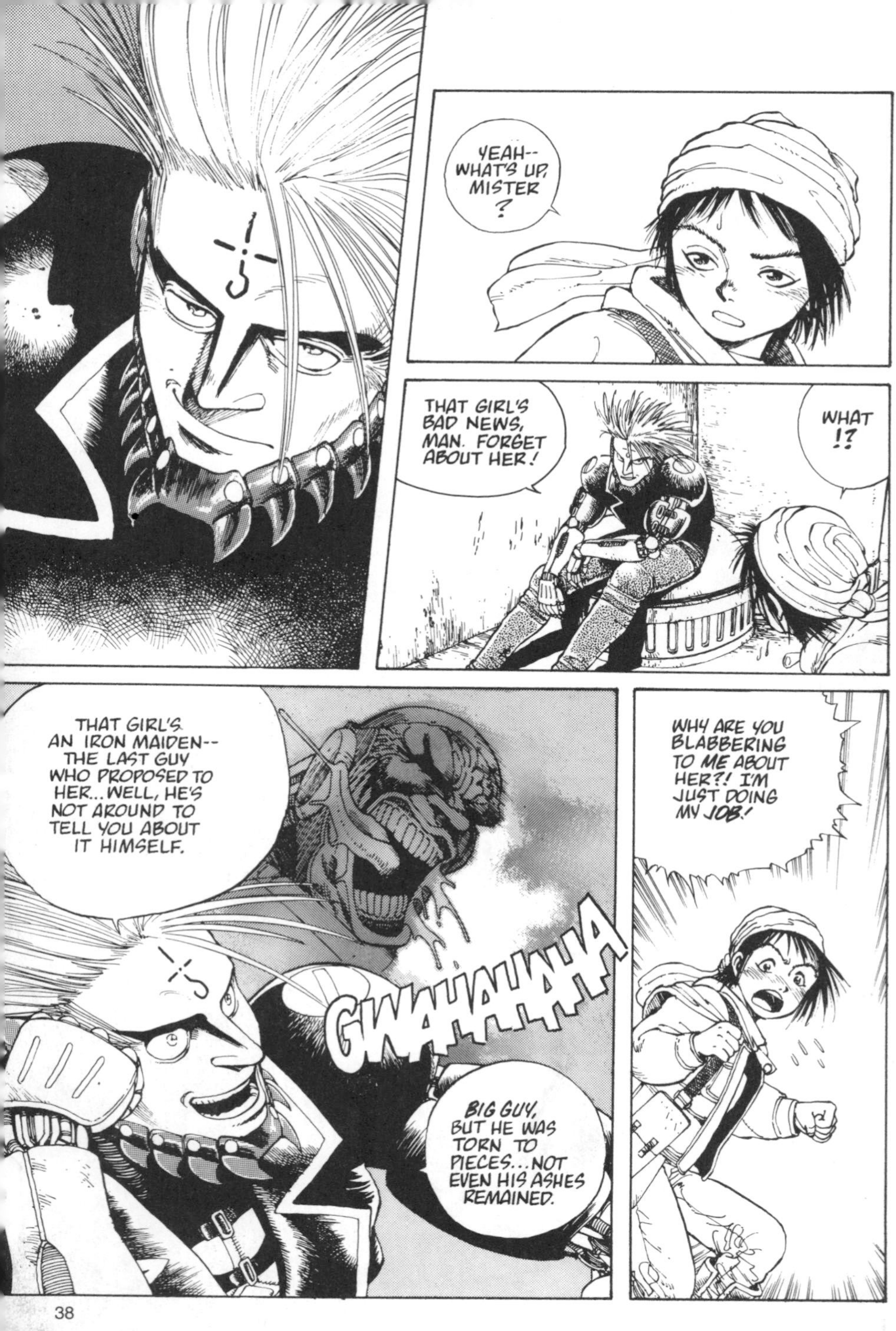
YEAH-- WHAT'S UP, MISTER ?
THAT GIRL'S BAD NEWS, MAN. FORGET ABOUT HER!
WHAT !?
THAT GIRL'S AN IRON MAIDEN-- THE LAST GUY WHO PROPOSED TO HER...WELL, HE'S NOT AROUND TO TELL YOU ABOUT IT HIMSELF.
GWAHAHAHAHA
BIG GUY, BUT HE WAS TORN TO PIECES...NOT EVEN HIS ASHES REMAINED.
WHY ARE YOU BLABBERING TO ME ABOUT HER?! I'M JUST DOING MY JOB!

HEH !

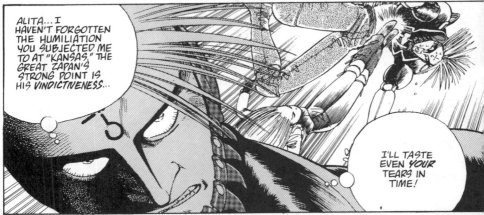

ALITA... I HAVEN'T FORGOTTEN THE HUMILIATION YOU SUBJECTED ME TO AT "KANSAS." THE GREAT ZAPAN'S STRONG POINT IS HIS *VINDICTIVENESS*...

I'LL TASTE EVEN *YOUR* TEARS IN TIME!

RMB RMB RMB

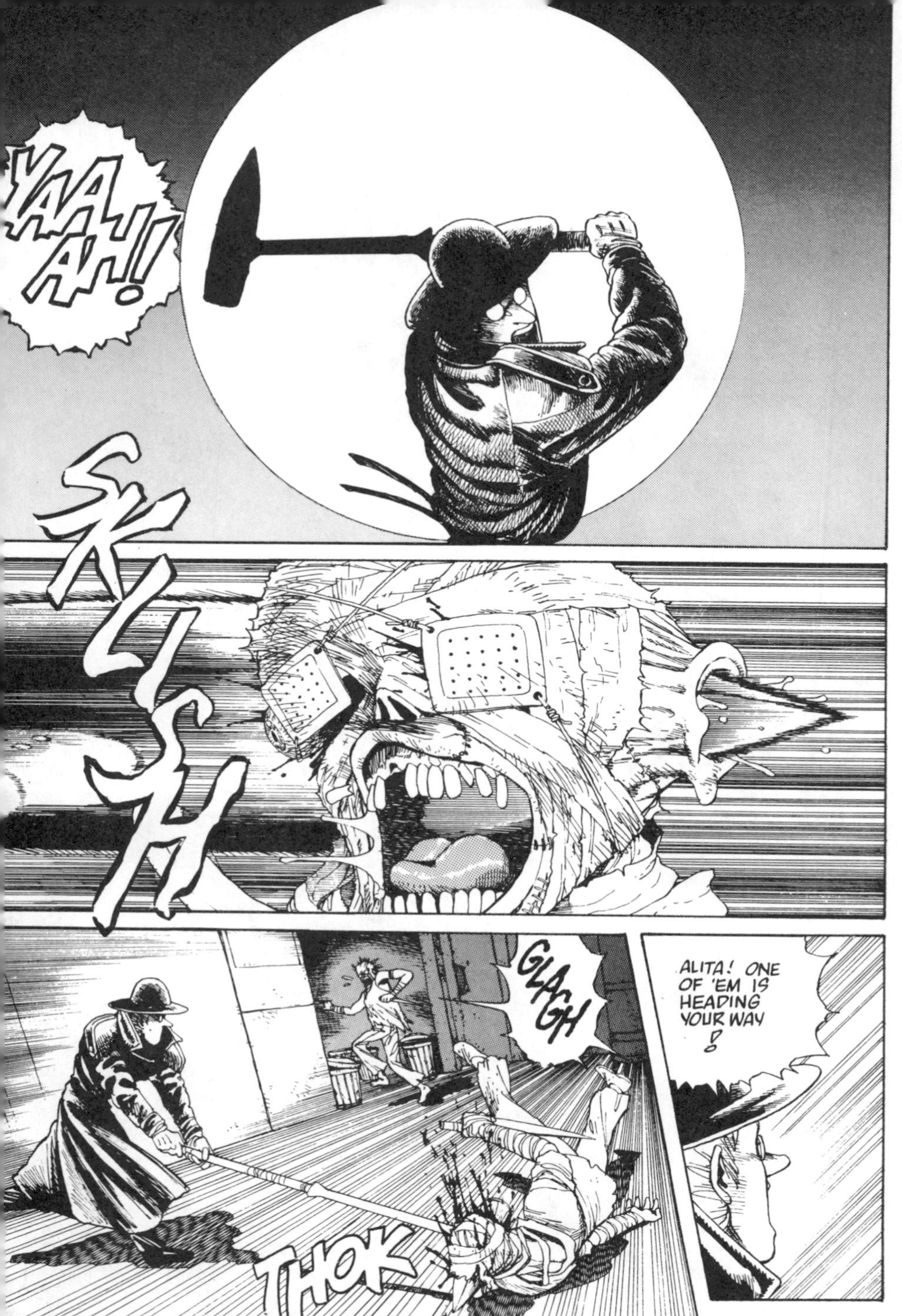
YAAAH!
SKLISH
GLAGH
THOK
ALITA! ONE OF 'EM IS HEADING YOUR WAY!

SIGH

TONKA
KRASH

.....?

GAAH

SLIK

AIEEEEE!
A
WOMAAAN!!

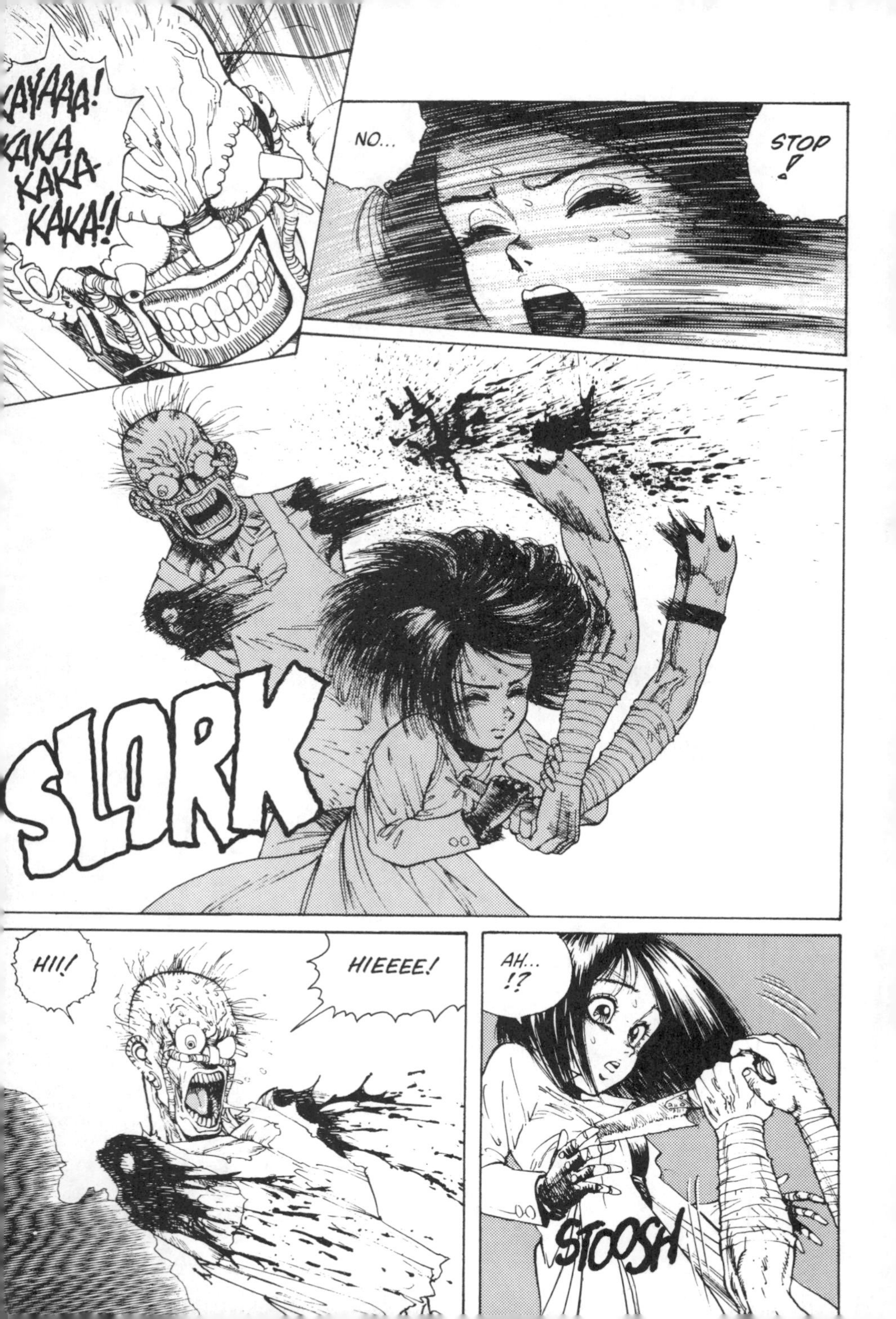
KAYAAA! KAKA KAKA KAKA!!
NO...
STOP!
SLORK
HII!
HIEEEE!
AH... !?
STOOSH

I ONLY MEANT TO SHAKE HIM OFF...

HOW FRAGILE...

HIIYAAAA

TONK

SKOOSH

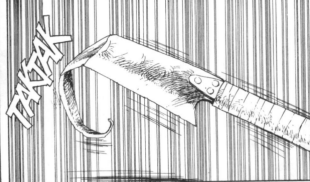

TAKTAK

DIDN'T DO MORE THAN SCRATCH MY BODY.

BUT THEN IT'S NOT EXACTLY THE BODY OF A HUMAN...

WHAT HAPPENED, ALITA!

KRESH

CRAK

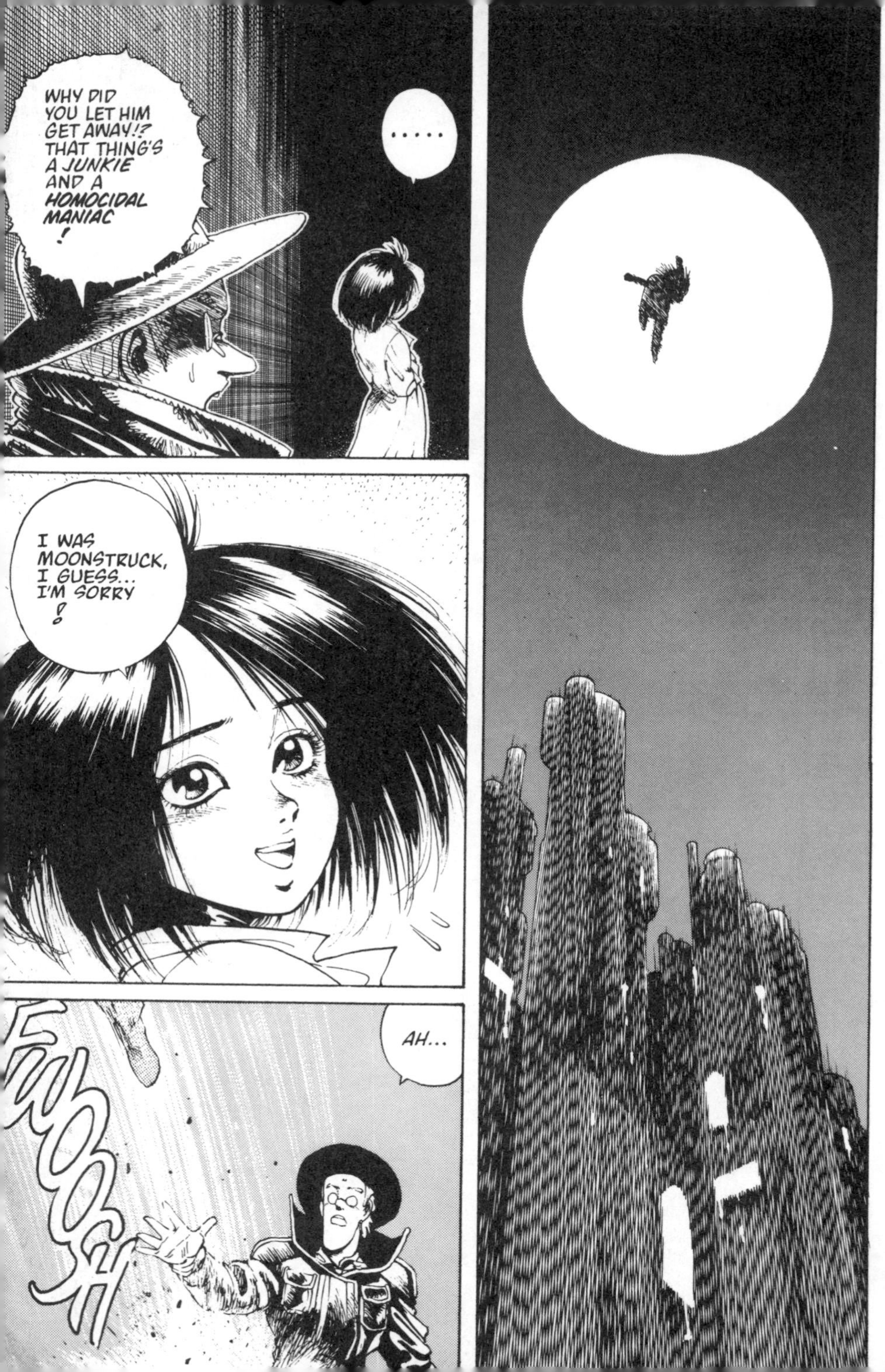
WHY DID YOU LET HIM GET AWAY!? THAT THING'S A JUNKIE AND A HOMOCIDAL MANIAC !
......
I WAS MOONSTRUCK, I GUESS... I'M SORRY !
AH...

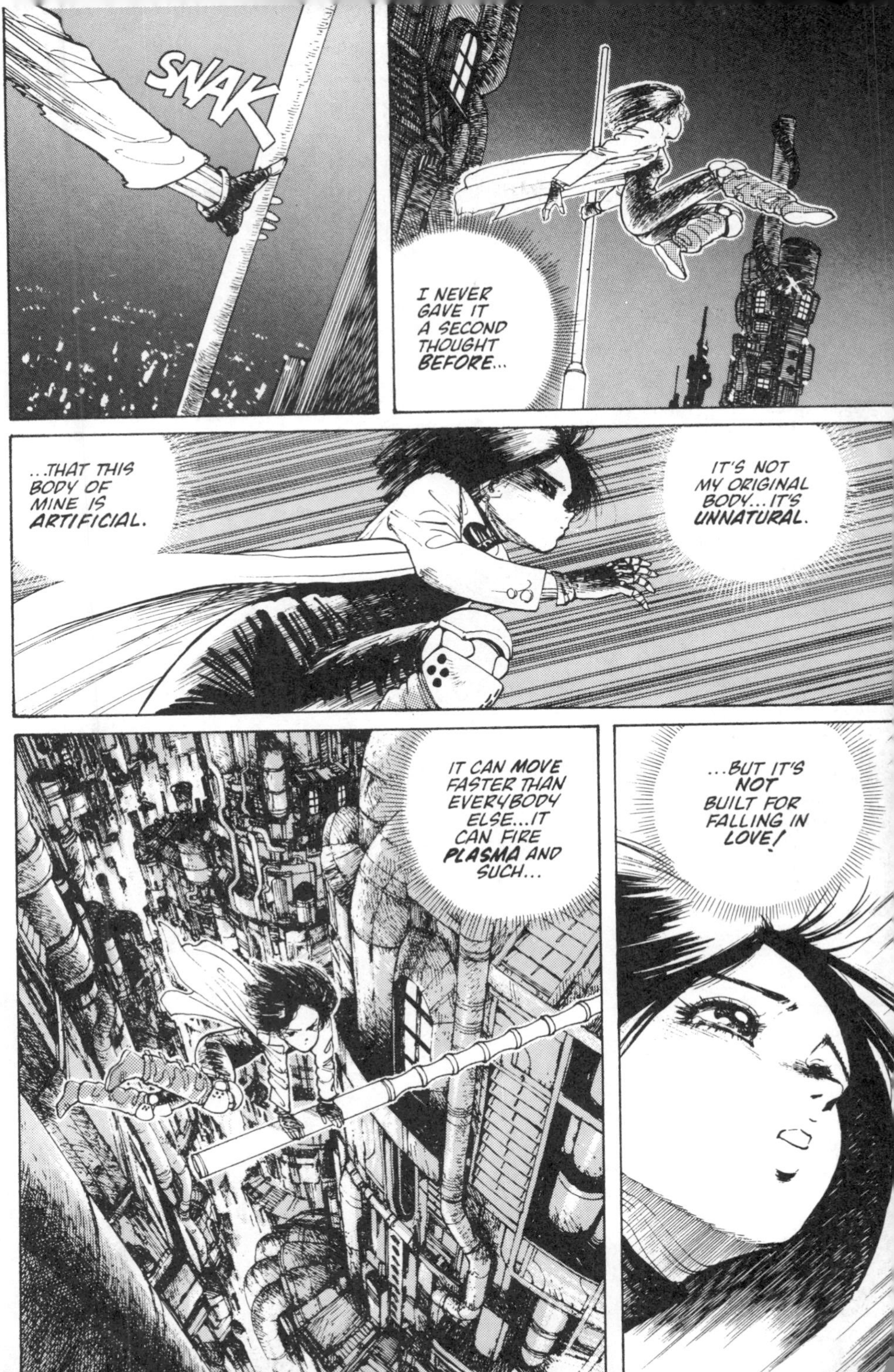
SNAK
I NEVER GAVE IT A SECOND THOUGHT BEFORE...
...THAT THIS BODY OF MINE IS ARTIFICIAL.
IT'S NOT MY ORIGINAL BODY... IT'S UNNATURAL.
IT CAN MOVE FASTER THAN EVERYBODY ELSE...IT CAN FIRE PLASMA AND SUCH...
...BUT IT'S NOT BUILT FOR FALLING IN LOVE!

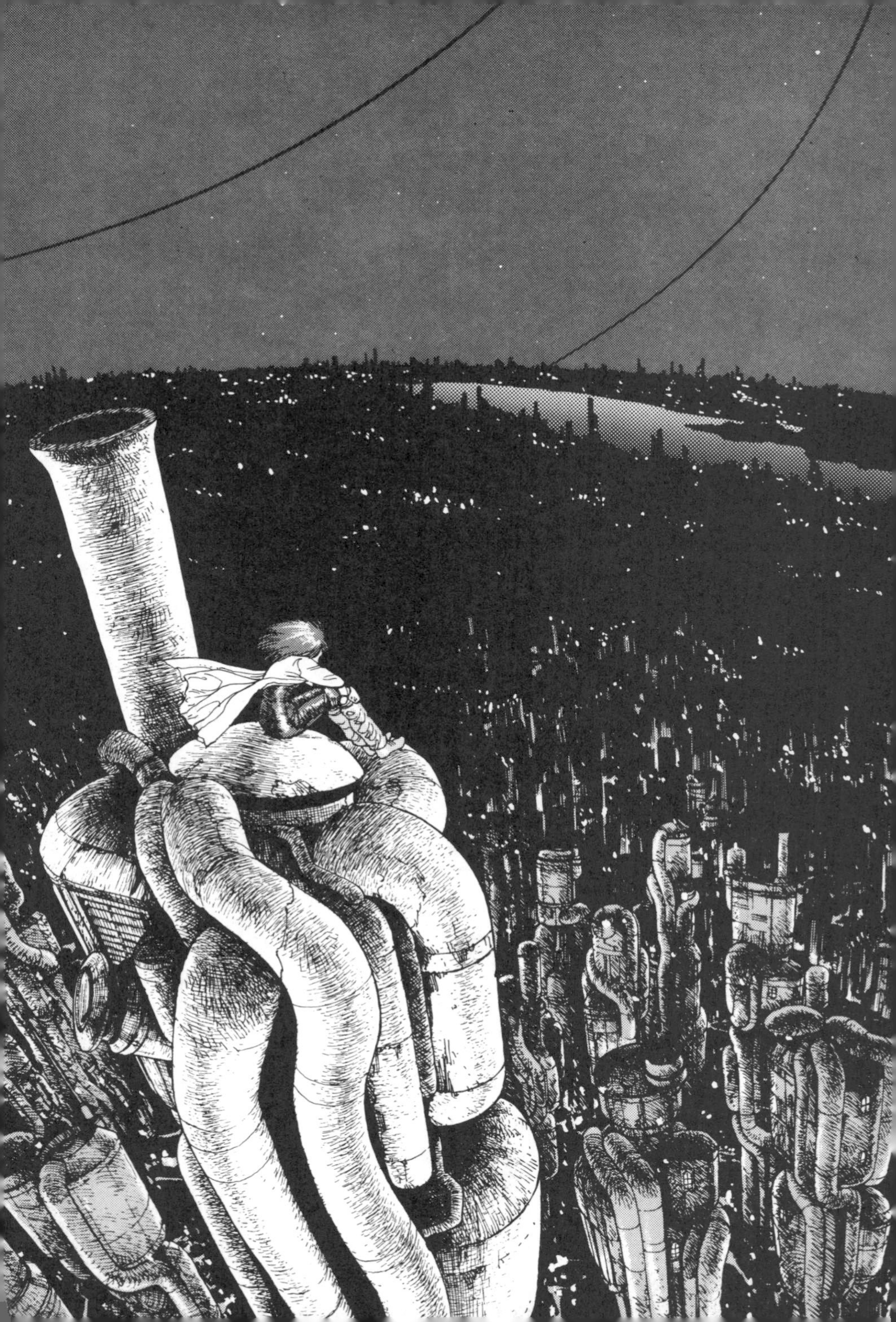

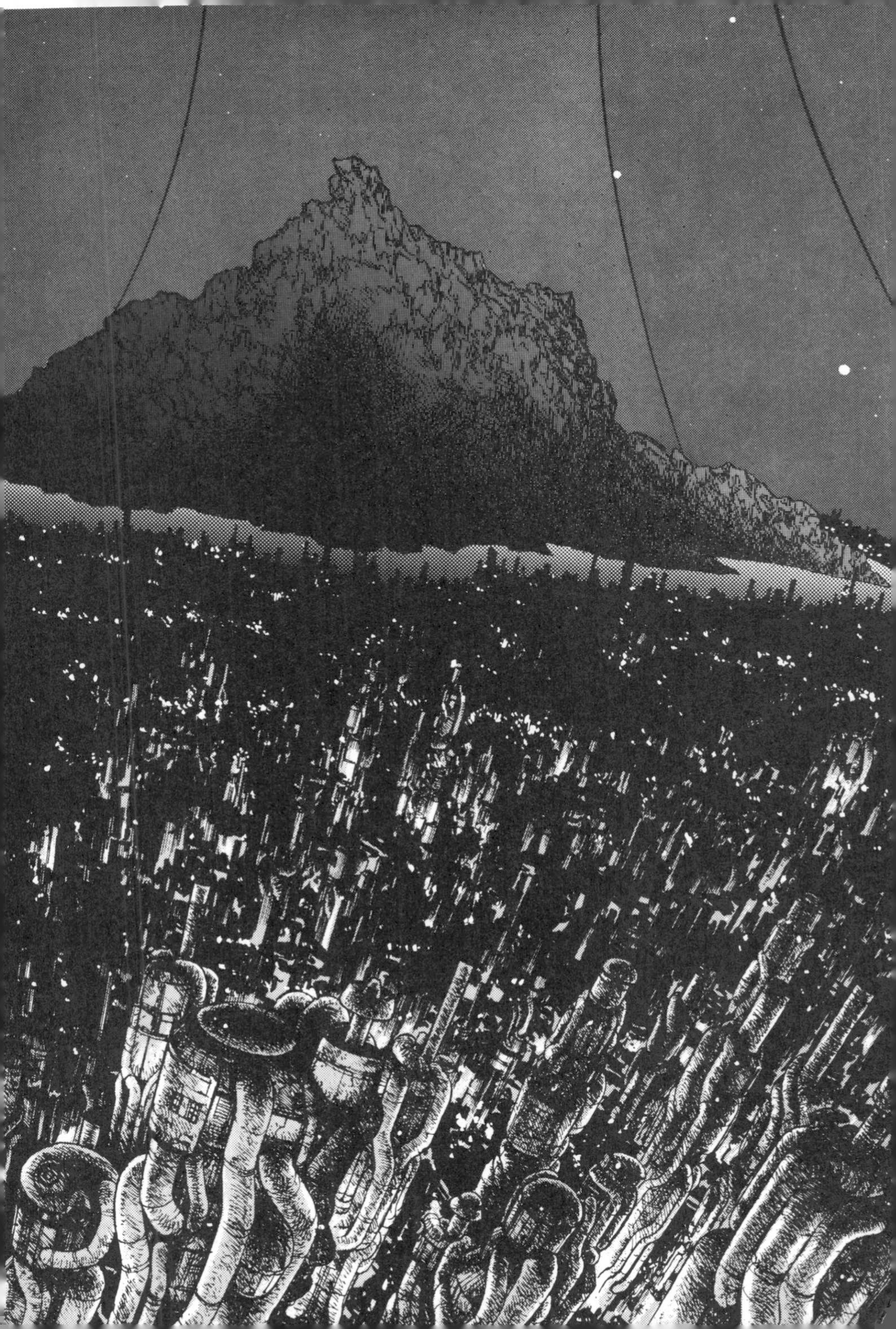

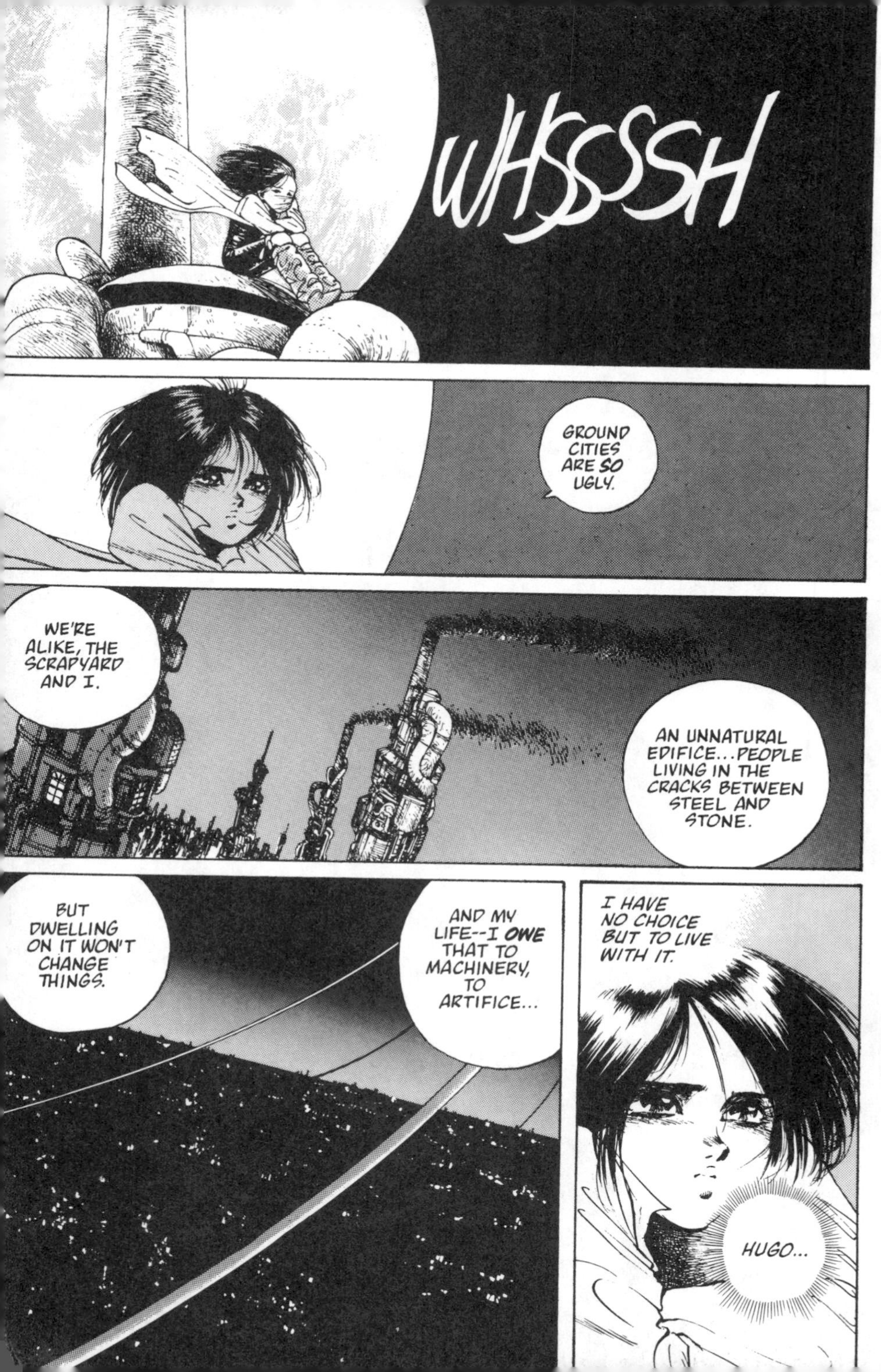

WHSSSSH
GROUND CITIES ARE SO UGLY.
WE'RE ALIKE, THE SCRAPYARD AND I.
AN UNNATURAL EDIFICE...PEOPLE LIVING IN THE CRACKS BETWEEN STEEL AND STONE.
BUT DWELLING ON IT WON'T CHANGE THINGS.
AND MY LIFE--I OWE THAT TO MACHINERY, TO ARTIFICE...
I HAVE NO CHOICE BUT TO LIVE WITH IT.
HUGO...

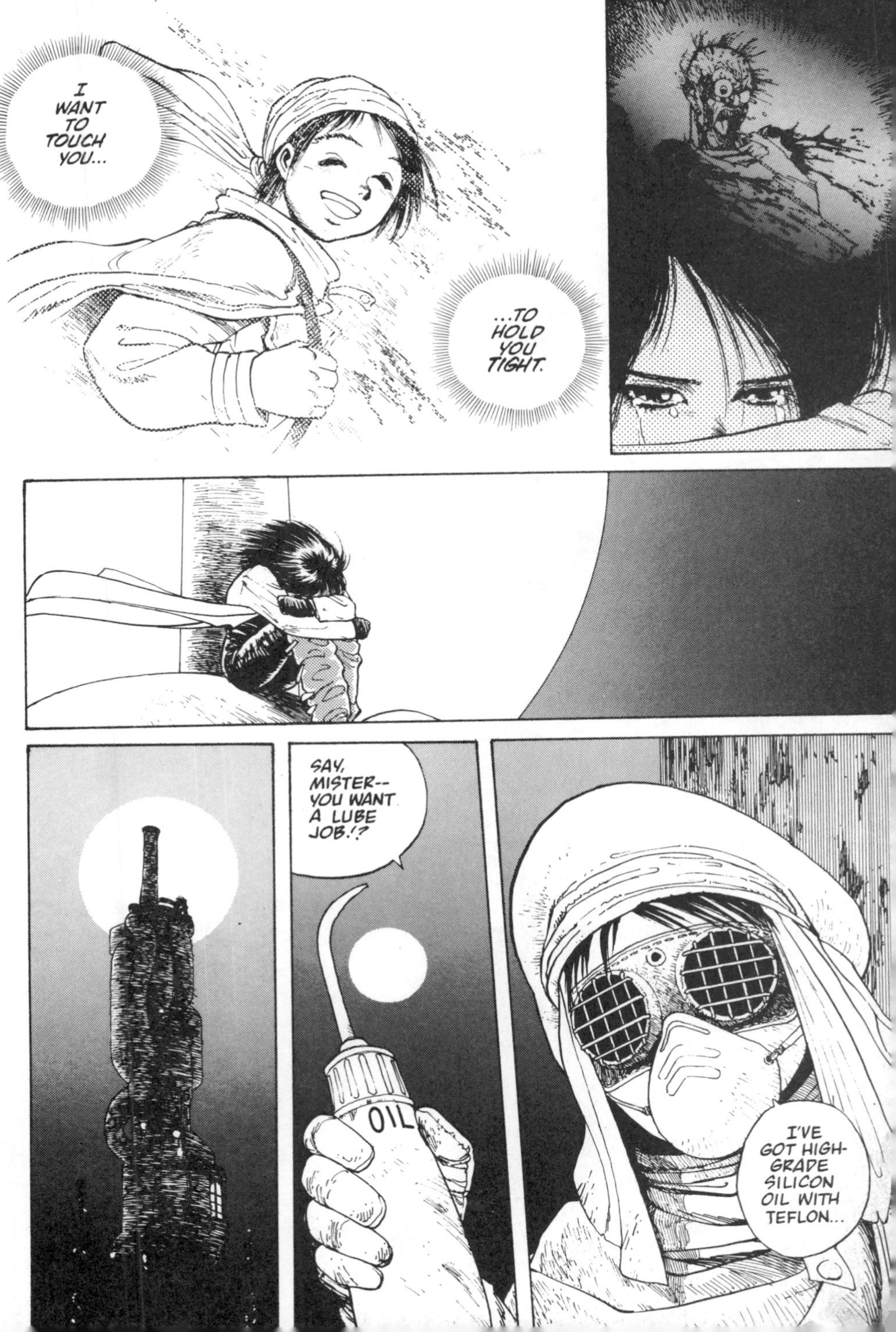
I WANT TO TOUCH YOU...
...TO HOLD YOU TIGHT.
SAY, MISTER-- YOU WANT A LUBE JOB!?
OIL
I'VE GOT HIGH-GRADE SILICON OIL WITH TEFLON...

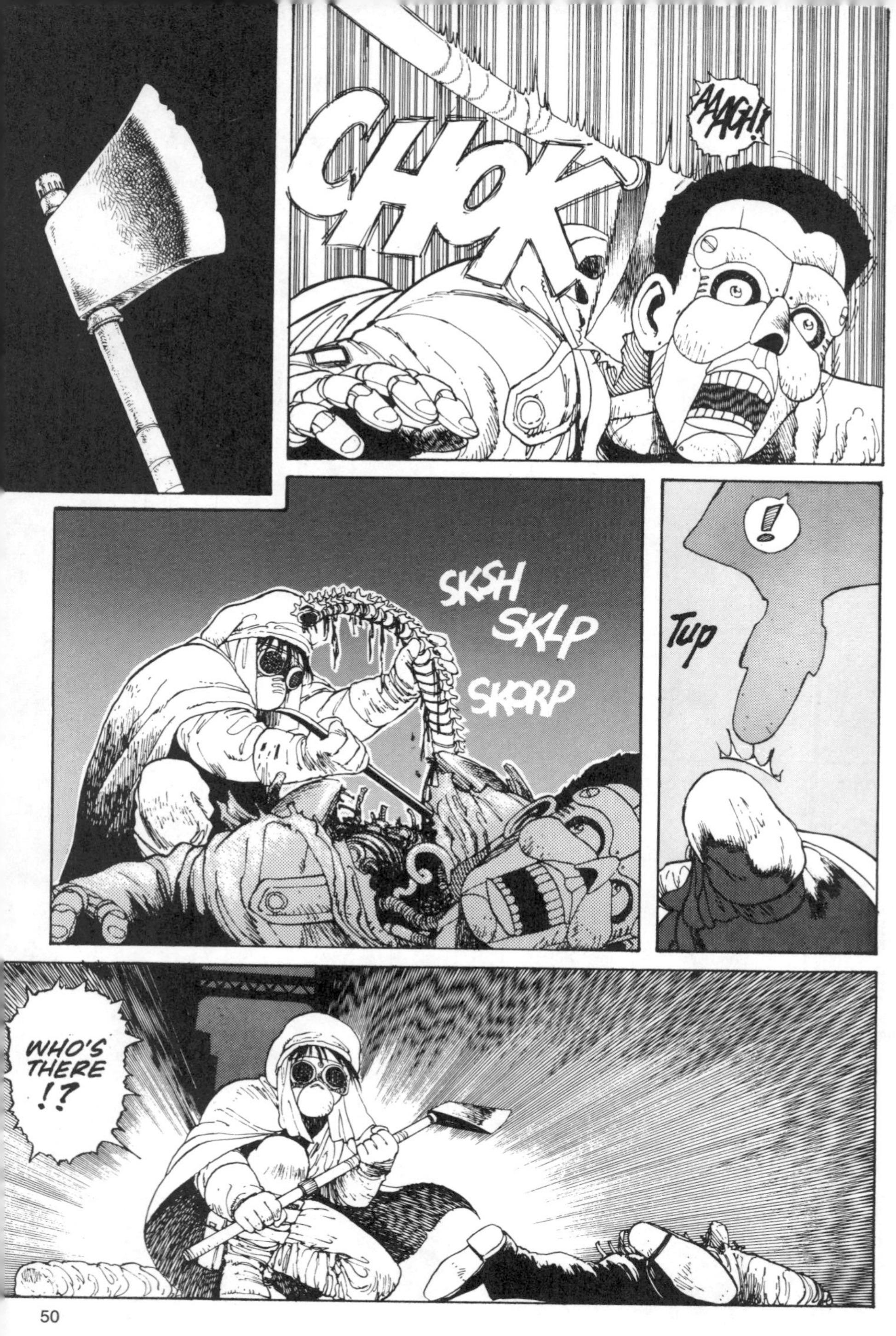
CHOK
AAAGH!!
SKSH
SKLP
SKORP
!
Tup
WHO'S THERE !?

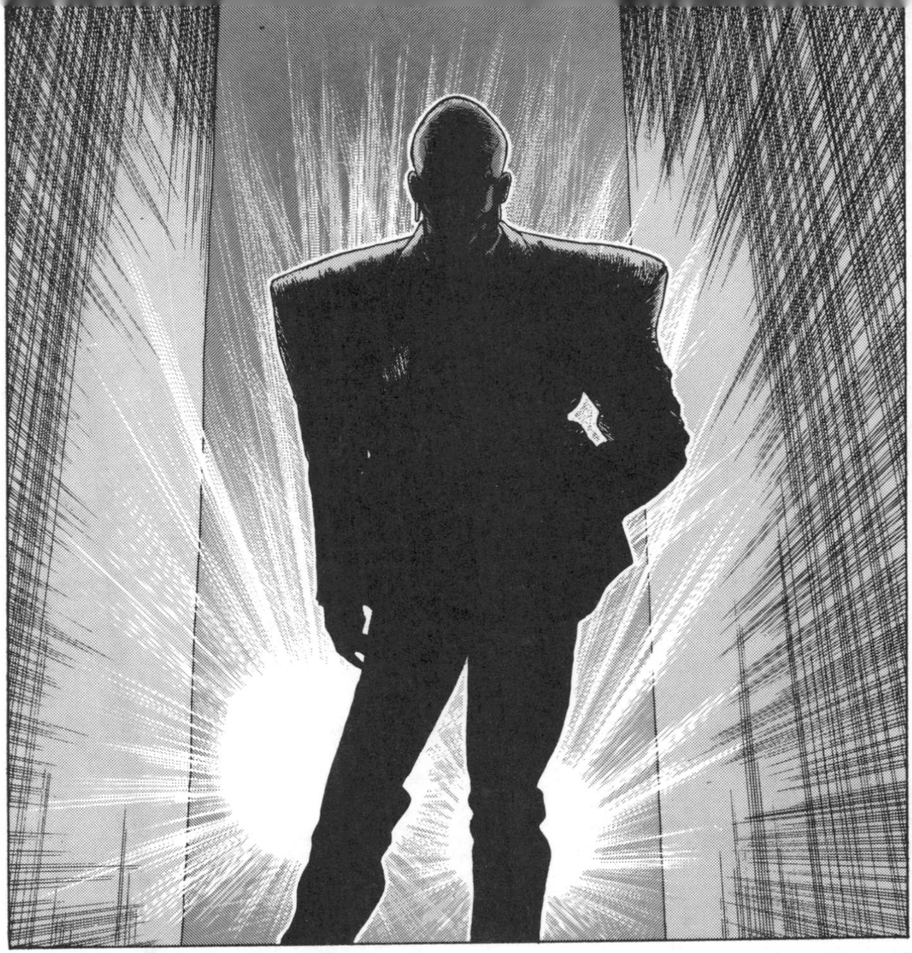
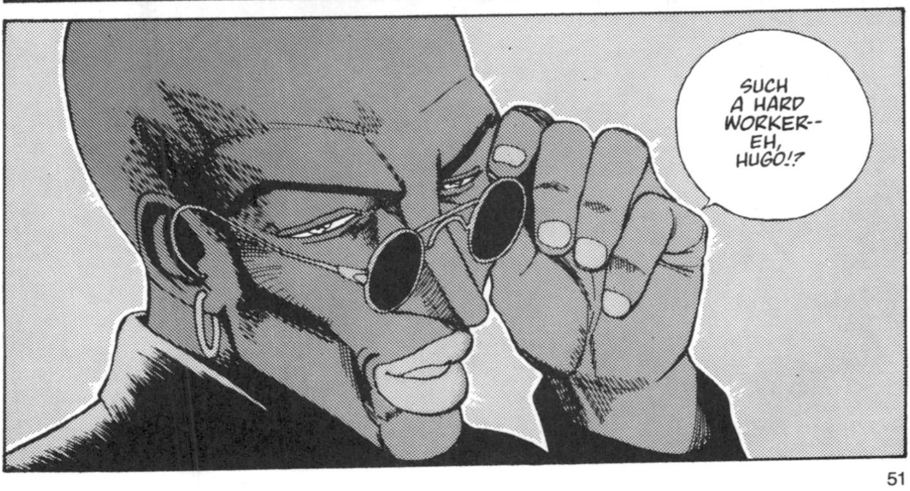
SUCH A HARD WORKER--EH, HUGO!?

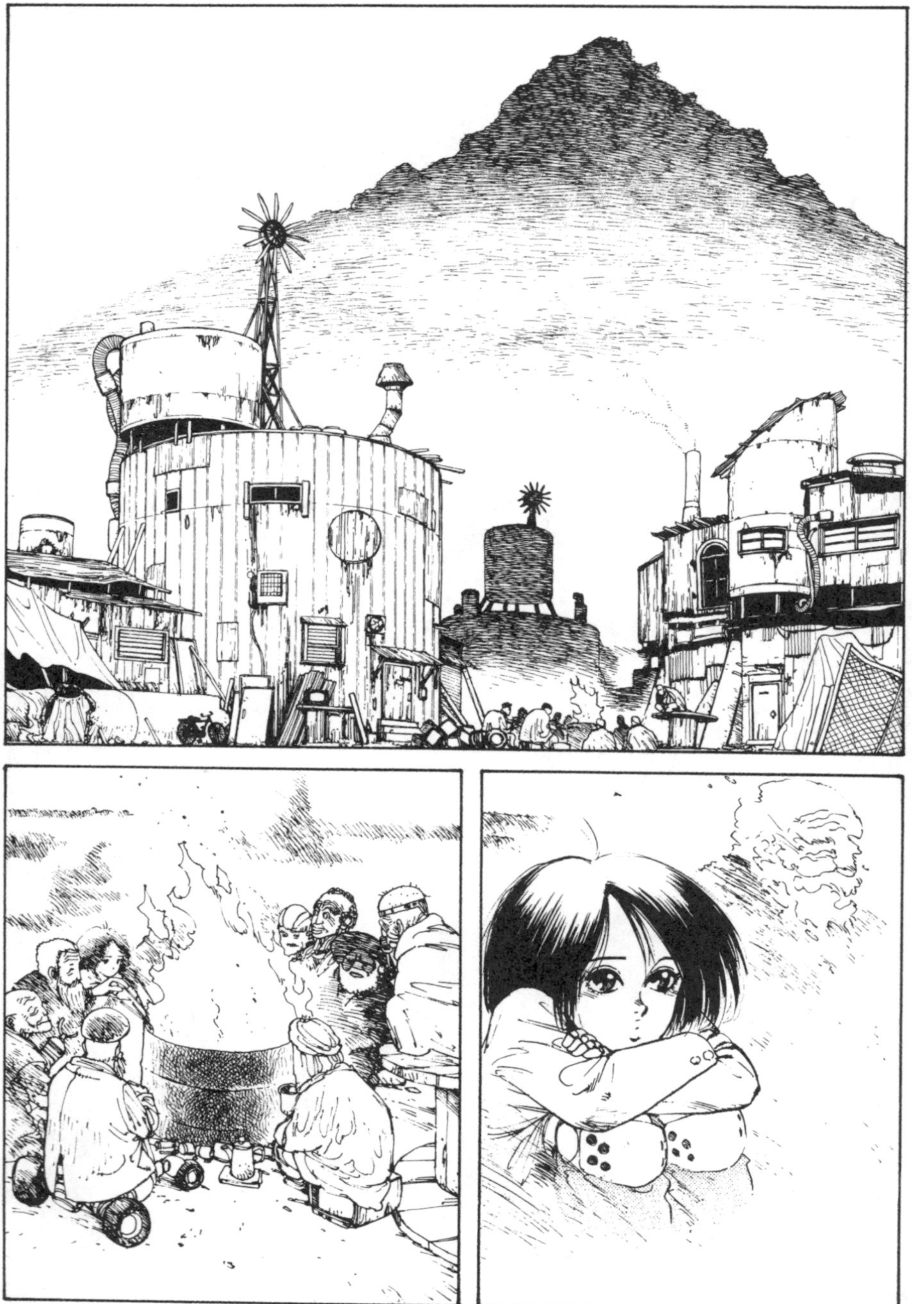

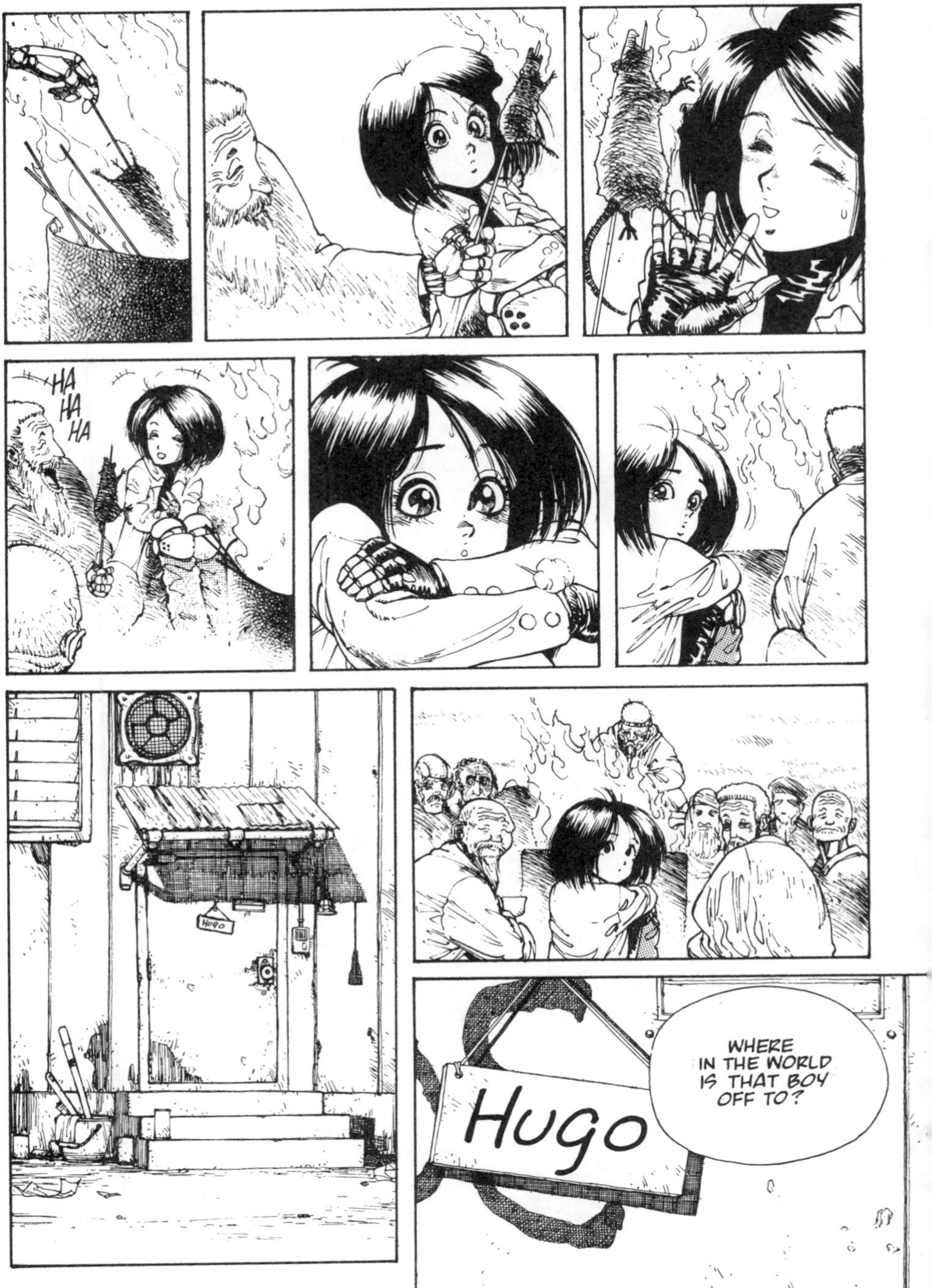
HA
HA
HA
Hugo
Hugo
WHERE IN THE WORLD IS THAT BOY OFF TO?

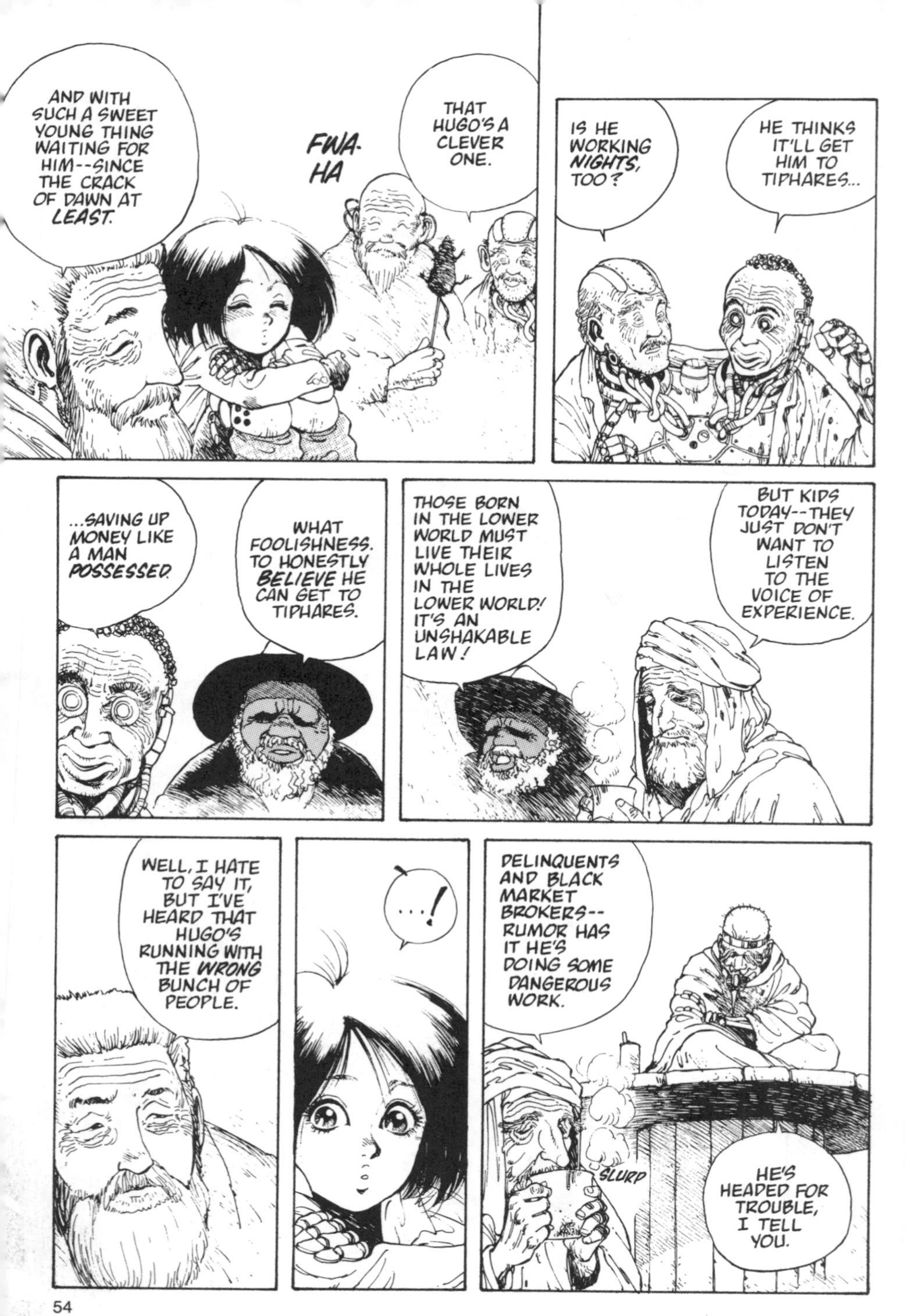
AND WITH SUCH A SWEET YOUNG THING WAITING FOR HIM--SINCE THE CRACK OF DAWN AT LEAST.
FWA-HA
THAT HUGO'S A CLEVER ONE.
IS HE WORKING NIGHTS, TOO?
HE THINKS IT'LL GET HIM TO TIPHARES...
...SAVING UP MONEY LIKE A MAN POSSESSED.
WHAT FOOLISHNESS. TO HONESTLY BELIEVE HE CAN GET TO TIPHARES.
THOSE BORN IN THE LOWER WORLD MUST LIVE THEIR WHOLE LIVES IN THE LOWER WORLD! IT'S AN UNSHAKABLE LAW!
BUT KIDS TODAY--THEY JUST DON'T WANT TO LISTEN TO THE VOICE OF EXPERIENCE.
WELL, I HATE TO SAY IT, BUT I'VE HEARD THAT HUGO'S RUNNING WITH THE WRONG BUNCH OF PEOPLE.
...!
DELINQUENTS AND BLACK MARKET BROKERS--RUMOR HAS IT HE'S DOING SOME DANGEROUS WORK.
SLURP
HE'S HEADED FOR TROUBLE, I TELL YOU.

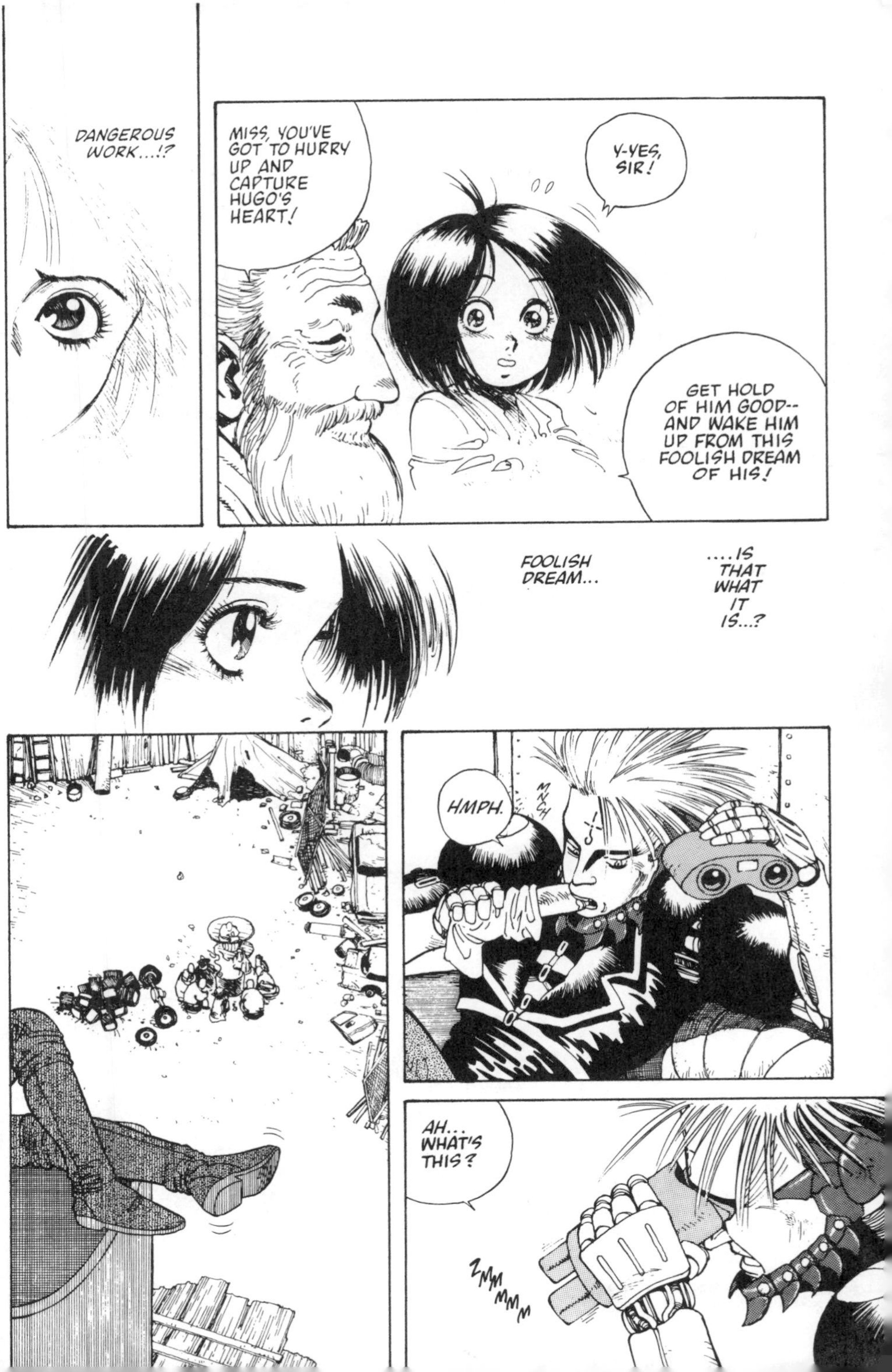
DANGEROUS WORK...!?
MISS, YOU'VE GOT TO HURRY UP AND CAPTURE HUGO'S HEART!
Y-YES, SIR!
GET HOLD OF HIM GOOD-- AND WAKE HIM UP FROM THIS FOOLISH DREAM OF HIS!
FOOLISH DREAM...
....IS THAT WHAT IT IS...?
HMPH.
MNCH
AH... WHAT'S THIS?
ZMM MMM

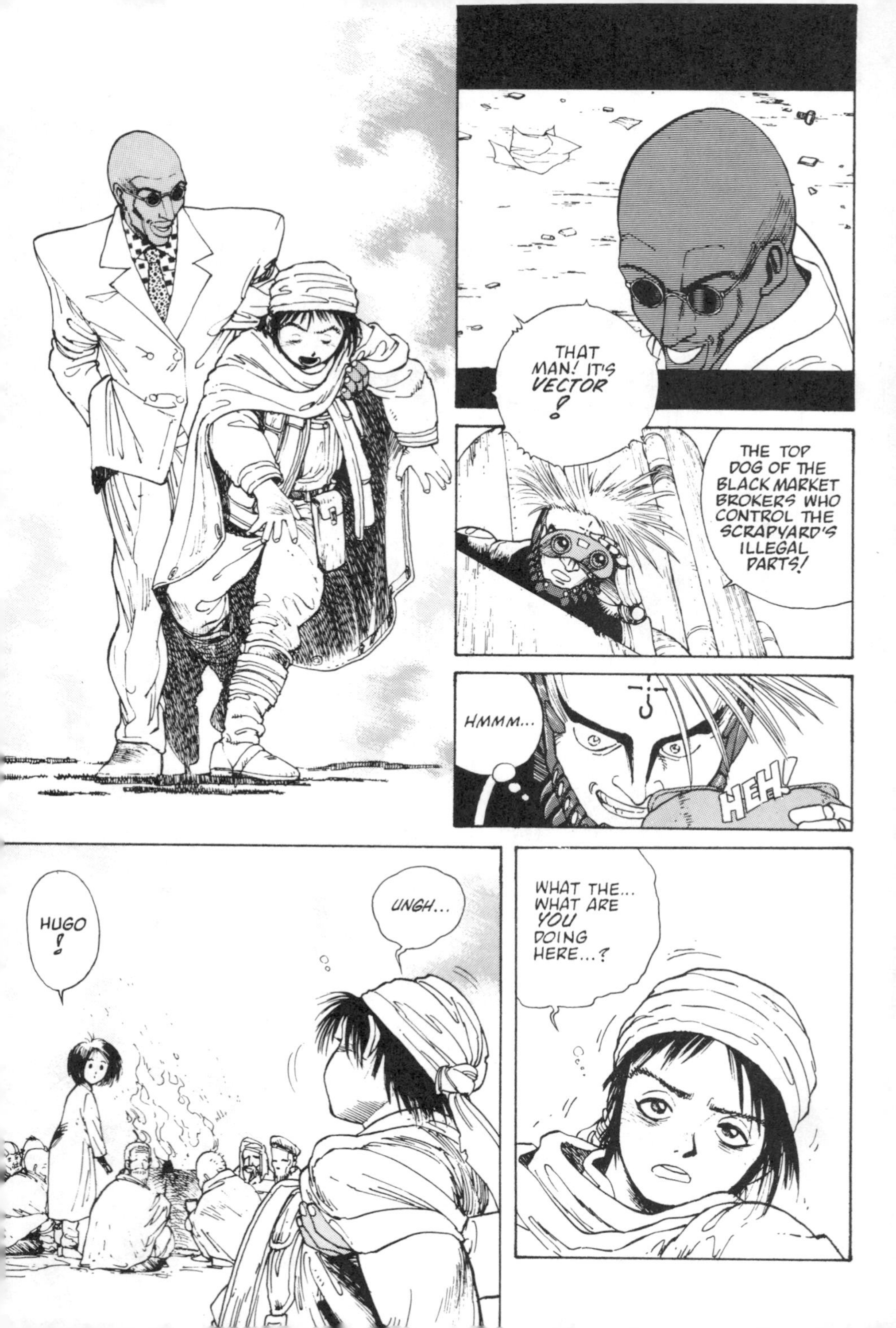
THAT MAN! IT'S VECTOR!
THE TOP DOG OF THE BLACK MARKET BROKERS WHO CONTROL THE SCRAPYARD'S ILLEGAL PARTS!
HMMM...
HEH!
HUGO!
UNGH...
WHAT THE... WHAT ARE YOU DOING HERE...?

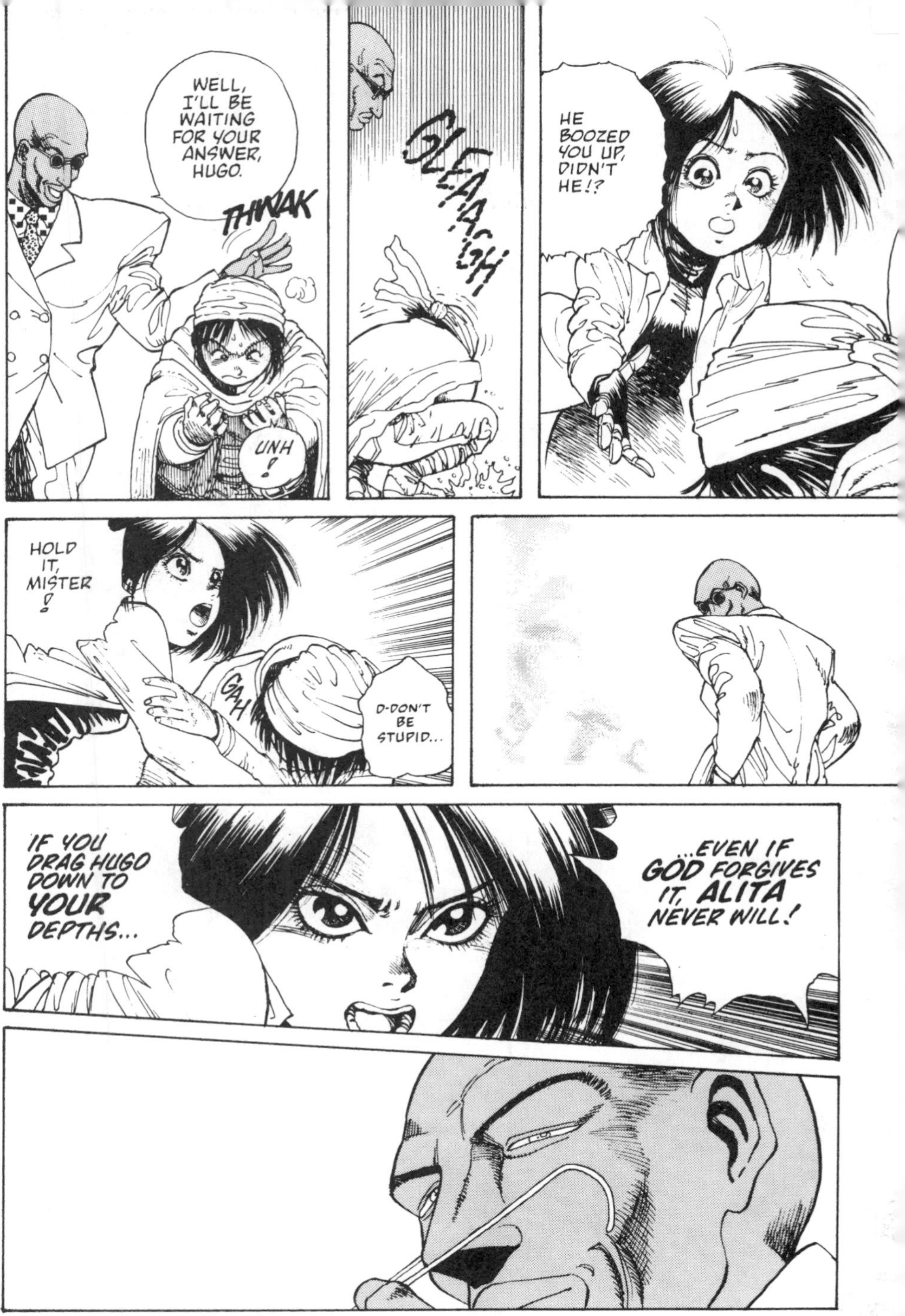
WELL, I'LL BE WAITING FOR YOUR ANSWER, HUGO.
THWAK
UNH!
GLEAAAGH
HE BOOZED YOU UP, DIDN'T HE!?
HOLD IT, MISTER!
GAH
D-DON'T BE STUPID...
IF YOU DRAG HUGO DOWN TO YOUR DEPTHS...
...EVEN IF GOD FORGIVES IT, ALITA NEVER WILL!

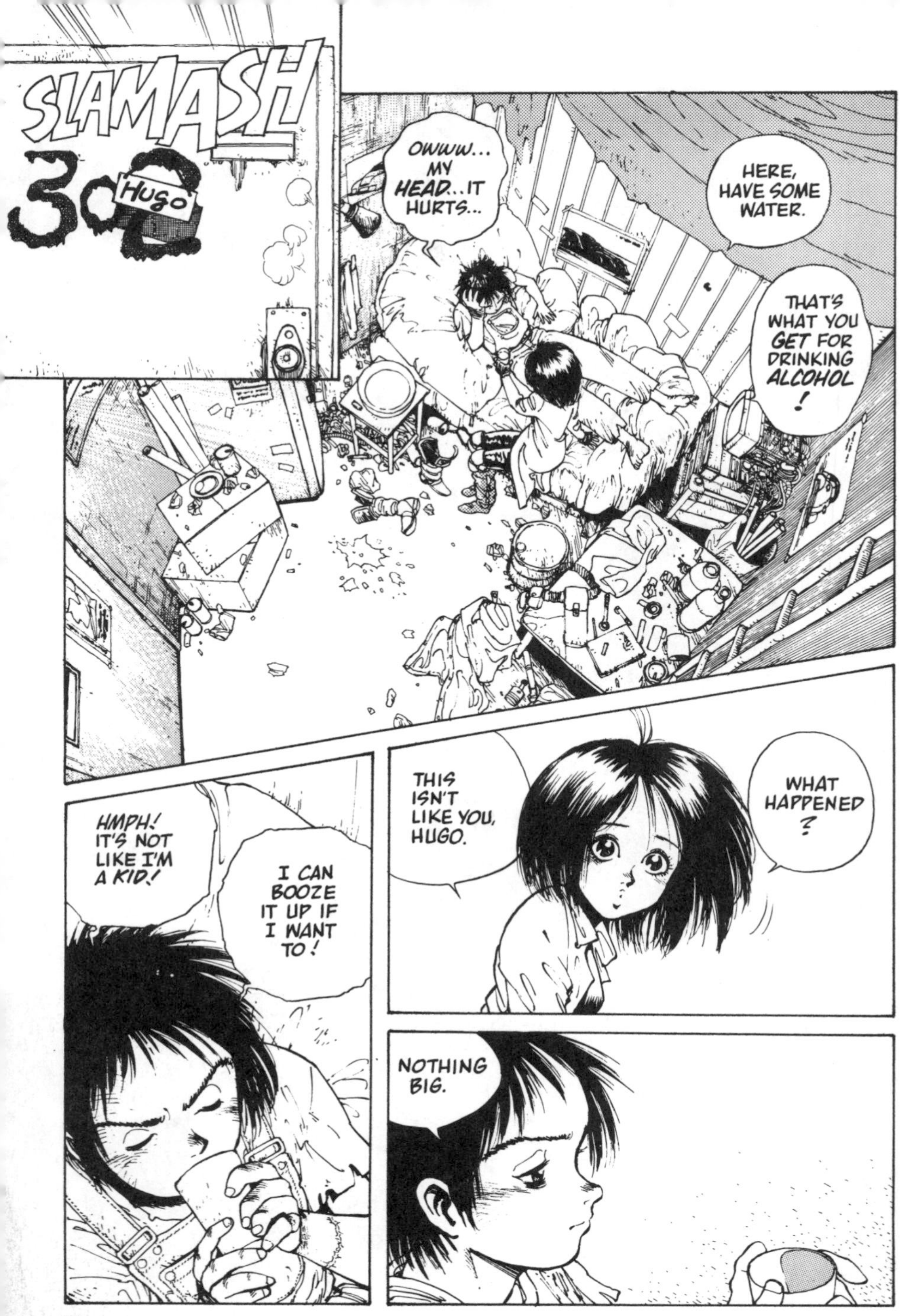
SLAMASH
30
HUGO
OWWW... MY HEAD...IT HURTS...
HERE, HAVE SOME WATER.
THAT'S WHAT YOU GET FOR DRINKING ALCOHOL!
HMPH! IT'S NOT LIKE I'M A KID!
I CAN BOOZE IT UP IF I WANT TO!
THIS ISN'T LIKE YOU, HUGO.
WHAT HAPPENED?
NOTHING BIG.

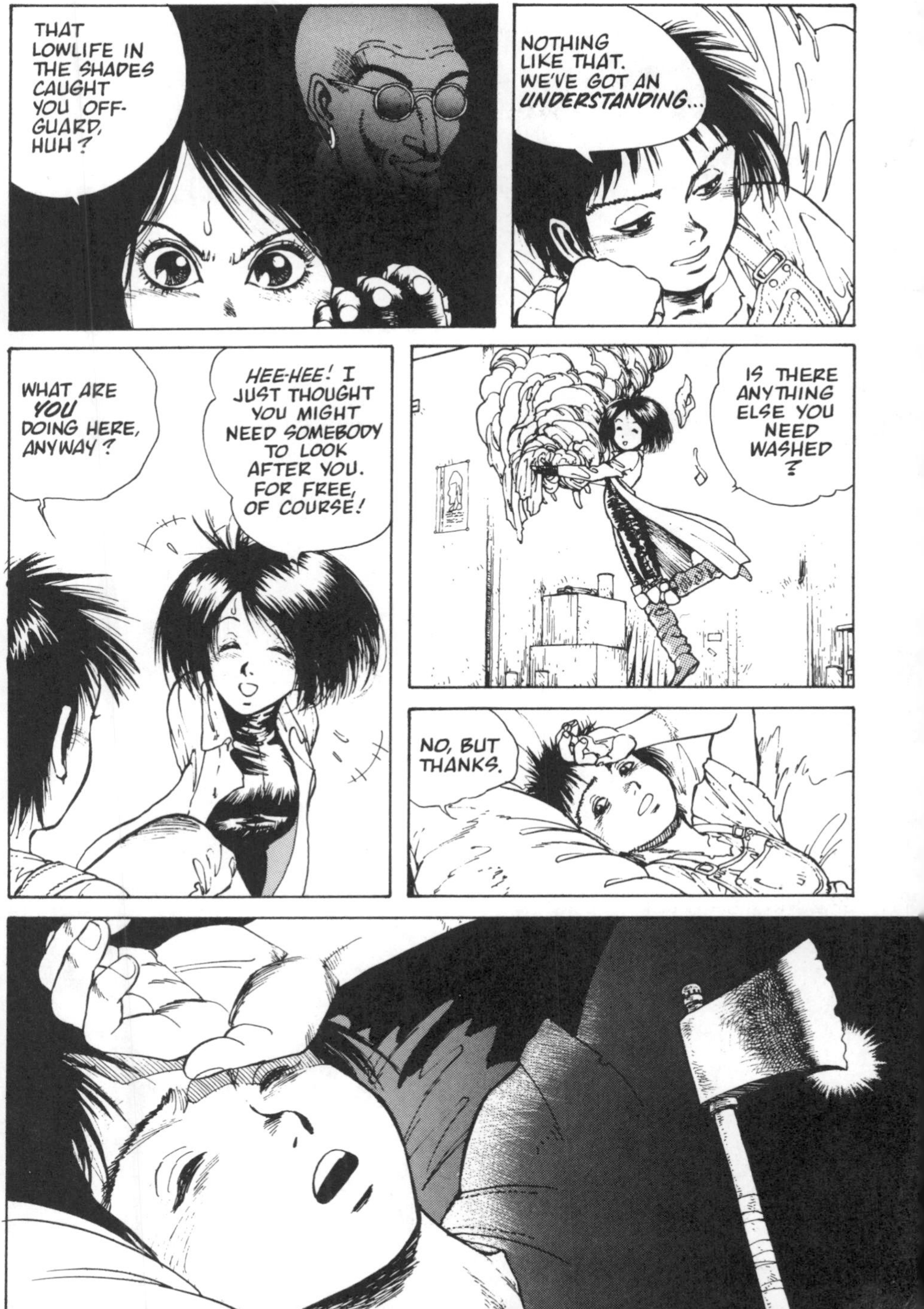
THAT LOWLIFE IN THE SHADES CAUGHT YOU OFF-GUARD, HUH?
NOTHING LIKE THAT. WE'VE GOT AN UNDERSTANDING...
WHAT ARE YOU DOING HERE, ANYWAY?
HEE-HEE! I JUST THOUGHT YOU MIGHT NEED SOMEBODY TO LOOK AFTER YOU. FOR FREE, OF COURSE!
IS THERE ANYTHING ELSE YOU NEED WASHED?
NO, BUT THANKS.

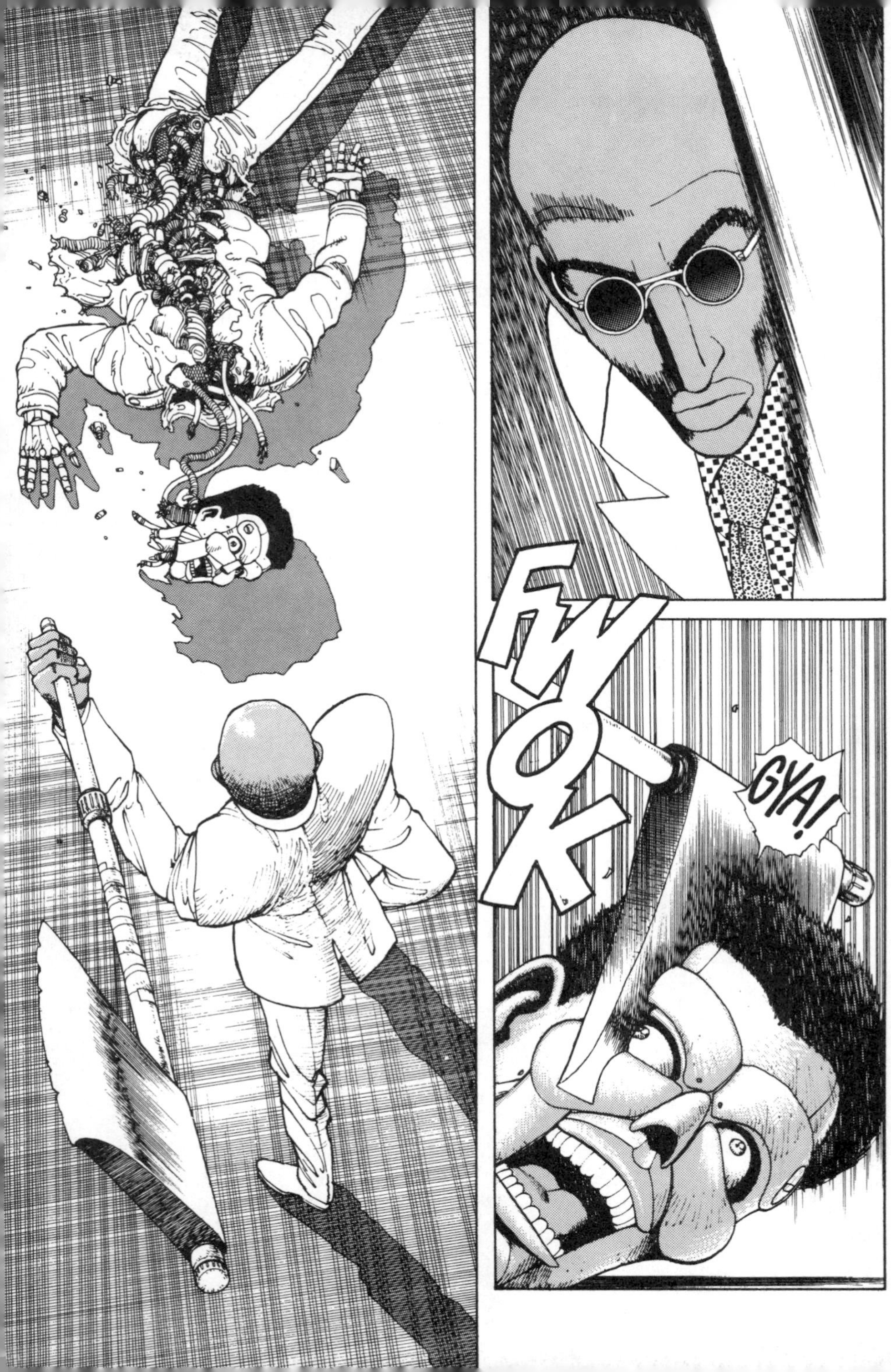
FWOK
GYA!

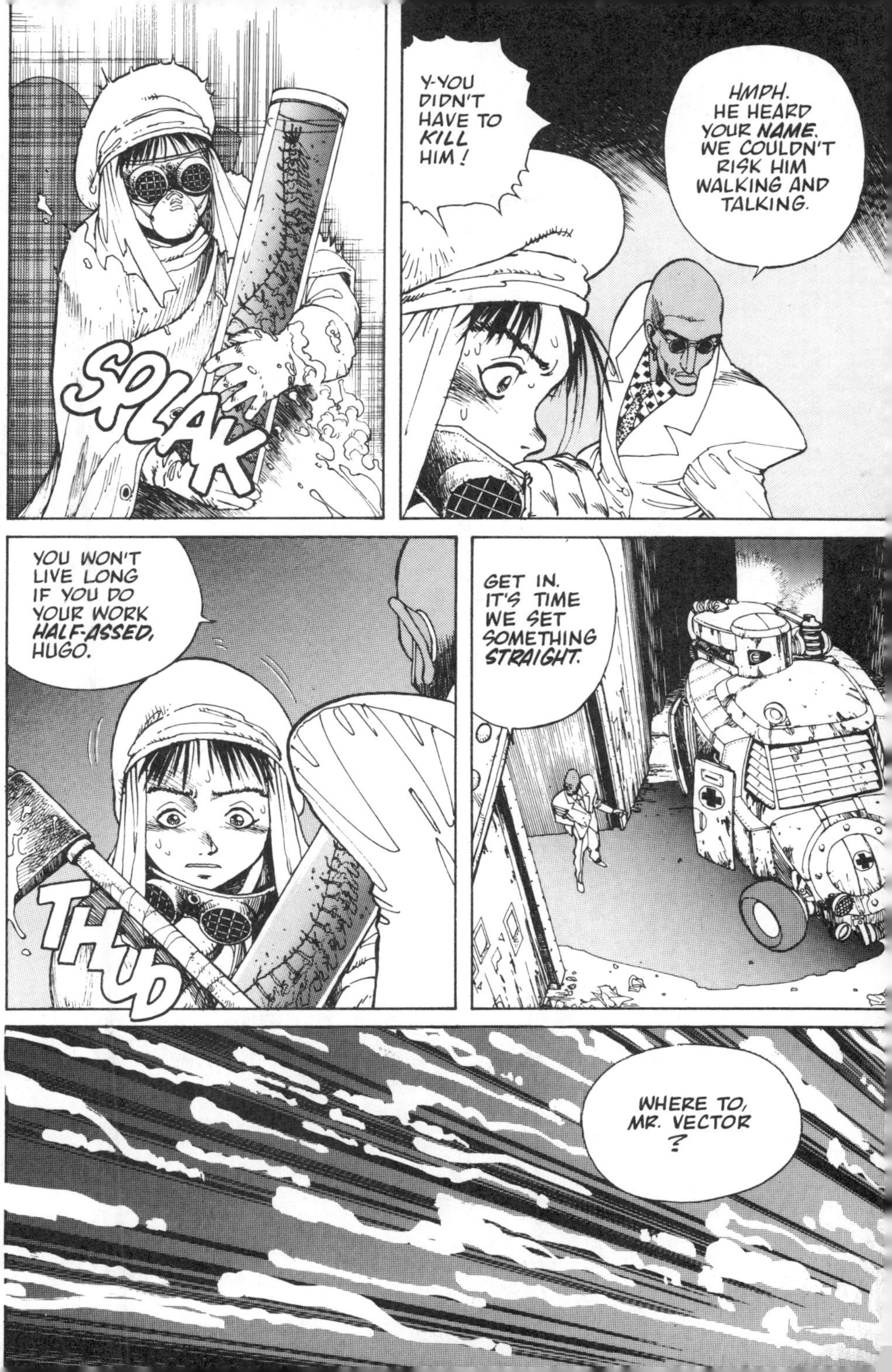
SPLAK
Y-YOU DIDN'T HAVE TO KILL HIM!
HMPH. HE HEARD YOUR NAME. WE COULDN'T RISK HIM WALKING AND TALKING.
YOU WON'T LIVE LONG IF YOU DO YOUR WORK HALF-ASSED, HUGO.
THUD
GET IN. IT'S TIME WE SET SOMETHING STRAIGHT.
WHERE TO, MR. VECTOR?

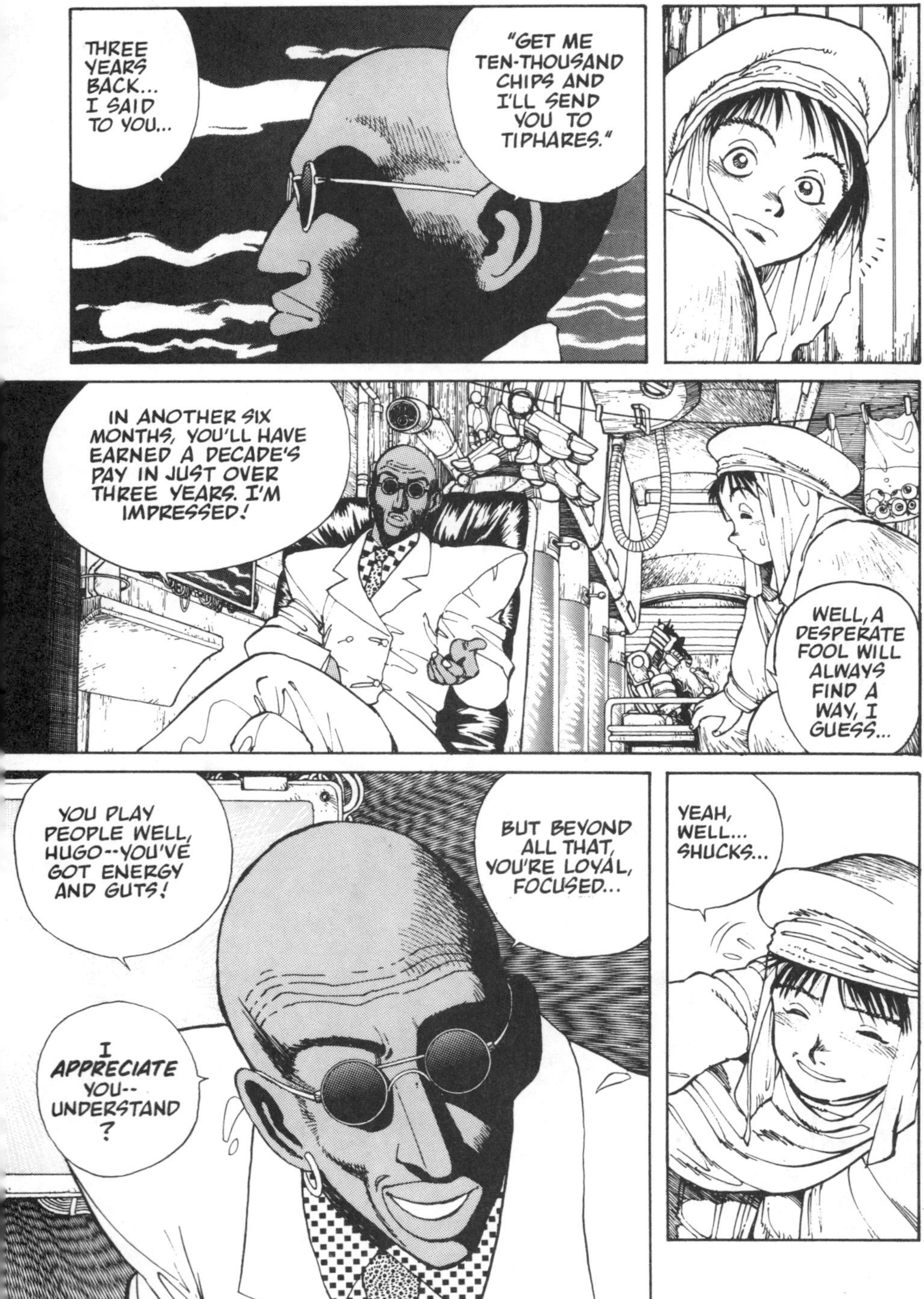
THREE YEARS BACK... I SAID TO YOU...
"GET ME TEN-THOUSAND CHIPS AND I'LL SEND YOU TO TIPHARES."
IN ANOTHER SIX MONTHS, YOU'LL HAVE EARNED A DECADE'S PAY IN JUST OVER THREE YEARS. I'M IMPRESSED!
WELL, A DESPERATE FOOL WILL ALWAYS FIND A WAY, I GUESS...
YOU PLAY PEOPLE WELL, HUGO--YOU'VE GOT ENERGY AND GUTS!
BUT BEYOND ALL THAT, YOU'RE LOYAL, FOCUSED...
I *APPRECIATE* YOU--UNDERSTAND?
YEAH, WELL... SHUCKS...

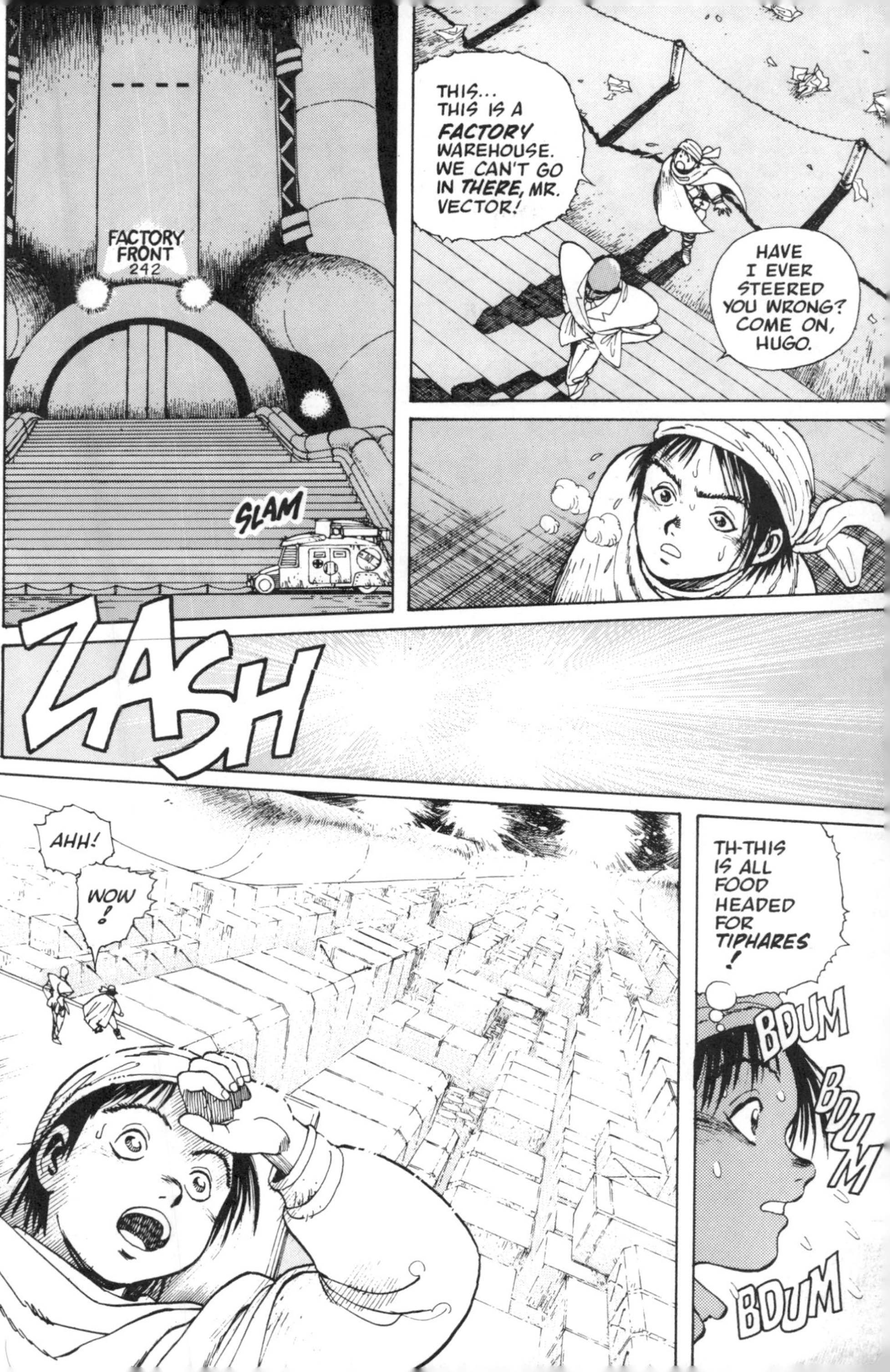
FACTORY FRONT 242
SLAM
THIS... THIS IS A FACTORY WAREHOUSE. WE CAN'T GO IN THERE, MR. VECTOR!
HAVE I EVER STEERED YOU WRONG? COME ON, HUGO.
ZASH
AHH!
WOW!
TH-THIS IS ALL FOOD HEADED FOR TIPHARES!
BDUM
BDUM
BDUM
BDUM

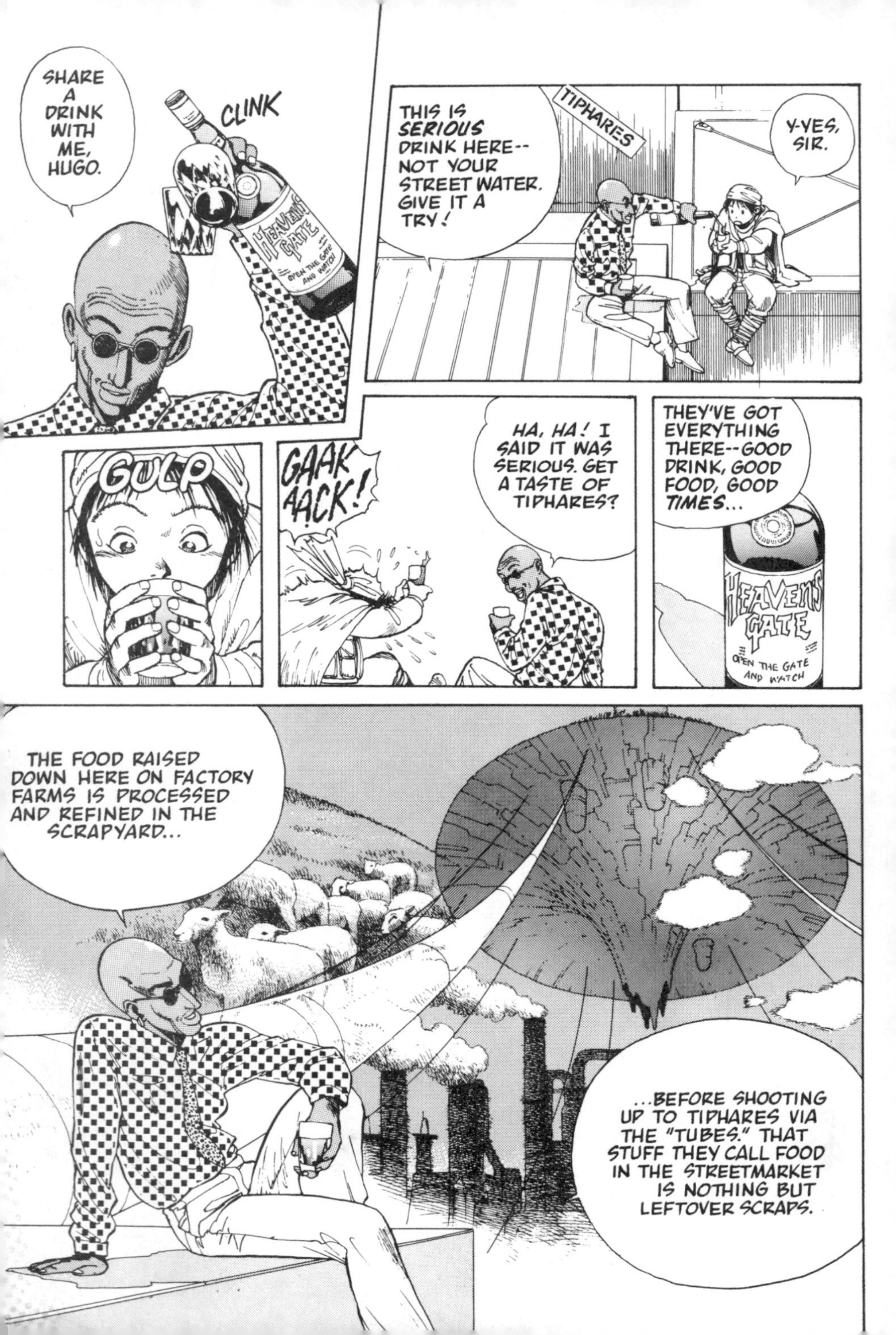
SHARE A DRINK WITH ME, HUGO.
CLINK
HEAVEN'S GATE
OPEN THE GATE AND WATCH
TIPHARES
THIS IS SERIOUS DRINK HERE-- NOT YOUR STREET WATER. GIVE IT A TRY!
Y-YES, SIR.
GULP
GAAK AACK!
HA, HA! I SAID IT WAS SERIOUS. GET A TASTE OF TIPHARES?
THEY'VE GOT EVERYTHING THERE--GOOD DRINK, GOOD FOOD, GOOD TIMES...
HEAVEN'S GATE
OPEN THE GATE AND WATCH
THE FOOD RAISED DOWN HERE ON FACTORY FARMS IS PROCESSED AND REFINED IN THE SCRAPYARD...
...BEFORE SHOOTING UP TO TIPHARES VIA THE "TUBES." THAT STUFF THEY CALL FOOD IN THE STREETMARKET IS NOTHING BUT LEFTOVER SCRAPS.

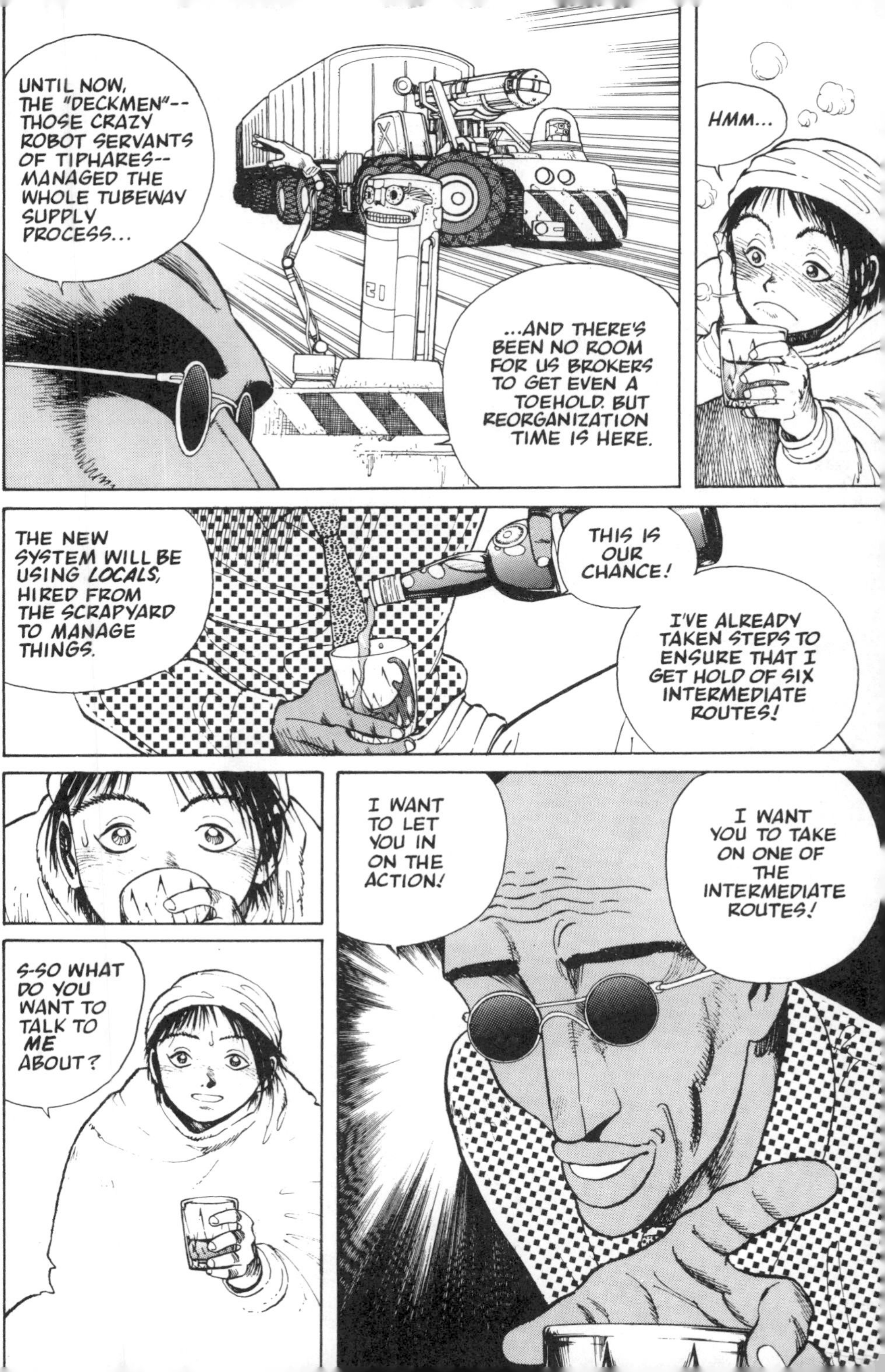
UNTIL NOW, THE "DECKMEN"-- THOSE CRAZY ROBOT SERVANTS OF TIPHARES-- MANAGED THE WHOLE TUBEWAY SUPPLY PROCESS...
...AND THERE'S BEEN NO ROOM FOR US BROKERS TO GET EVEN A TOEHOLD. BUT REORGANIZATION TIME IS HERE.
HMM...
THE NEW SYSTEM WILL BE USING *LOCALS*, HIRED FROM THE SCRAPYARD TO MANAGE THINGS.
THIS IS OUR CHANCE!
I'VE ALREADY TAKEN STEPS TO ENSURE THAT I GET HOLD OF SIX INTERMEDIATE ROUTES!
I WANT YOU TO TAKE ON ONE OF THE INTERMEDIATE ROUTES!
I WANT TO LET YOU IN ON THE ACTION!
S-SO WHAT DO YOU WANT TO TALK TO *ME* ABOUT?

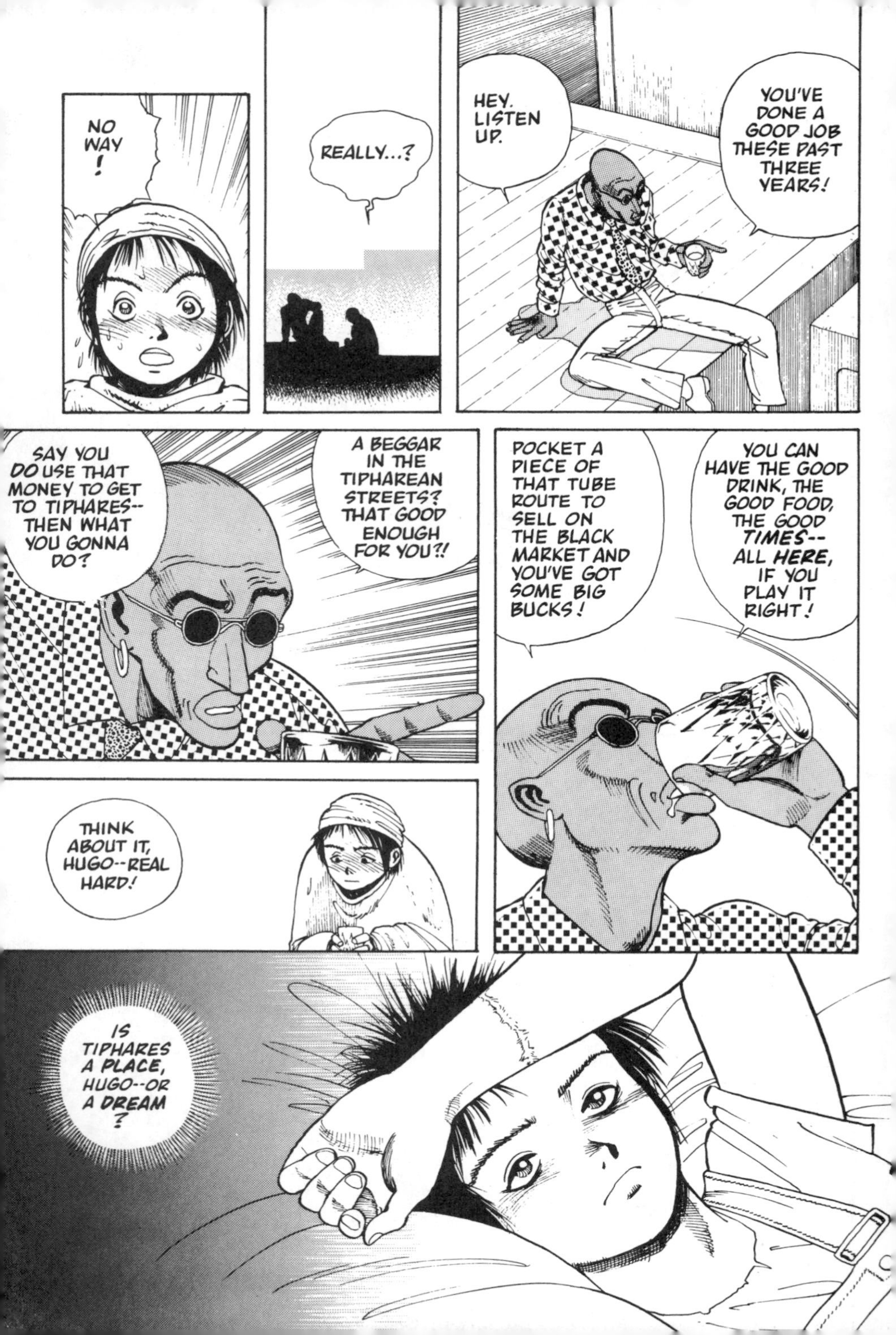
NO WAY !
REALLY...?
HEY. LISTEN UP.
YOU'VE DONE A GOOD JOB THESE PAST THREE YEARS!
SAY YOU DO USE THAT MONEY TO GET TO TIPHARES-- THEN WHAT YOU GONNA DO?
A BEGGAR IN THE TIPHAREAN STREETS? THAT GOOD ENOUGH FOR YOU?!
POCKET A PIECE OF THAT TUBE ROUTE TO SELL ON THE BLACK MARKET AND YOU'VE GOT SOME BIG BUCKS!
YOU CAN HAVE THE GOOD DRINK, THE GOOD FOOD, THE GOOD TIMES-- ALL HERE, IF YOU PLAY IT RIGHT!
THINK ABOUT IT, HUGO--REAL HARD!
IS TIPHARES A PLACE, HUGO--OR A DREAM ?

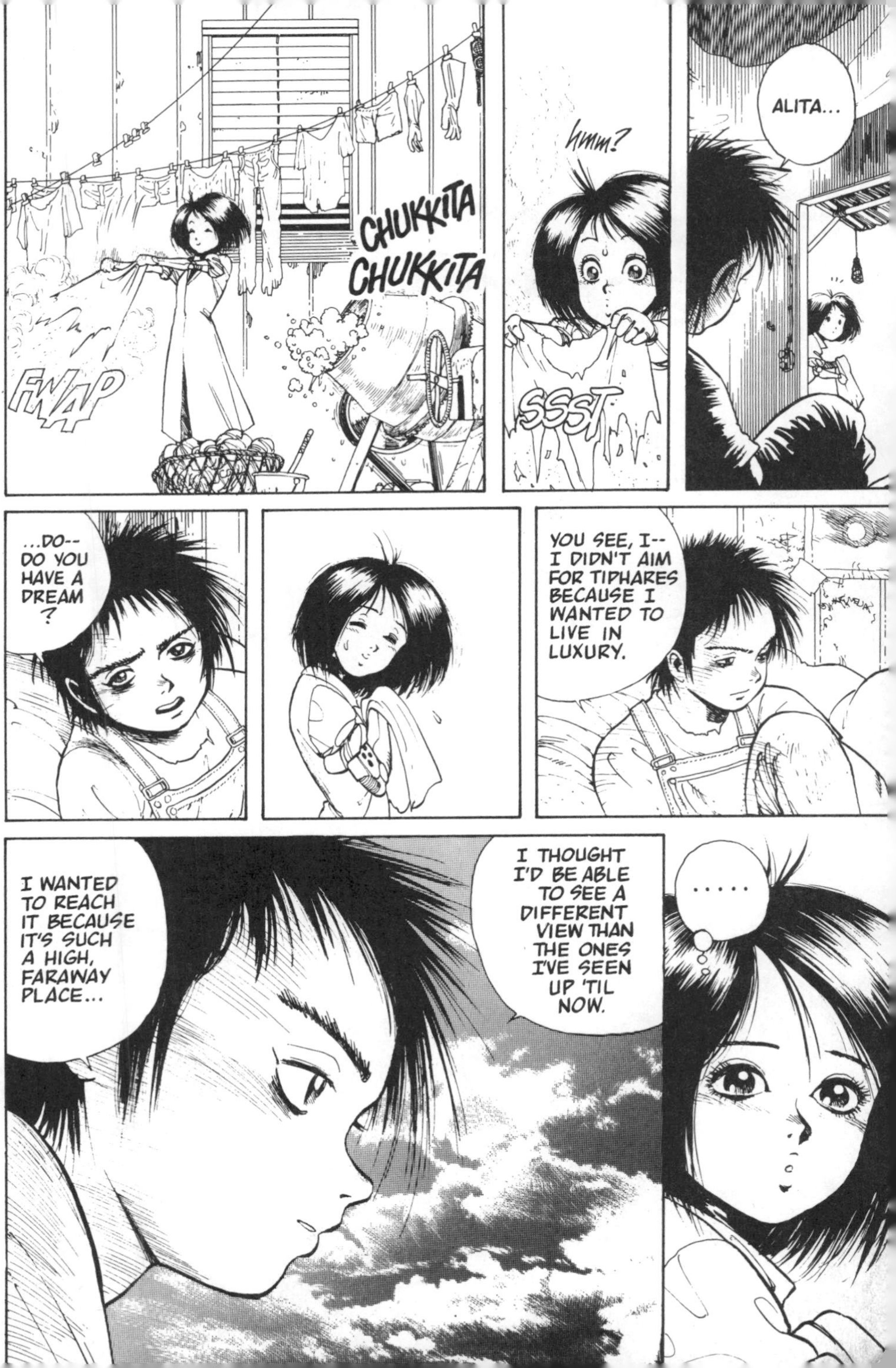
CHUKKITA
CHUKKITA
FWAP
hmm?
SSST
ALITA...
...DO-- DO YOU HAVE A DREAM ?
YOU SEE, I-- I DIDN'T AIM FOR TIPHARES BECAUSE I WANTED TO LIVE IN LUXURY.
I WANTED TO REACH IT BECAUSE IT'S SUCH A HIGH, FARAWAY PLACE...
I THOUGHT I'D BE ABLE TO SEE A DIFFERENT VIEW THAN THE ONES I'VE SEEN UP 'TIL NOW.
.....

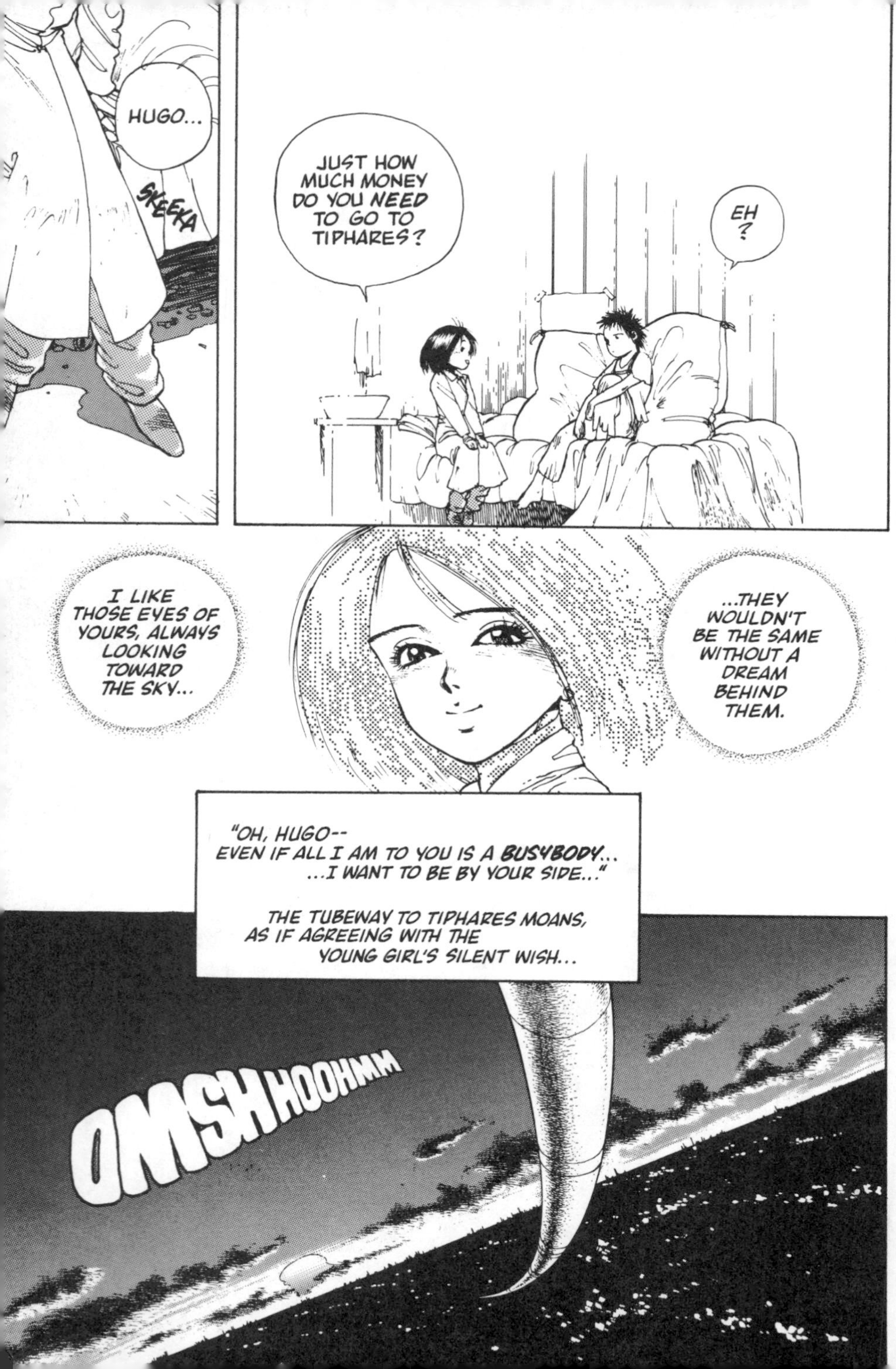
HUGO...
SKEEKA
JUST HOW MUCH MONEY DO YOU NEED TO GO TO TIPHARES?
EH?
I LIKE THOSE EYES OF YOURS, ALWAYS LOOKING TOWARD THE SKY...
...THEY WOULDN'T BE THE SAME WITHOUT A DREAM BEHIND THEM.
"OH, HUGO-- EVEN IF ALL I AM TO YOU IS A BUSYBODY... ...I WANT TO BE BY YOUR SIDE..."
THE TUBEWAY TO TIPHARES MOANS, AS IF AGREEING WITH THE YOUNG GIRL'S SILENT WISH...
OMSHHOOHMM

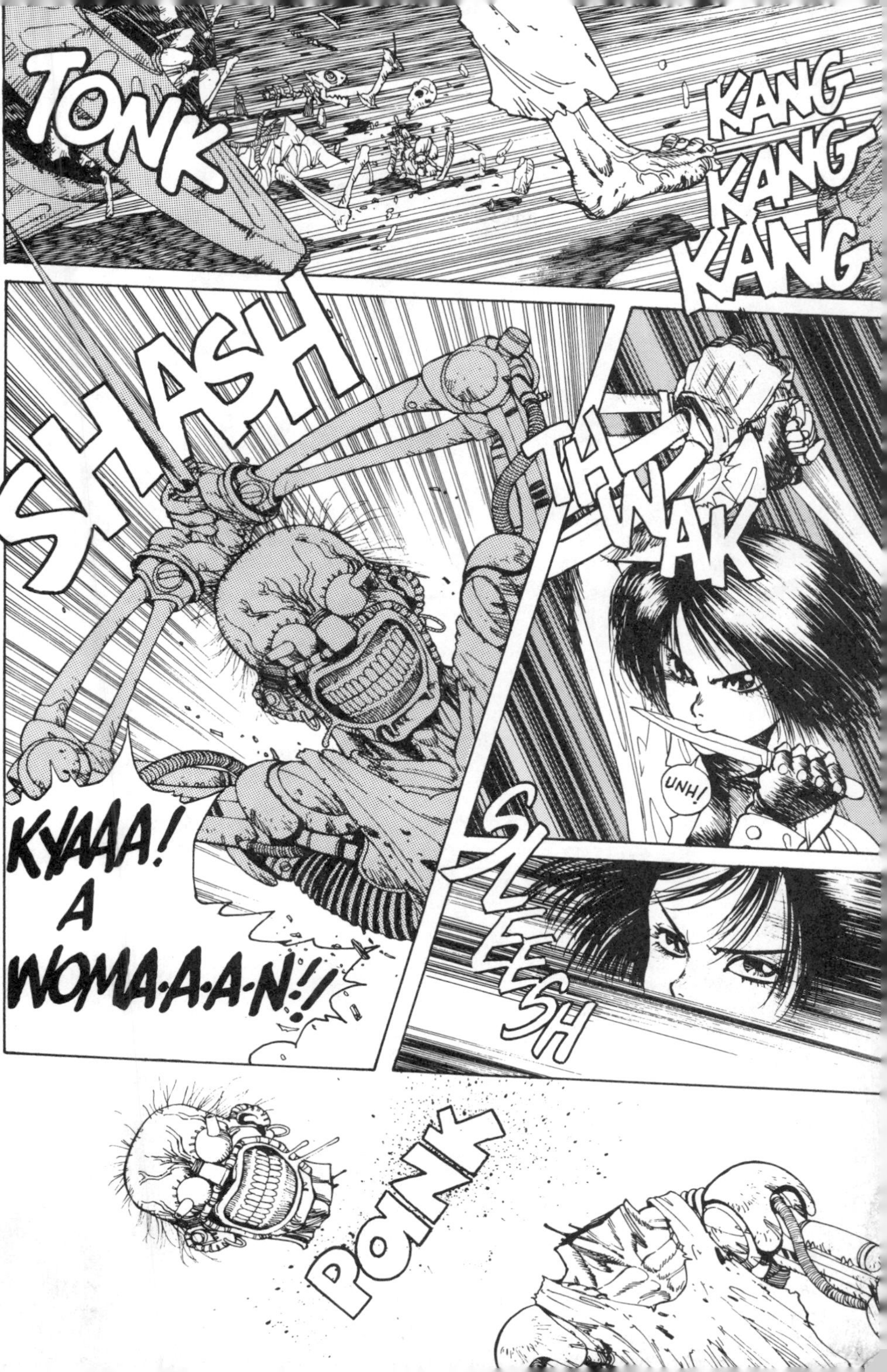
TONK
KANG KANG KANG
SHASH
KYAAA! A WOMA-A-A-N!!
THWAK
UNH!
SLEESH
POINK

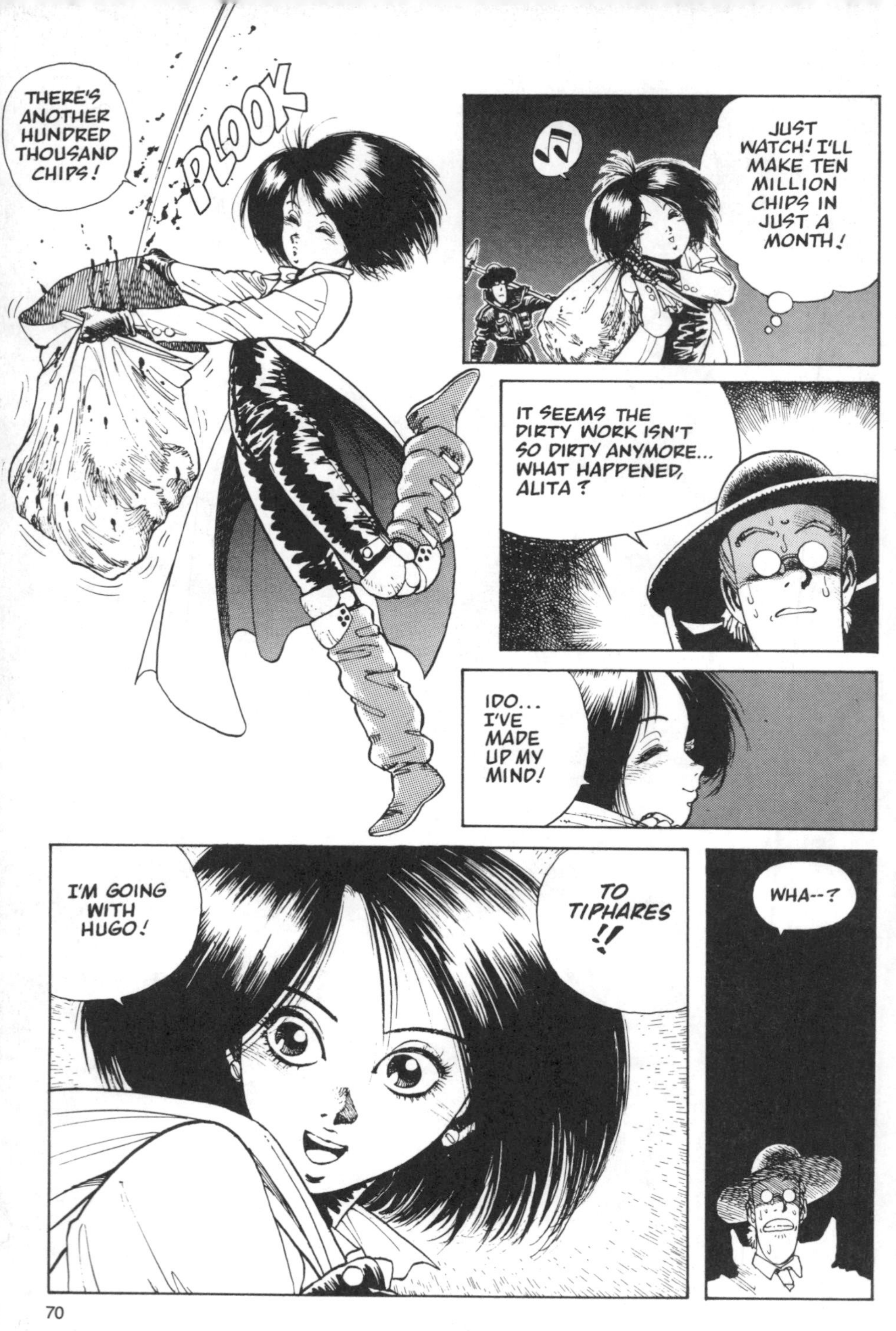

THERE'S ANOTHER HUNDRED THOUSAND CHIPS!
PLOOK
♫
JUST WATCH! I'LL MAKE TEN MILLION CHIPS IN JUST A MONTH!
IT SEEMS THE DIRTY WORK ISN'T SO DIRTY ANYMORE... WHAT HAPPENED, ALITA?
IDO... I'VE MADE UP MY MIND!
I'M GOING WITH HUGO!
TO TIPHARES!!
WHA--?

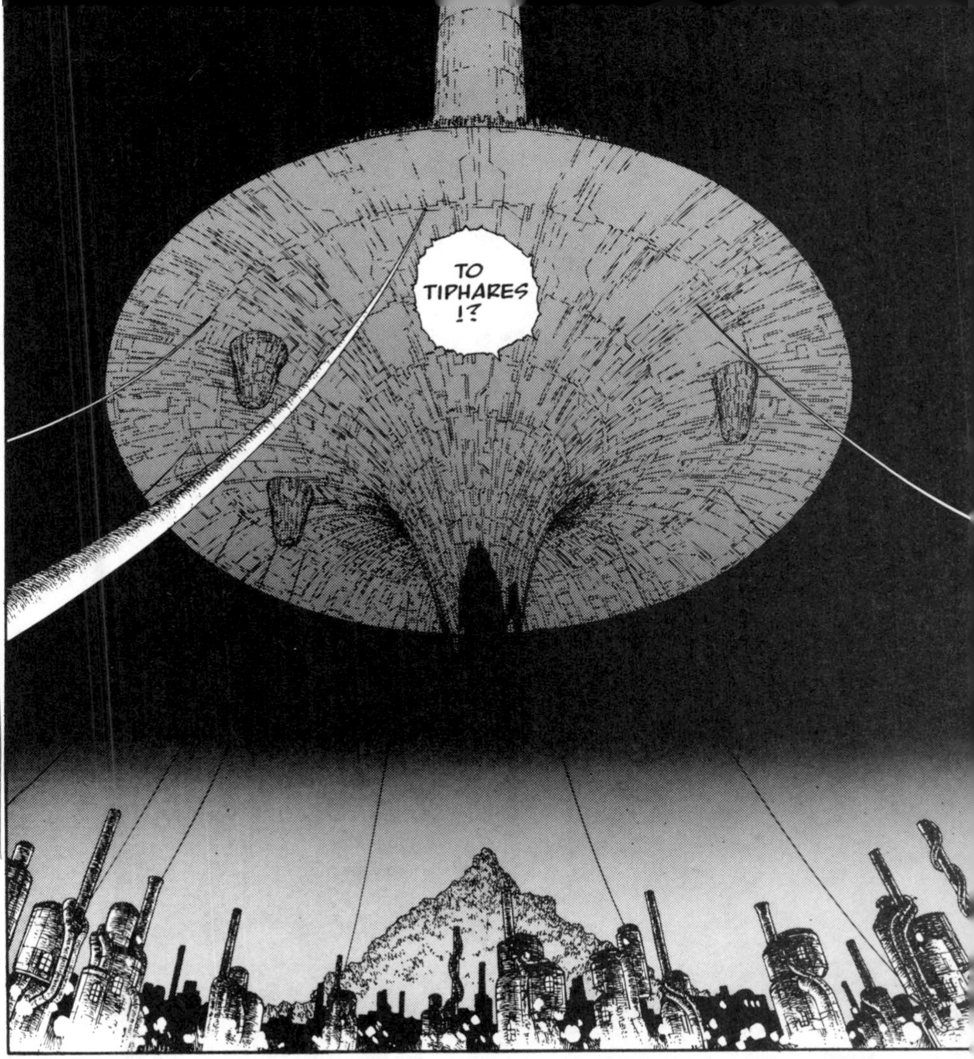
TO TIPHARES !?
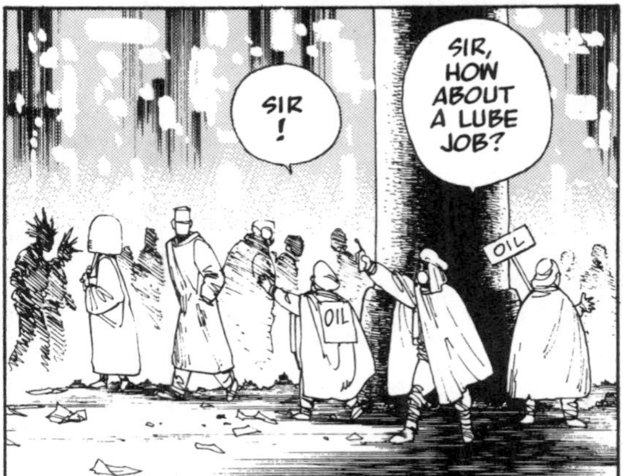
SIR !
SIR, HOW ABOUT A LUBE JOB?
OIL
OIL
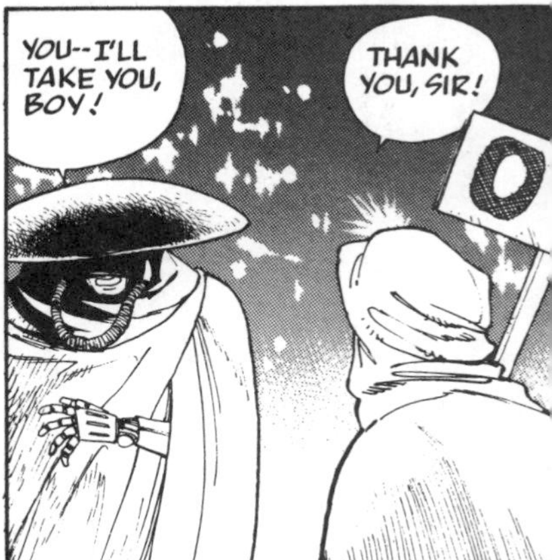
YOU--I'LL TAKE YOU, BOY !
THANK YOU, SIR!

TEE-
HEE

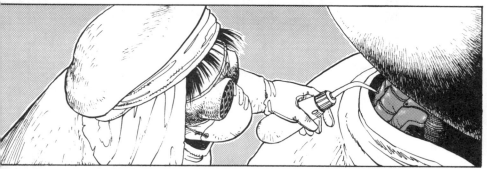

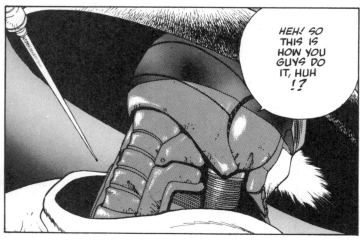

HEH! SO THIS IS HOW YOU GUYS DO IT, HUH !?

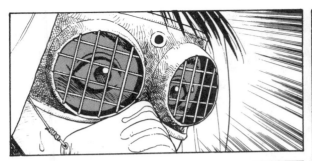

SKATCH

WHEN *YOUR* FACE SHOWS UP ON THE BOUNTY LIST...

...I BET IT WILL REALLY MESS UP THAT LITTLE *ALITA* OF YOURS-- DON'T YOU, *HUGO*?

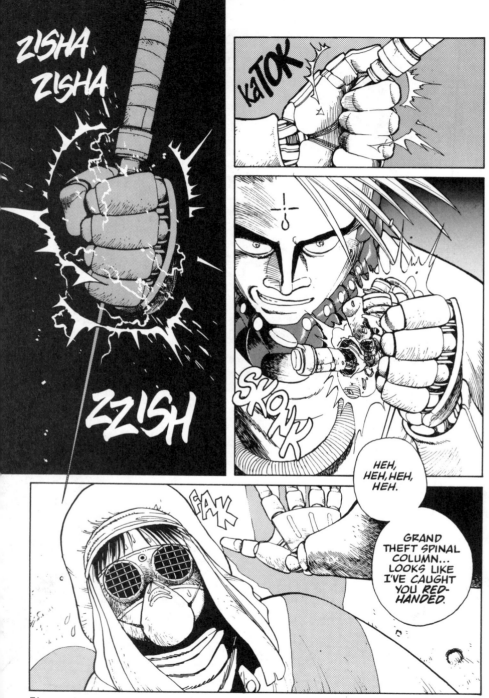

ZISHA
ZISHA

ZZISH

KATOK

SKONK

FAK

HEH, HEH, HEH, HEH.

GRAND THEFT SPINAL COLUMN... LOOKS LIKE I'VE CAUGHT YOU RED-HANDED.

ACCORDING TO "FACTORY LAW"... ...ROBBING A LIVING BEING OF HIS CENTRAL NERVOUS SYSTEM IS A BOUNTY LIST-GRADE OFFENSE, ISN'T IT?

A HUNTER-WARRIOR!

WE'RE IN FOR IT NOW...

LET'S SEE YOUR FACE...

...LITTLE HUGO!

I'M TELLING YOU, TAKE OFF YOUR MASK!

UNGH!

SKNCH

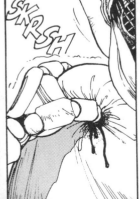

SKRSH

HEE, HEE, HEE.

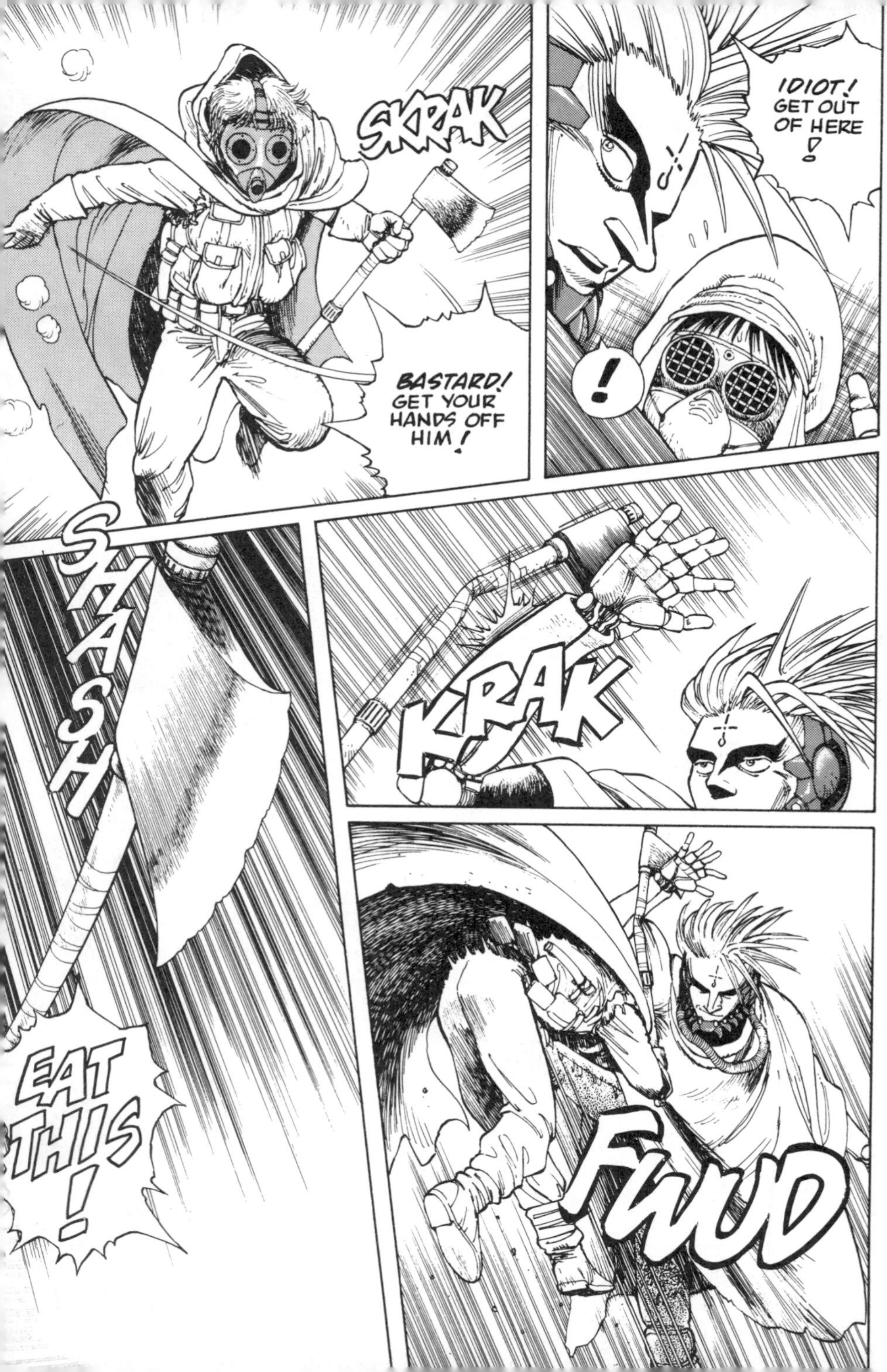
SKRAK
BASTARD! GET YOUR HANDS OFF HIM!
IDIOT! GET OUT OF HERE!
!
SHASH
KRAK
EAT THIS!
FWUD

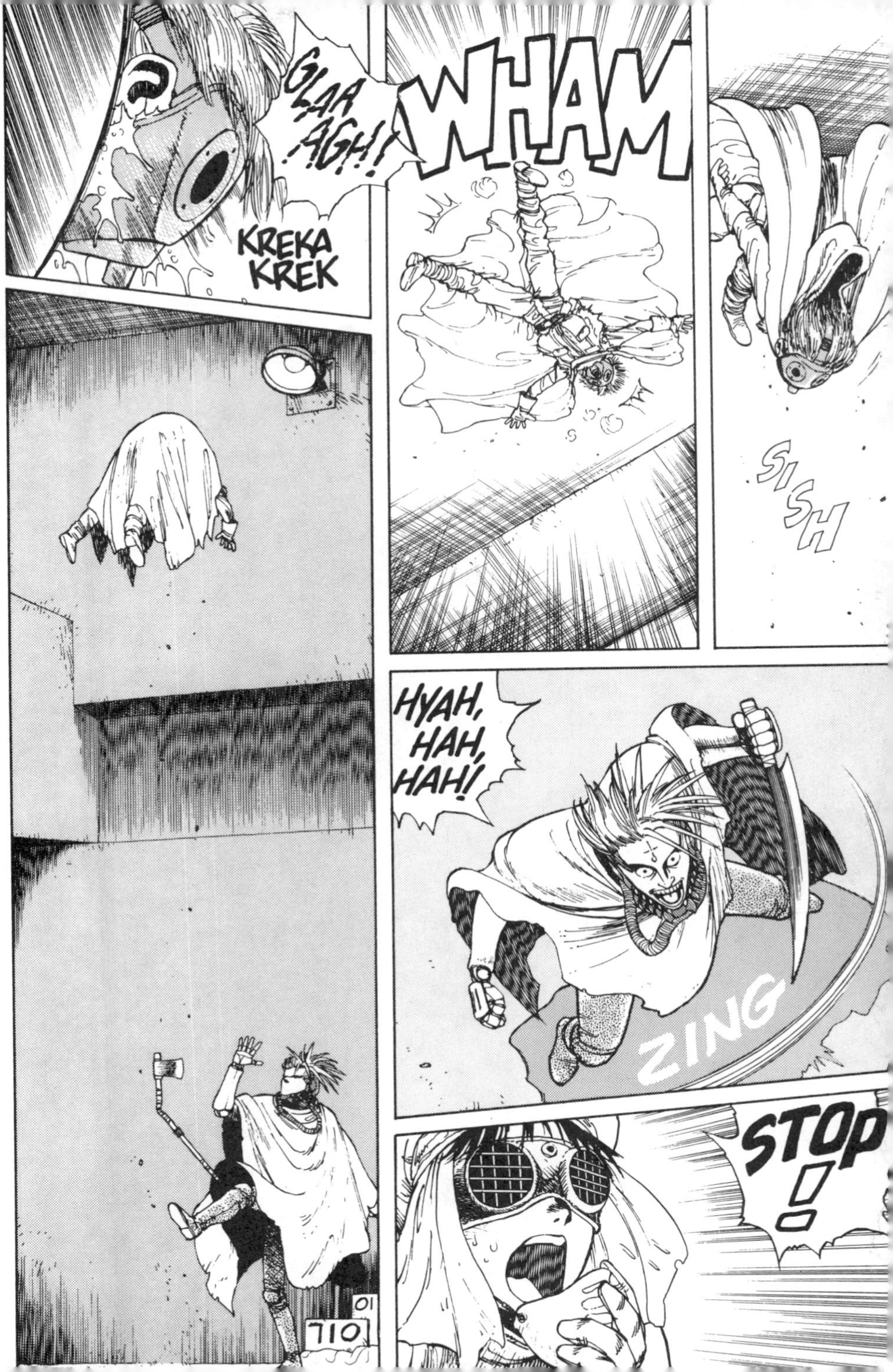
GLARAGH!!
KREKA KREK
WHAM
SISH
HYAH, HAH, HAH!
ZING
STOP!

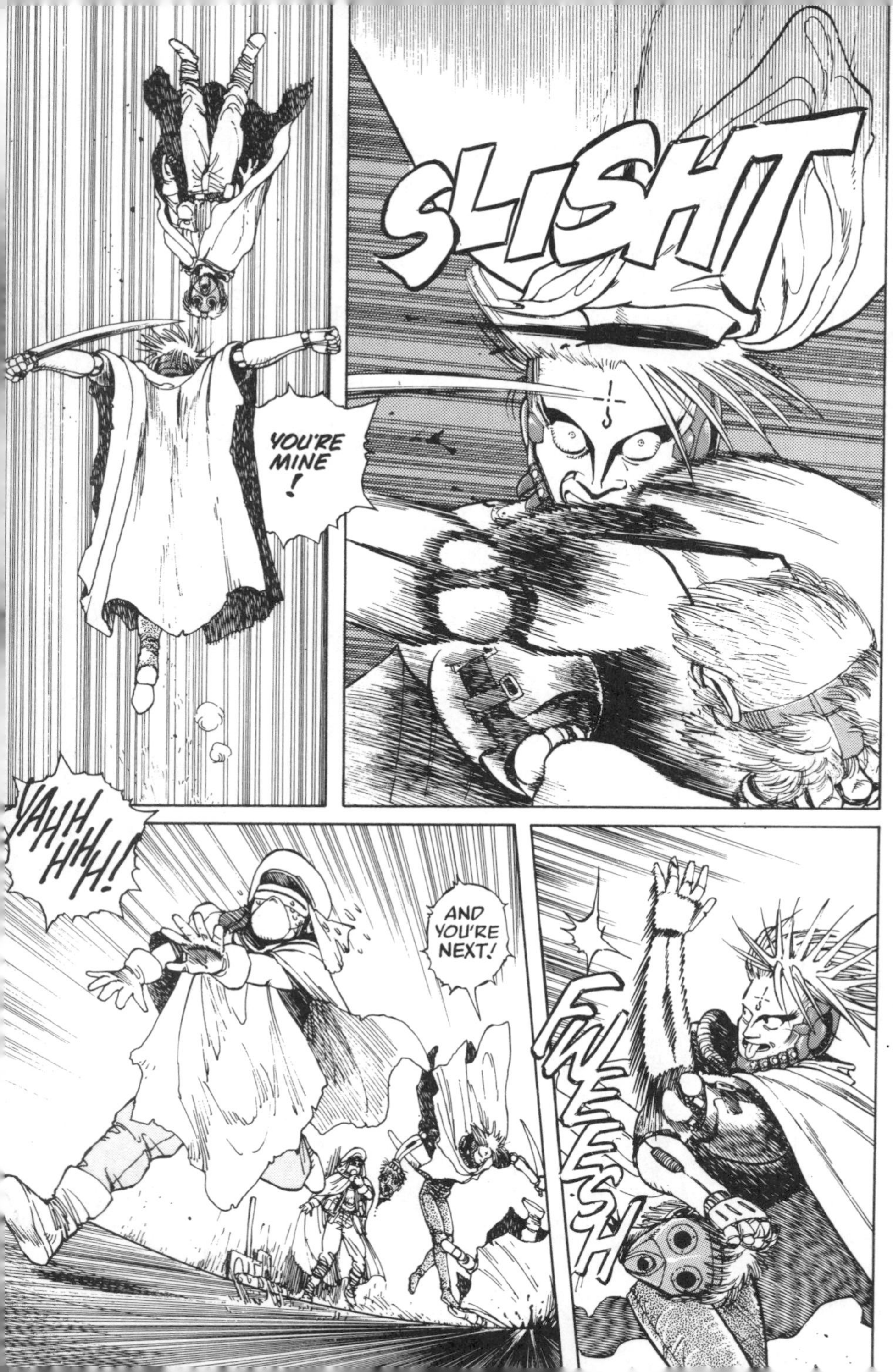
YOU'RE MINE!
SLISHT
YAHHHHHH!
AND YOU'RE NEXT!
FWEEESH

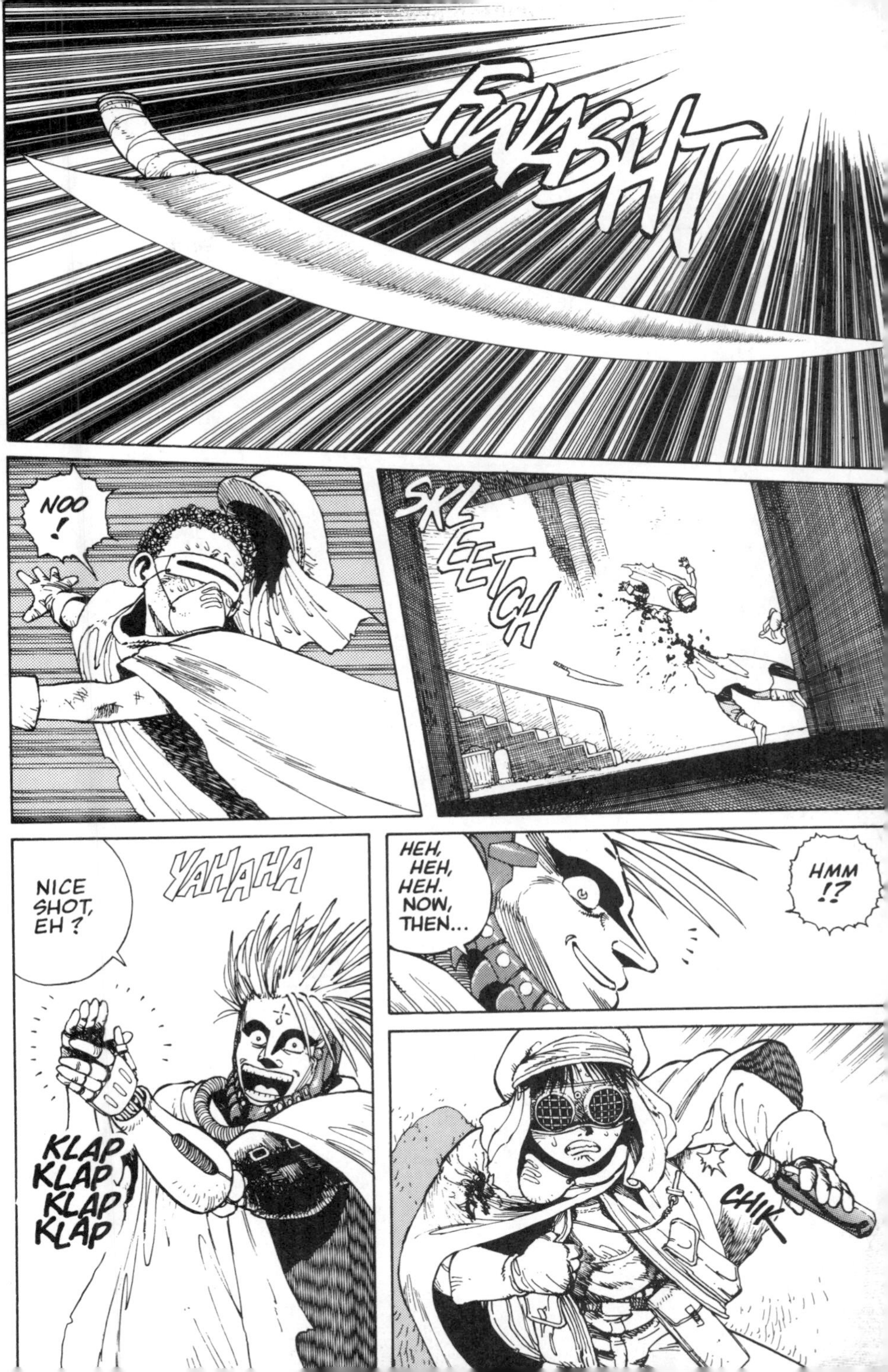
FWASHT
NOO!
SKLEETCH
NICE SHOT, EH?
YAHAHA
KLAP KLAP KLAP KLAP
HEH, HEH, HEH. NOW, THEN...
HMM !?
CHIK

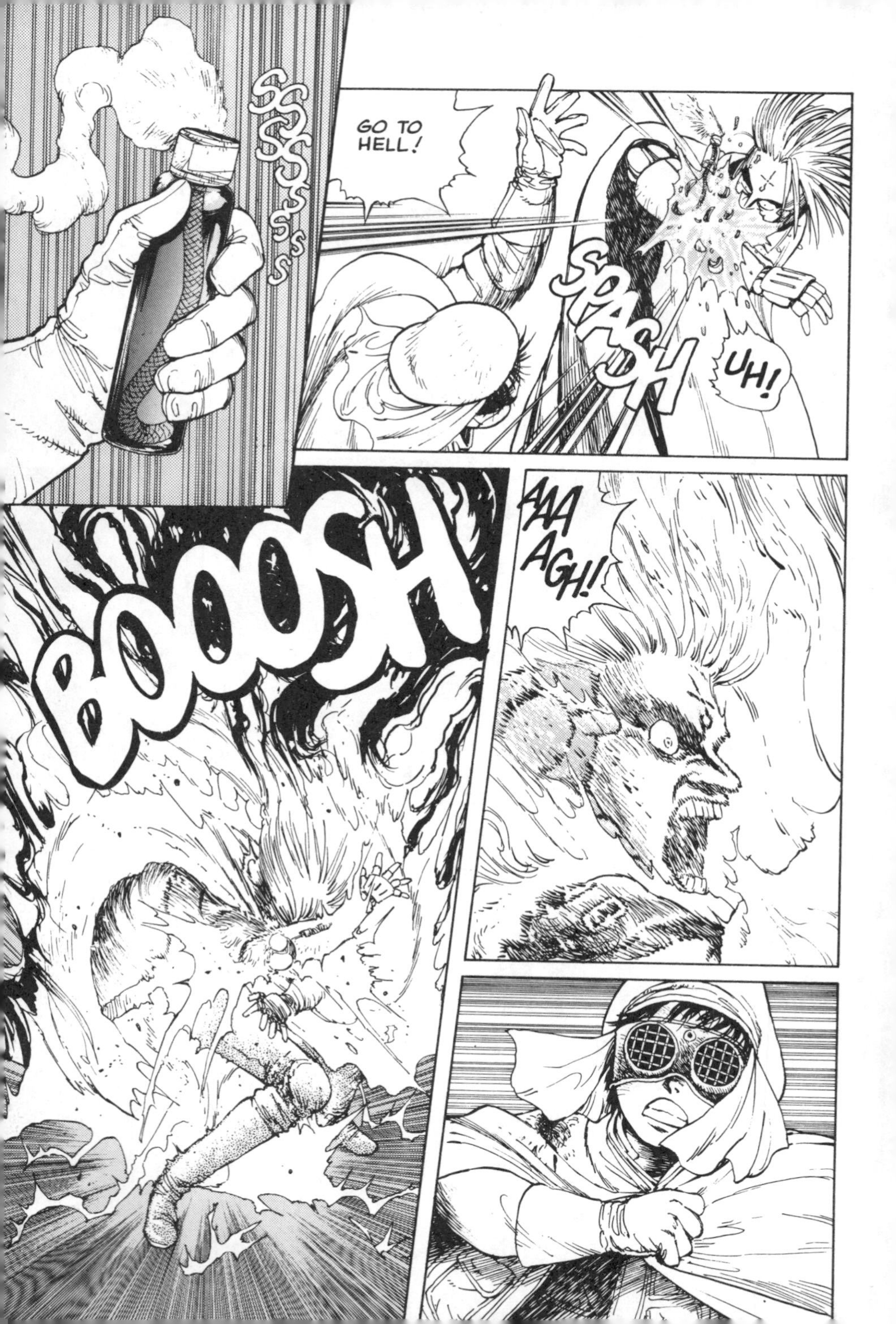
SSSSSSSSS
GO TO HELL!
SPASH
UH!
BOOOSH
AAA AGH!

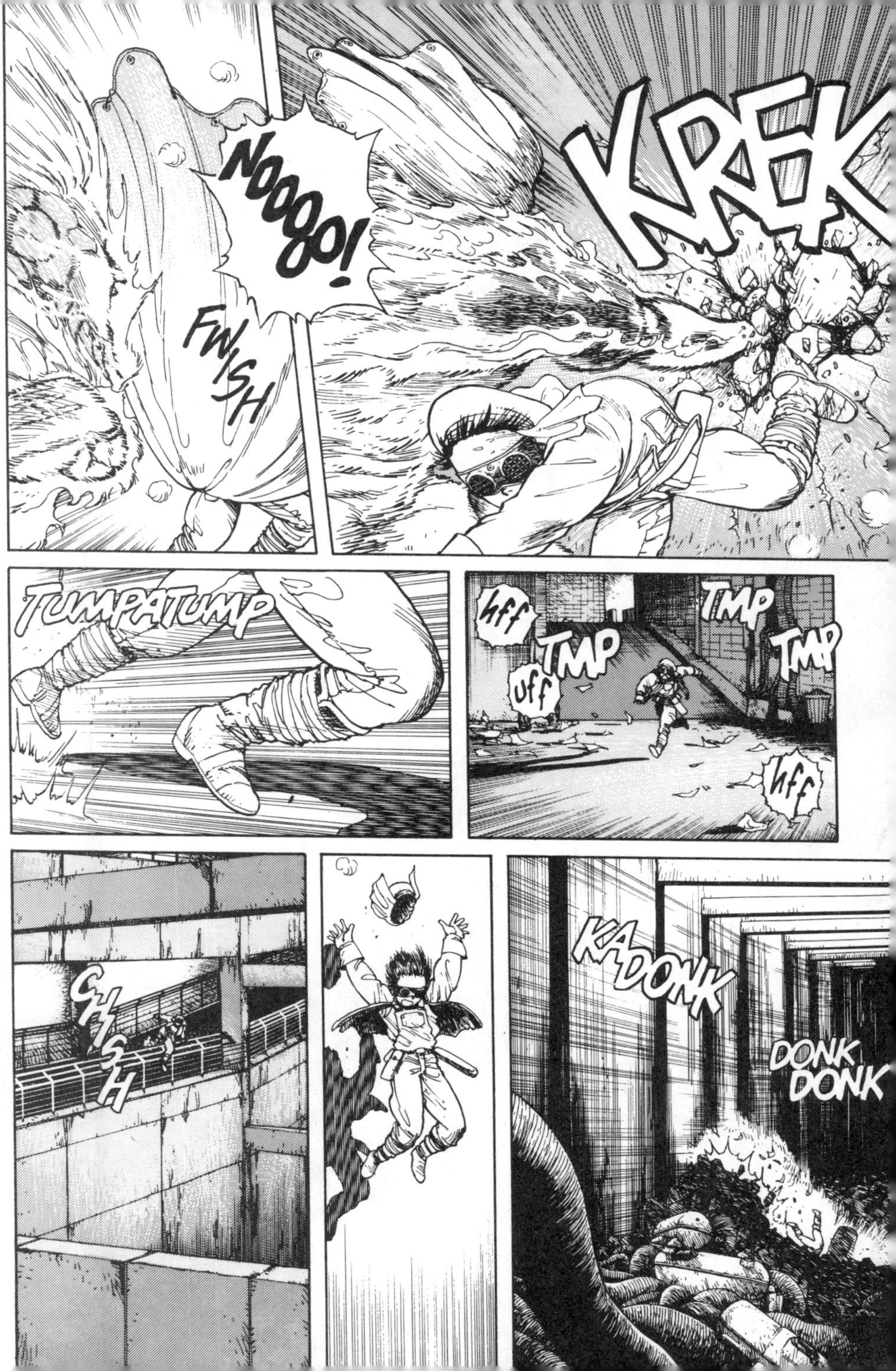
NOOOOOO!
FWISH
KREK
TUMPATUMP
hff
TMP
uff
TMP
TMP
TMP
hff
CHSH
KADONK
DONK DONK

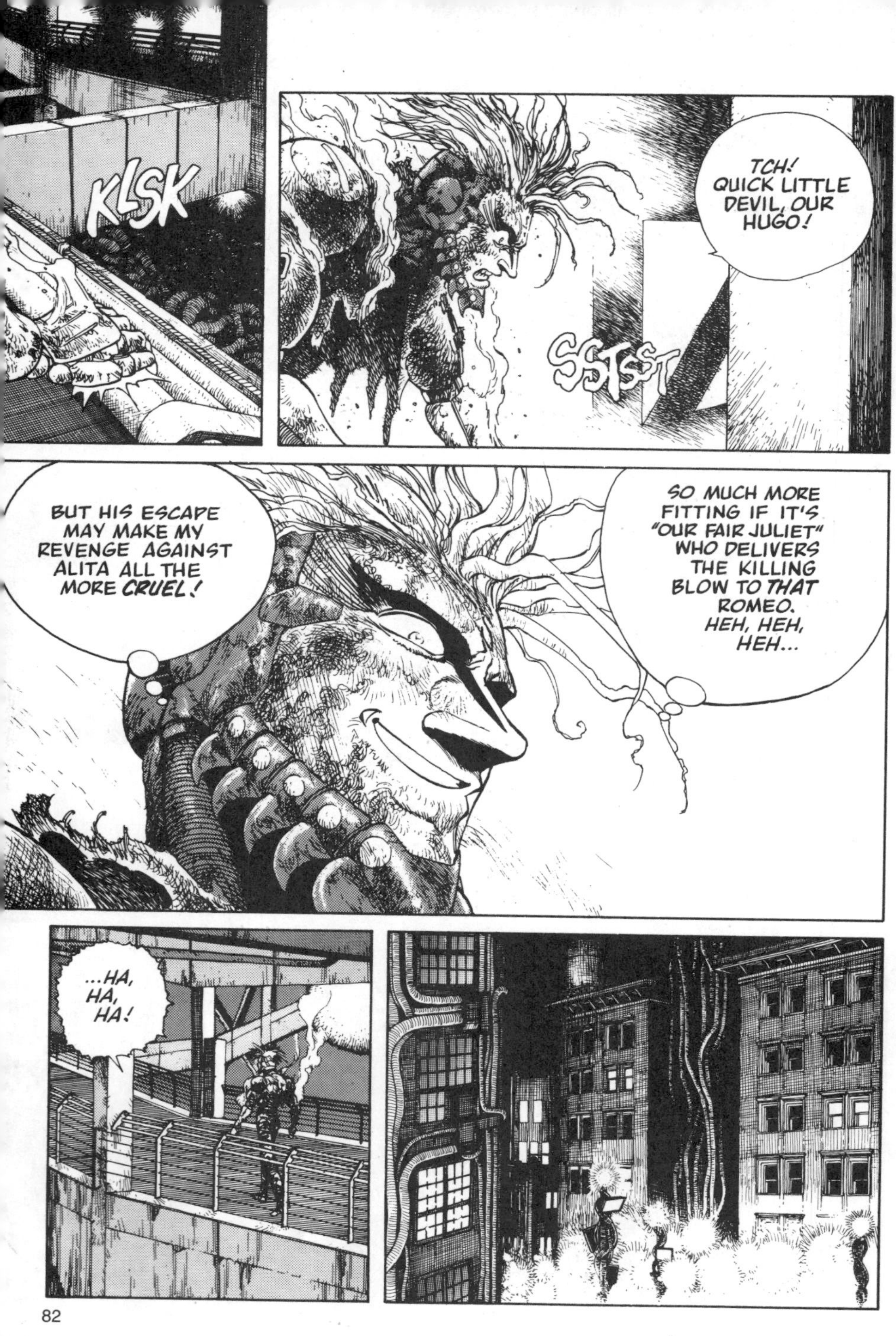
KLSK
TCH! QUICK LITTLE DEVIL, OUR HUGO!
SSTSST
BUT HIS ESCAPE MAY MAKE MY REVENGE AGAINST ALITA ALL THE MORE CRUEL!
SO MUCH MORE FITTING IF IT'S "OUR FAIR JULIET" WHO DELIVERS THE KILLING BLOW TO THAT ROMEO. HEH, HEH, HEH...
...HA, HA, HA!

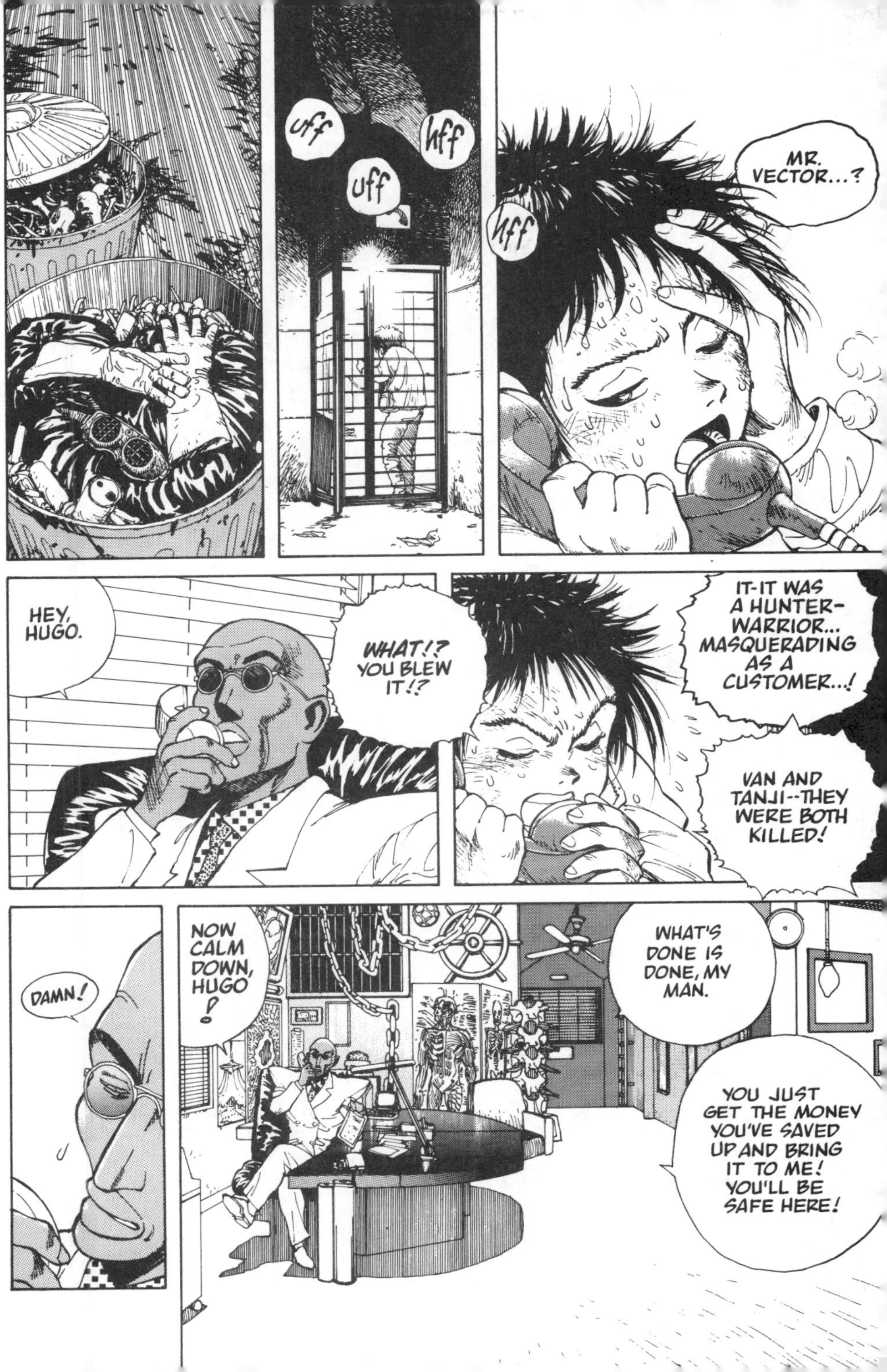
uff
hff
uff
hff
MR. VECTOR...?
HEY, HUGO.
WHAT!? YOU BLEW IT!?
IT-IT WAS A HUNTER-WARRIOR... MASQUERADING AS A CUSTOMER...!
VAN AND TANJI--THEY WERE BOTH KILLED!
DAMN!
NOW CALM DOWN, HUGO!
WHAT'S DONE IS DONE, MY MAN.
YOU JUST GET THE MONEY YOU'VE SAVED UP AND BRING IT TO ME! YOU'LL BE SAFE HERE!

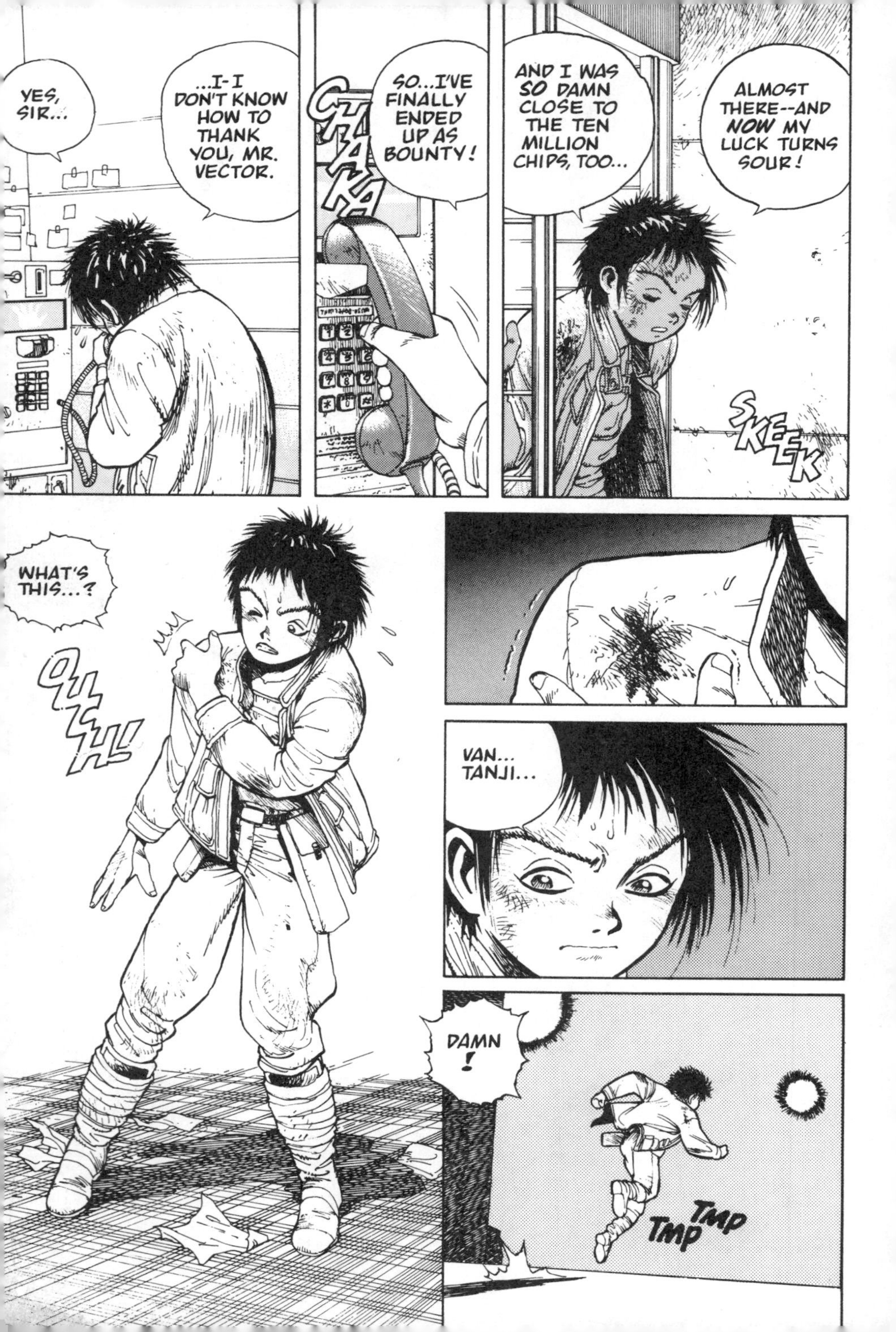
YES, SIR...
...I-I DON'T KNOW HOW TO THANK YOU, MR. VECTOR.
CHAKA
SO...I'VE FINALLY ENDED UP AS BOUNTY!
AND I WAS SO DAMN CLOSE TO THE TEN MILLION CHIPS, TOO...
ALMOST THERE--AND NOW MY LUCK TURNS SOUR!
SKEEK
WHAT'S THIS...?
OUCHH!
VAN... TANJI...
DAMN!
Tmp Tmp

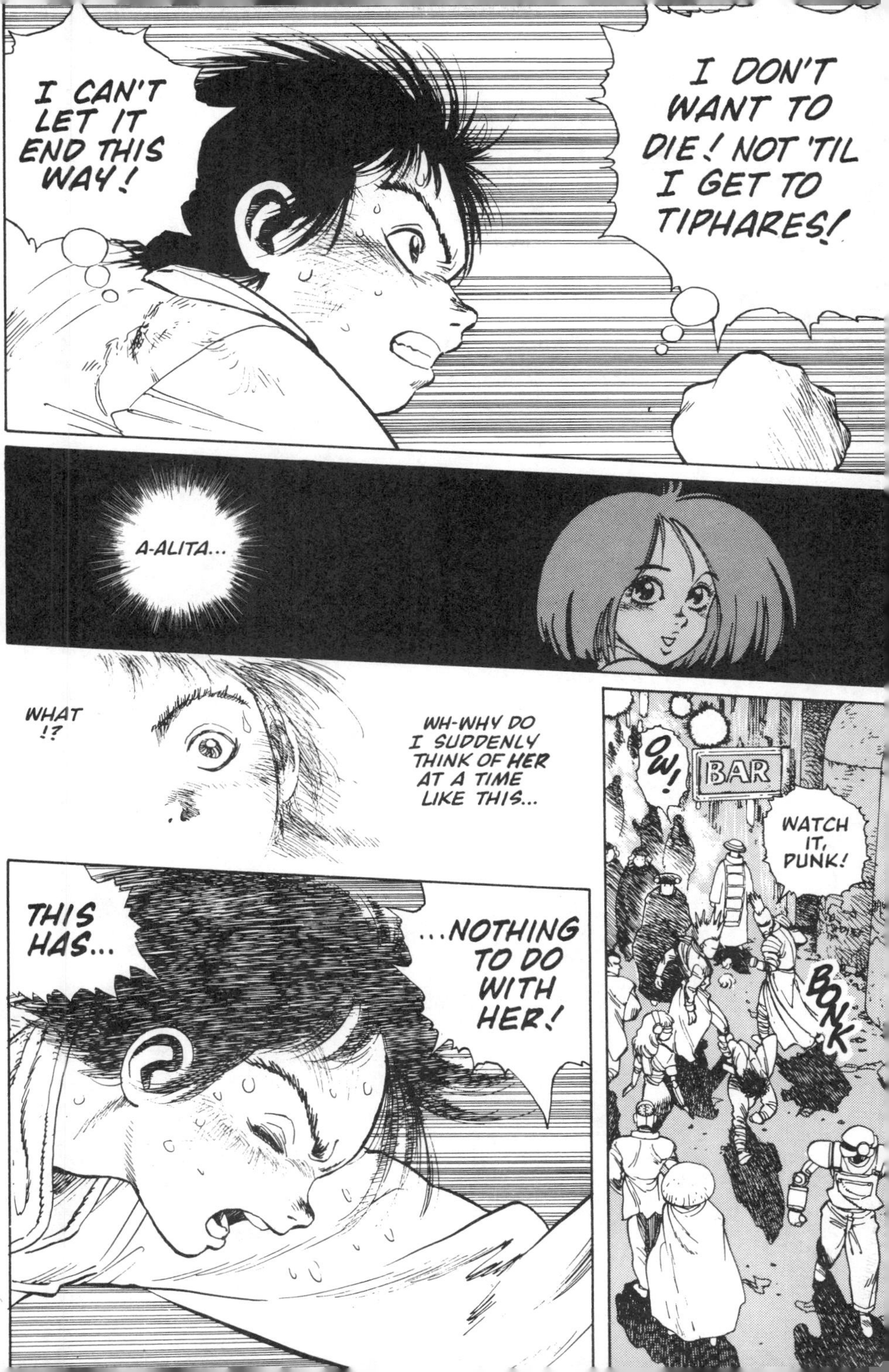
I CAN'T LET IT END THIS WAY!
I DON'T WANT TO DIE! NOT 'TIL I GET TO TIPHARES!
A-ALITA...
WHAT !?
WH-WHY DO I SUDDENLY THINK OF HER AT A TIME LIKE THIS...
OW!
BAR
WATCH IT, PUNK!
BONK
THIS HAS...
...NOTHING TO DO WITH HER!

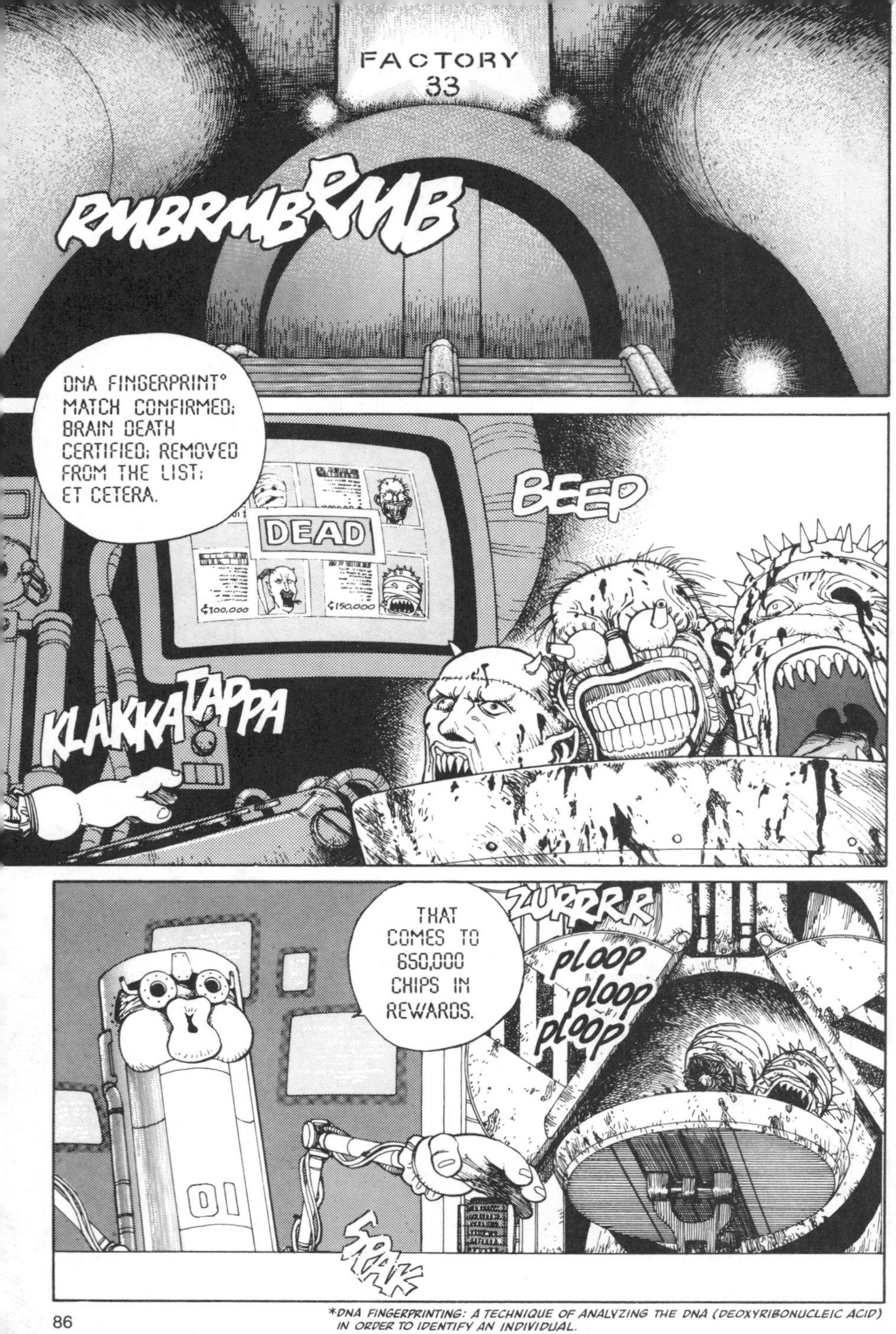

FACTORY 33
RMBRMBRMB
DNA FINGERPRINT* MATCH CONFIRMED; BRAIN DEATH CERTIFIED; REMOVED FROM THE LIST; ET CETERA.
DEAD
$100,000
$150,000
BEEP
KLAKKATAPPA
ZURRRR
THAT COMES TO 650,000 CHIPS IN REWARDS.
ploop ploop ploop
01

*DNA FINGERPRINTING: A TECHNIQUE OF ANALYZING THE DNA (DEOXYRIBONUCLEIC ACID) IN ORDER TO IDENTIFY AN INDIVIDUAL.

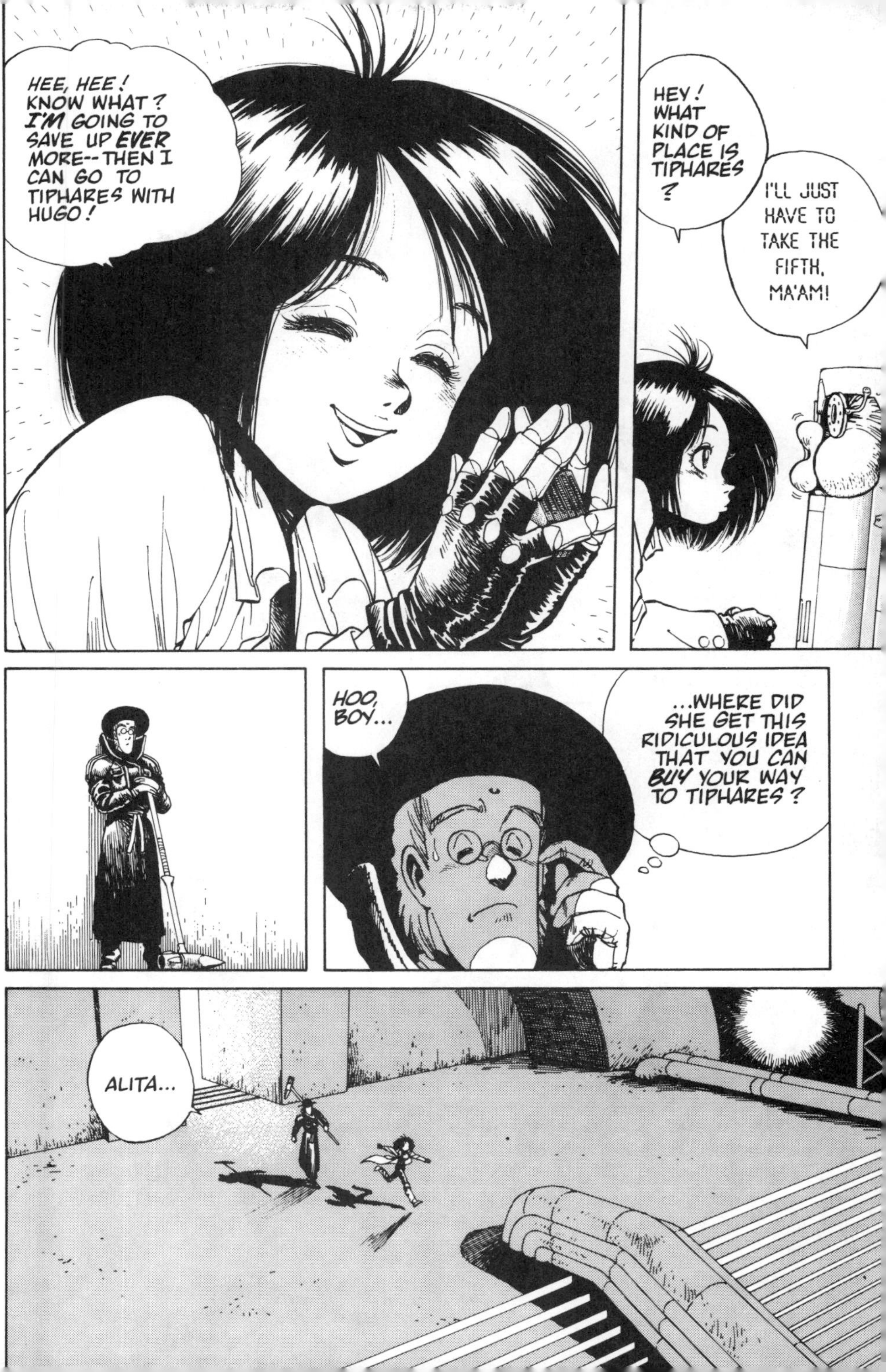
HEE, HEE! KNOW WHAT? I'M GOING TO SAVE UP EVER MORE--THEN I CAN GO TO TIPHARES WITH HUGO!
HEY! WHAT KIND OF PLACE IS TIPHARES?
I'LL JUST HAVE TO TAKE THE FIFTH, MA'AM!
HOO, BOY...
...WHERE DID SHE GET THIS RIDICULOUS IDEA THAT YOU CAN BUY YOUR WAY TO TIPHARES?
ALITA...

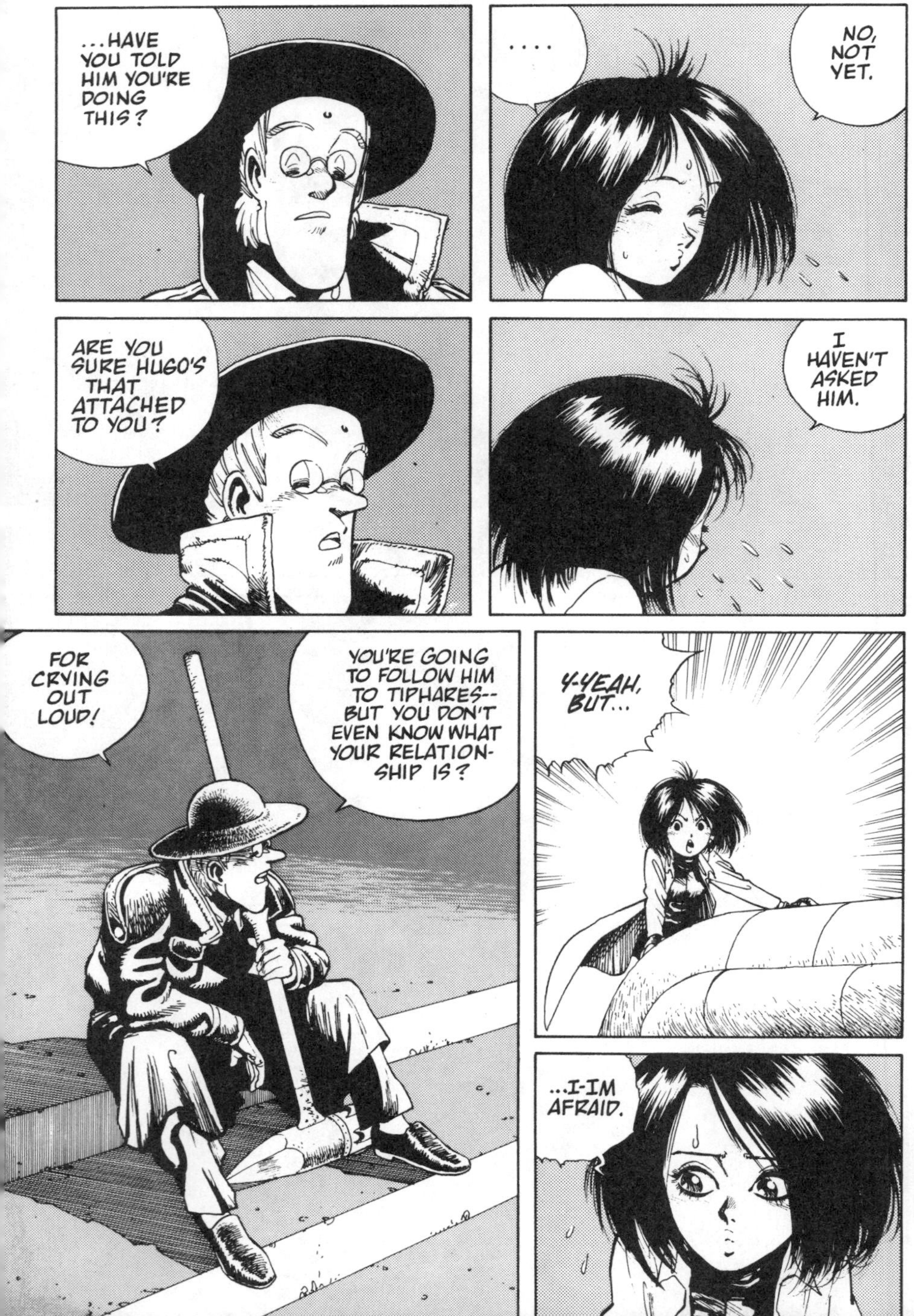
...HAVE YOU TOLD HIM YOU'RE DOING THIS?
....
NO, NOT YET.
ARE YOU SURE HUGO'S THAT ATTACHED TO YOU?
I HAVEN'T ASKED HIM.
FOR CRYING OUT LOUD!
YOU'RE GOING TO FOLLOW HIM TO TIPHARES-- BUT YOU DON'T EVEN KNOW WHAT YOUR RELATION-SHIP IS?
Y-YEAH, BUT...
...I-IM AFRAID.

I UNDERSTAND THAT. EVERYONE'S AFRAID TO CONFRONT REALITY.

YOU DON'T WANT TO TOUCH IT. YOU WANT TO KEEP LOOKING AWAY.

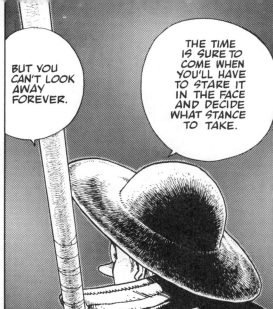

BUT YOU CAN'T LOOK AWAY FOREVER.

THE TIME IS SURE TO COME WHEN YOU'LL HAVE TO STARE IT IN THE FACE AND DECIDE WHAT STANCE TO TAKE.

WHAT DO YOU KNOW ABOUT *MY* REALITY!? WHAT DO *YOU* KNOW!?

YOU DON'T UNDERSTAND HOW I FEEL! YOU WOULDN'T WANT TO BE A HUMAN BEING IN A MECHANICAL BODY!

BUT THAT'S ALL YOU *HAVE*, ALITA. AND NOW YOU'RE RUNNING AWAY.

WHERE HAS MY BRAVE LITTLE ALITA GONE?

YOU'RE WRONG... IT'S NOT LIKE THAT... I'M ONLY HOLDING BACK...

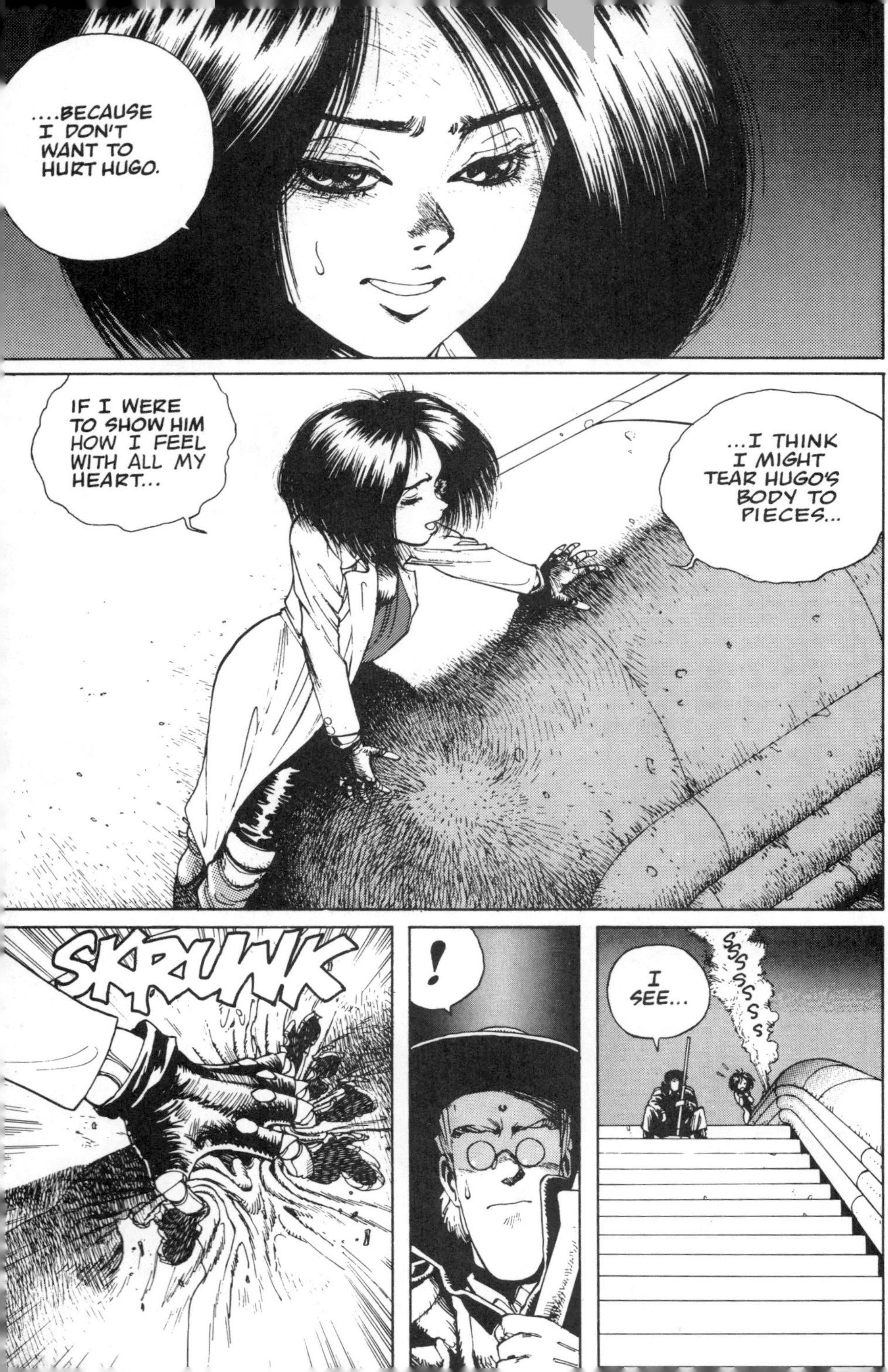
....BECAUSE I DON'T WANT TO HURT HUGO.
IF I WERE TO SHOW HIM HOW I FEEL WITH ALL MY HEART...
...I THINK I MIGHT TEAR HUGO'S BODY TO PIECES...
SKRUNK
!
I SEE...
SSSSSSSS

GOOD EVENING.

SUCH PERFECT TIMING, IDO. I DIDN'T EXPECT TO RUN INTO YOU...

...OR LITTLE ALITA! I'VE GOT SOME... INTERESTING... NEWS FOR YOU, GIRL!

?!

DO I... DO I KNOW YOU?

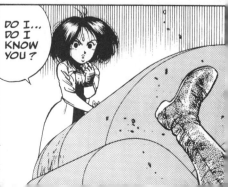

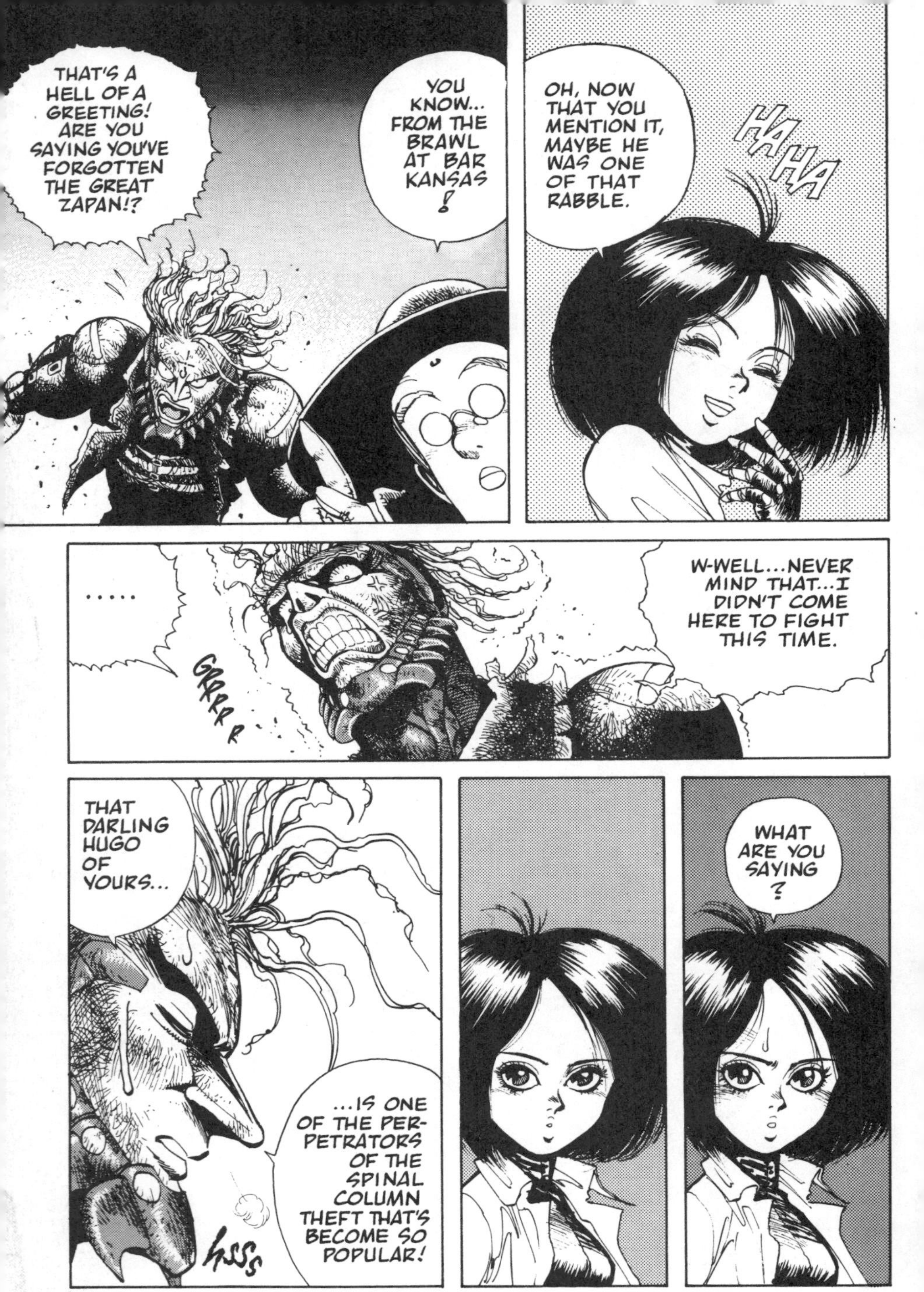
THAT'S A HELL OF A GREETING! ARE YOU SAYING YOU'VE FORGOTTEN THE GREAT ZAPAN!?
YOU KNOW... FROM THE BRAWL AT BAR KANSAS!
OH, NOW THAT YOU MENTION IT, MAYBE HE WAS ONE OF THAT RABBLE.
HAHA
.....
GRRRR R
W-WELL...NEVER MIND THAT...I DIDN'T COME HERE TO FIGHT THIS TIME.
THAT DARLING HUGO OF YOURS...
...IS ONE OF THE PERPETRATORS OF THE SPINAL COLUMN THEFT THAT'S BECOME SO POPULAR!
HSSS
WHAT ARE YOU SAYING?

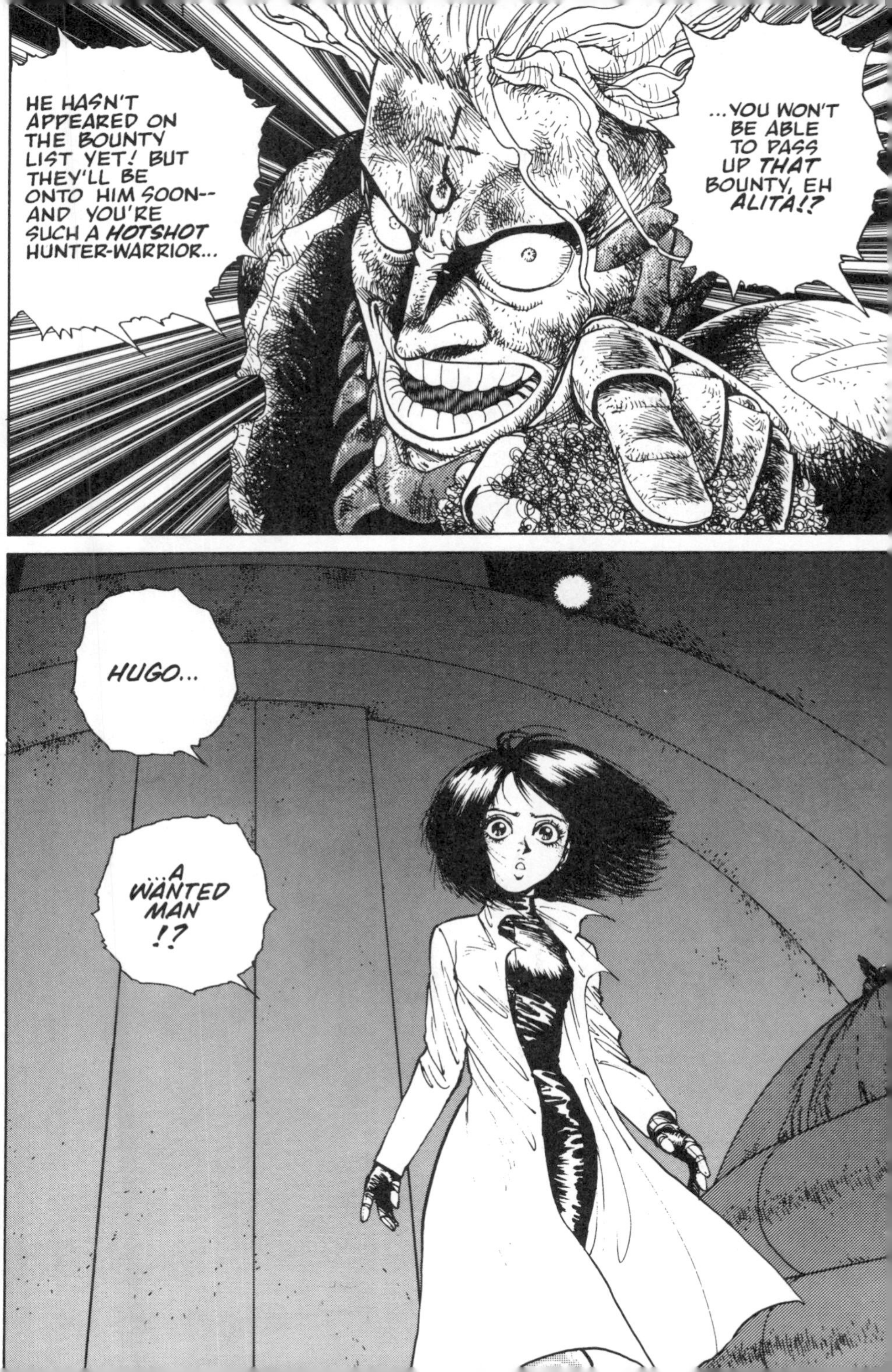
HE HASN'T APPEARED ON THE BOUNTY LIST YET! BUT THEY'LL BE ONTO HIM SOON-- AND YOU'RE SUCH A HOTSHOT HUNTER-WARRIOR...
...YOU WON'T BE ABLE TO PASS UP THAT BOUNTY, EH ALITA!?
HUGO...
...A WANTED MAN !?

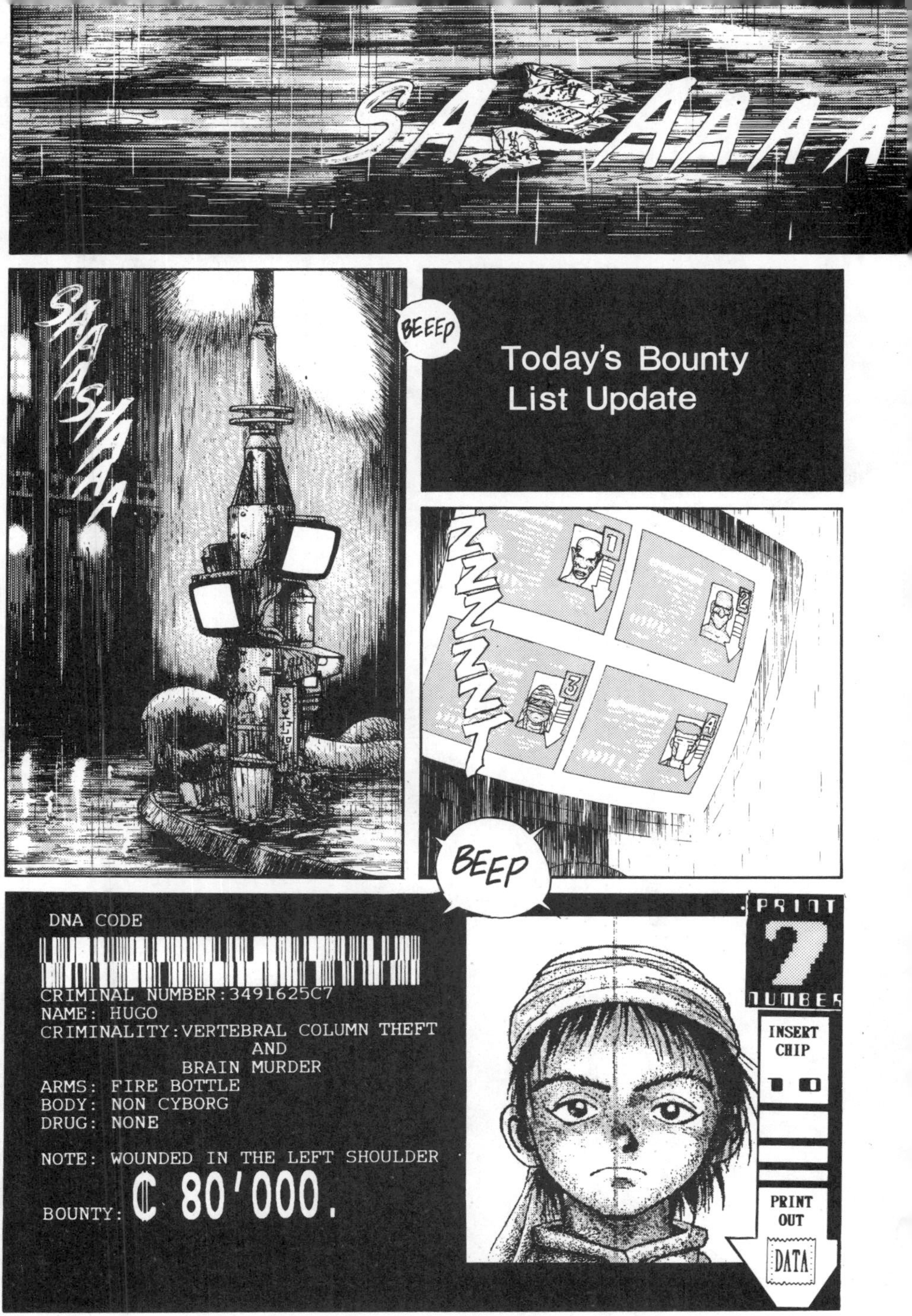
SA-AAAAA
SAAASHAAAA
BEEEP
Today's Bounty List Update
ZZZZZT
BEEP
DNA CODE
CRIMINAL NUMBER:3491625C7
NAME: HUGO
CRIMINALITY:VERTEBRAL COLUMN THEFT AND BRAIN MURDER
ARMS: FIRE BOTTLE
BODY: NON CYBORG
DRUG: NONE
NOTE: WOUNDED IN THE LEFT SHOULDER
BOUNTY: ₵ 80'000.
PRINT
7
NUMBER
INSERT CHIP
PRINT OUT
DATA

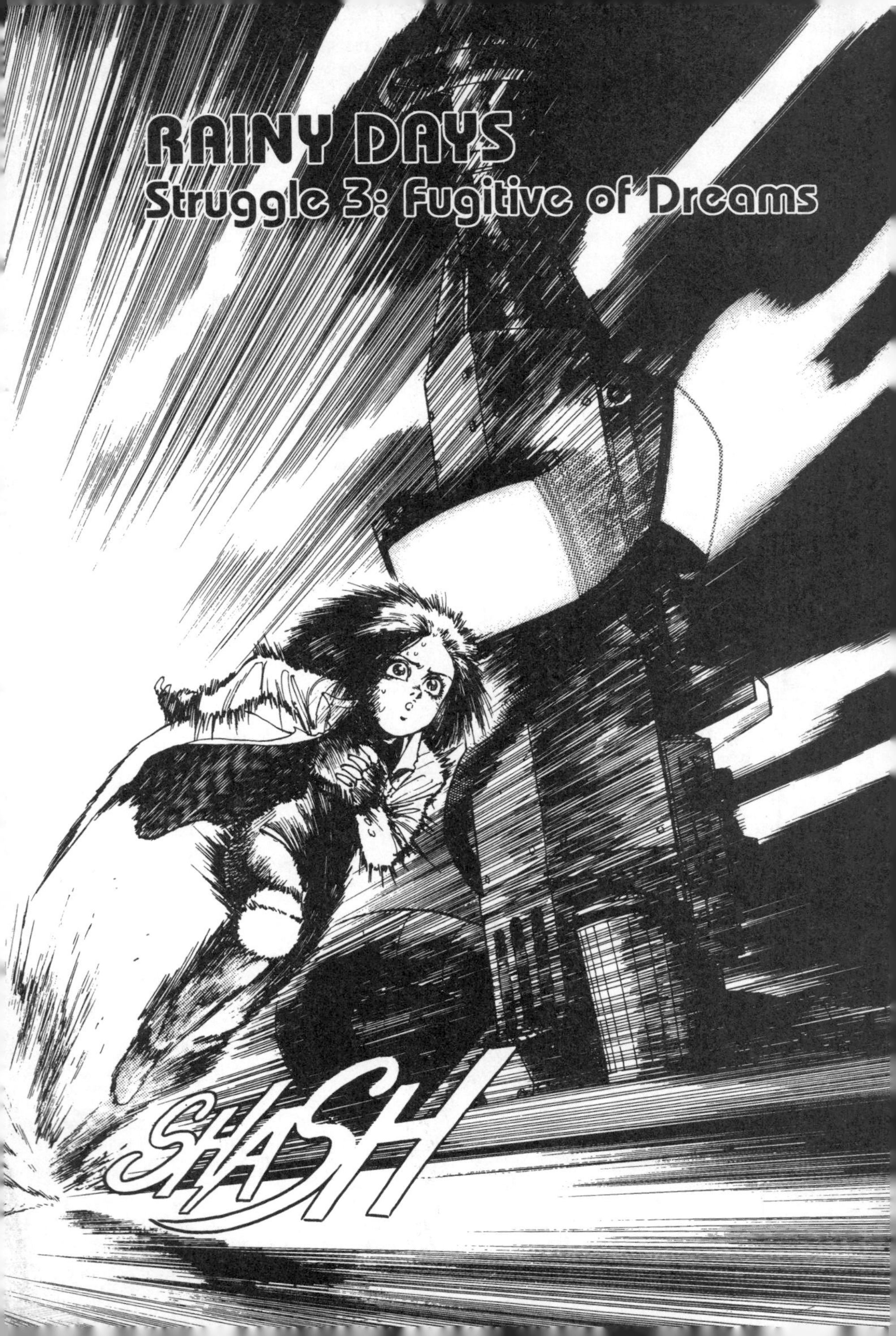
RAINY DAYS
Struggle 3: Fugitive of Dreams
SHASH

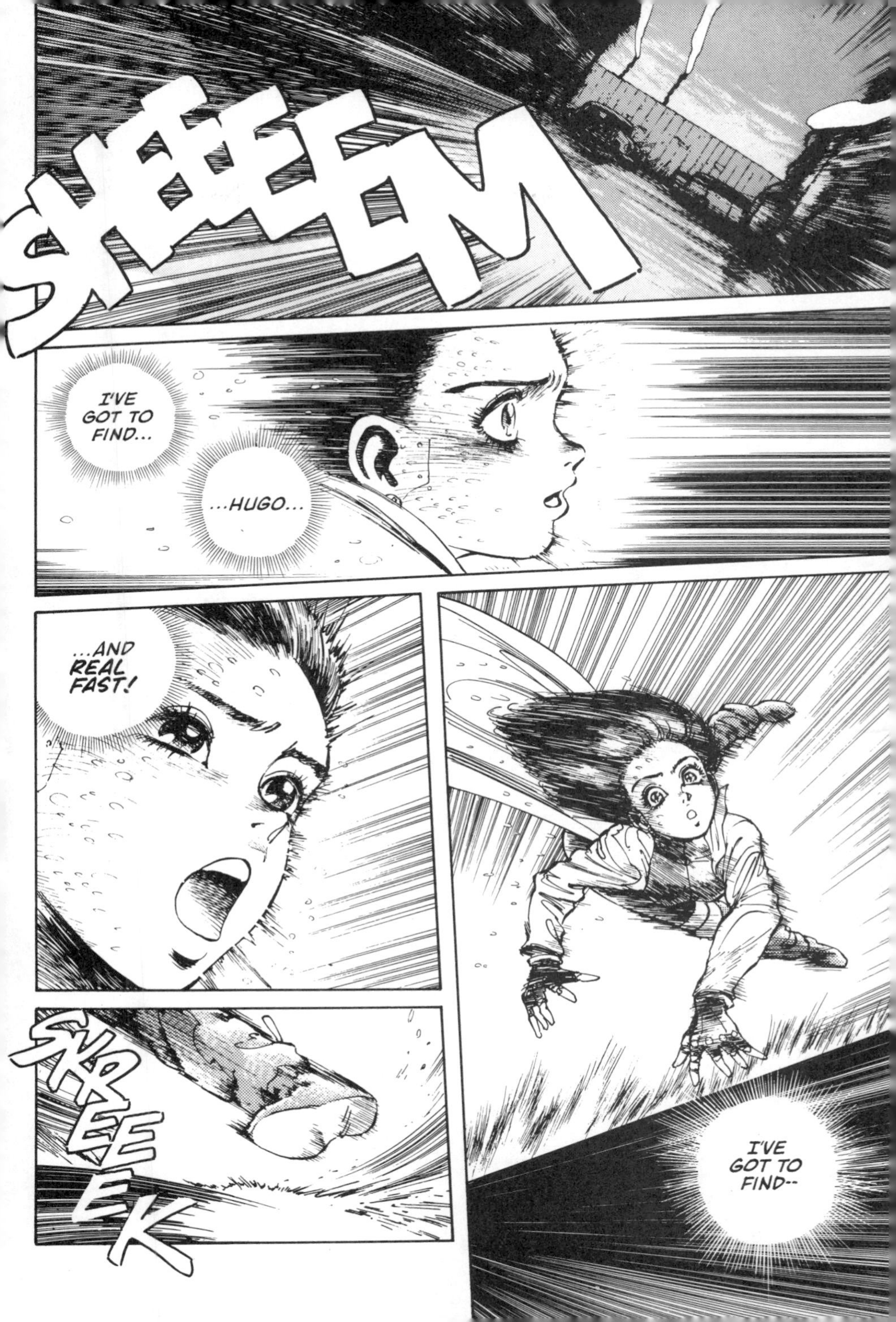
SHEEEM
I'VE GOT TO FIND...
...HUGO...
...AND REAL FAST!
SKREEEK
I'VE GOT TO FIND--

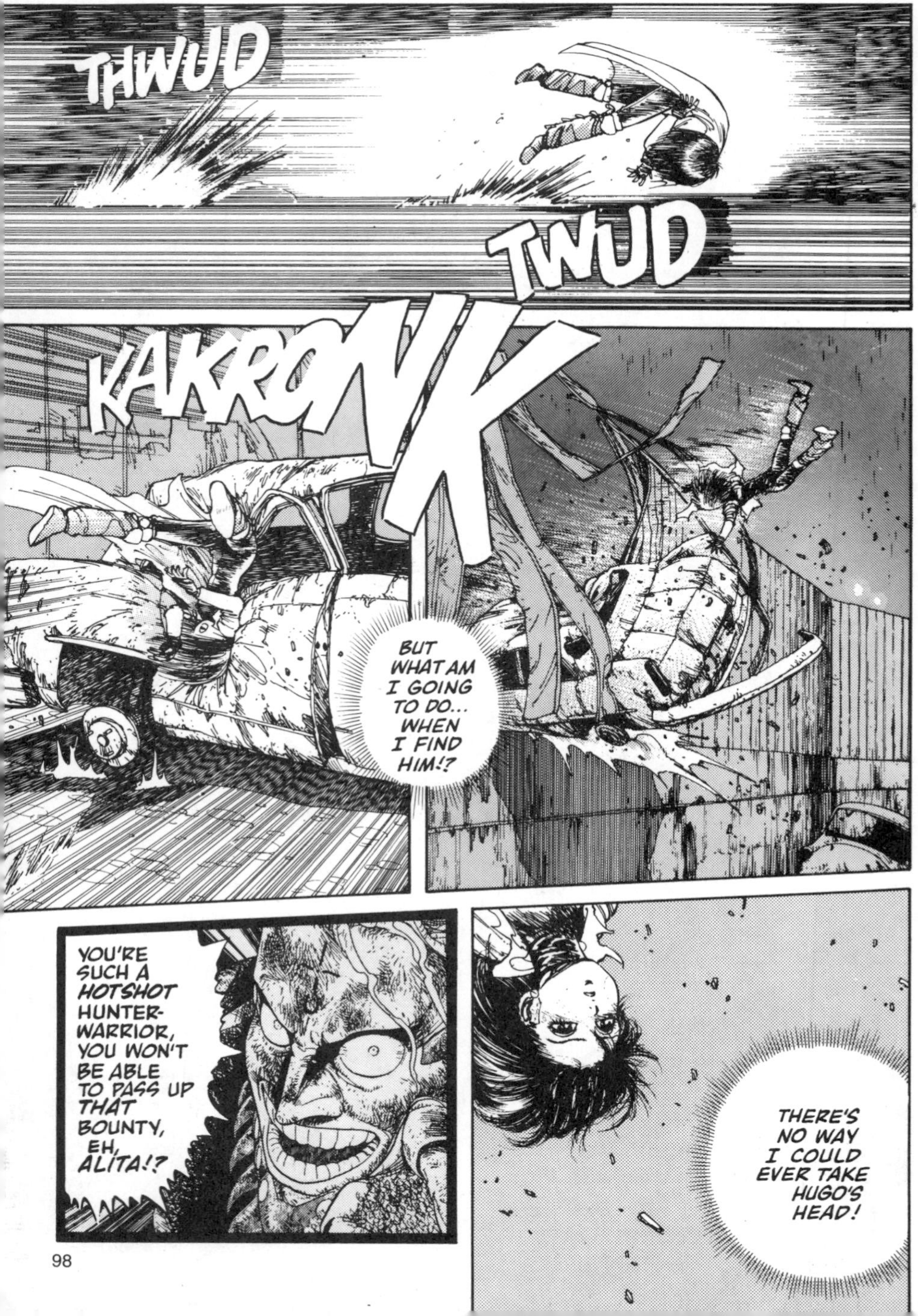
THWUD
TWUD
KAKRONK
BUT WHAT AM I GOING TO DO... WHEN I FIND HIM!?
YOU'RE SUCH A HOTSHOT HUNTER-WARRIOR, YOU WON'T BE ABLE TO PASS UP THAT BOUNTY, EH, ALITA!?
THERE'S NO WAY I COULD EVER TAKE HUGO'S HEAD!

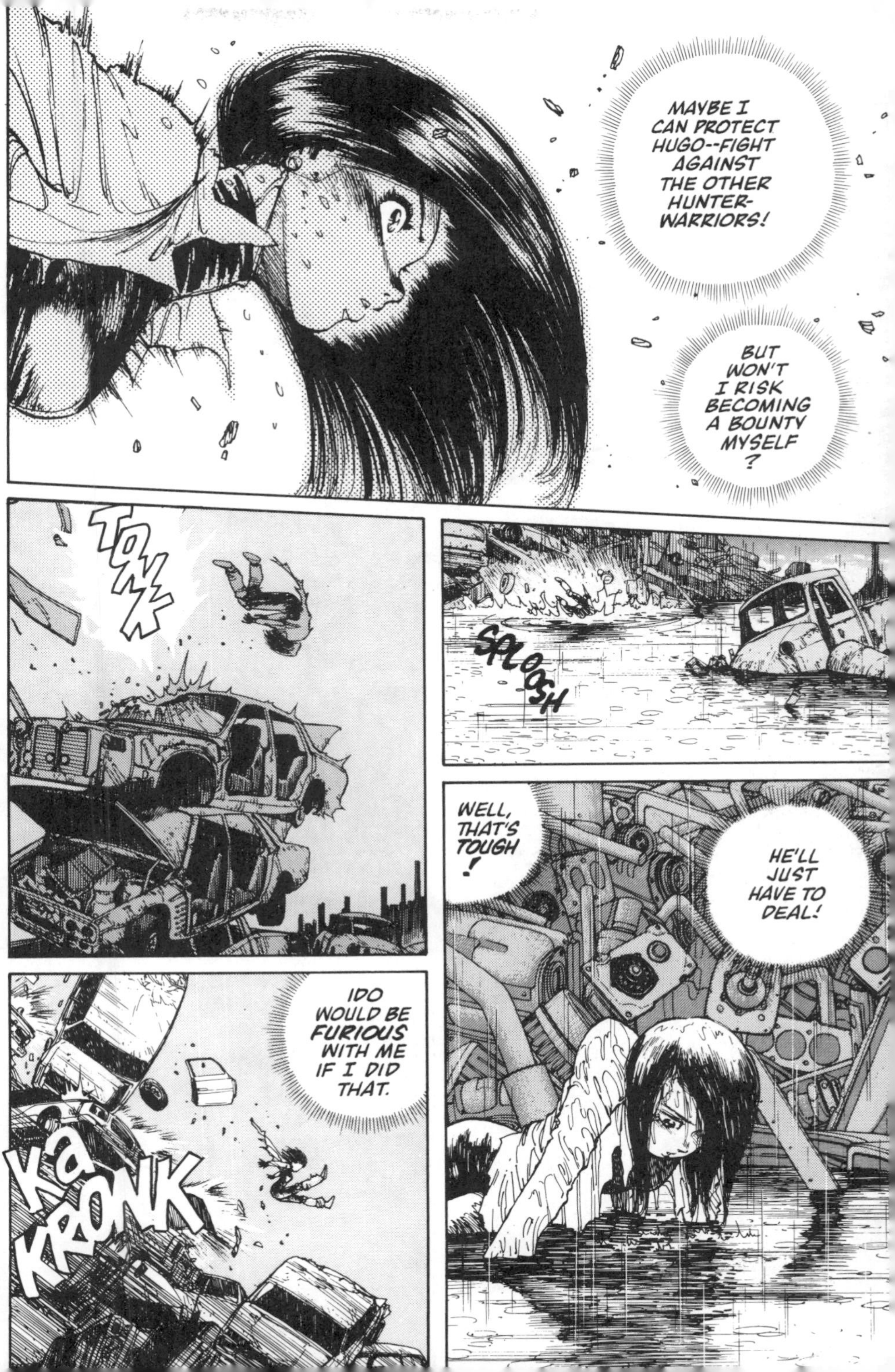
MAYBE I CAN PROTECT HUGO--FIGHT AGAINST THE OTHER HUNTER-WARRIORS!
BUT WON'T I RISK BECOMING A BOUNTY MYSELF?
TONK
SPLOOSH
IDO WOULD BE FURIOUS WITH ME IF I DID THAT.
KA KRONK
WELL, THAT'S TOUGH!
HE'LL JUST HAVE TO DEAL!

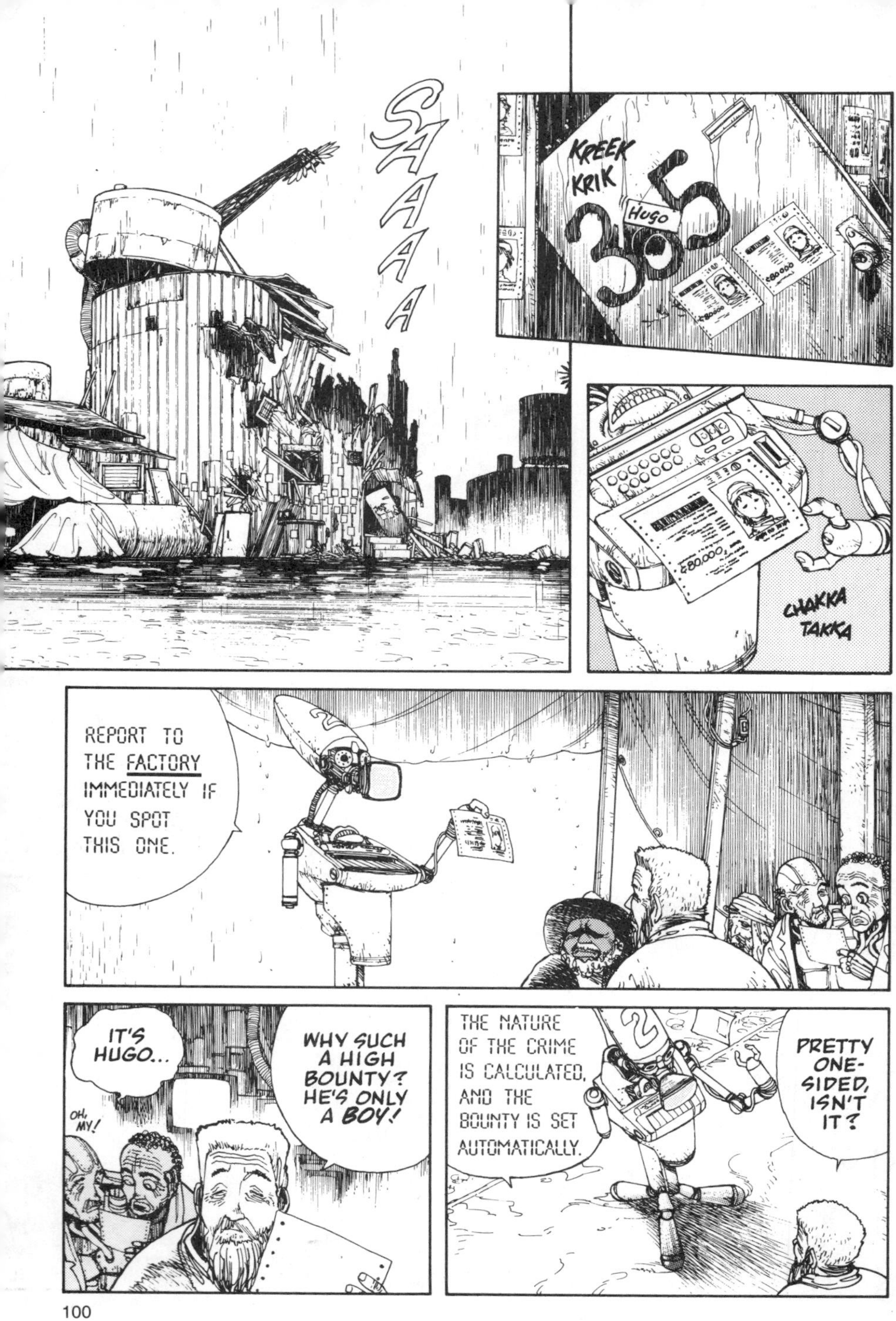

SAAAAA
KREEK KRIK
HUGO
CHAKKA TAKKA
REPORT TO THE FACTORY IMMEDIATELY IF YOU SPOT THIS ONE.
IT'S HUGO...
OH, MY!
WHY SUCH A HIGH BOUNTY? HE'S ONLY A BOY!
THE NATURE OF THE CRIME IS CALCULATED, AND THE BOUNTY IS SET AUTOMATICALLY.
PRETTY ONE-SIDED, ISN'T IT?

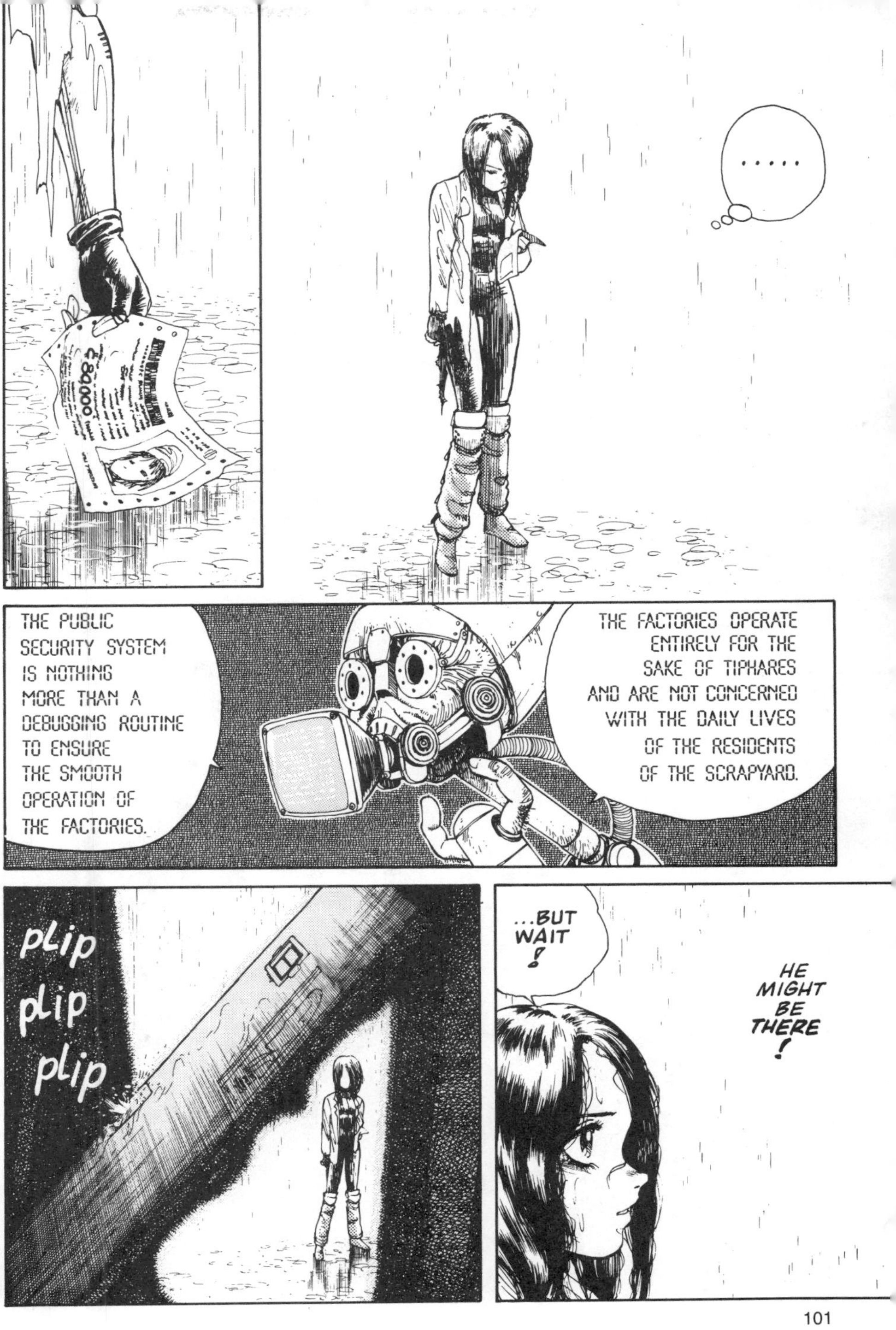
......
THE PUBLIC SECURITY SYSTEM IS NOTHING MORE THAN A DEBUGGING ROUTINE TO ENSURE THE SMOOTH OPERATION OF THE FACTORIES.
THE FACTORIES OPERATE ENTIRELY FOR THE SAKE OF TIPHARES AND ARE NOT CONCERNED WITH THE DAILY LIVES OF THE RESIDENTS OF THE SCRAPYARD.
plip plip plip
...BUT WAIT!
HE MIGHT BE THERE!

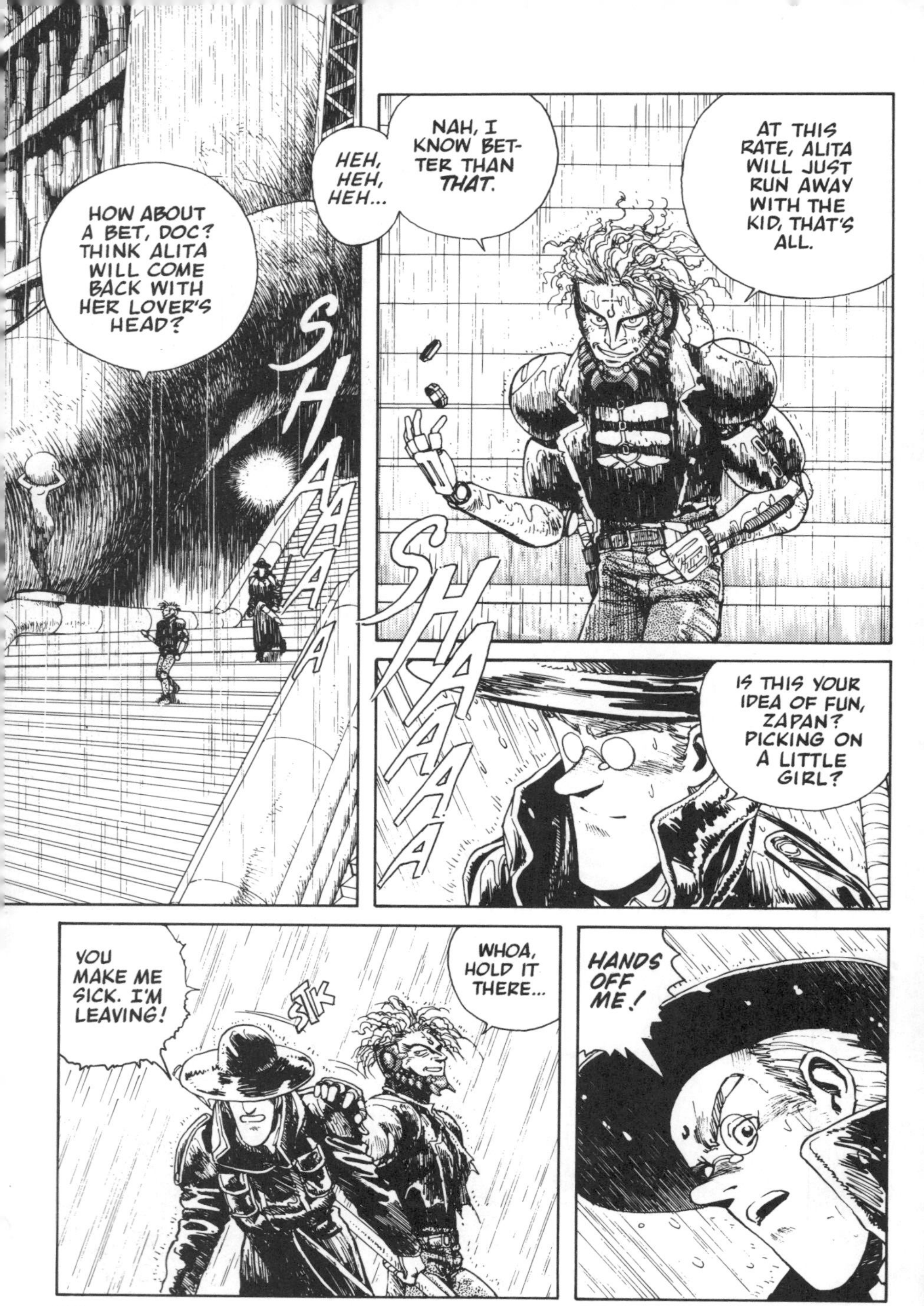
HOW ABOUT A BET, DOC? THINK ALITA WILL COME BACK WITH HER LOVER'S HEAD?
SHAAAAAA
HEH, HEH, HEH...
NAH, I KNOW BETTER THAN THAT.
AT THIS RATE, ALITA WILL JUST RUN AWAY WITH THE KID, THAT'S ALL.
SHAAAAAA
IS THIS YOUR IDEA OF FUN, ZAPAN? PICKING ON A LITTLE GIRL?
YOU MAKE ME SICK. I'M LEAVING!
STK
WHOA, HOLD IT THERE...
HANDS OFF ME!

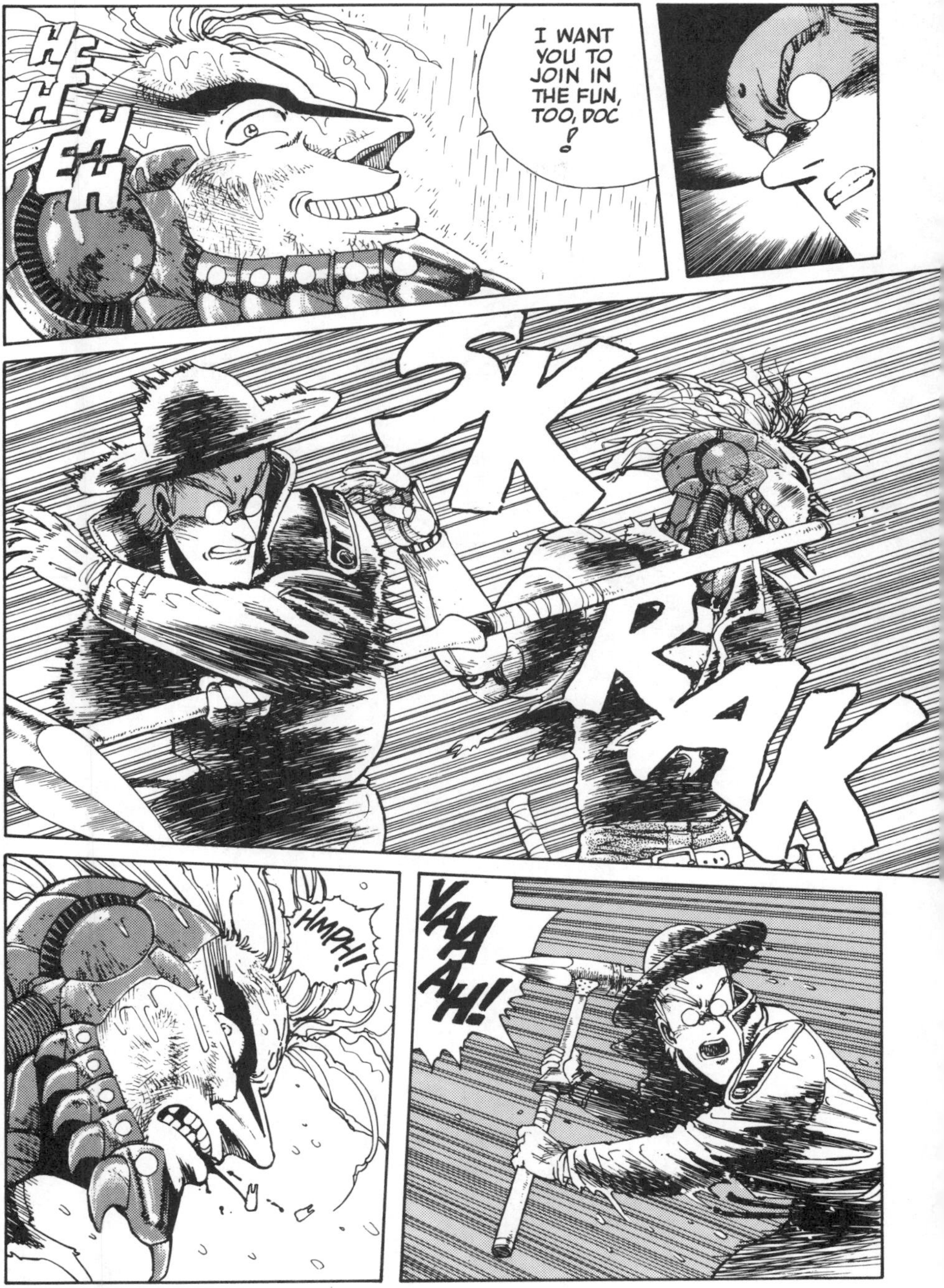
HEH HEH HEH HEH
I WANT YOU TO JOIN IN THE FUN, TOO, DOC!
SKRAK
HMPH!
YAAAAH!

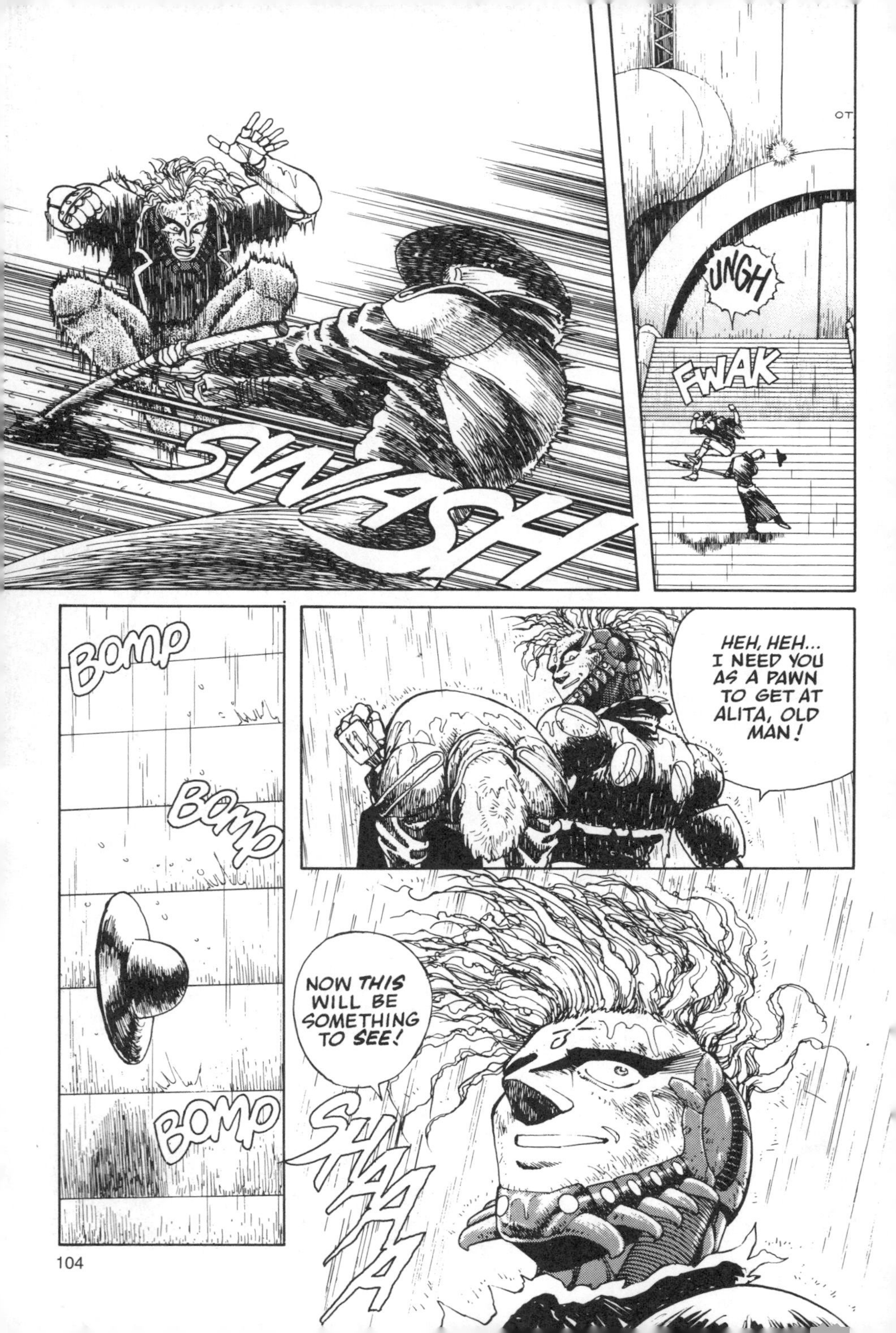
SWASH
OT
UNGH
FWAK
BOMP
BOMP
BOMP
HEH, HEH... I NEED YOU AS A PAWN TO GET AT ALITA, OLD MAN!
NOW THIS WILL BE SOMETHING TO SEE!
SHAAA

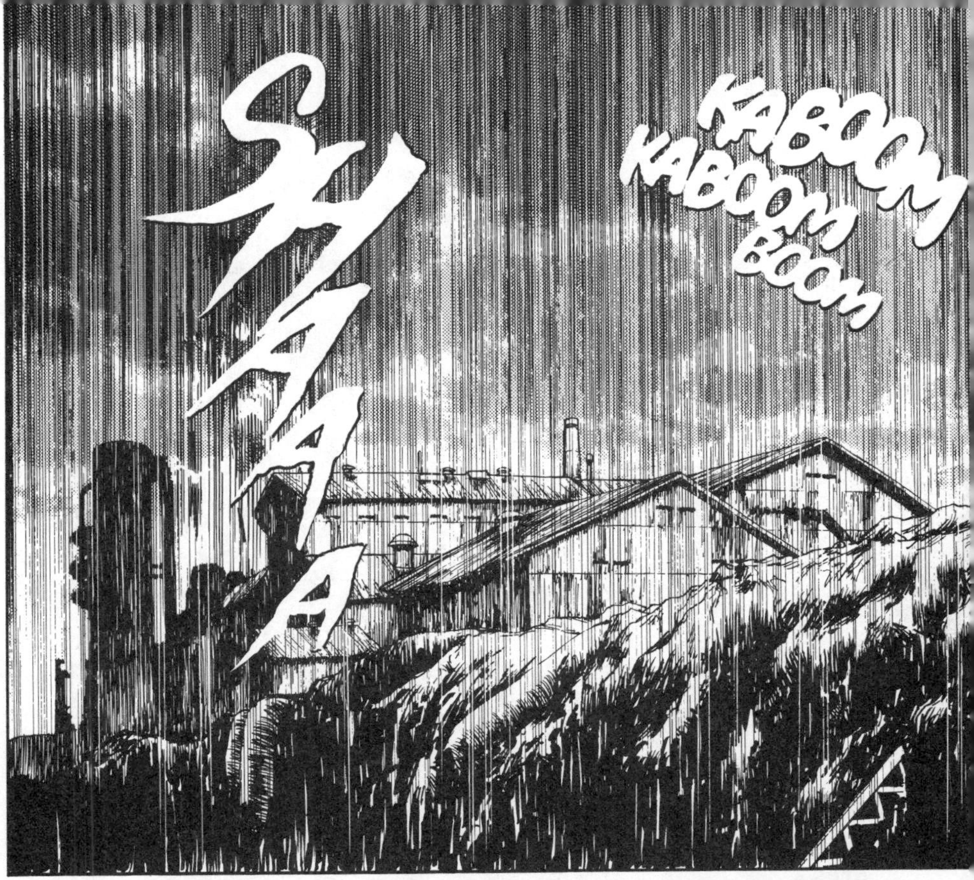
SHAAAA
KABOOM
KABOOM
BOOM

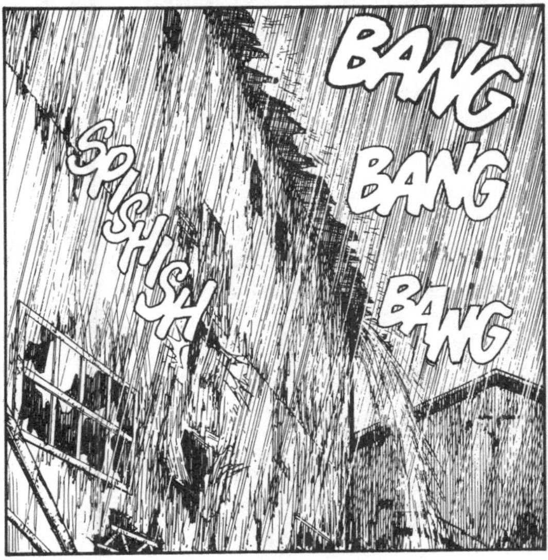
BANG
BANG
BANG
SPISHISH

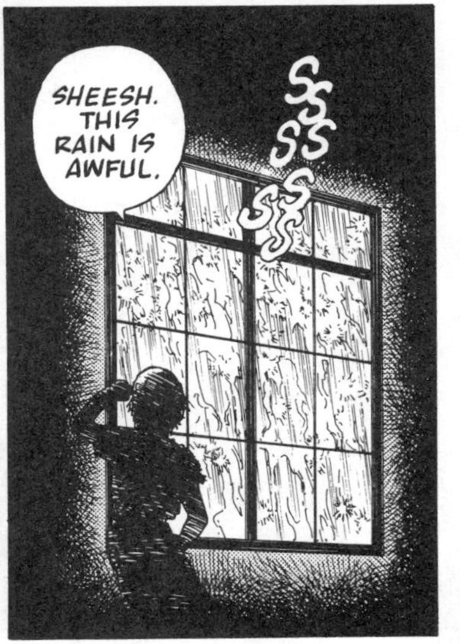
SHEESH. THIS RAIN IS AWFUL.
SSSSSS

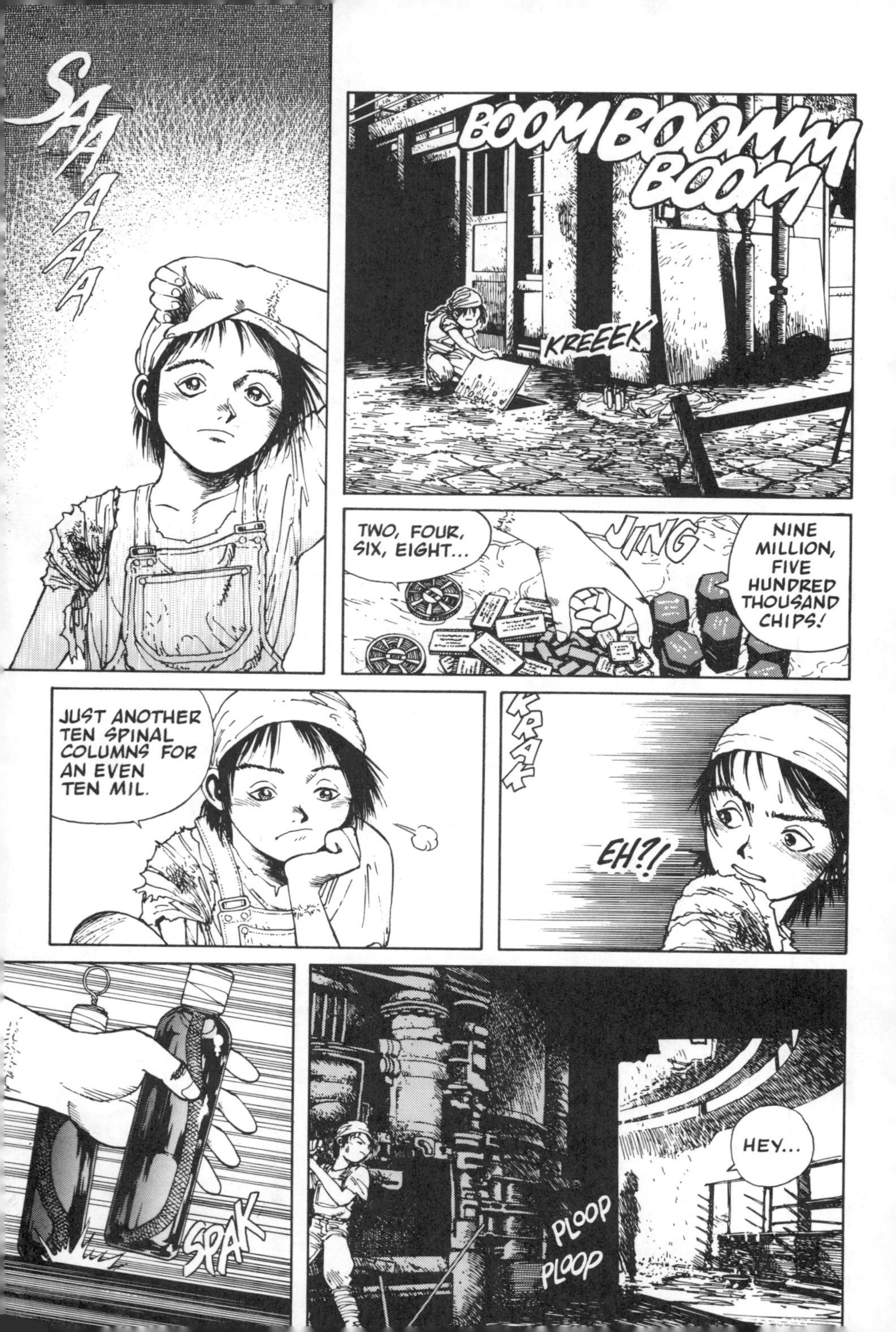
SAAAAAA
BOOM BOOMM BOOM
KREEEK
TWO, FOUR, SIX, EIGHT...
JING
NINE MILLION, FIVE HUNDRED THOUSAND CHIPS!
JUST ANOTHER TEN SPINAL COLUMNS FOR AN EVEN TEN MIL.
KRAK
EH?!
SPAK
PLOOP PLOOP
HEY...

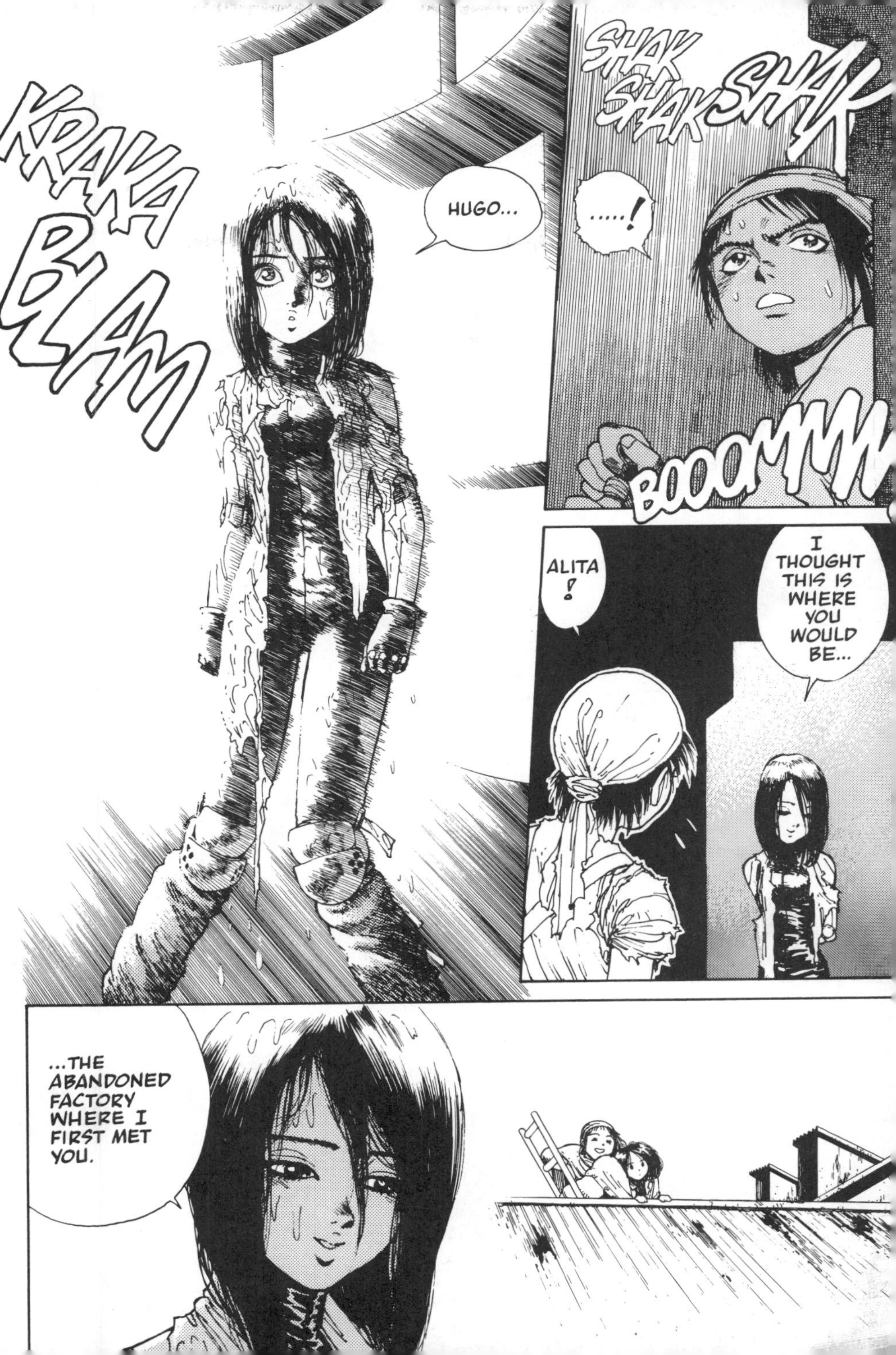
KRAKA BLAM
HUGO...
SHAK SHAK SHAK SHAK
.....!
BOOOMMM
ALITA!
I THOUGHT THIS IS WHERE YOU WOULD BE...
...THE ABANDONED FACTORY WHERE I FIRST MET YOU.

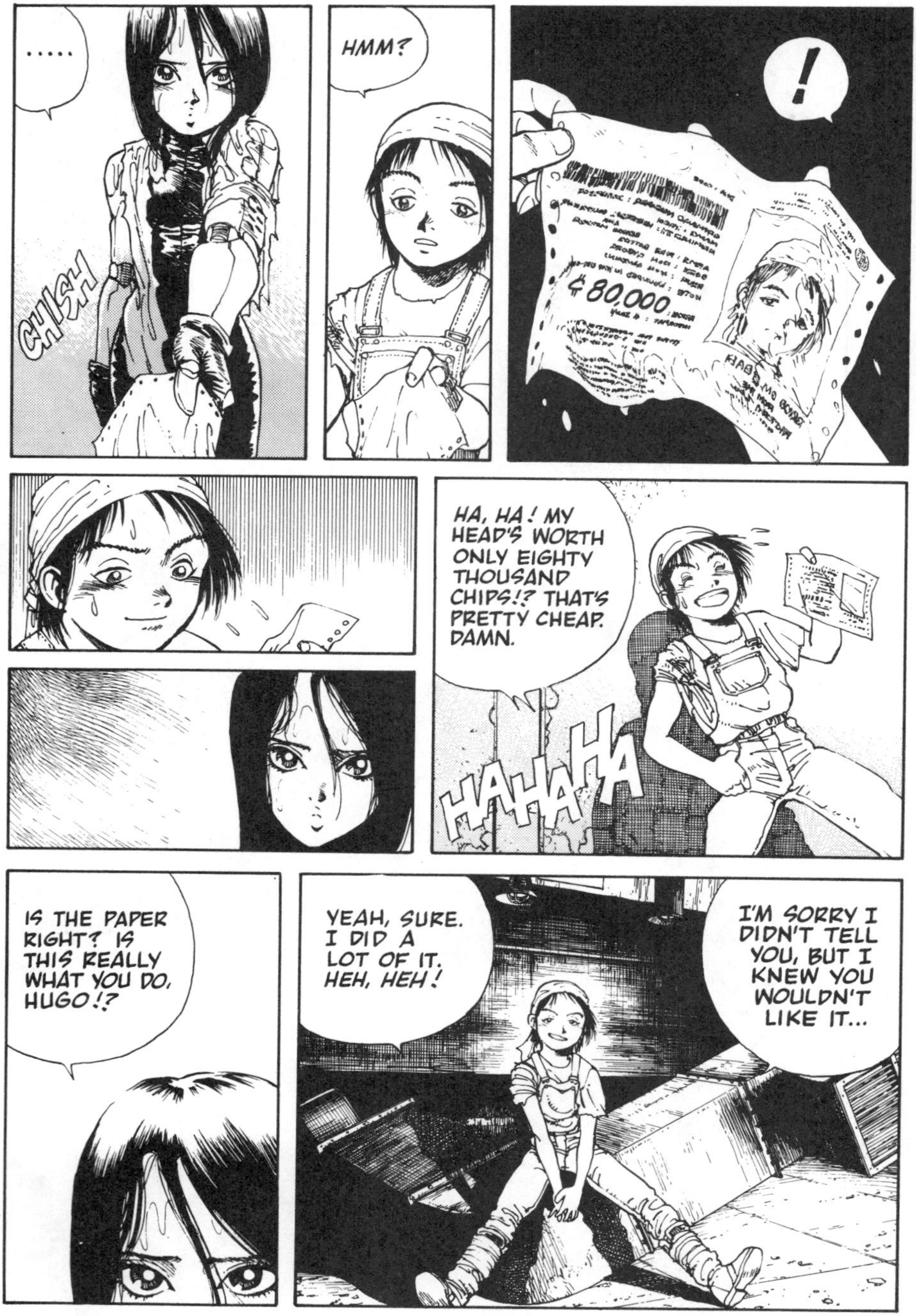
......
CHISH
HMM?
!
¢80,000
HA, HA! MY HEAD'S WORTH ONLY EIGHTY THOUSAND CHIPS!? THAT'S PRETTY CHEAP. DAMN.
HAHAHA
IS THE PAPER RIGHT? IS THIS REALLY WHAT YOU DO, HUGO!?
YEAH, SURE. I DID A LOT OF IT. HEH, HEH!
I'M SORRY I DIDN'T TELL YOU, BUT I KNEW YOU WOULDN'T LIKE IT...

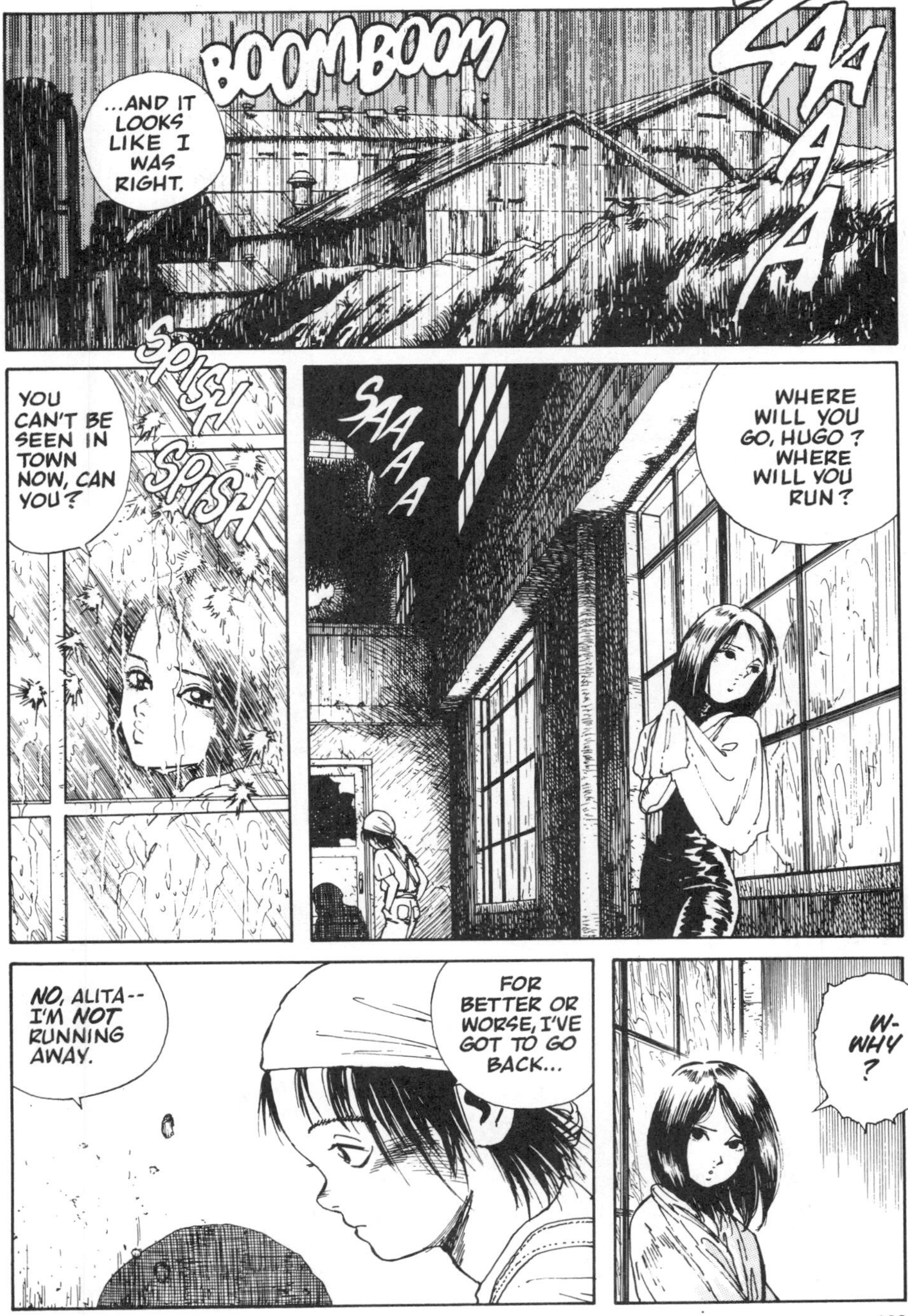
BOOMBOOM
ZAAAA
...AND IT LOOKS LIKE I WAS RIGHT.
SPISH SPISH
YOU CAN'T BE SEEN IN TOWN NOW, CAN YOU?
SAAAAA
WHERE WILL YOU GO, HUGO? WHERE WILL YOU RUN?
NO, ALITA-- I'M NOT RUNNING AWAY.
FOR BETTER OR WORSE, I'VE GOT TO GO BACK...
W-WHY?

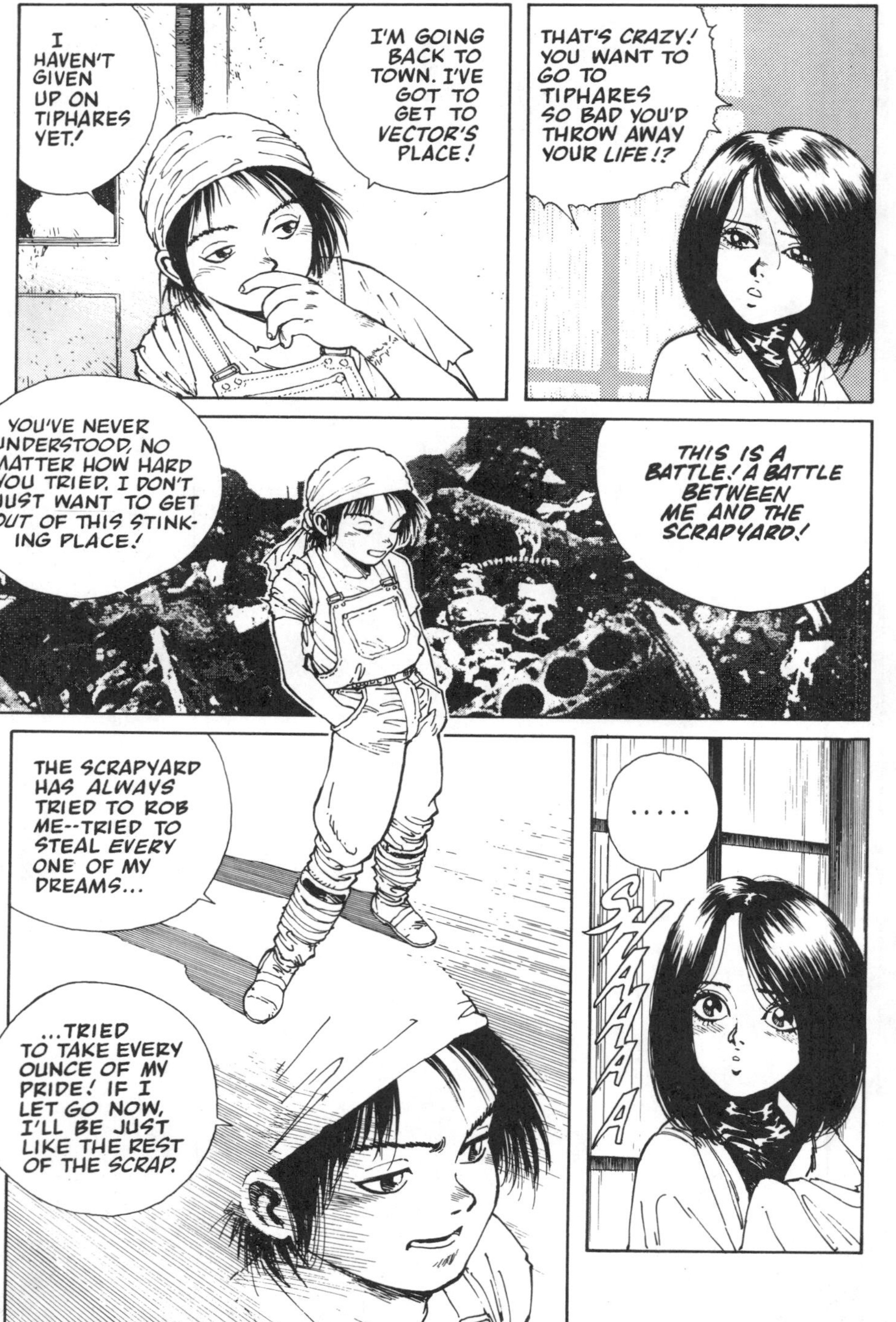
I HAVEN'T GIVEN UP ON TIPHARES YET!
I'M GOING BACK TO TOWN. I'VE GOT TO GET TO VECTOR'S PLACE!
THAT'S CRAZY! YOU WANT TO GO TO TIPHARES SO BAD YOU'D THROW AWAY YOUR LIFE!?
YOU'VE NEVER UNDERSTOOD, NO MATTER HOW HARD YOU TRIED. I DON'T JUST WANT TO GET OUT OF THIS STINKING PLACE!
THIS IS A BATTLE! A BATTLE BETWEEN ME AND THE SCRAPYARD!
THE SCRAPYARD HAS ALWAYS TRIED TO ROB ME--TRIED TO STEAL EVERY ONE OF MY DREAMS...
...TRIED TO TAKE EVERY OUNCE OF MY PRIDE! IF I LET GO NOW, I'LL BE JUST LIKE THE REST OF THE SCRAP.
.....
SHAAAAAA

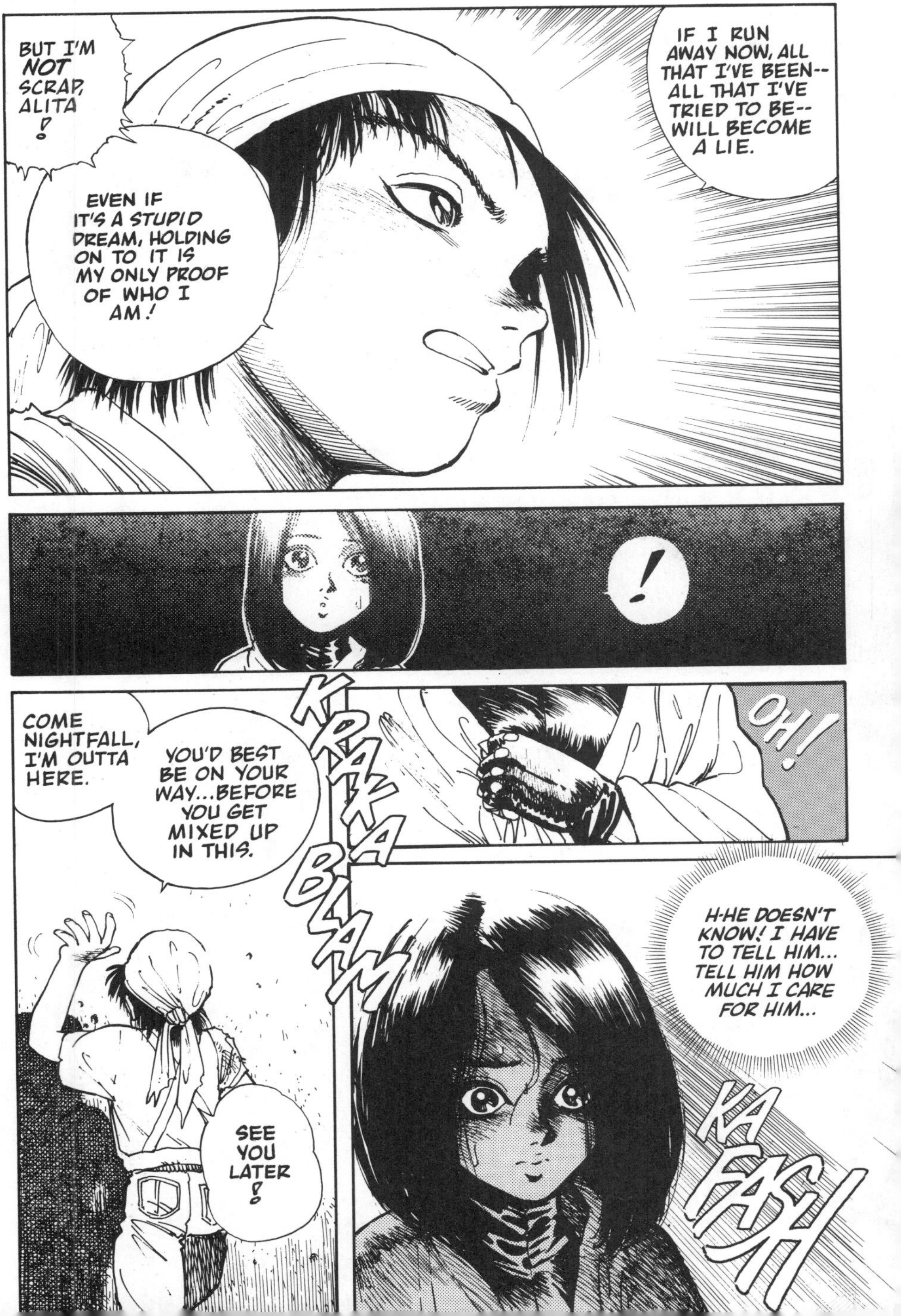
BUT I'M NOT SCRAP, ALITA!
EVEN IF IT'S A STUPID DREAM, HOLDING ON TO IT IS MY ONLY PROOF OF WHO I AM!
IF I RUN AWAY NOW, ALL THAT I'VE BEEN-- ALL THAT I'VE TRIED TO BE-- WILL BECOME A LIE.
!
COME NIGHTFALL, I'M OUTTA HERE.
YOU'D BEST BE ON YOUR WAY...BEFORE YOU GET MIXED UP IN THIS.
KRAKABLAM
OH!
SEE YOU LATER!
H-HE DOESN'T KNOW! I HAVE TO TELL HIM... TELL HIM HOW MUCH I CARE FOR HIM...
KA FASH

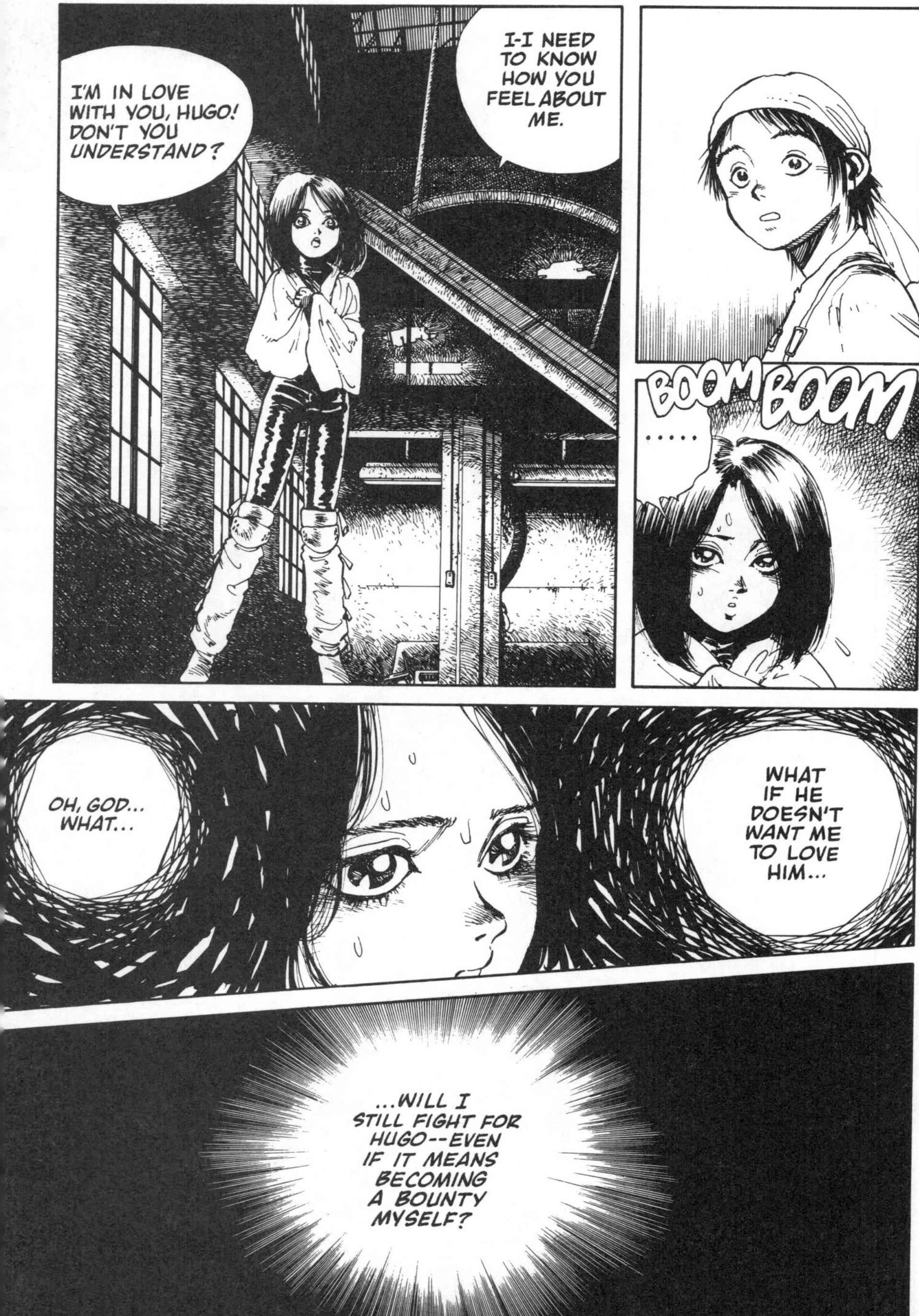
I'M IN LOVE WITH YOU, HUGO! DON'T YOU UNDERSTAND?
I-I NEED TO KNOW HOW YOU FEEL ABOUT ME.
BOOM BOOM
.....
OH, GOD... WHAT...
WHAT IF HE DOESN'T WANT ME TO LOVE HIM...
...WILL I STILL FIGHT FOR HUGO--EVEN IF IT MEANS BECOMING A BOUNTY MYSELF?

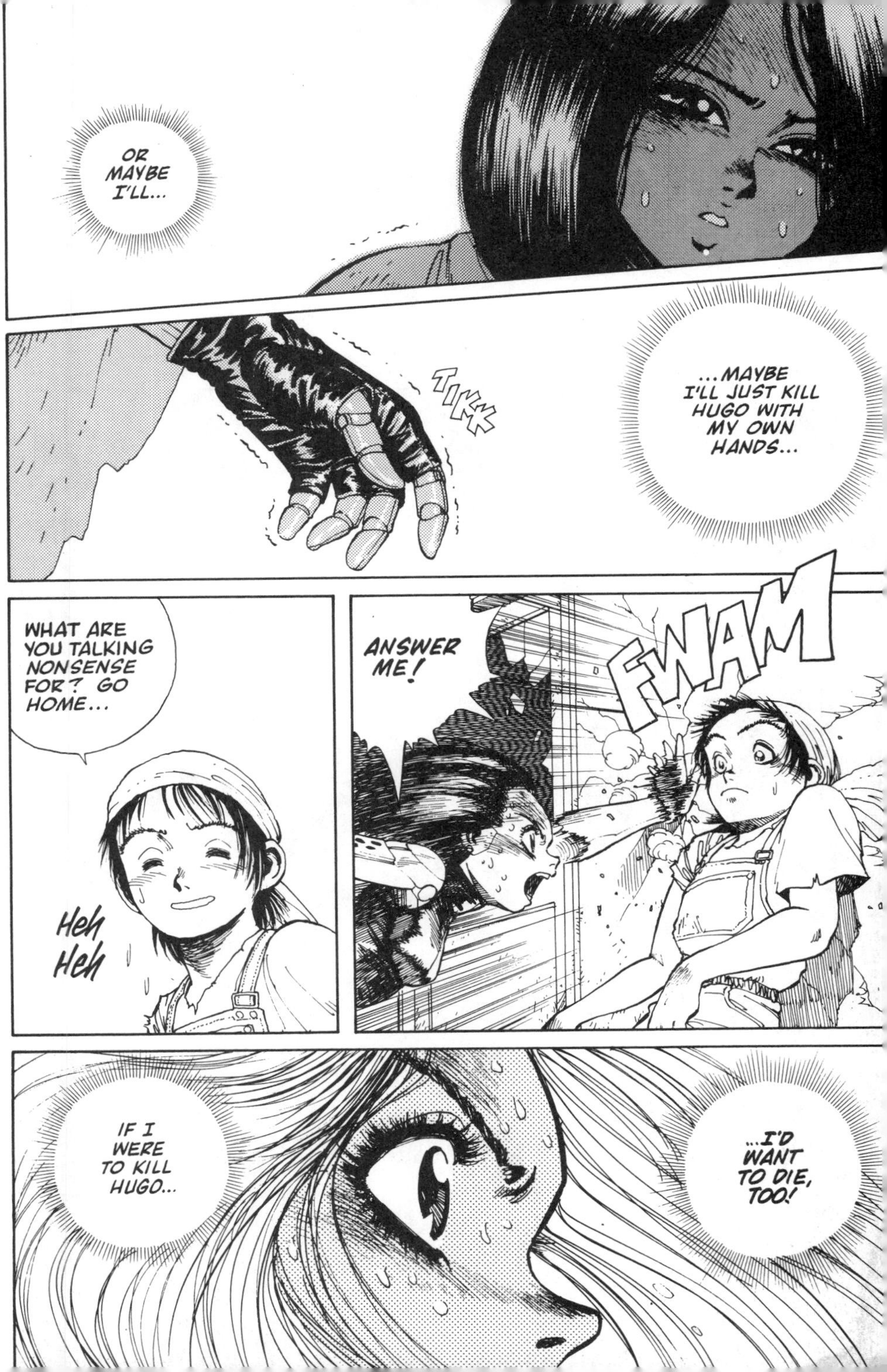
OR MAYBE I'LL...
TIKK
...MAYBE I'LL JUST KILL HUGO WITH MY OWN HANDS...
WHAT ARE YOU TALKING NONSENSE FOR? GO HOME...
Heh Heh
ANSWER ME!
FWAM
IF I WERE TO KILL HUGO...
...I'D WANT TO DIE, TOO!

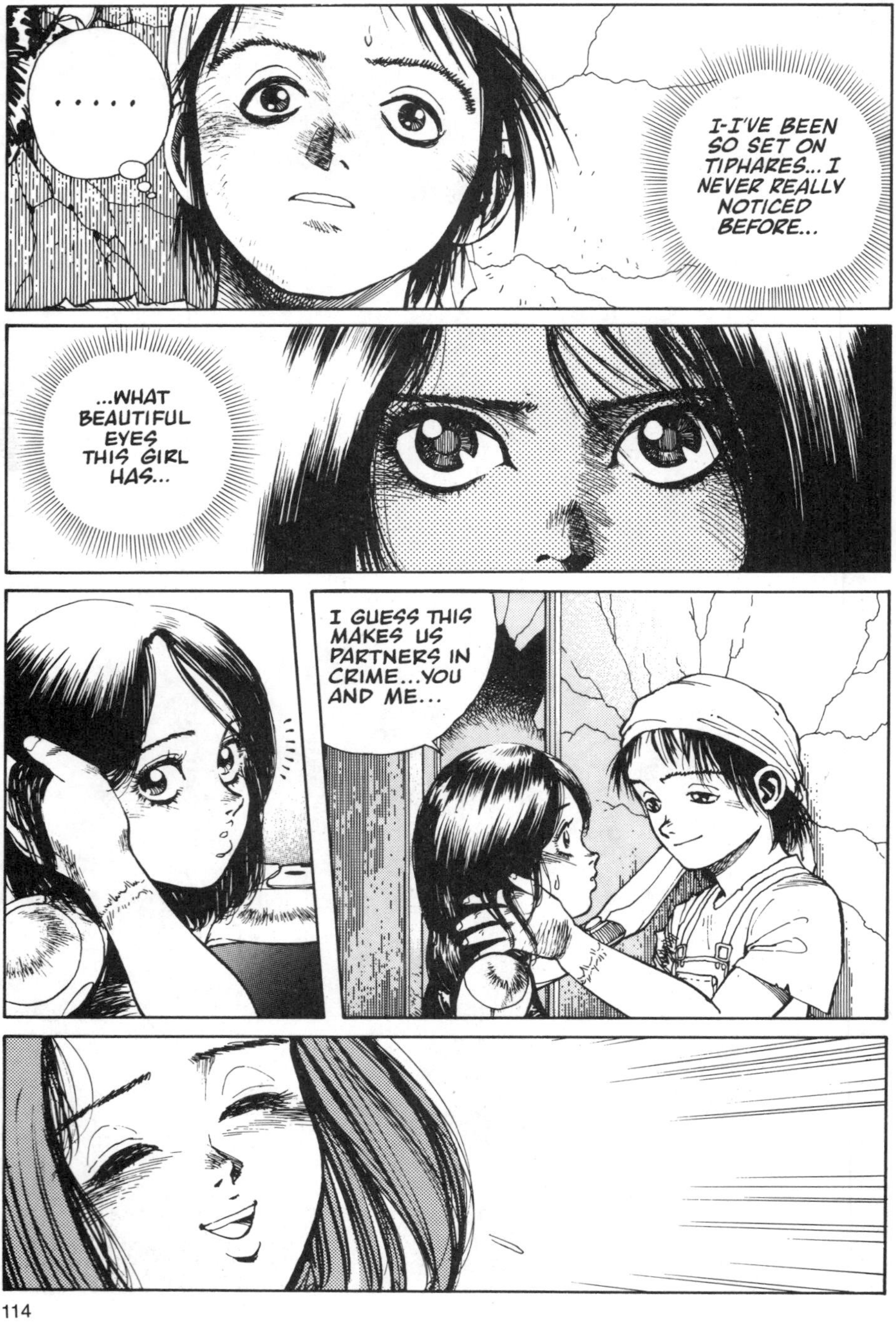
.....
I-I'VE BEEN SO SET ON TIPHARES... I NEVER REALLY NOTICED BEFORE...
...WHAT BEAUTIFUL EYES THIS GIRL HAS...
I GUESS THIS MAKES US PARTNERS IN CRIME...YOU AND ME...

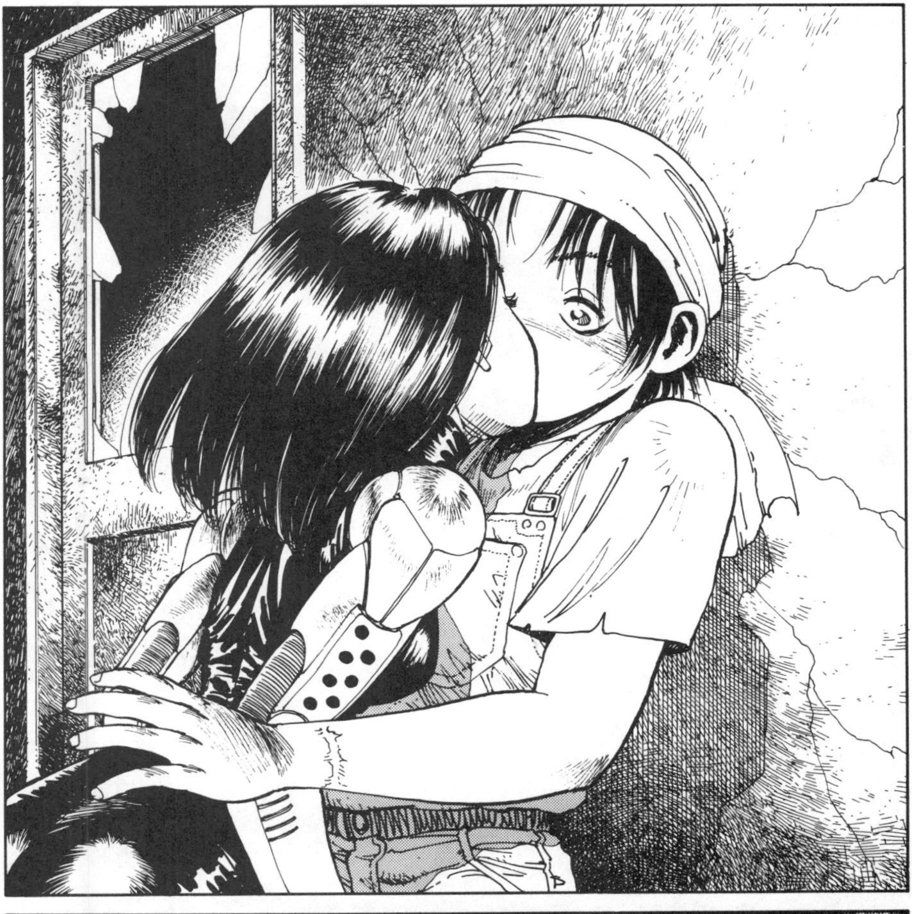

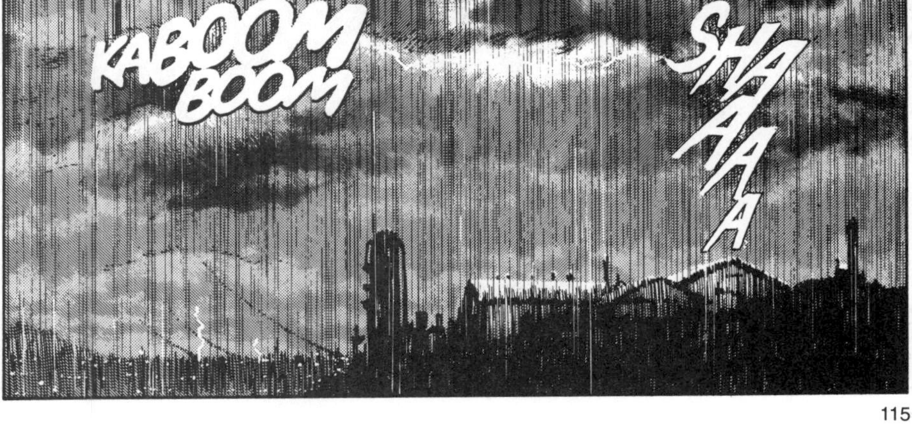
KABOOM BOOM
SHAAAAA

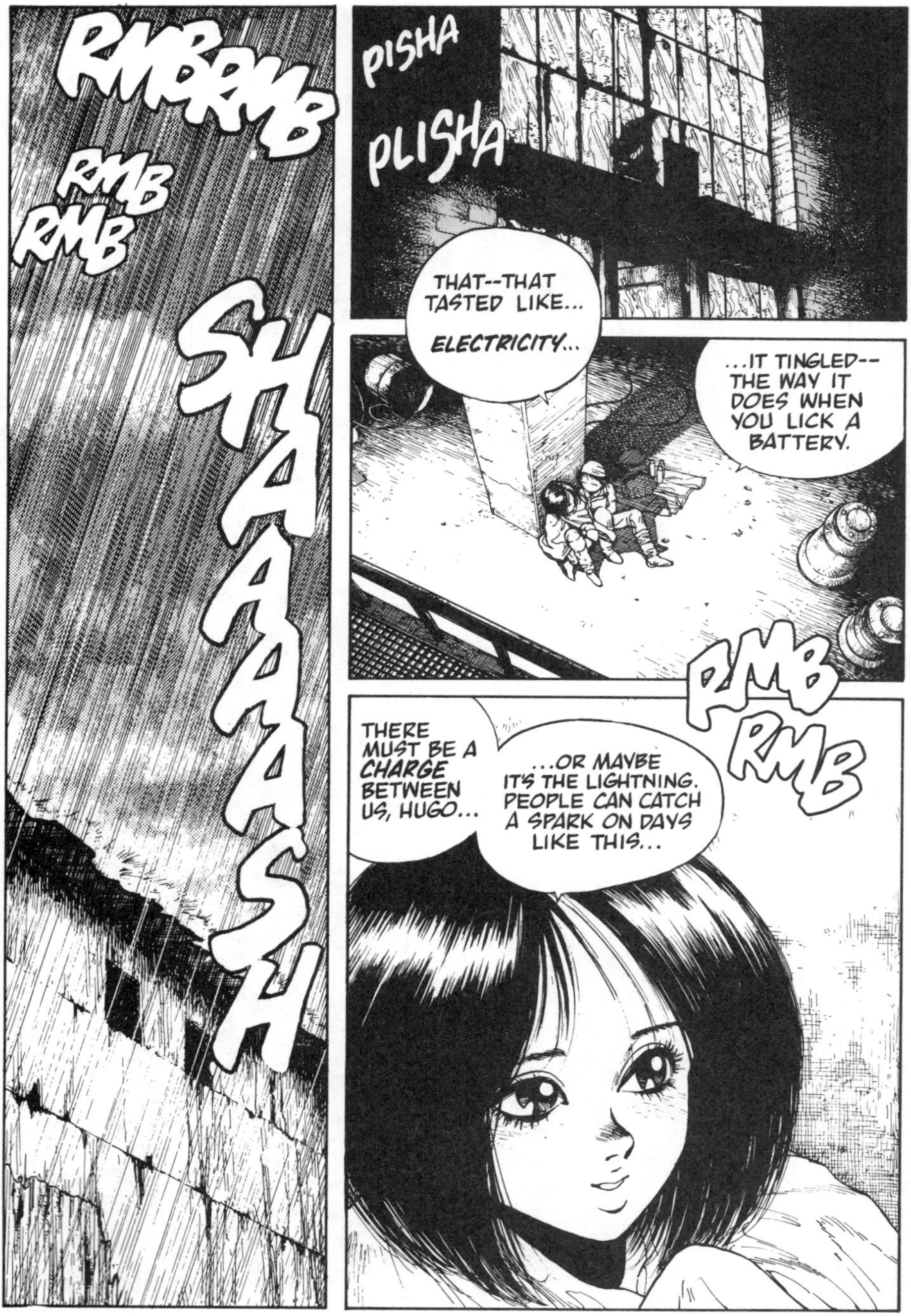

RMBRMB
RMB
RMB
SHAAAASH
PISHA
PLISHA
THAT--THAT TASTED LIKE... ELECTRICITY...
...IT TINGLED-- THE WAY IT DOES WHEN YOU LICK A BATTERY.
RMB RMB
THERE MUST BE A CHARGE BETWEEN US, HUGO...
...OR MAYBE IT'S THE LIGHTNING. PEOPLE CAN CATCH A SPARK ON DAYS LIKE THIS...

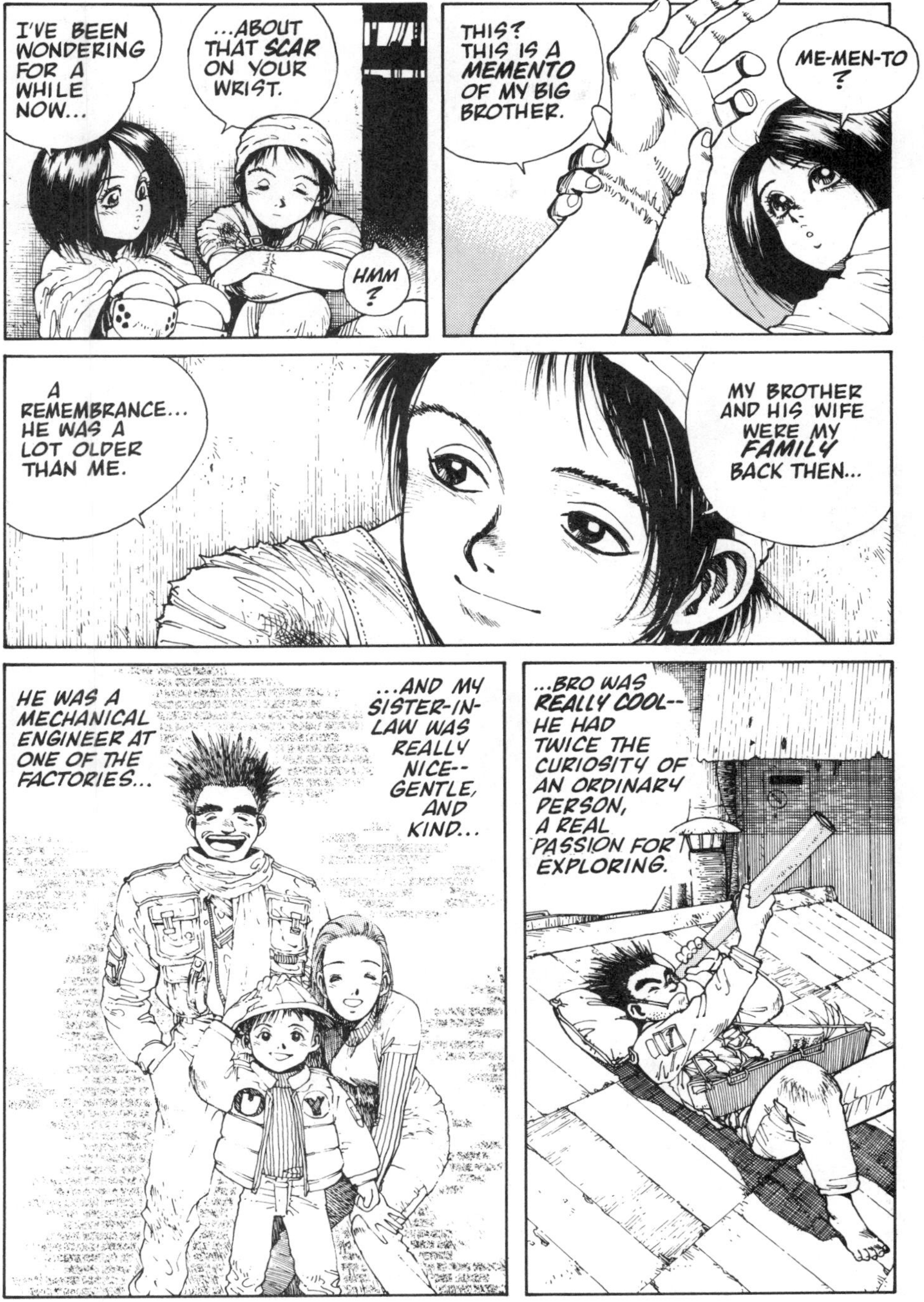
I'VE BEEN WONDERING FOR A WHILE NOW...
...ABOUT THAT SCAR ON YOUR WRIST.
HMM?
THIS? THIS IS A MEMENTO OF MY BIG BROTHER.
ME-MEN-TO?
A REMEMBRANCE... HE WAS A LOT OLDER THAN ME.
MY BROTHER AND HIS WIFE WERE MY FAMILY BACK THEN...
HE WAS A MECHANICAL ENGINEER AT ONE OF THE FACTORIES...
...AND MY SISTER-IN-LAW WAS REALLY NICE-- GENTLE, AND KIND...
...BRO WAS REALLY COOL-- HE HAD TWICE THE CURIOSITY OF AN ORDINARY PERSON, A REAL PASSION FOR EXPLORING.

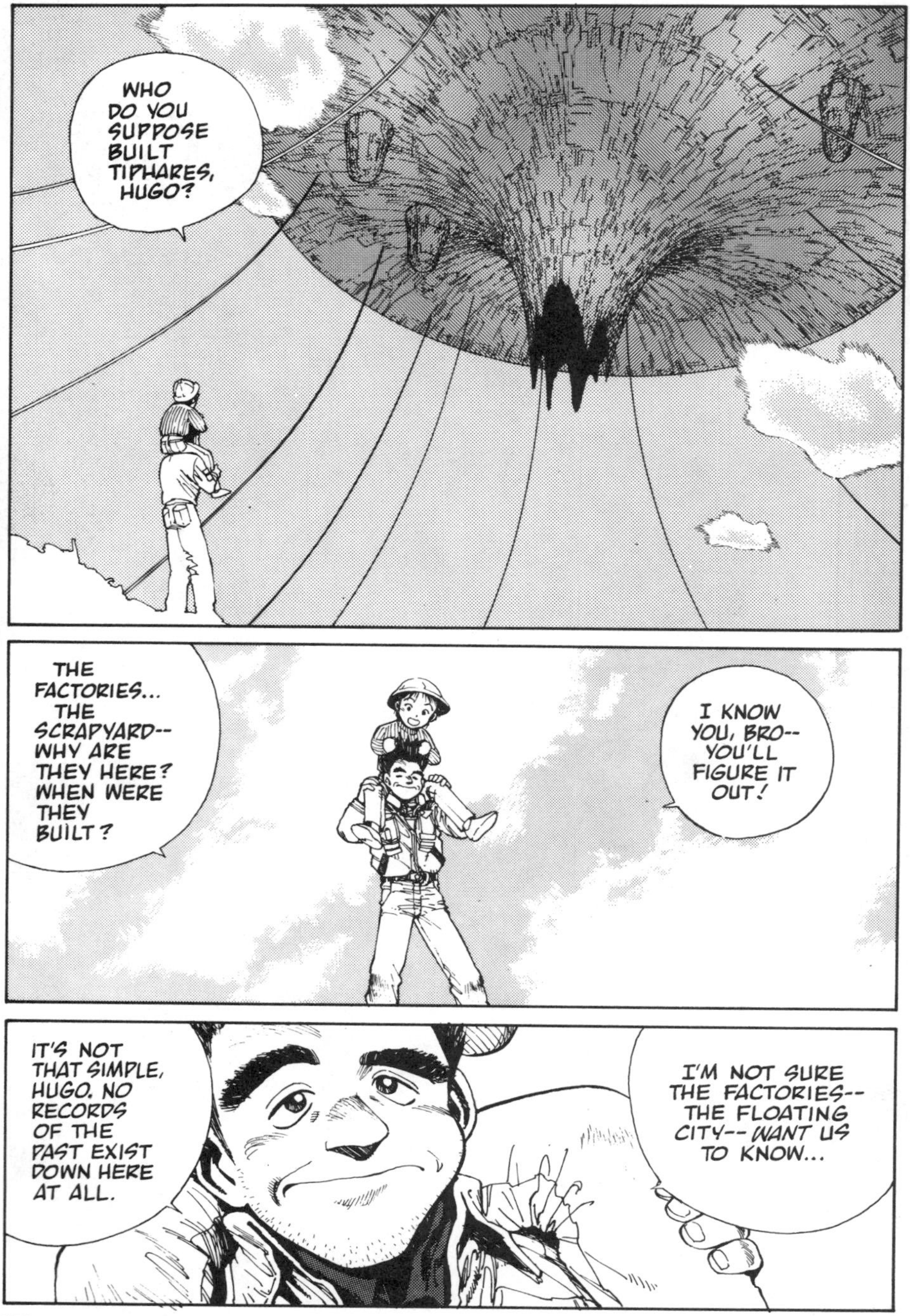
WHO DO YOU SUPPOSE BUILT TIPHARES, HUGO?
THE FACTORIES... THE SCRAPYARD-- WHY ARE THEY HERE? WHEN WERE THEY BUILT?
I KNOW YOU, BRO-- YOU'LL FIGURE IT OUT!
IT'S NOT THAT SIMPLE, HUGO. NO RECORDS OF THE PAST EXIST DOWN HERE AT ALL.
I'M NOT SURE THE FACTORIES-- THE FLOATING CITY-- WANT US TO KNOW...

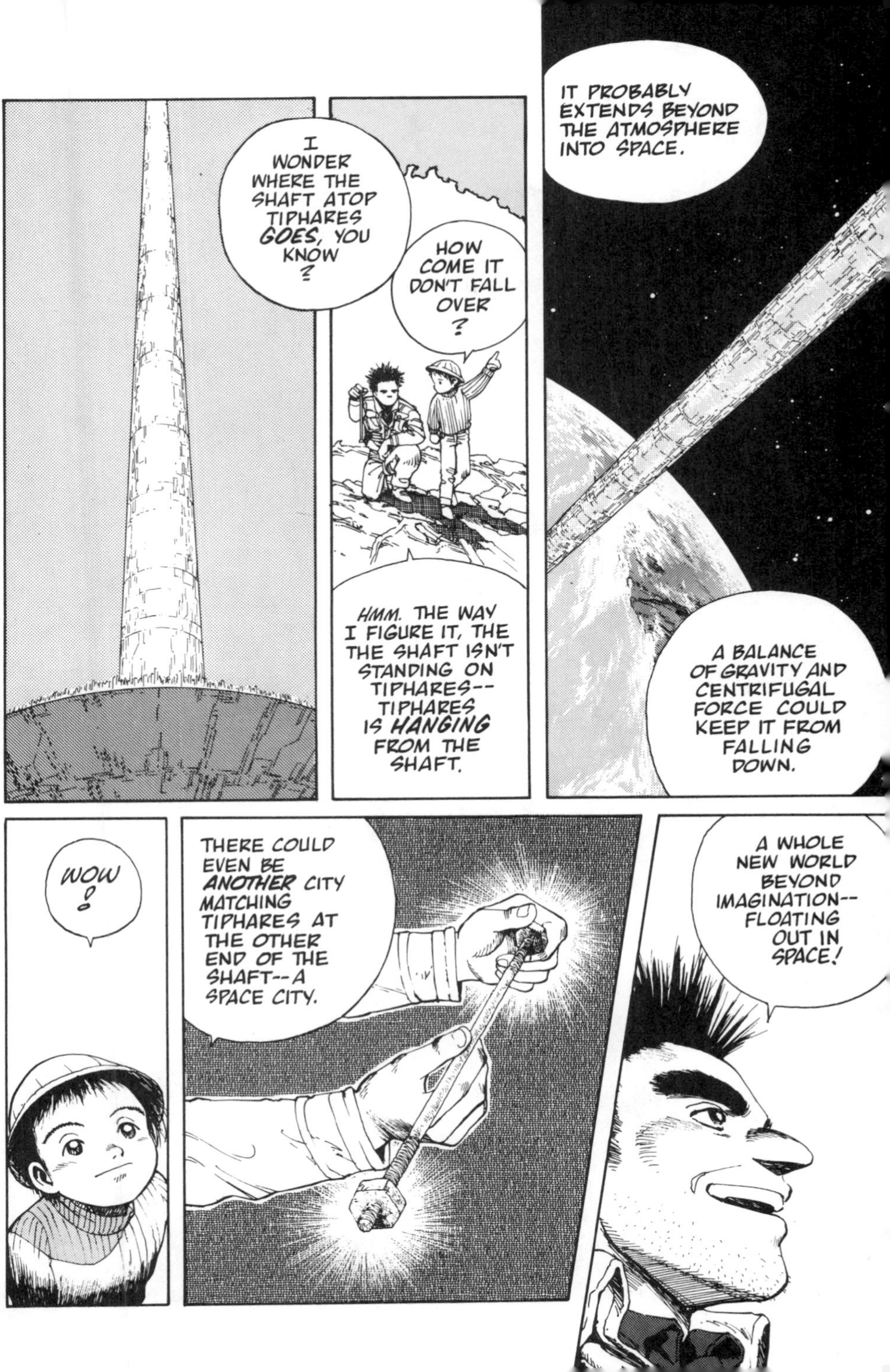
I WONDER WHERE THE SHAFT ATOP TIPHARES GOES, YOU KNOW?
HOW COME IT DON'T FALL OVER?
HMM. THE WAY I FIGURE IT, THE THE SHAFT ISN'T STANDING ON TIPHARES-- TIPHARES IS HANGING FROM THE SHAFT.
IT PROBABLY EXTENDS BEYOND THE ATMOSPHERE INTO SPACE.
A BALANCE OF GRAVITY AND CENTRIFUGAL FORCE COULD KEEP IT FROM FALLING DOWN.
WOW!
THERE COULD EVEN BE ANOTHER CITY MATCHING TIPHARES AT THE OTHER END OF THE SHAFT--A SPACE CITY.
A WHOLE NEW WORLD BEYOND IMAGINATION-- FLOATING OUT IN SPACE!

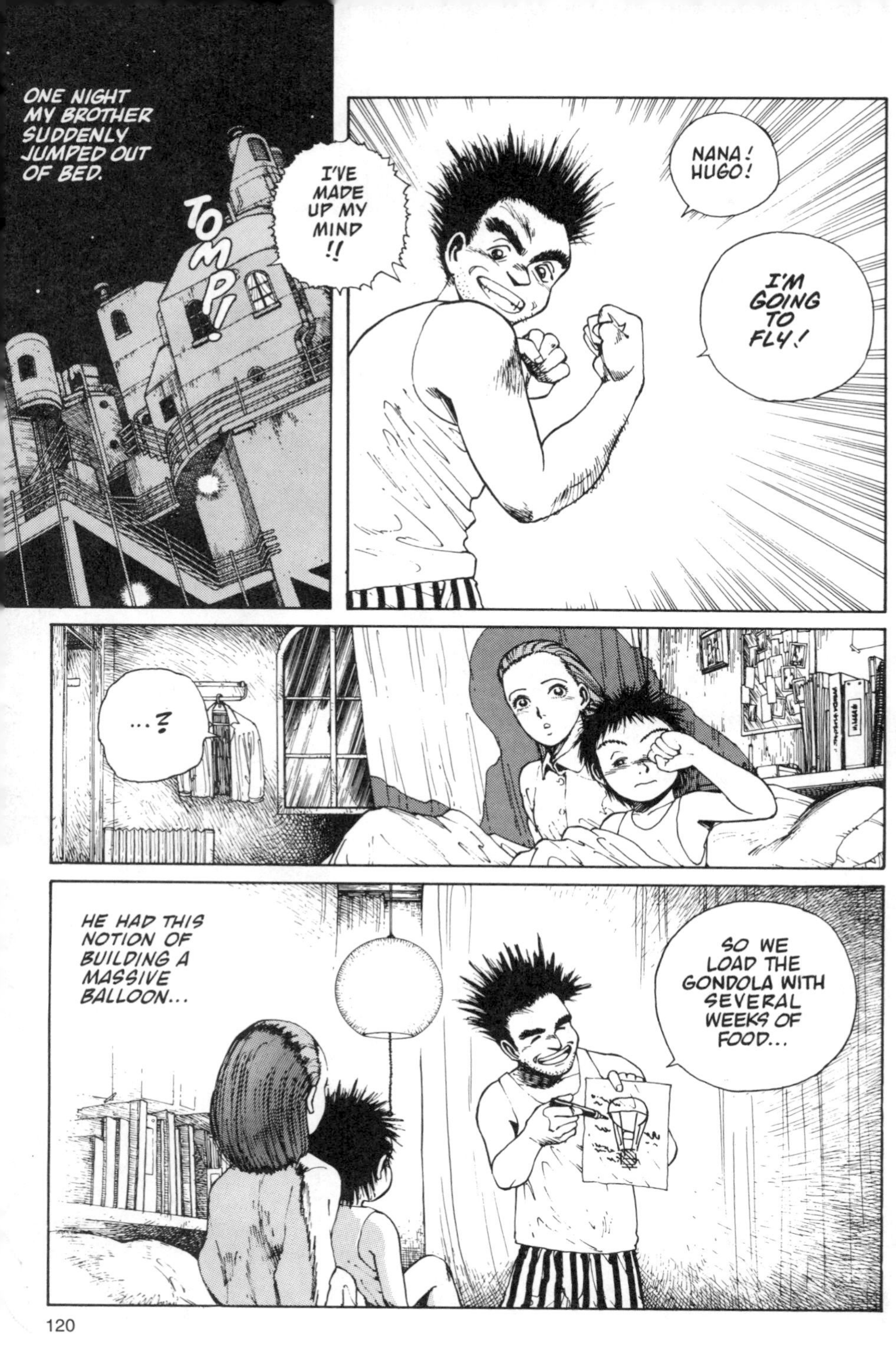
ONE NIGHT MY BROTHER SUDDENLY JUMPED OUT OF BED.
TOMP!
I'VE MADE UP MY MIND !!
NANA! HUGO!
I'M GOING TO FLY!
...?
HE HAD THIS NOTION OF BUILDING A MASSIVE BALLOON...
SO WE LOAD THE GONDOLA WITH SEVERAL WEEKS OF FOOD...

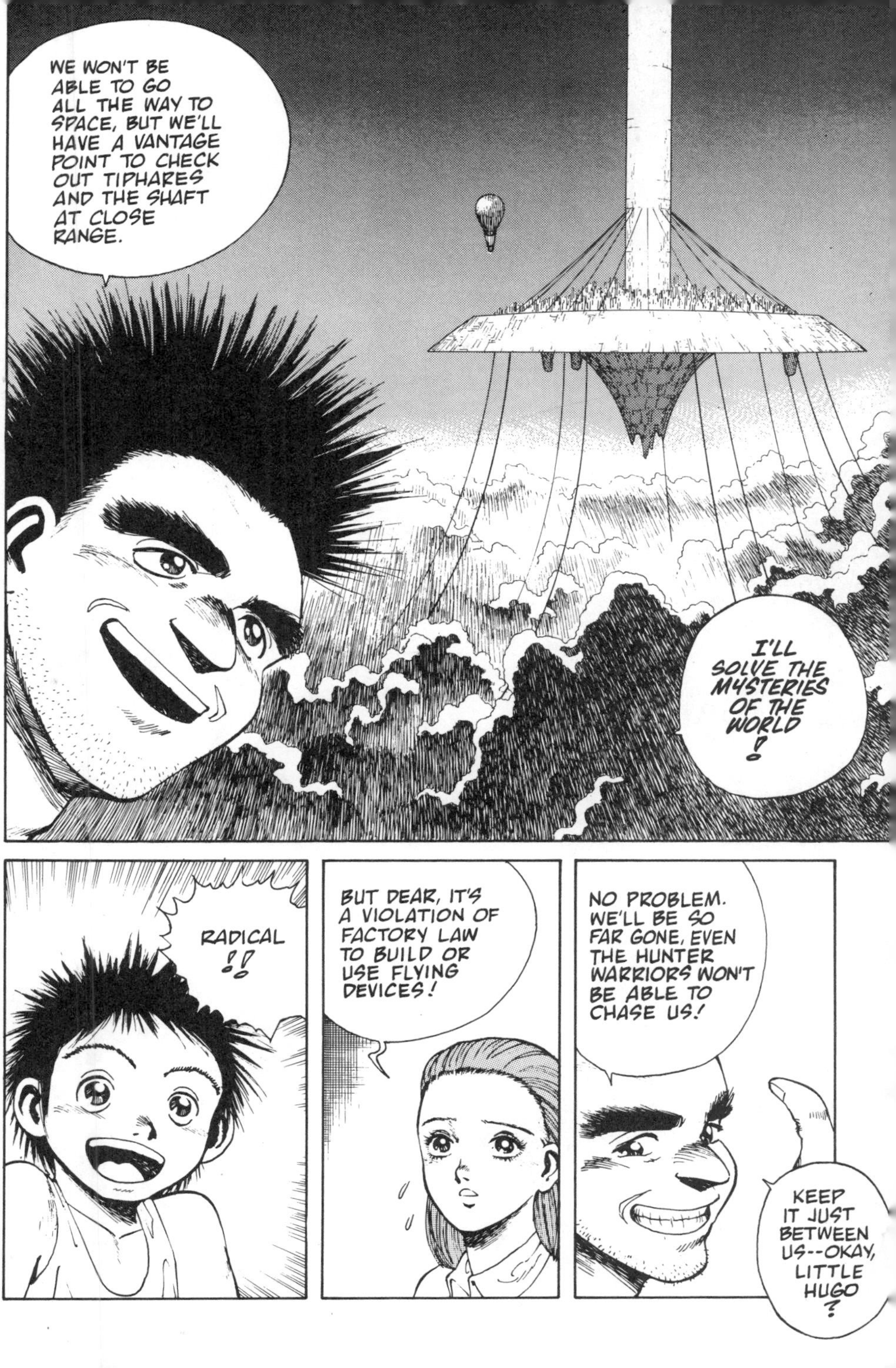
WE WON'T BE ABLE TO GO ALL THE WAY TO SPACE, BUT WE'LL HAVE A VANTAGE POINT TO CHECK OUT TIPHARES AND THE SHAFT AT CLOSE RANGE.
I'LL SOLVE THE MYSTERIES OF THE WORLD!
RADICAL!!
BUT DEAR, IT'S A VIOLATION OF FACTORY LAW TO BUILD OR USE FLYING DEVICES!
NO PROBLEM. WE'LL BE SO FAR GONE, EVEN THE HUNTER WARRIORS WON'T BE ABLE TO CHASE US!
KEEP IT JUST BETWEEN US--OKAY, LITTLE HUGO?

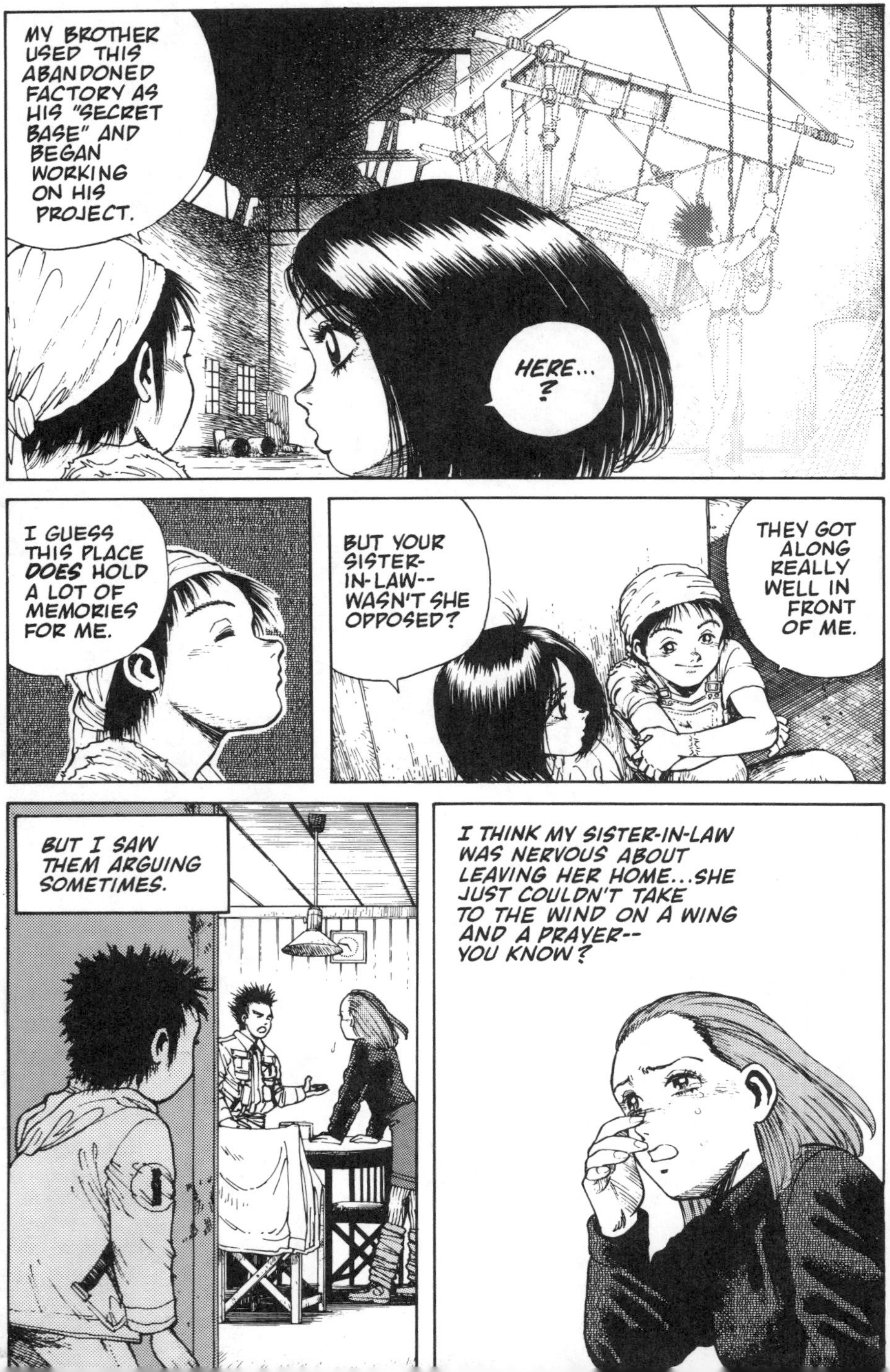
MY BROTHER USED THIS ABANDONED FACTORY AS HIS "SECRET BASE" AND BEGAN WORKING ON HIS PROJECT.
HERE...?
I GUESS THIS PLACE DOES HOLD A LOT OF MEMORIES FOR ME.
BUT YOUR SISTER-IN-LAW--WASN'T SHE OPPOSED?
THEY GOT ALONG REALLY WELL IN FRONT OF ME.
BUT I SAW THEM ARGUING SOMETIMES.
I THINK MY SISTER-IN-LAW WAS NERVOUS ABOUT LEAVING HER HOME...SHE JUST COULDN'T TAKE TO THE WIND ON A WING AND A PRAYER--YOU KNOW?

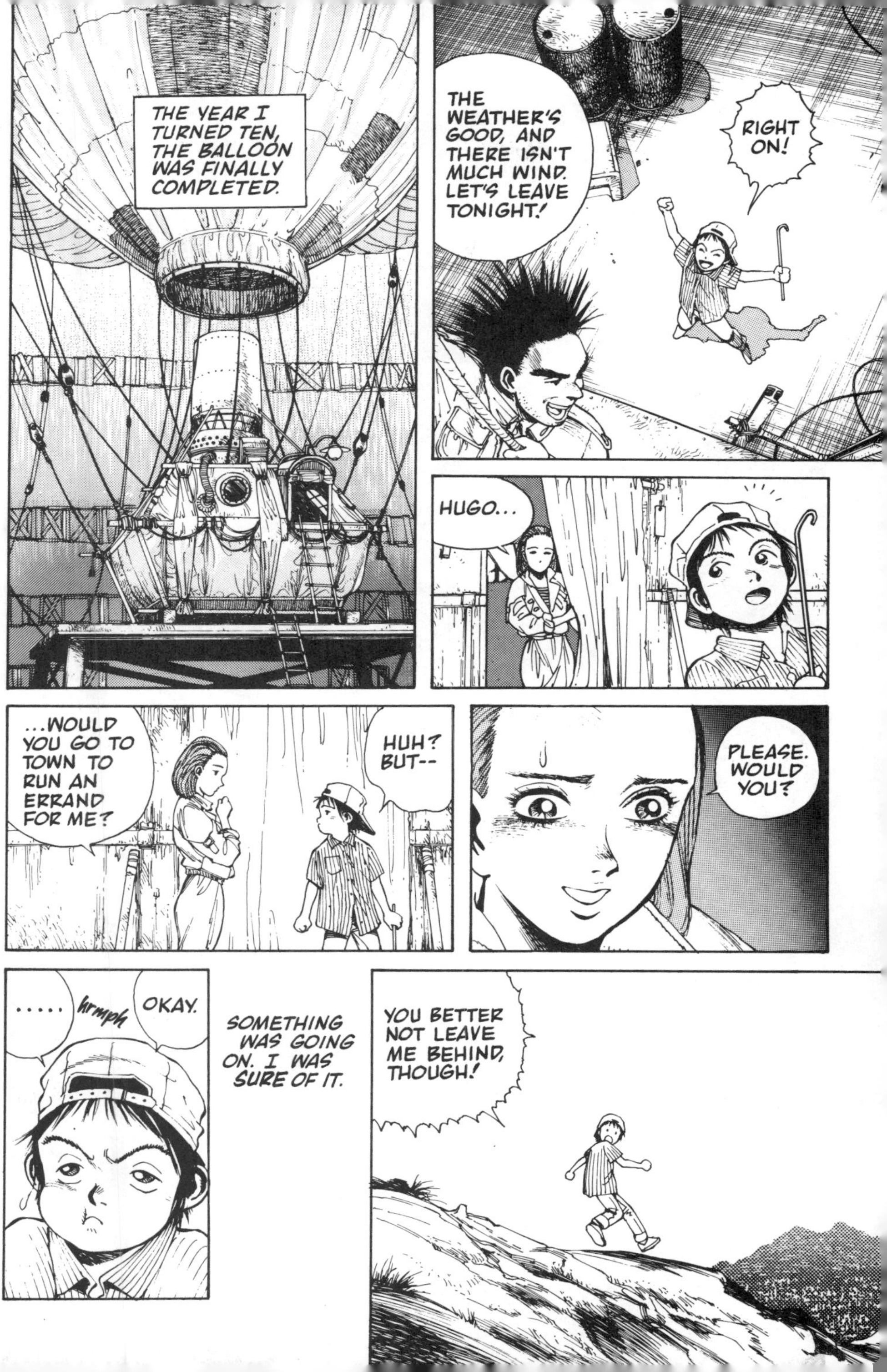
THE YEAR I TURNED TEN, THE BALLOON WAS FINALLY COMPLETED.
THE WEATHER'S GOOD, AND THERE ISN'T MUCH WIND. LET'S LEAVE TONIGHT!
RIGHT ON!
HUGO...
...WOULD YOU GO TO TOWN TO RUN AN ERRAND FOR ME?
HUH? BUT--
PLEASE. WOULD YOU?
.....
hrmph
OKAY.
SOMETHING WAS GOING ON. I WAS SURE OF IT.
YOU BETTER NOT LEAVE ME BEHIND, THOUGH!

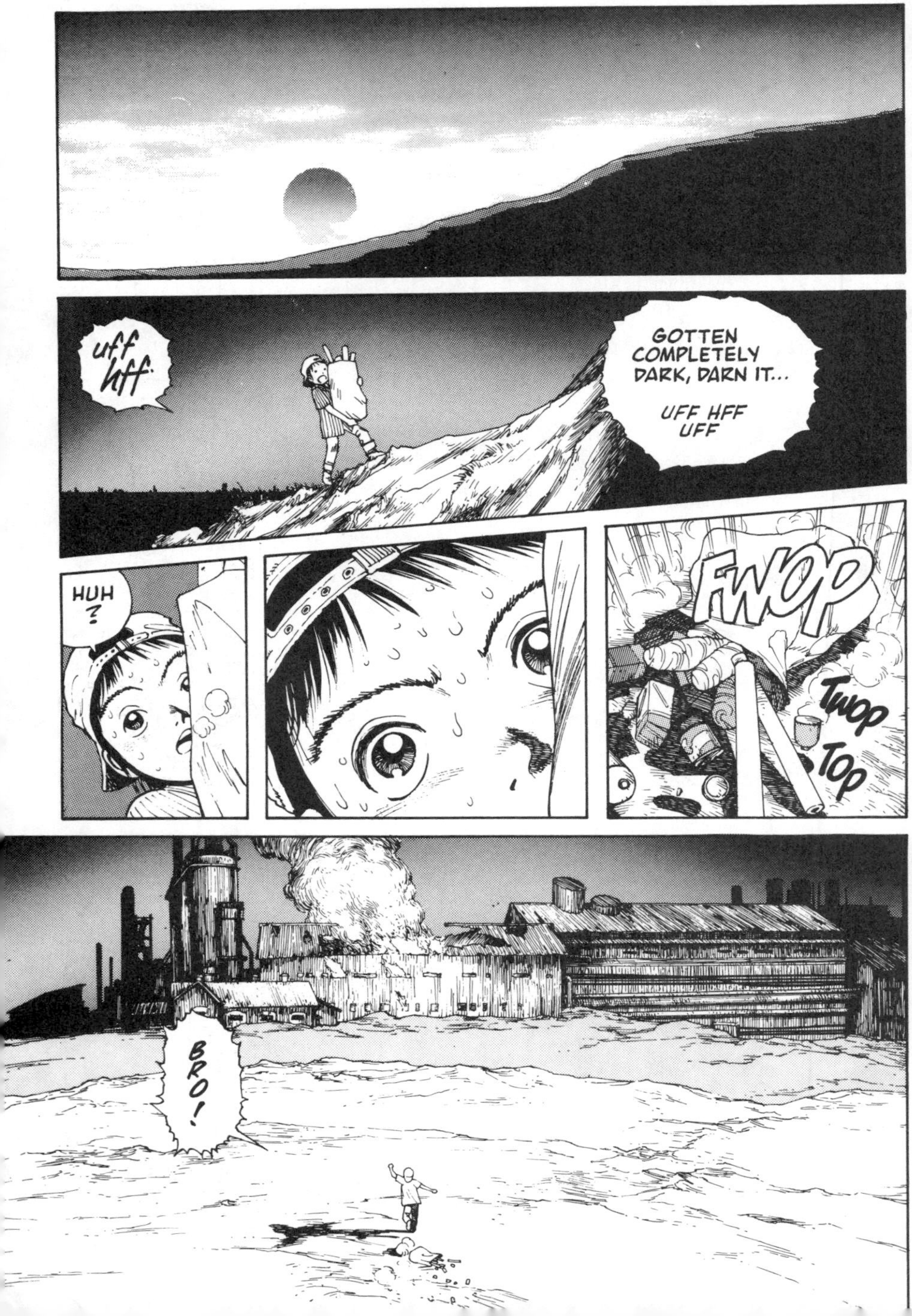
uff hff
GOTTEN COMPLETELY DARK, DARN IT...
UFF HFF UFF
HUH?
FWOP
TWOP TOP
BRO!

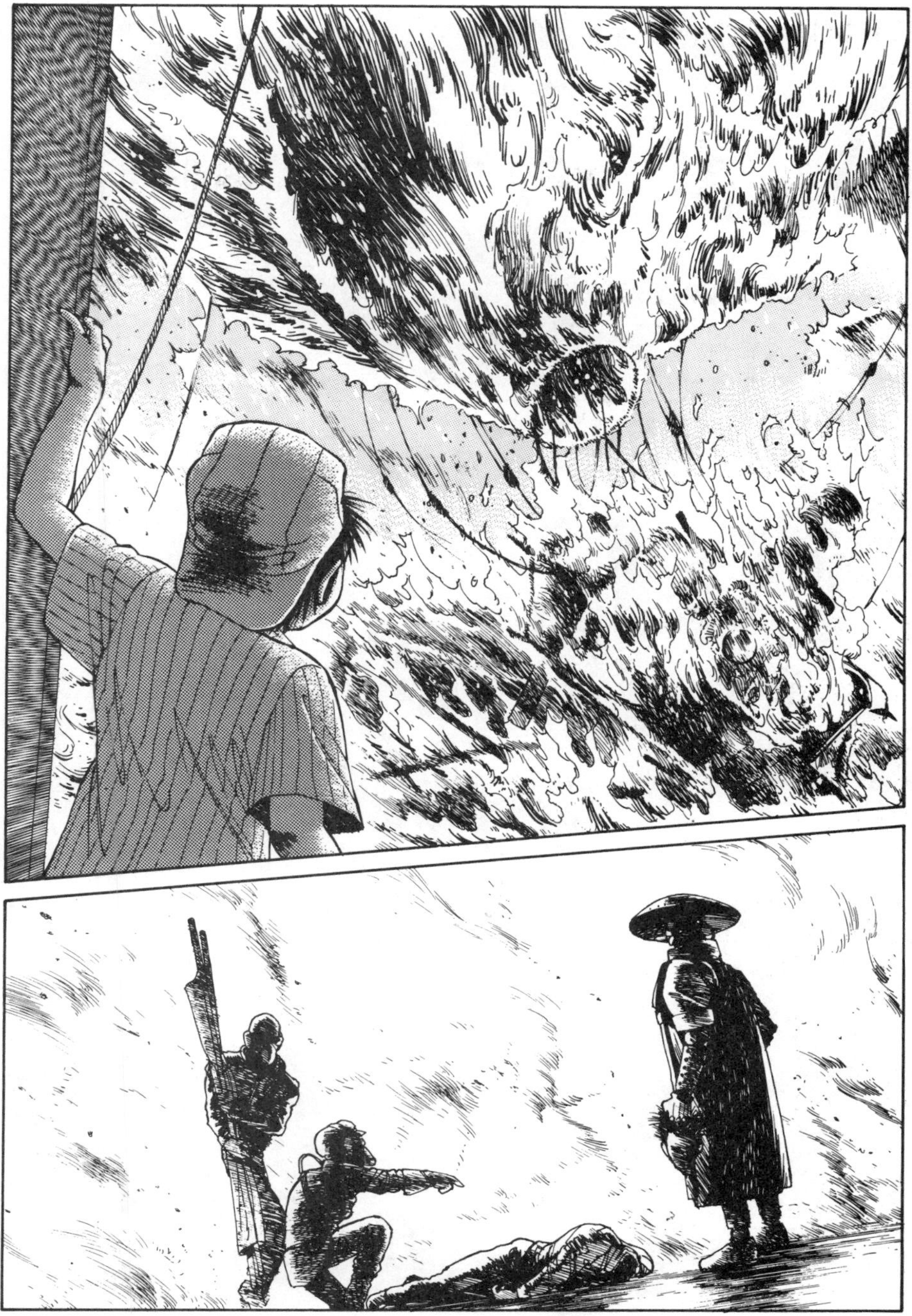

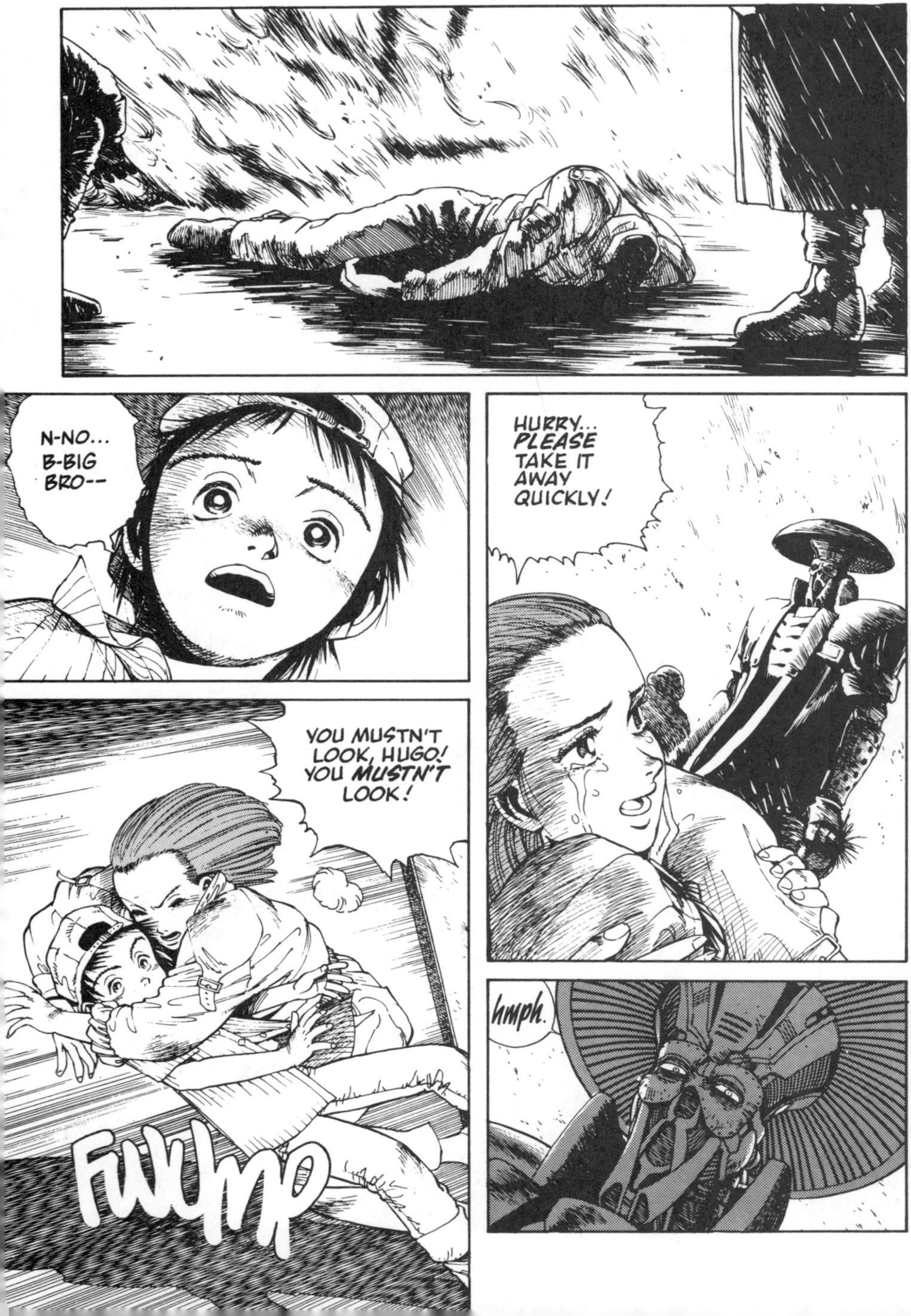
N-NO... B-BIG BRO--
HURRY... PLEASE TAKE IT AWAY QUICKLY!
YOU MUSTN'T LOOK, HUGO! YOU MUSTN'T LOOK!
FWUMP
hmph.

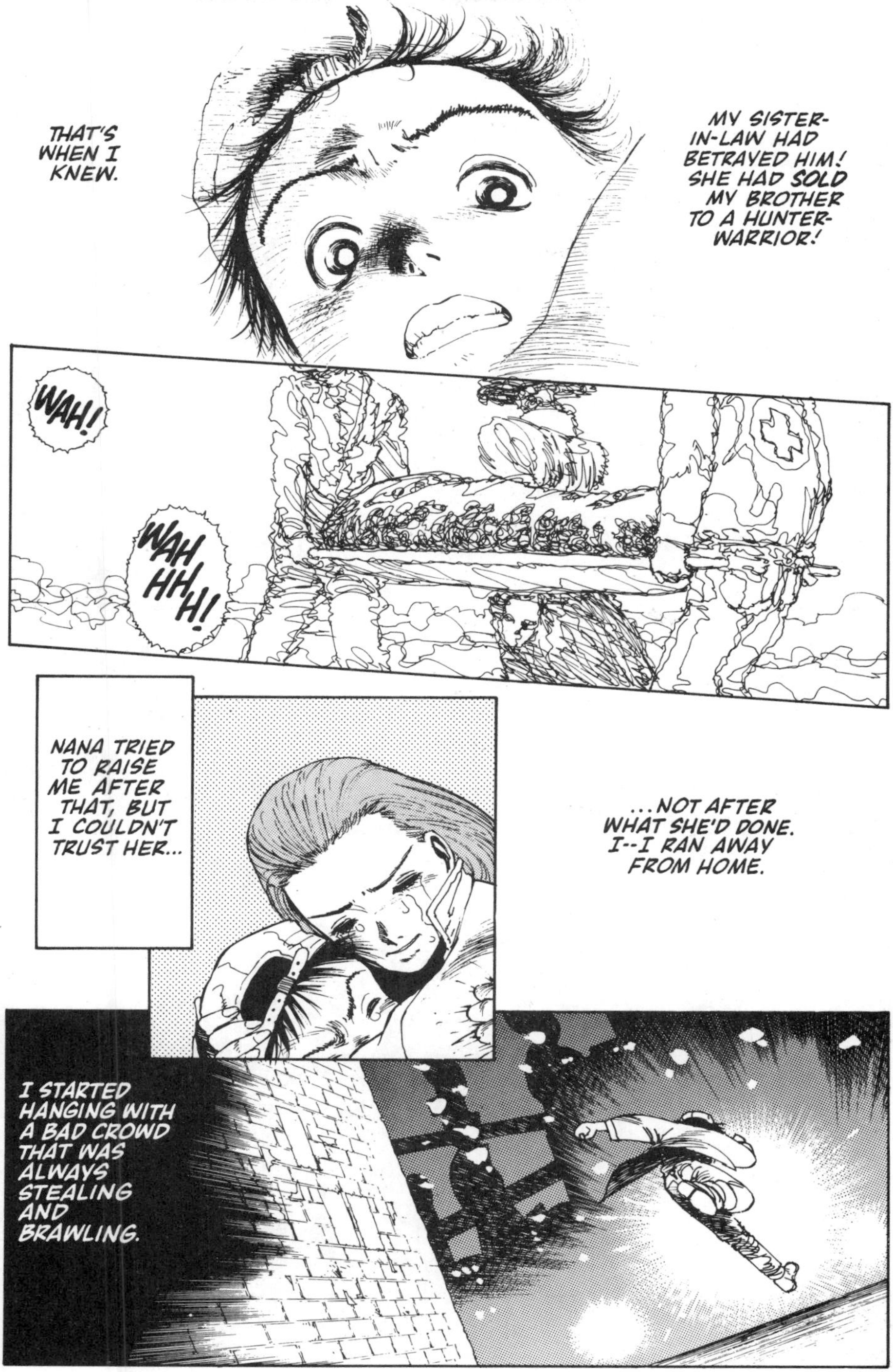

THAT'S WHEN I KNEW.
MY SISTER-IN-LAW HAD BETRAYED HIM! SHE HAD SOLD MY BROTHER TO A HUNTER-WARRIOR!
WAH!
WAHHHH!
NANA TRIED TO RAISE ME AFTER THAT, BUT I COULDN'T TRUST HER...
...NOT AFTER WHAT SHE'D DONE. I--I RAN AWAY FROM HOME.
I STARTED HANGING WITH A BAD CROWD THAT WAS ALWAYS STEALING AND BRAWLING.

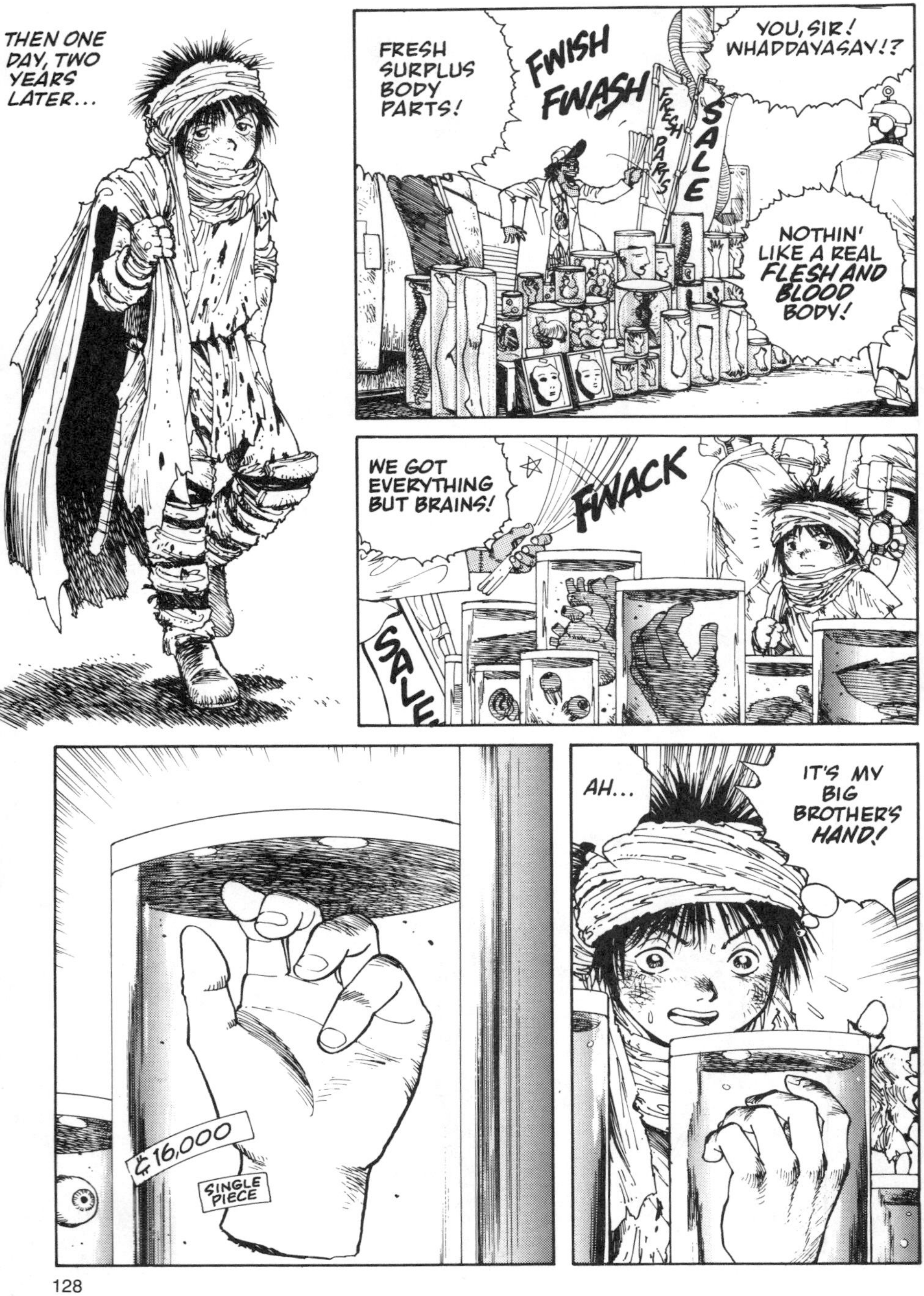
THEN ONE DAY, TWO YEARS LATER...
FRESH SURPLUS BODY PARTS!
FWISH
FWASH
FRESH PARTS
SALE
YOU, SIR! WHADDAYASAY!?
NOTHIN' LIKE A REAL FLESH AND BLOOD BODY!
WE GOT EVERYTHING BUT BRAINS!
FWACK
SALE
₲16,000
SINGLE PIECE
AH...
IT'S MY BIG BROTHER'S HAND!

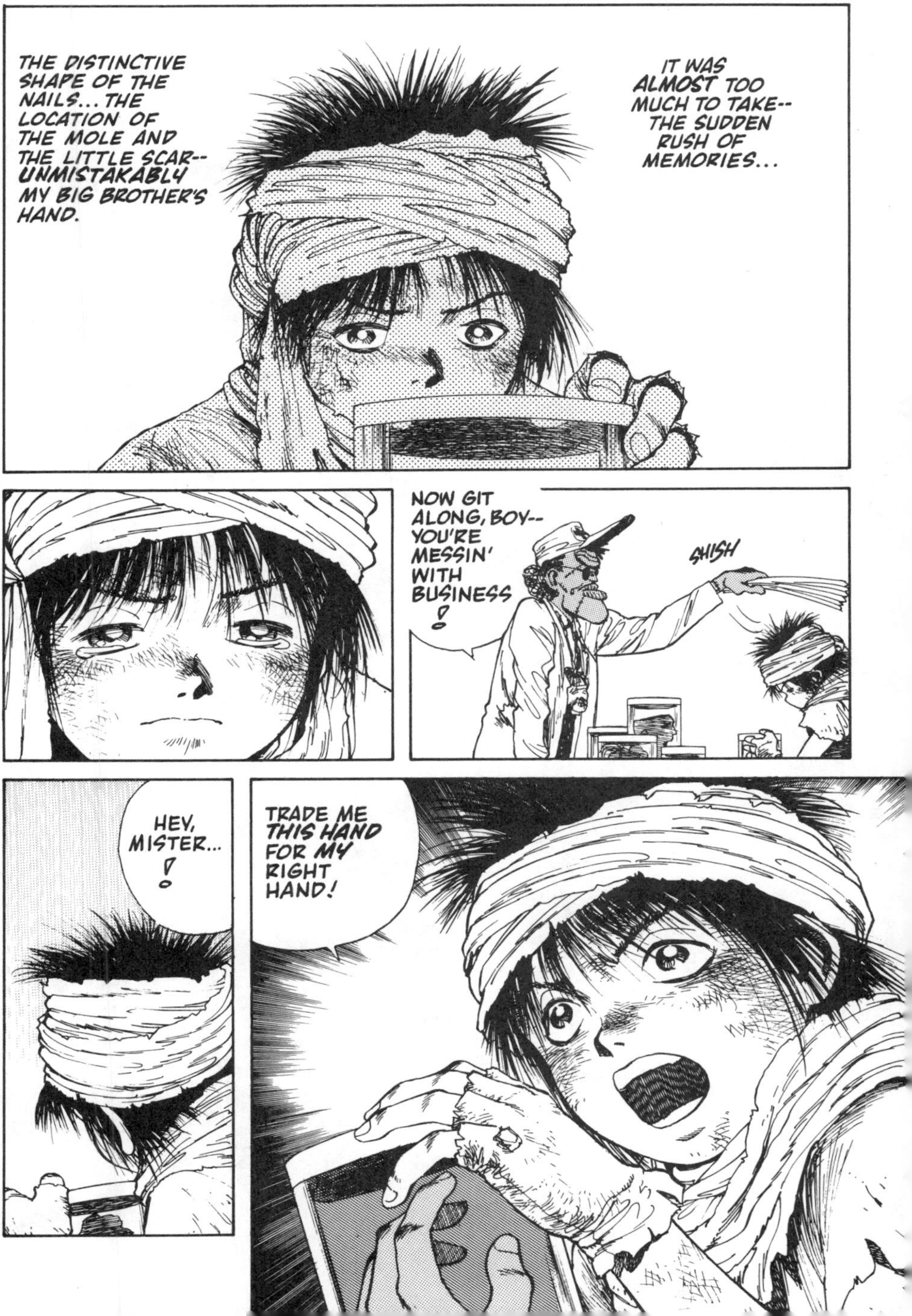
THE DISTINCTIVE SHAPE OF THE NAILS... THE LOCATION OF THE MOLE AND THE LITTLE SCAR-- UNMISTAKABLY MY BIG BROTHER'S HAND.
IT WAS ALMOST TOO MUCH TO TAKE-- THE SUDDEN RUSH OF MEMORIES...
NOW GIT ALONG, BOY-- YOU'RE MESSIN' WITH BUSINESS!
SHISH
HEY, MISTER...!
TRADE ME THIS HAND FOR MY RIGHT HAND!

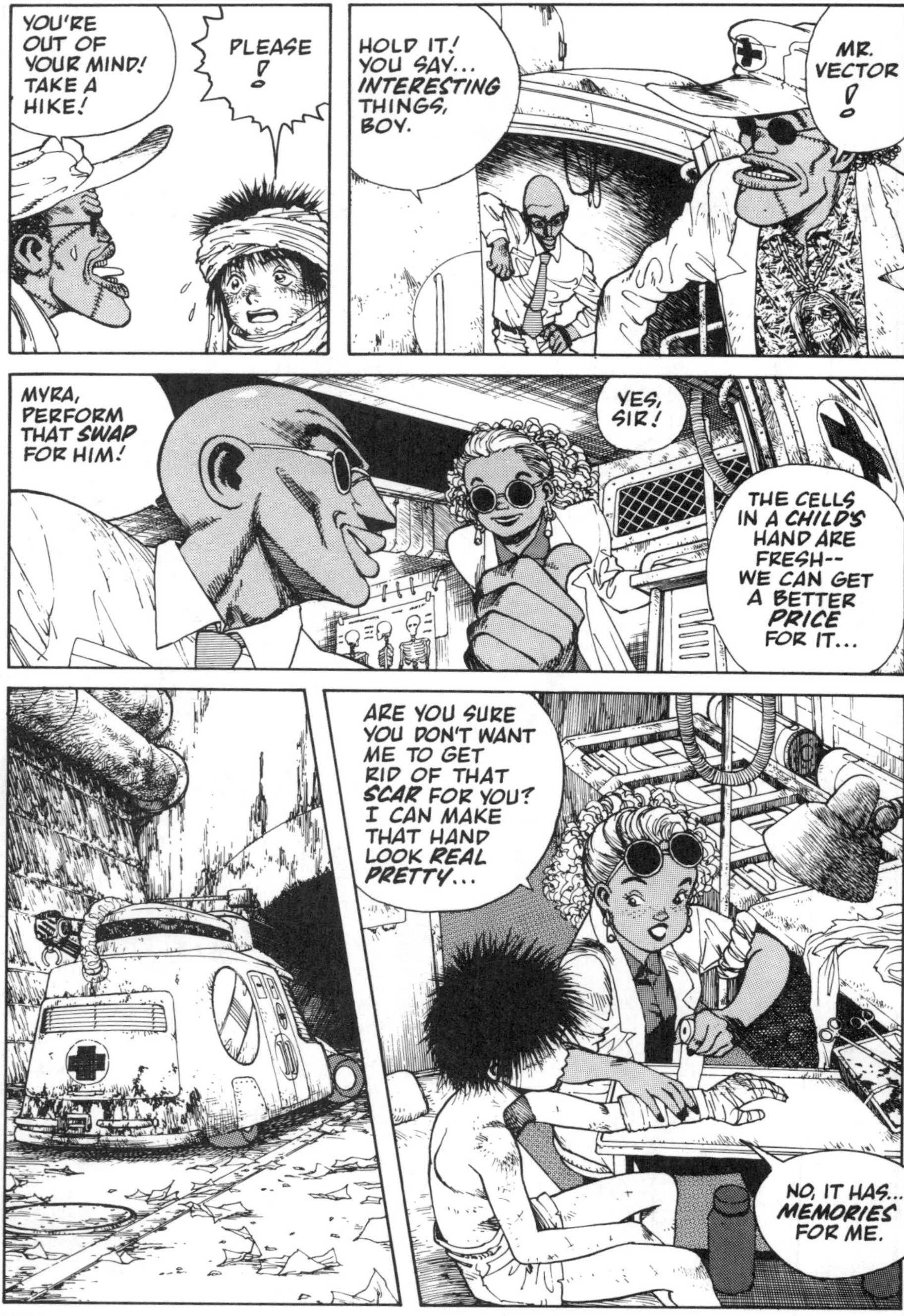
YOU'RE OUT OF YOUR MIND! TAKE A HIKE!
PLEASE!
HOLD IT! YOU SAY... INTERESTING THINGS, BOY.
MR. VECTOR!
MYRA, PERFORM THAT SWAP FOR HIM!
YES, SIR!
THE CELLS IN A CHILD'S HAND ARE FRESH-- WE CAN GET A BETTER PRICE FOR IT...
ARE YOU SURE YOU DON'T WANT ME TO GET RID OF THAT SCAR FOR YOU? I CAN MAKE THAT HAND LOOK REAL PRETTY...
NO, IT HAS... MEMORIES FOR ME.

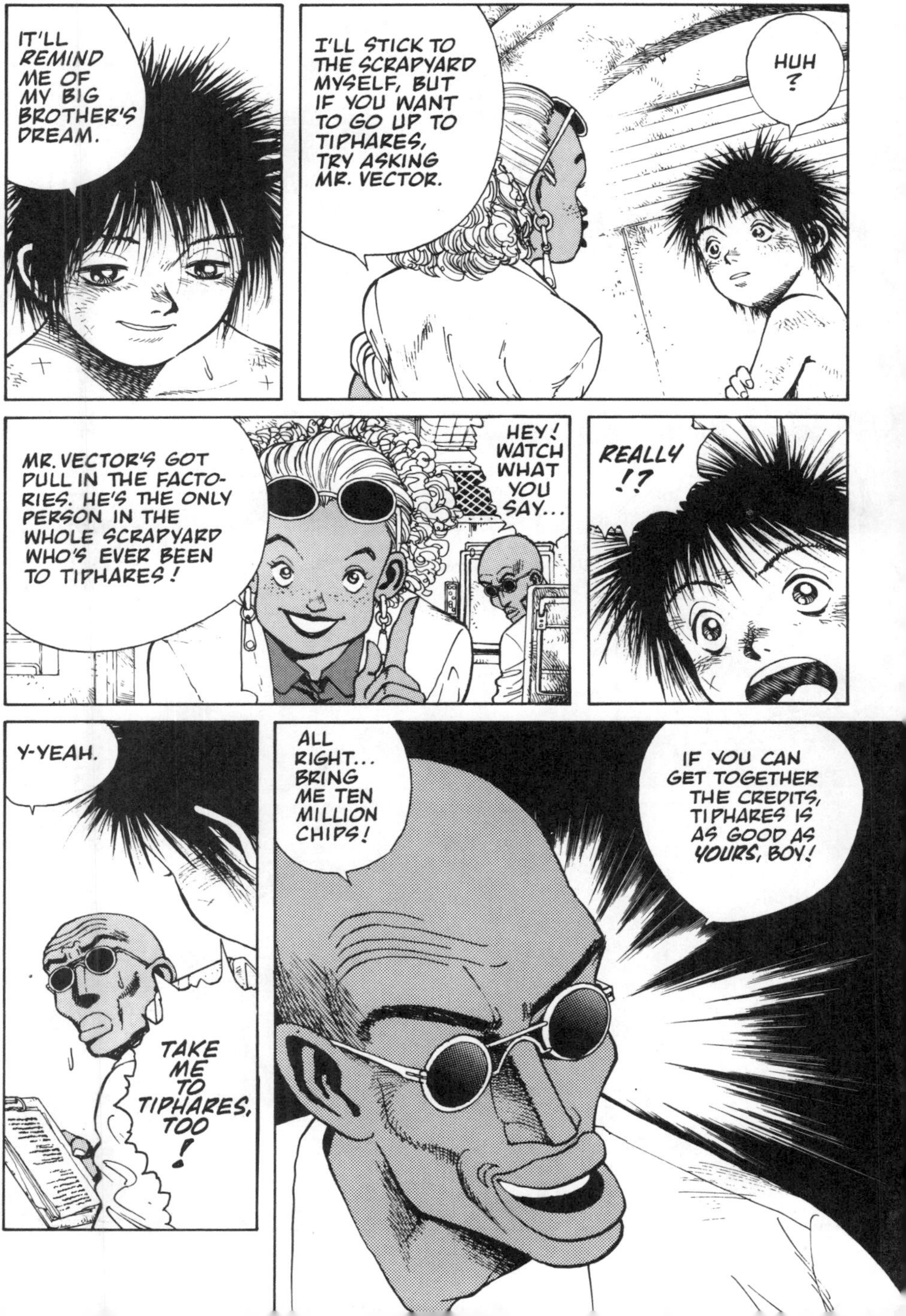
IT'LL REMIND ME OF MY BIG BROTHER'S DREAM.
I'LL STICK TO THE SCRAPYARD MYSELF, BUT IF YOU WANT TO GO UP TO TIPHARES, TRY ASKING MR. VECTOR.
HUH?
MR. VECTOR'S GOT PULL IN THE FACTO-RIES. HE'S THE ONLY PERSON IN THE WHOLE SCRAPYARD WHO'S EVER BEEN TO TIPHARES!
HEY! WATCH WHAT YOU SAY...
REALLY!?
Y-YEAH.
TAKE ME TO TIPHARES, TOO!
ALL RIGHT... BRING ME TEN MILLION CHIPS!
IF YOU CAN GET TOGETHER THE CREDITS, TIPHARES IS AS GOOD AS YOURS, BOY!

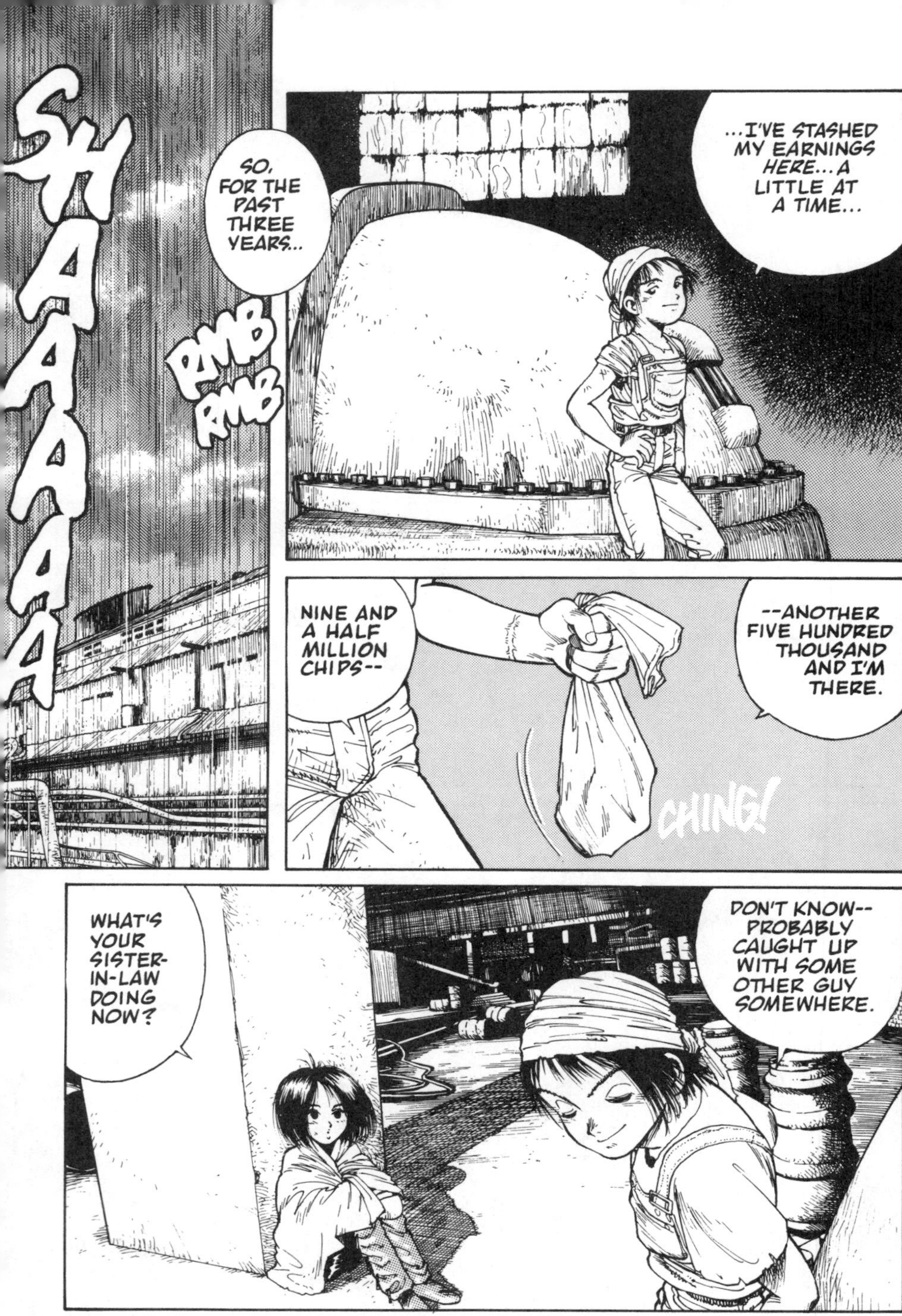
SHAAAAAA
RMB RMB
SO, FOR THE PAST THREE YEARS...
...I'VE STASHED MY EARNINGS HERE... A LITTLE AT A TIME...
NINE AND A HALF MILLION CHIPS--
--ANOTHER FIVE HUNDRED THOUSAND AND I'M THERE.
CHING!
WHAT'S YOUR SISTER-IN-LAW DOING NOW?
DON'T KNOW-- PROBABLY CAUGHT UP WITH SOME OTHER GUY SOMEWHERE.

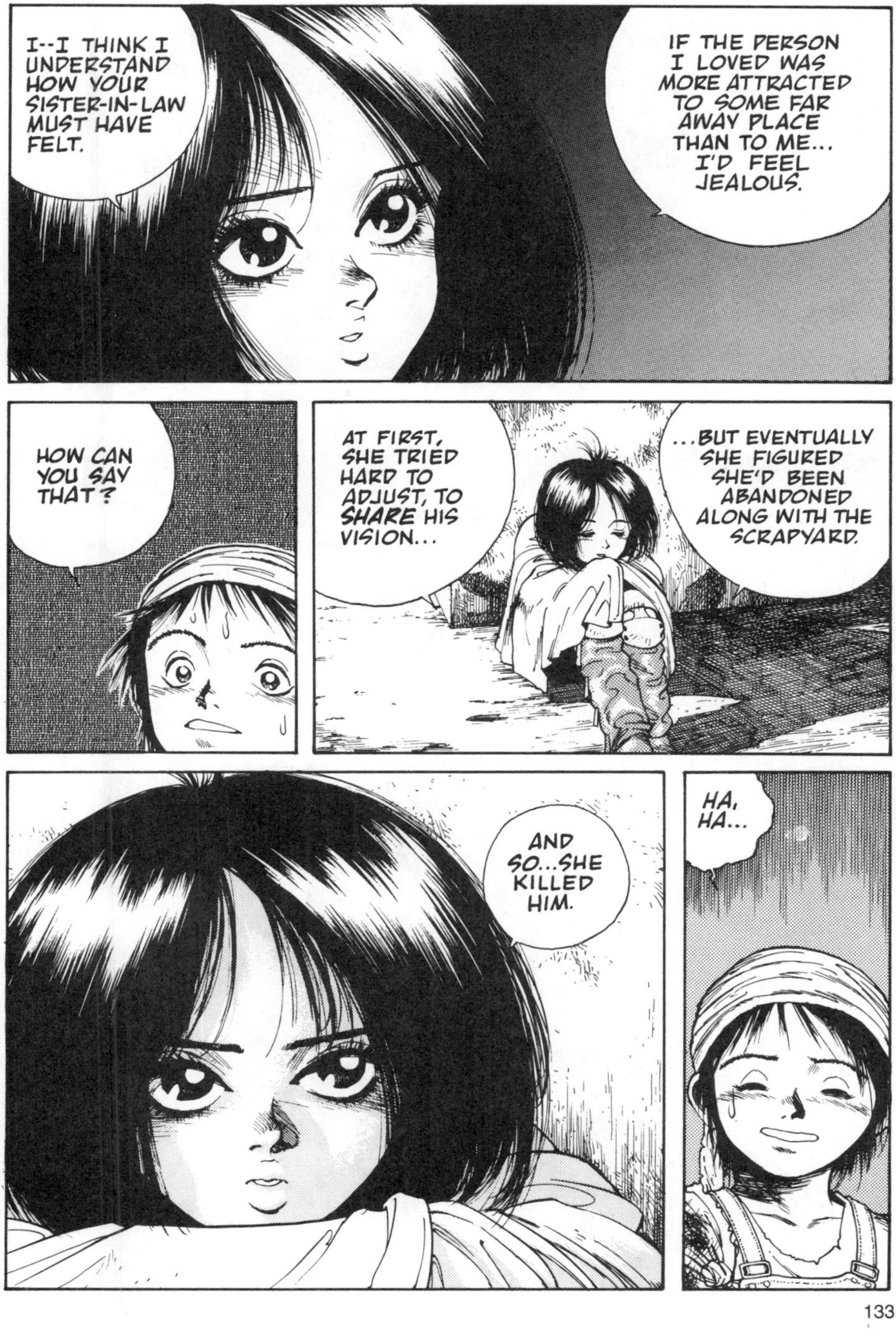
I--I THINK I UNDERSTAND HOW YOUR SISTER-IN-LAW MUST HAVE FELT.
IF THE PERSON I LOVED WAS MORE ATTRACTED TO SOME FAR AWAY PLACE THAN TO ME... I'D FEEL JEALOUS.
HOW CAN YOU SAY THAT?
AT FIRST, SHE TRIED HARD TO ADJUST, TO SHARE HIS VISION...
...BUT EVENTUALLY SHE FIGURED SHE'D BEEN ABANDONED ALONG WITH THE SCRAPYARD.
AND SO...SHE KILLED HIM.
HA, HA...

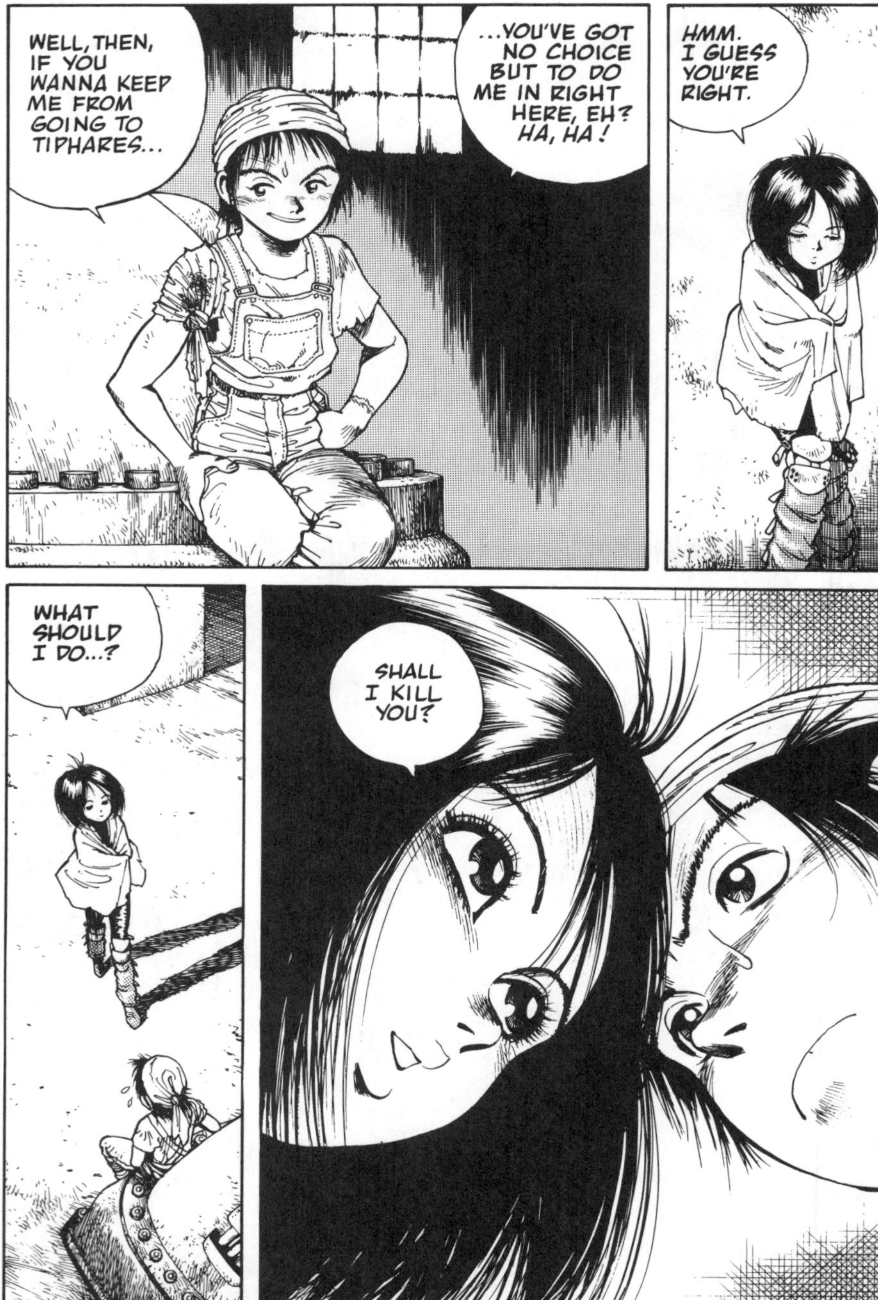
WELL, THEN, IF YOU WANNA KEEP ME FROM GOING TO TIPHARES...
...YOU'VE GOT NO CHOICE BUT TO DO ME IN RIGHT HERE, EH? HA, HA!
HMM. I GUESS YOU'RE RIGHT.
WHAT SHOULD I DO...?
SHALL I KILL YOU?

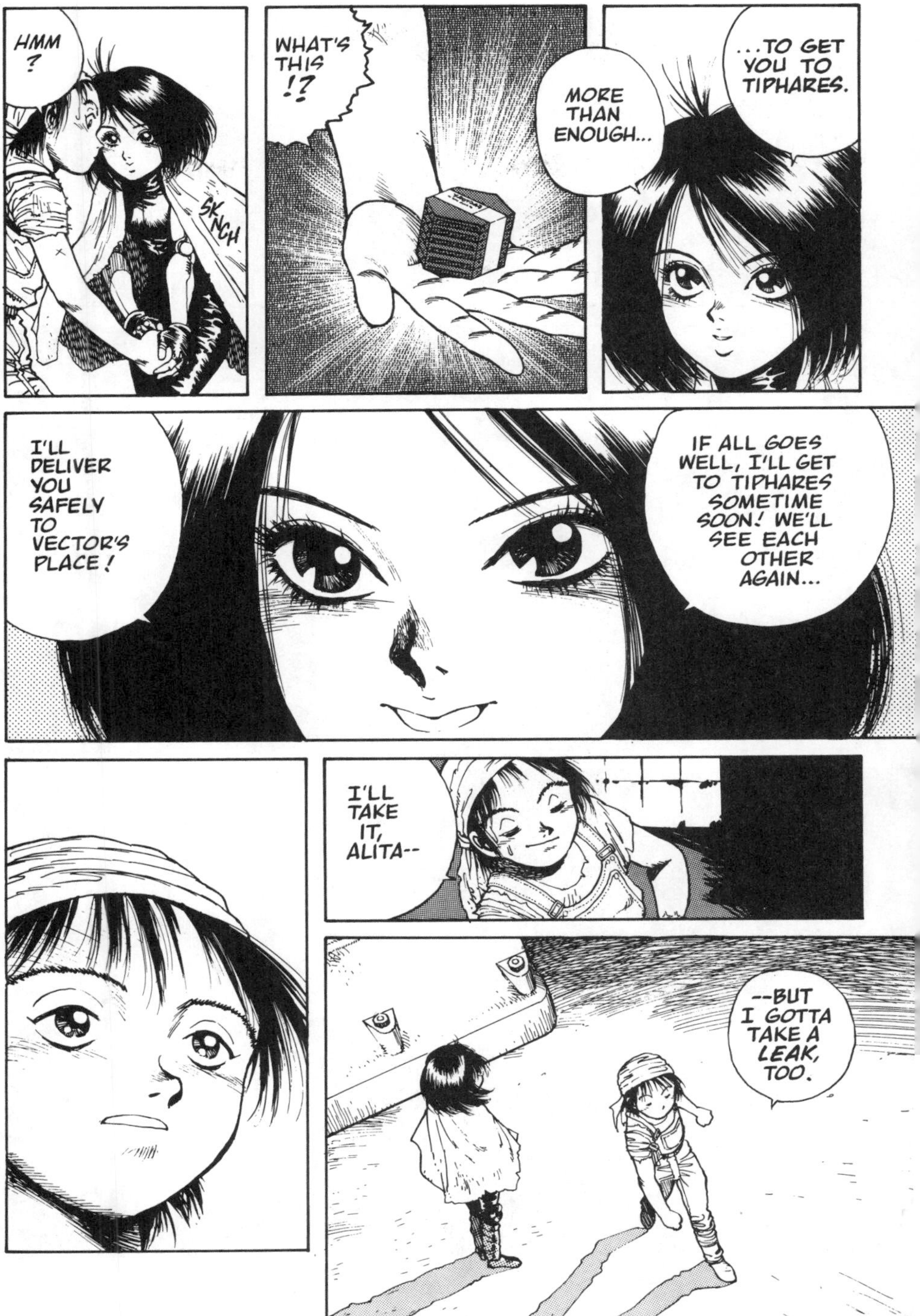
HMM ?
SKNCH
WHAT'S THIS !?
MORE THAN ENOUGH...
...TO GET YOU TO TIPHARES.
I'LL DELIVER YOU SAFELY TO VECTOR'S PLACE!
IF ALL GOES WELL, I'LL GET TO TIPHARES SOMETIME SOON! WE'LL SEE EACH OTHER AGAIN...
I'LL TAKE IT, ALITA--
--BUT I GOTTA TAKE A LEAK, TOO.

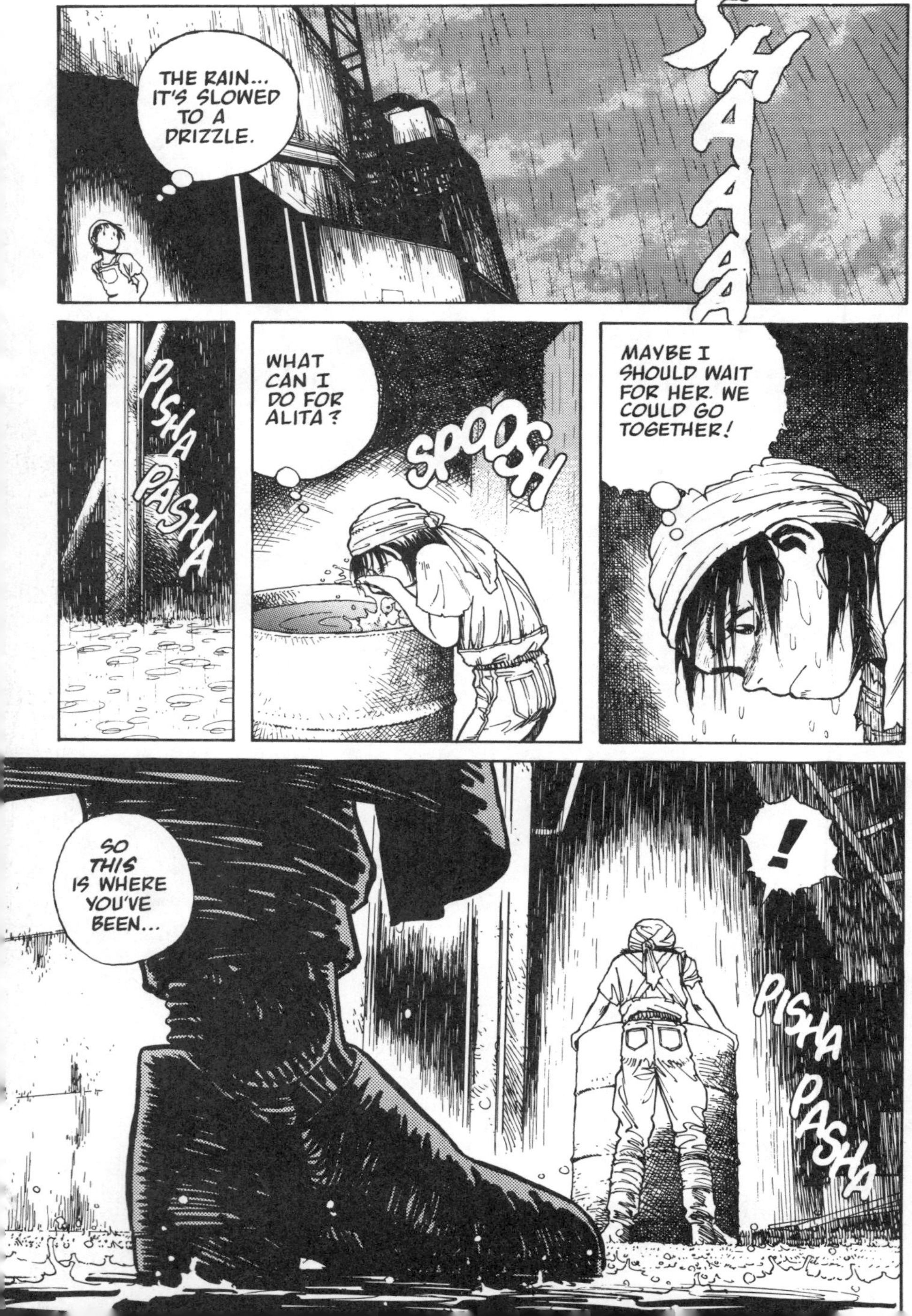
THE RAIN... IT'S SLOWED TO A DRIZZLE.
SHAAAAA
PISHA PASHA
WHAT CAN I DO FOR ALITA?
SPOOSH
MAYBE I SHOULD WAIT FOR HER. WE COULD GO TOGETHER!
SO THIS IS WHERE YOU'VE BEEN...
!
PISHA PASHA

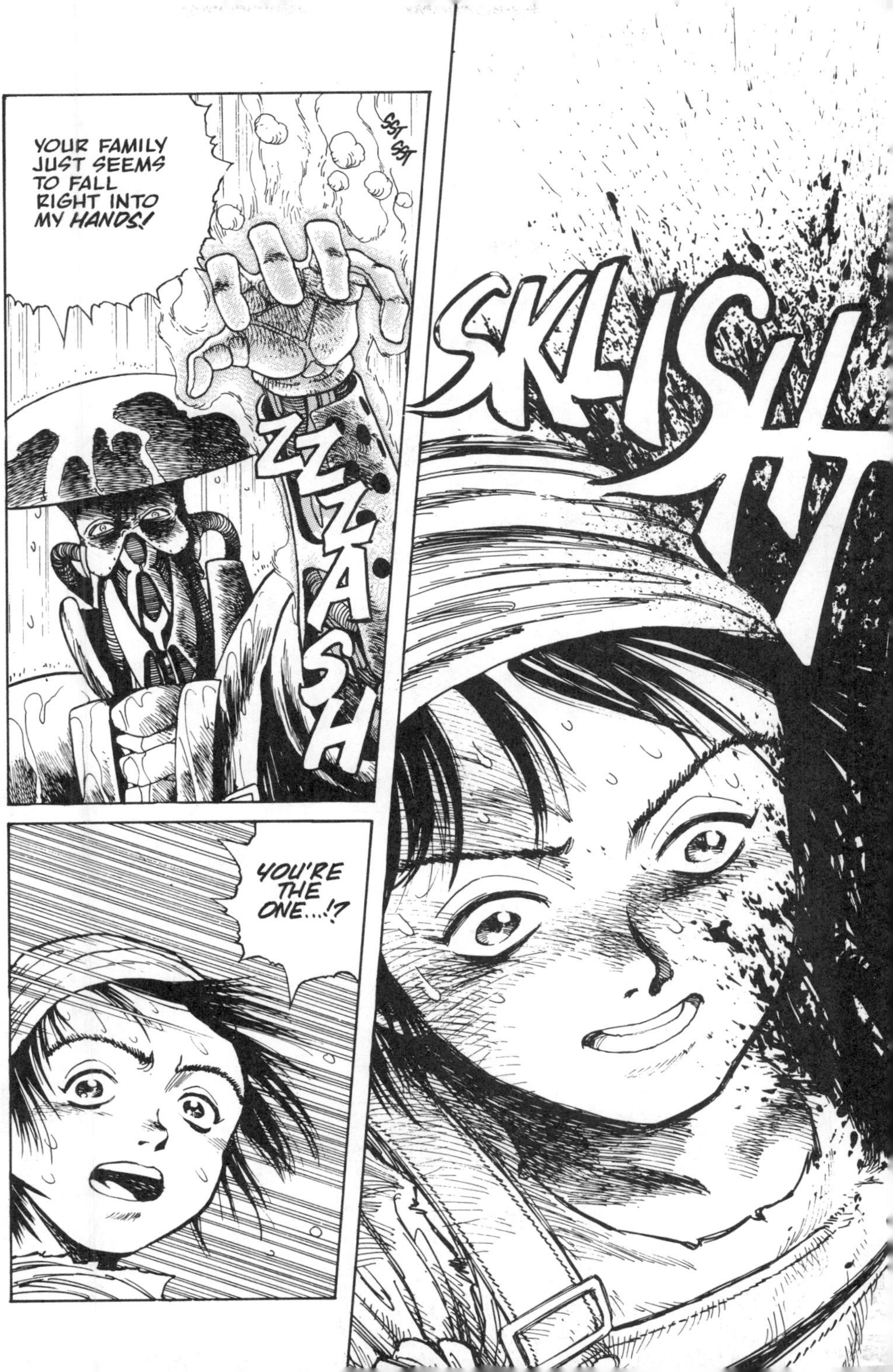
YOUR FAMILY JUST SEEMS TO FALL RIGHT INTO MY *HANDS!*
SSST SSST
ZZZASH
SKLISH
YOU'RE THE ONE...!?

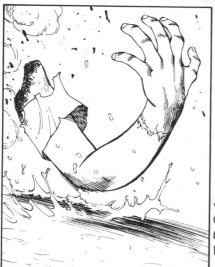

NO,
I...

SPSSST

ZZZLASH

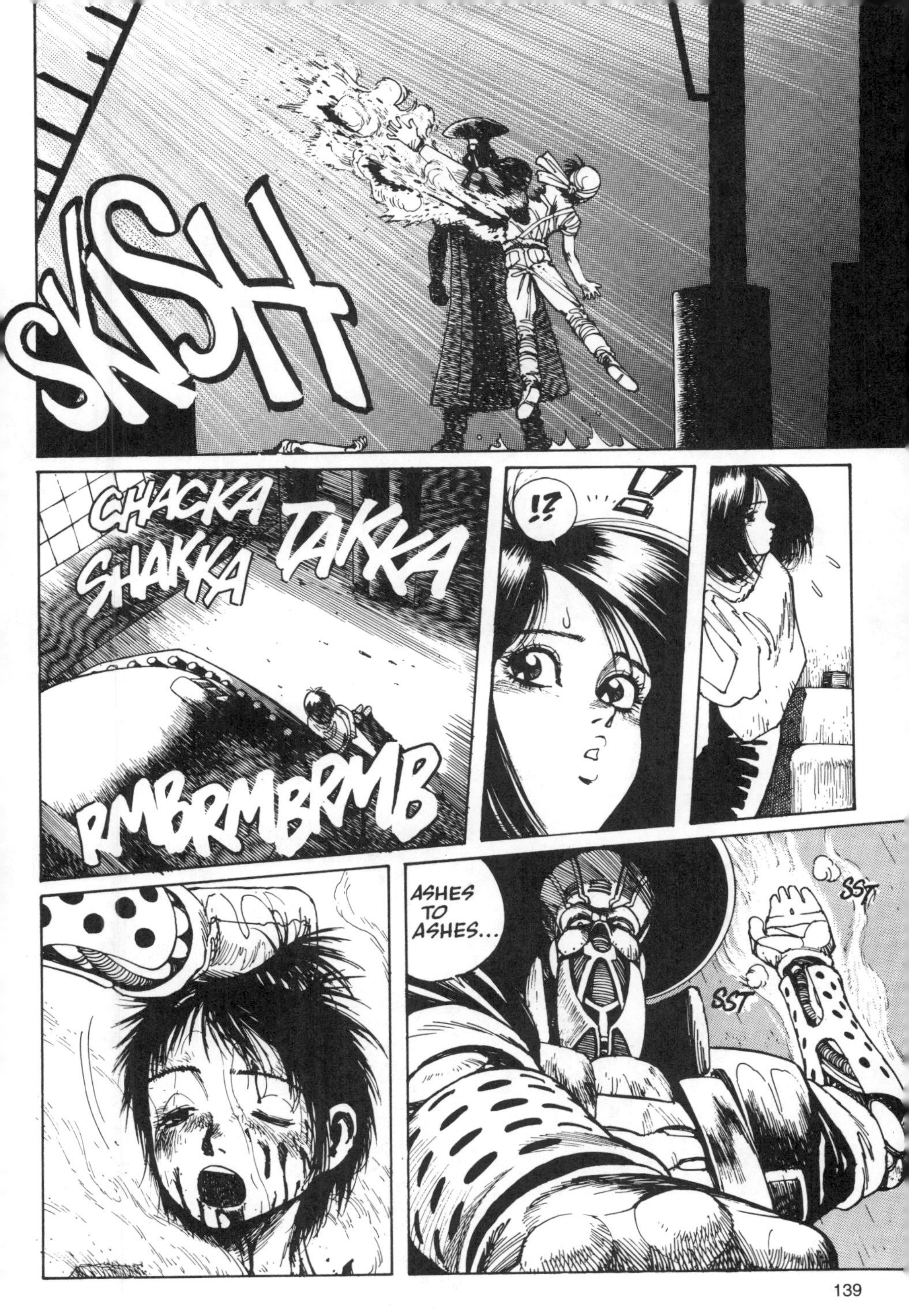
SKSH
CHACKA SHAKKA TAKKA
RMBRMBRMB
!?
ASHES TO ASHES...
SST
SST

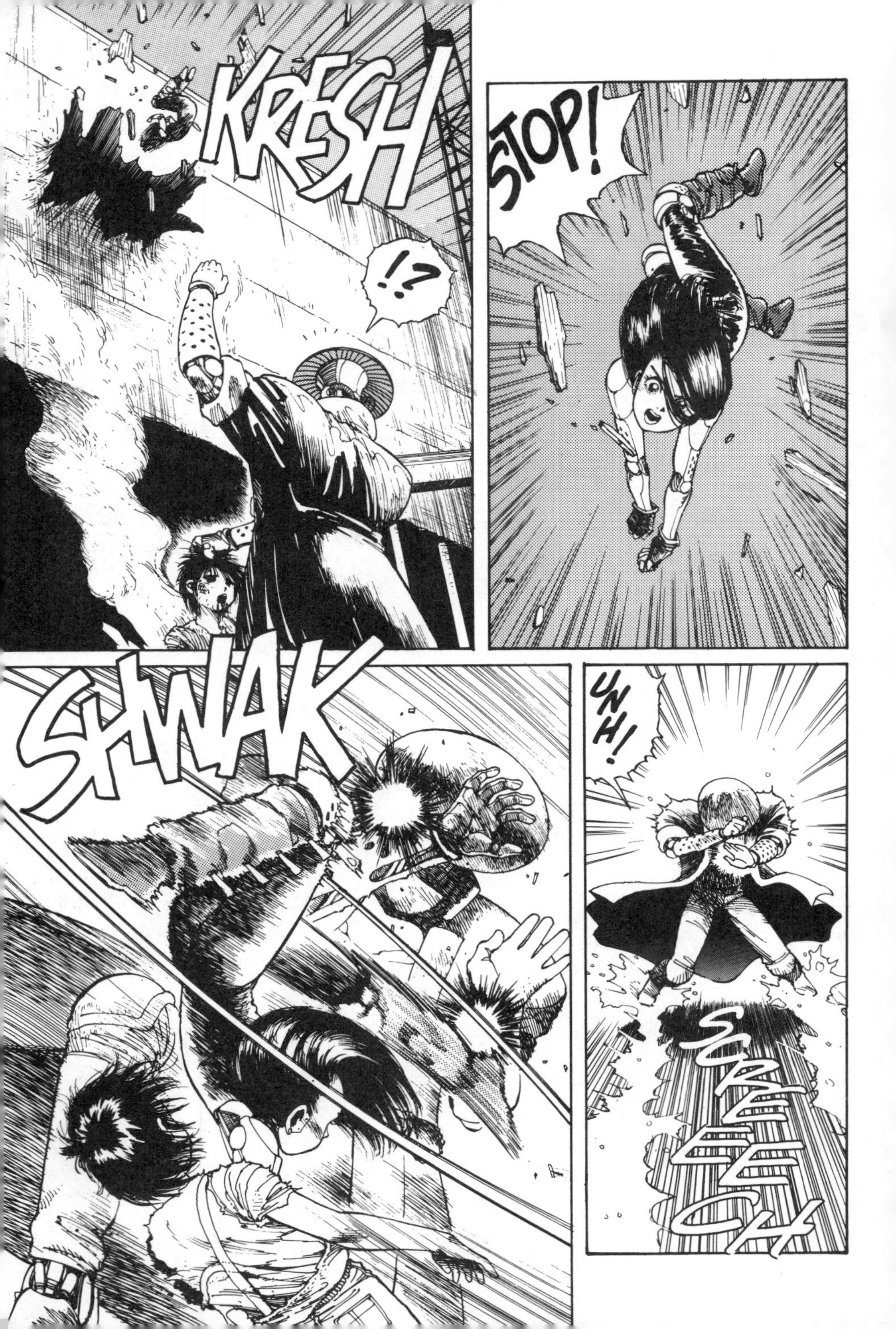
KRESH
!?
STOP!
SHWAK
UNH!
SKREEECH

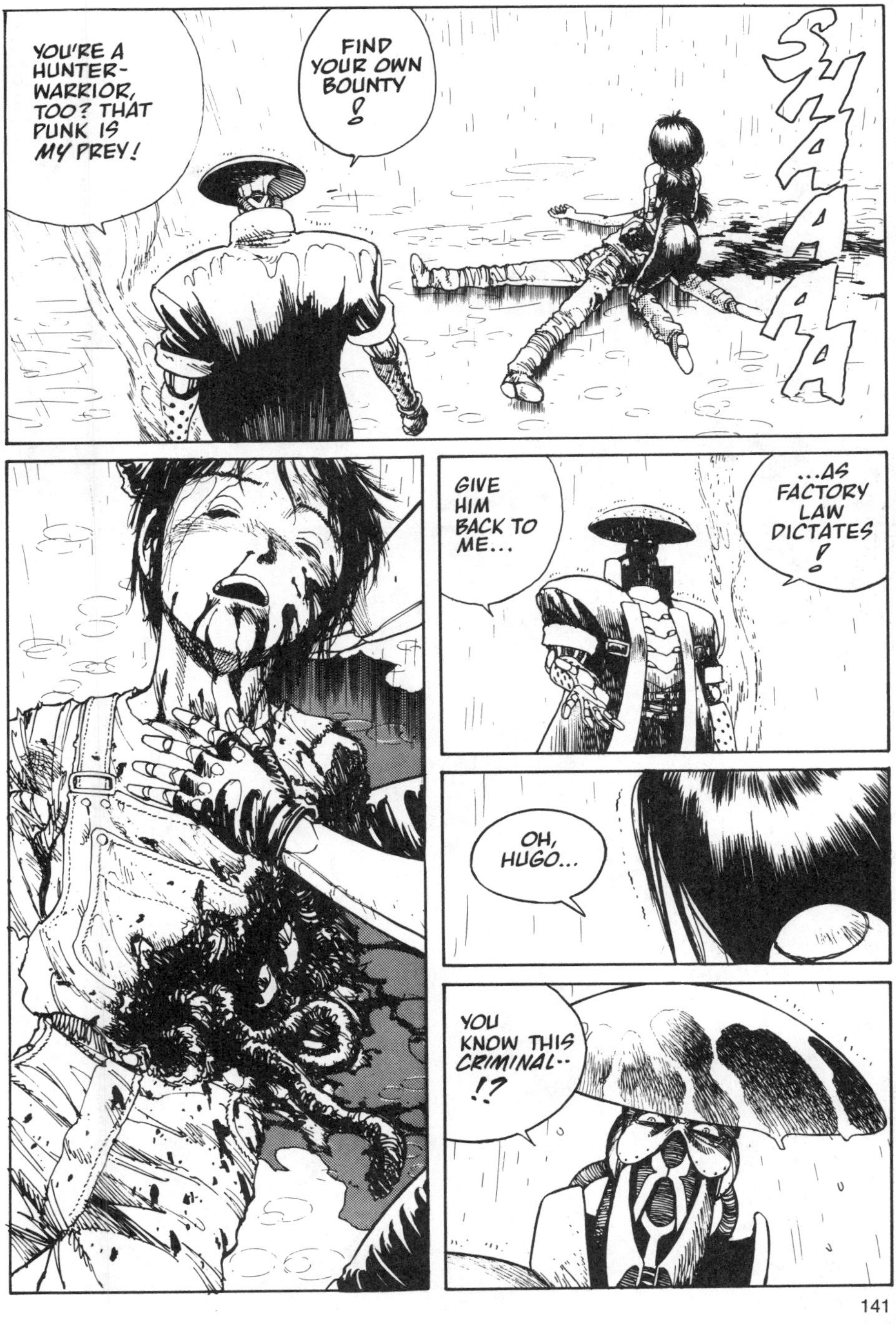
YOU'RE A HUNTER-WARRIOR, TOO? THAT PUNK IS MY PREY!
FIND YOUR OWN BOUNTY!
SHAAAAA
GIVE HIM BACK TO ME...
...AS FACTORY LAW DICTATES!
OH, HUGO...
YOU KNOW THIS CRIMINAL..!?

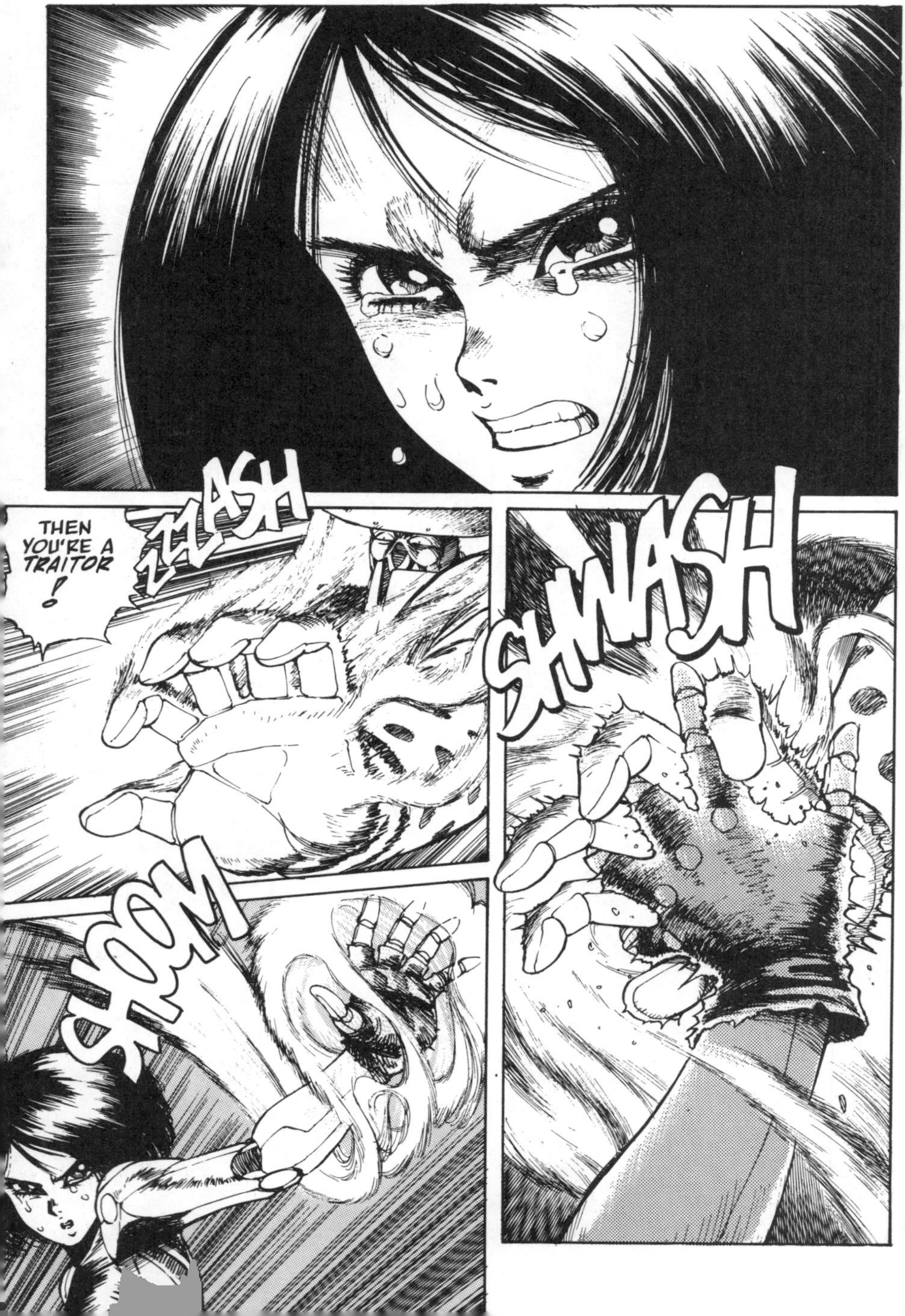
THEN YOU'RE A TRAITOR!
ZZZASH
SHWASH
SHOOM

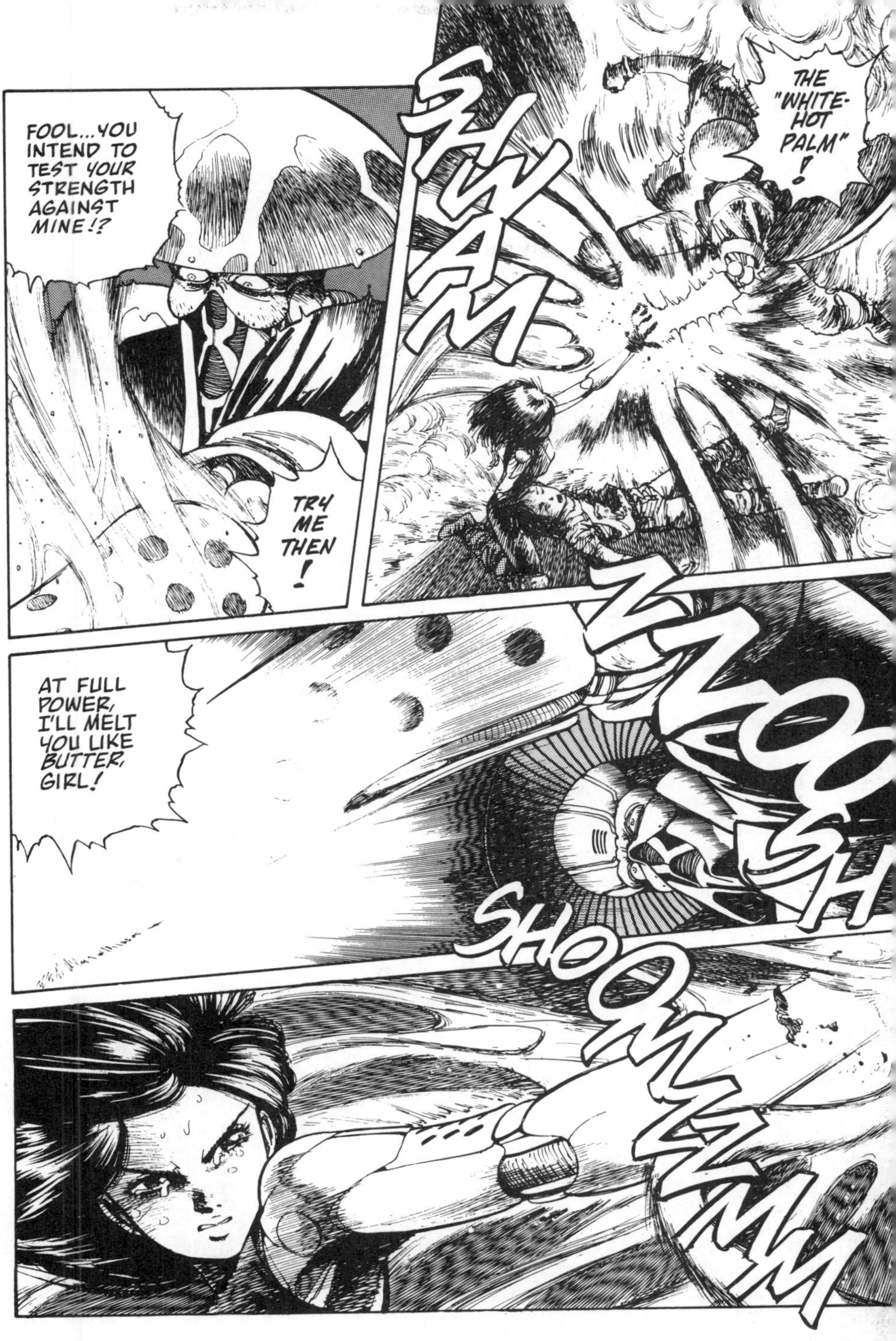
FOOL...YOU INTEND TO TEST YOUR STRENGTH AGAINST MINE!?
TRY ME THEN!
SHWAM
THE "WHITE-HOT PALM"!
AT FULL POWER, I'LL MELT YOU LIKE BUTTER, GIRL!
VVVOOOSH
SHOOMMMMM

CHIK

CHIK
CHIK

ZZMM

!?

ZZZMM

HA, HA, HA...
YOU THINK
SOME LAST DITCH
*ELECTRICAL
ATTACK* WILL
AFFECT ME*!?*

WHA-- !?

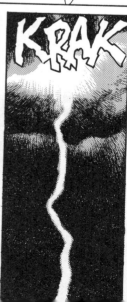

KRAK

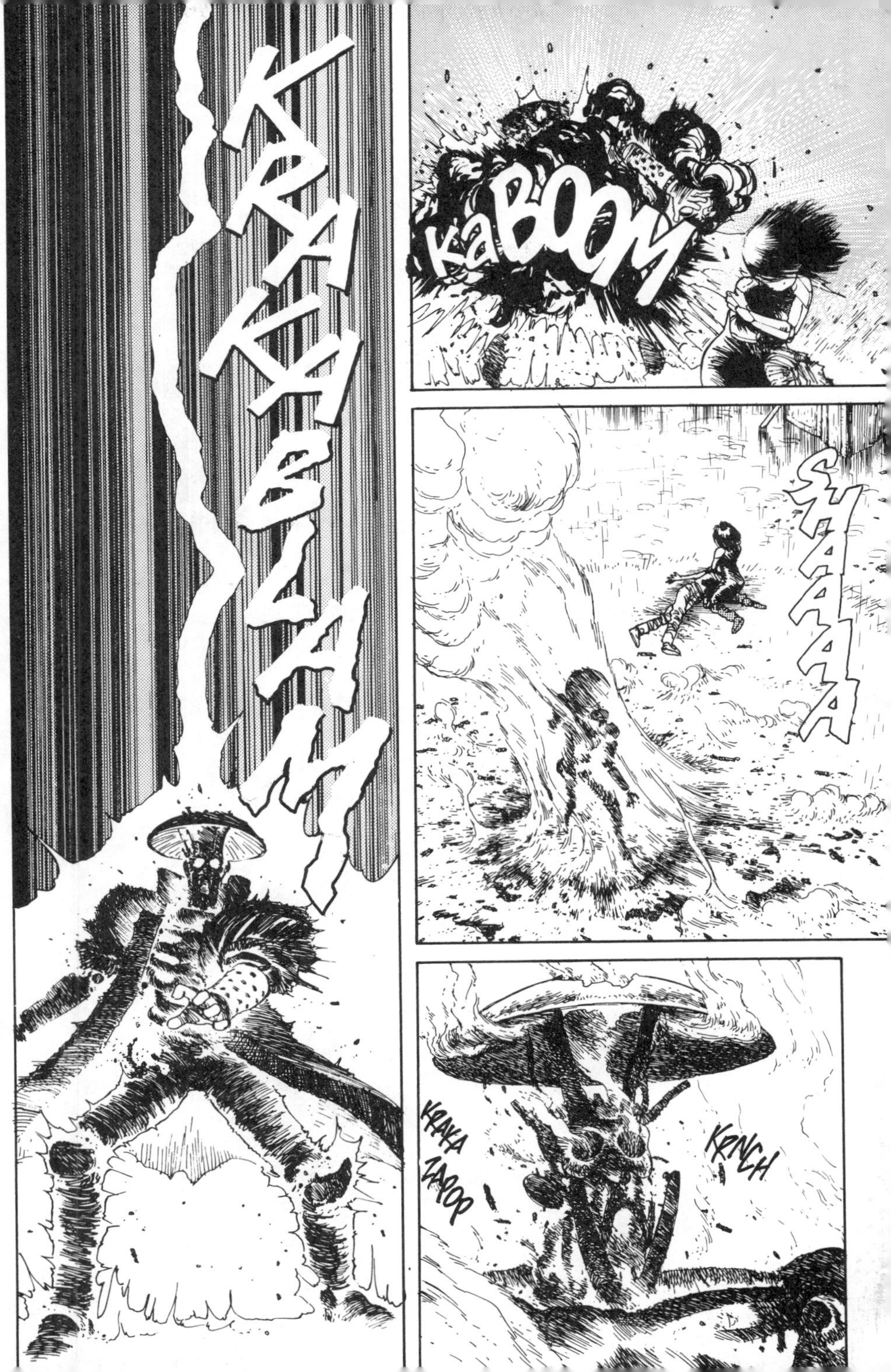
KAKABLAM
KaBOOM
SHAAAAA
KRAKA ZAPOP
KRNCH

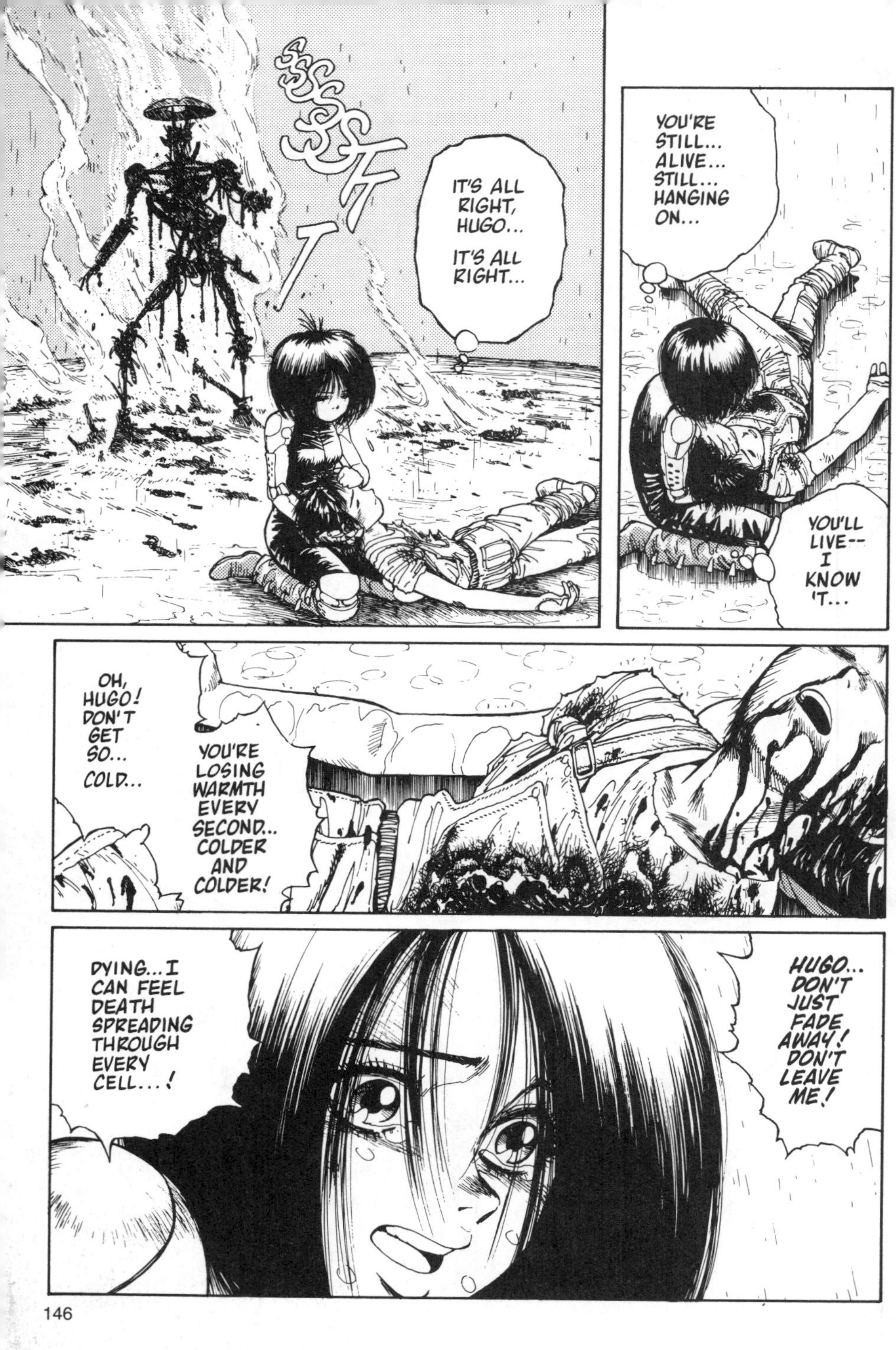
SSSSSK
IT'S ALL RIGHT, HUGO...
IT'S ALL RIGHT...
YOU'RE STILL... ALIVE... STILL... HANGING ON...
YOU'LL LIVE-- I KNOW IT...
OH, HUGO! DON'T GET SO... COLD...
YOU'RE LOSING WARMTH EVERY SECOND... COLDER AND COLDER!
DYING...I CAN FEEL DEATH SPREADING THROUGH EVERY CELL...!
HUGO... DON'T JUST FADE AWAY! DON'T LEAVE ME!

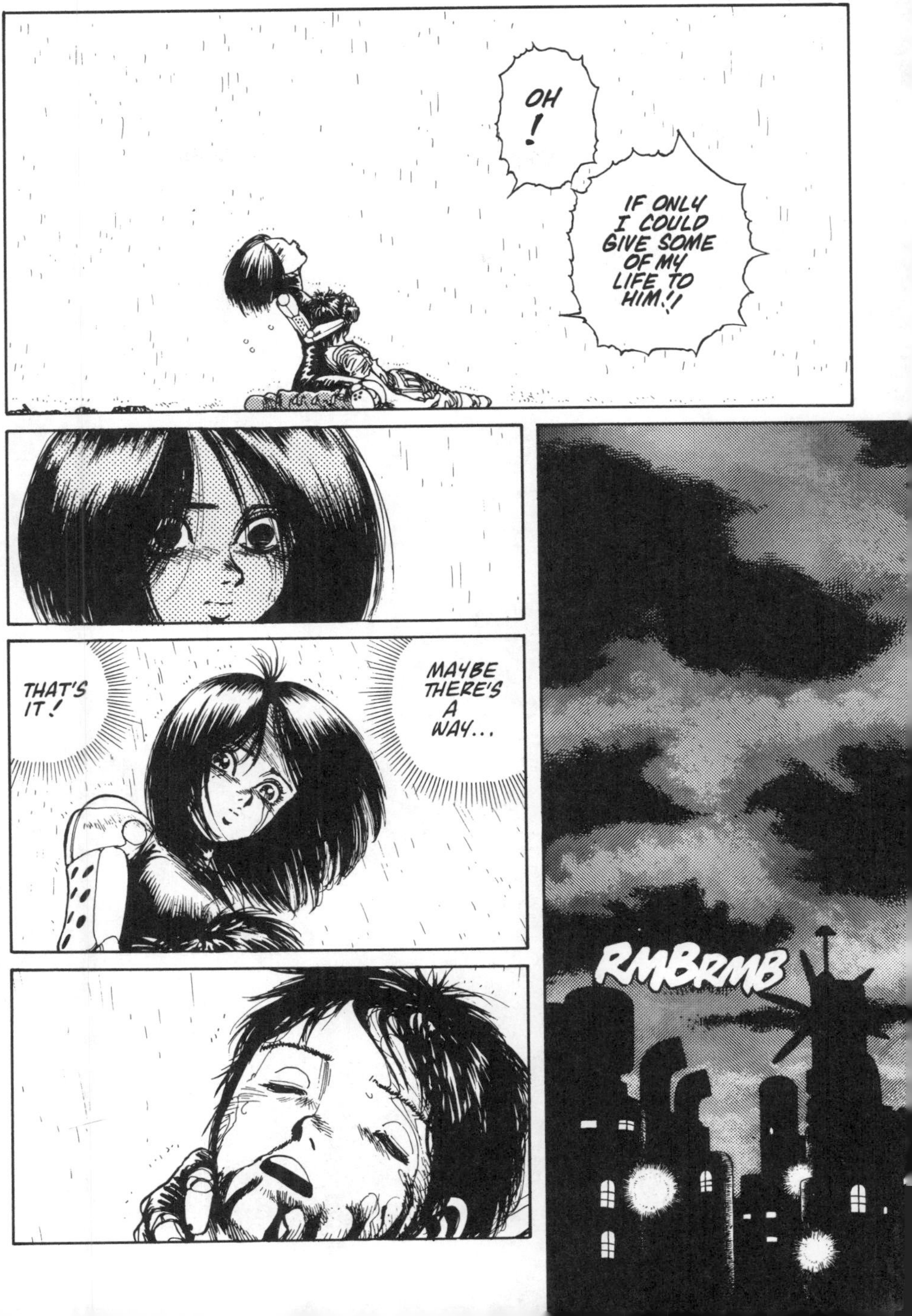
OH !
IF ONLY I COULD GIVE SOME OF MY LIFE TO HIM!!
THAT'S IT!
MAYBE THERE'S A WAY...
RMBRMB

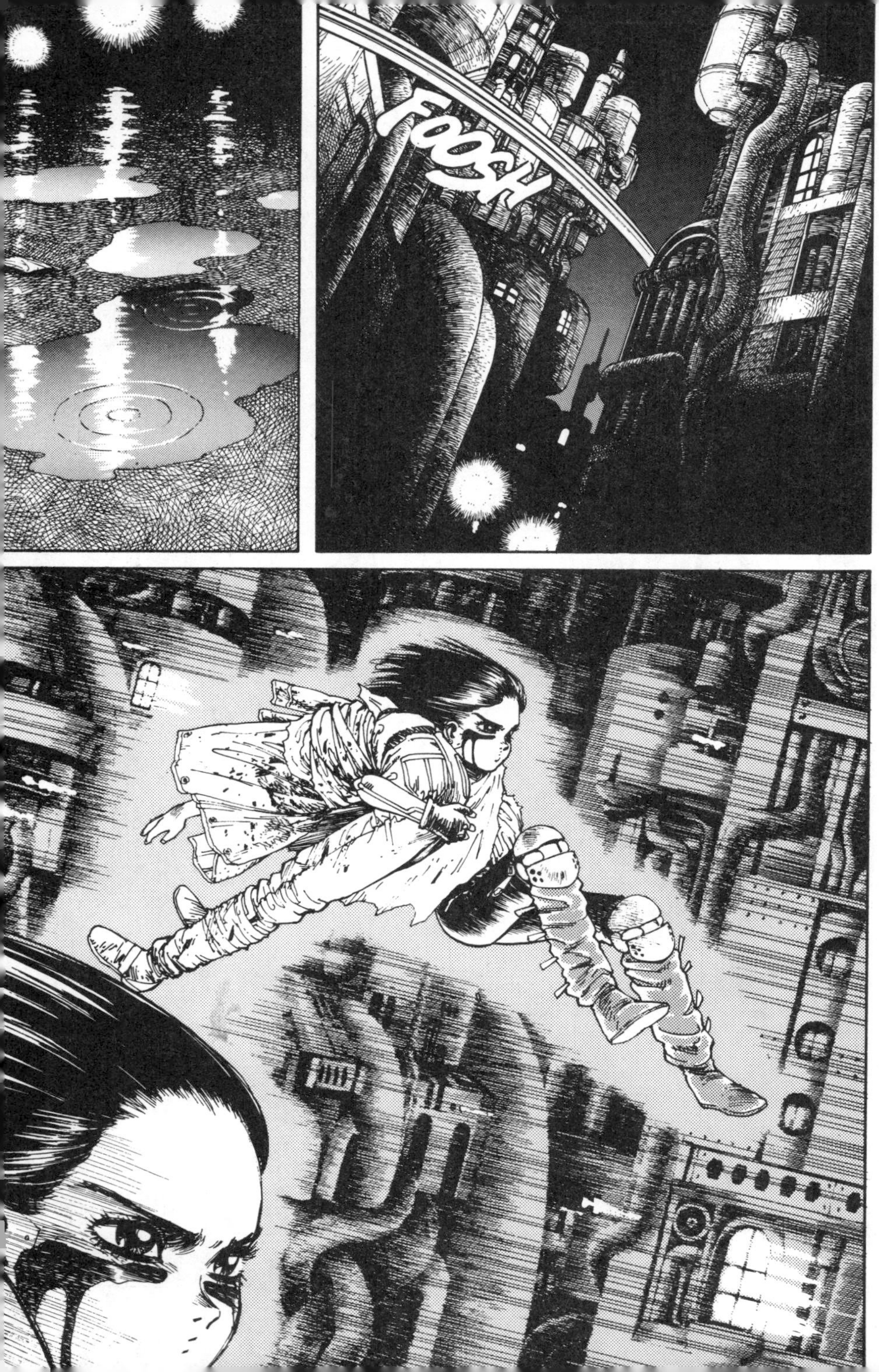
FOOSH

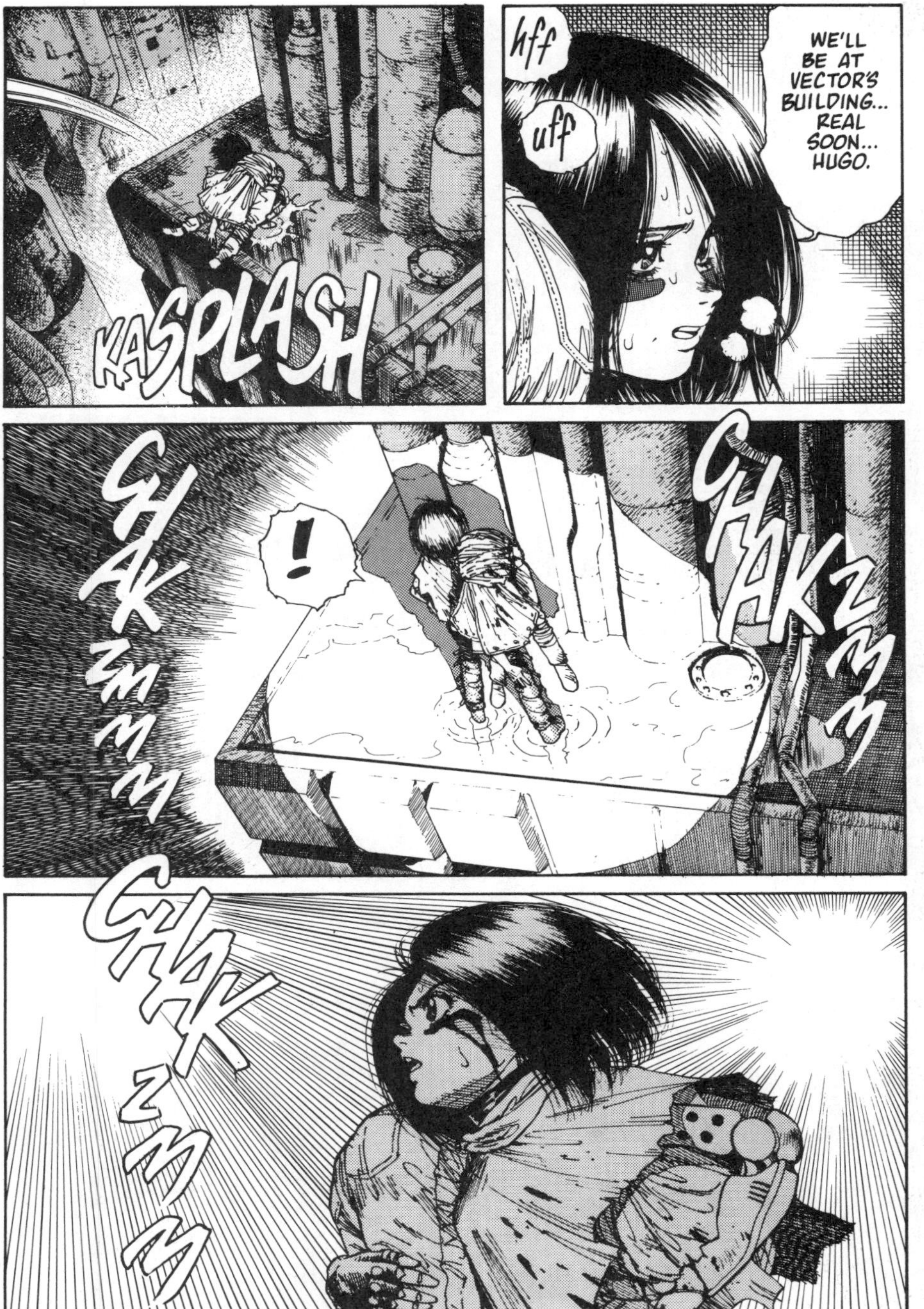
KASPLASH
hff
uff
WE'LL BE AT VECTOR'S BUILDING... REAL SOON... HUGO.
CHAKMMMMM
!
CHAKZMM
CHAKZMM

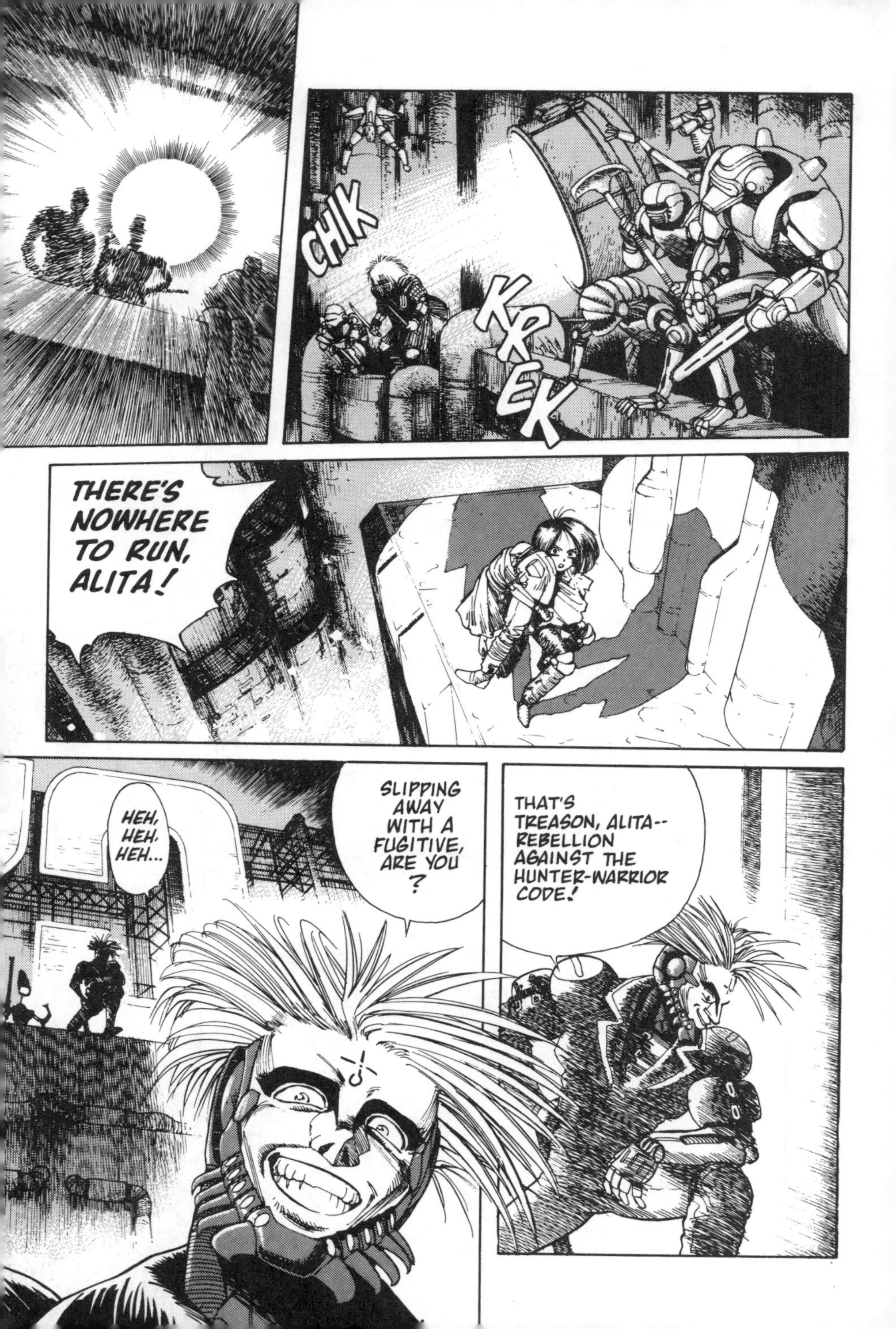
CHIK
KREK
THERE'S NOWHERE TO RUN, ALITA!
HEH, HEH, HEH...
SLIPPING AWAY WITH A FUGITIVE, ARE YOU?
THAT'S TREASON, ALITA-- REBELLION AGAINST THE HUNTER-WARRIOR CODE!

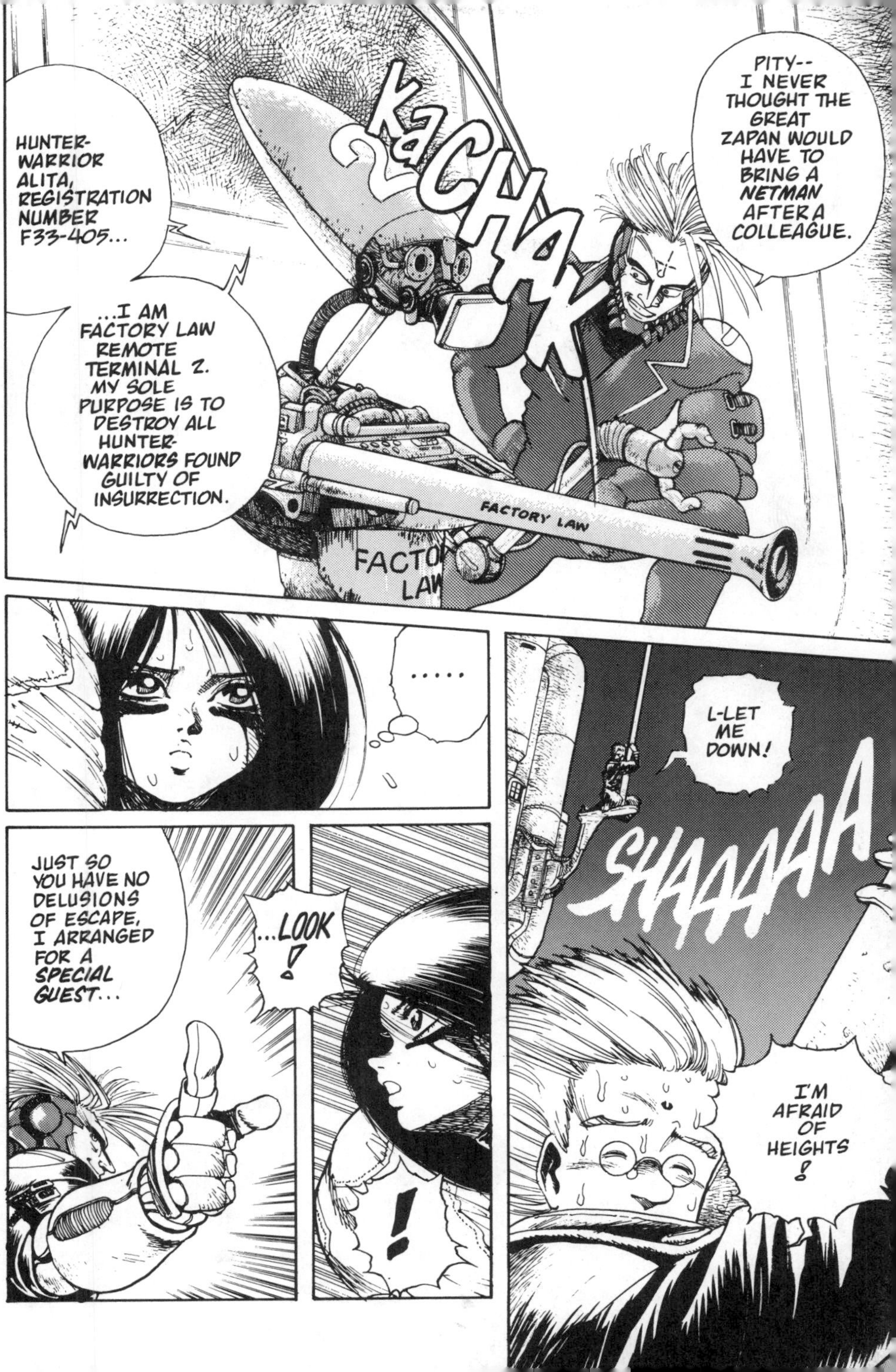
HUNTER-WARRIOR ALITA, REGISTRATION NUMBER F33-405...
...I AM FACTORY LAW REMOTE TERMINAL 2. MY SOLE PURPOSE IS TO DESTROY ALL HUNTER-WARRIORS FOUND GUILTY OF INSURRECTION.
KaCHAK
PITY-- I NEVER THOUGHT THE GREAT ZAPAN WOULD HAVE TO BRING A NETMAN AFTER A COLLEAGUE.
FACTORY LAW
FACTORY LAW
.....
JUST SO YOU HAVE NO DELUSIONS OF ESCAPE, I ARRANGED FOR A SPECIAL GUEST...
...LOOK!
!
L-LET ME DOWN!
SHAAAAAA
I'M AFRAID OF HEIGHTS!

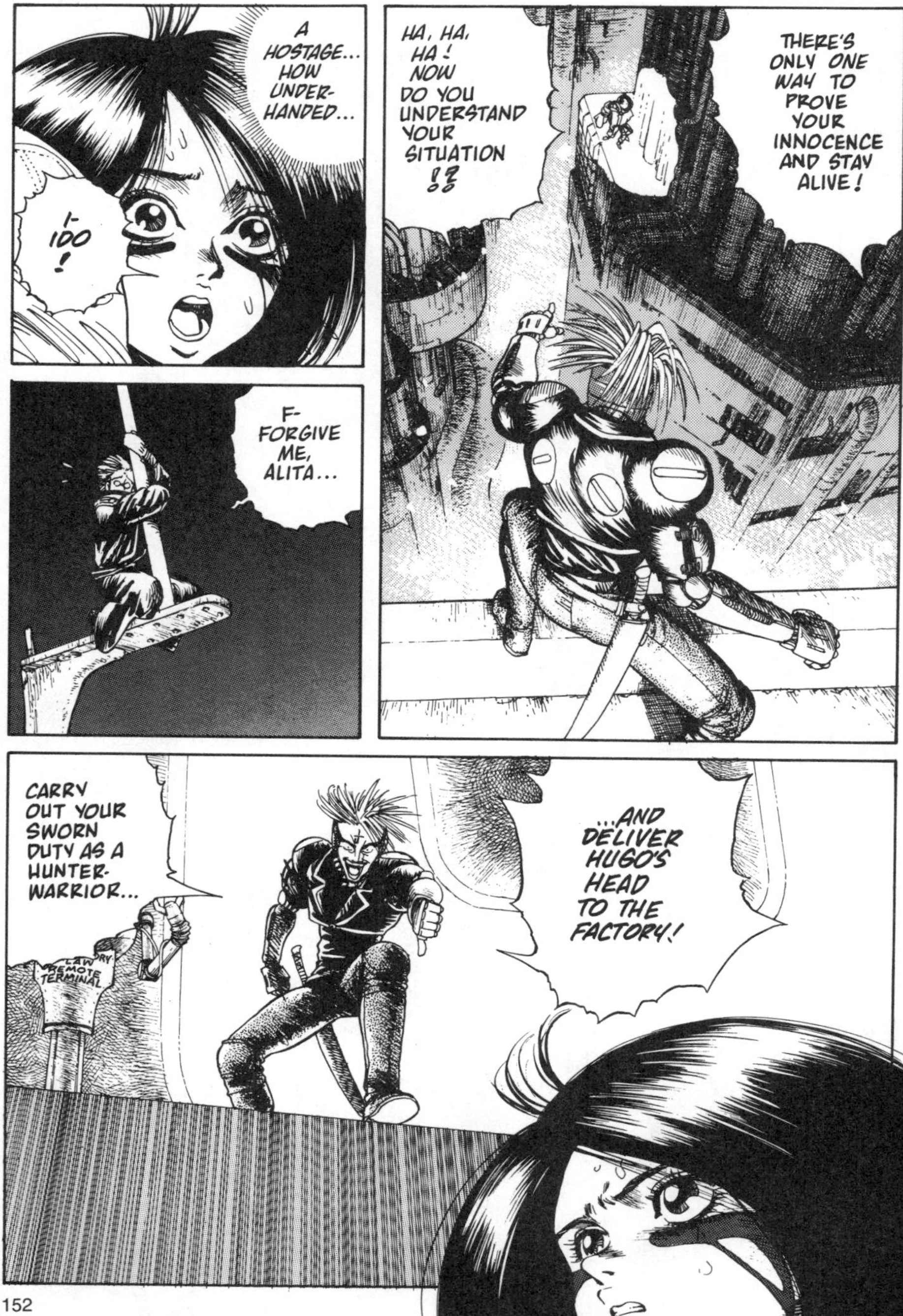

A HOSTAGE... HOW UNDER-HANDED...
I- IDO!
F- FORGIVE ME, ALITA...
HA, HA, HA! NOW DO YOU UNDERSTAND YOUR SITUATION!?
THERE'S ONLY ONE WAY TO PROVE YOUR INNOCENCE AND STAY ALIVE!
CARRY OUT YOUR SWORN DUTY AS A HUNTER-WARRIOR...
LAW REMOTE TERMINAL
...AND DELIVER HUGO'S HEAD TO THE FACTORY!

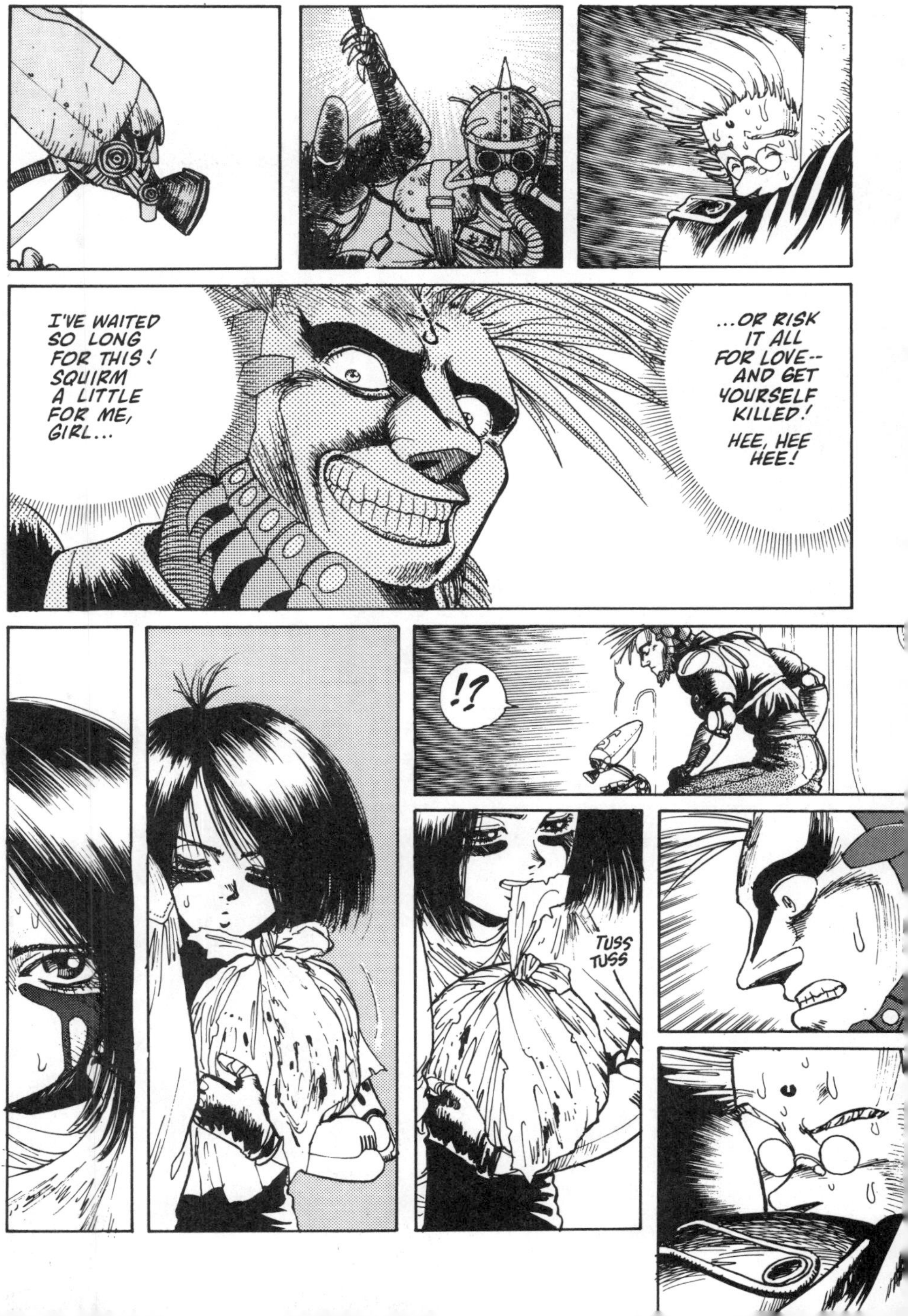
I'VE WAITED SO LONG FOR THIS! SQUIRM A LITTLE FOR ME, GIRL...
...OR RISK IT ALL FOR LOVE-- AND GET YOURSELF KILLED!
HEE, HEE HEE!
!?
TUSS TUSS

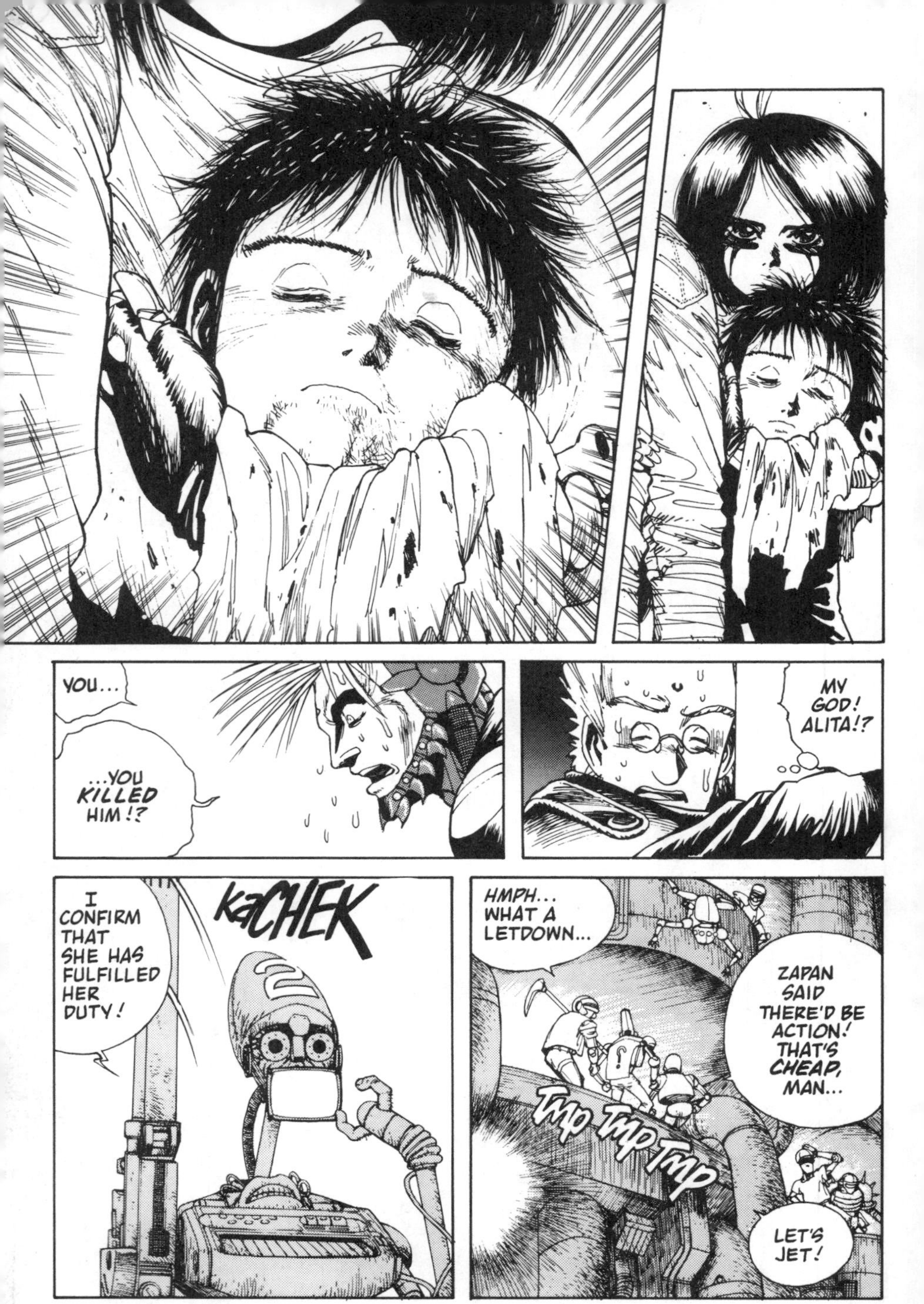
YOU...
...YOU KILLED HIM!?
MY GOD! ALITA!?
I CONFIRM THAT SHE HAS FULFILLED HER DUTY!
kaCHEK
HMPH... WHAT A LETDOWN...
ZAPAN SAID THERE'D BE ACTION! THAT'S CHEAP, MAN...
Tmp Tmp Tmp Tmp
LET'S JET!

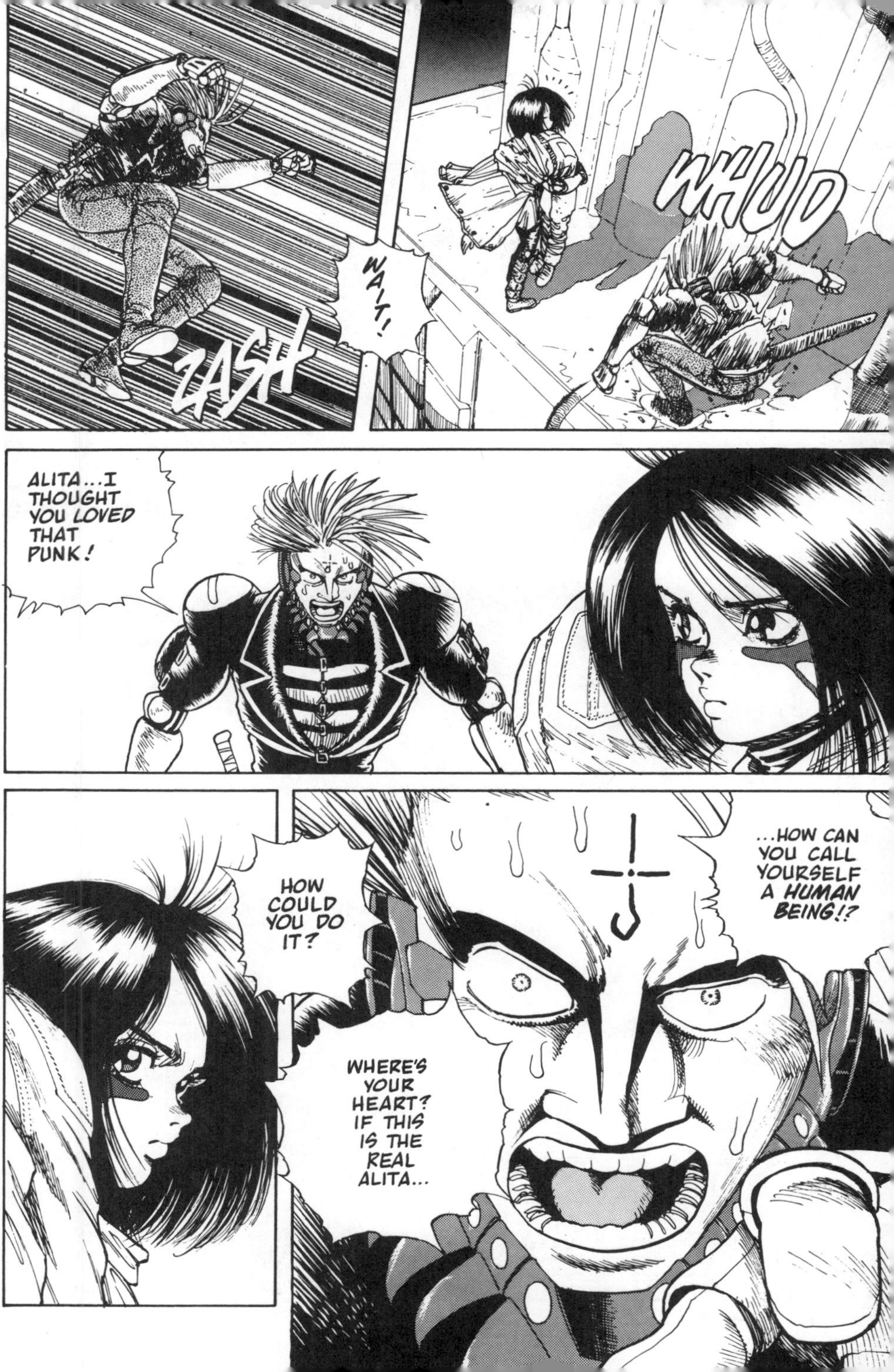
ZASH
WAIT!
WHUD
ALITA...I THOUGHT YOU LOVED THAT PUNK!
HOW COULD YOU DO IT?
...HOW CAN YOU CALL YOURSELF A HUMAN BEING!?
WHERE'S YOUR HEART? IF THIS IS THE REAL ALITA...

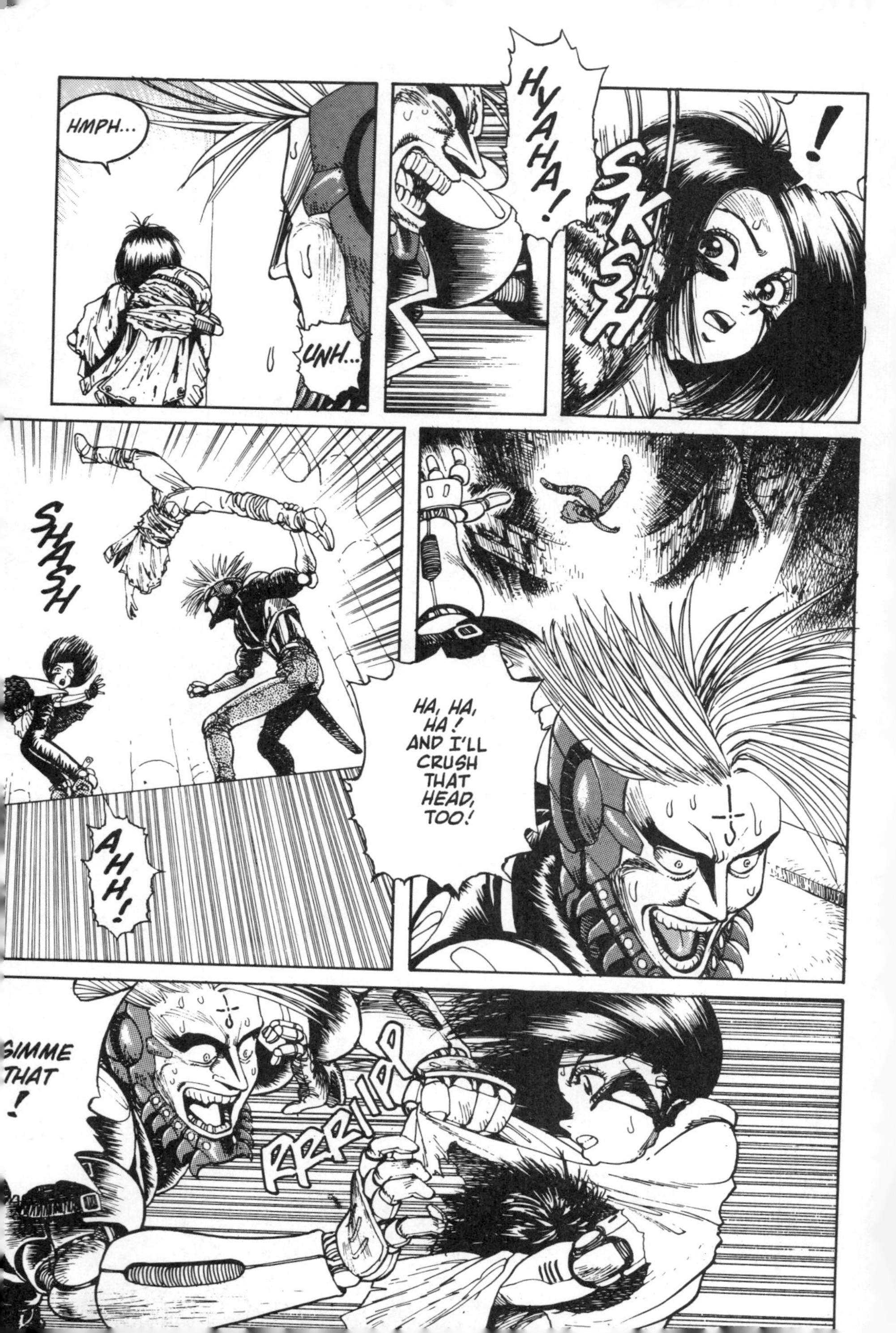
HMPH...
UNH...
HYAHAHA!
SKSSH
!
SHASH
AHH!
HA, HA, HA! AND I'LL CRUSH THAT HEAD, TOO!
GIMME THAT!
RRRIIP

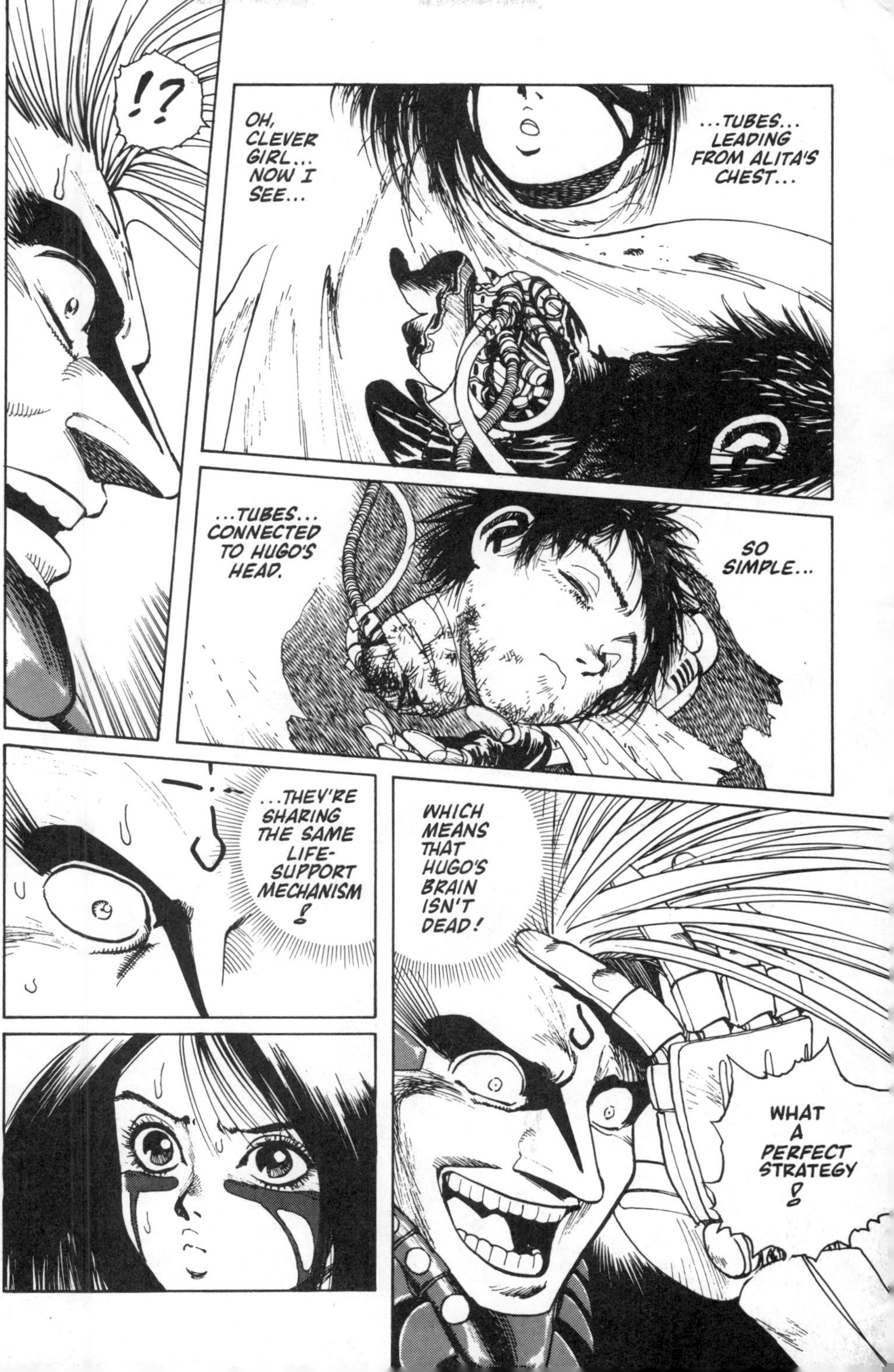
!?
OH, CLEVER GIRL... NOW I SEE...
...TUBES... LEADING FROM ALITA'S CHEST...
...TUBES... CONNECTED TO HUGO'S HEAD.
SO SIMPLE...
...THEY'RE SHARING THE SAME LIFE-SUPPORT MECHANISM!
WHICH MEANS THAT HUGO'S BRAIN ISN'T DEAD!
WHAT A PERFECT STRATEGY!

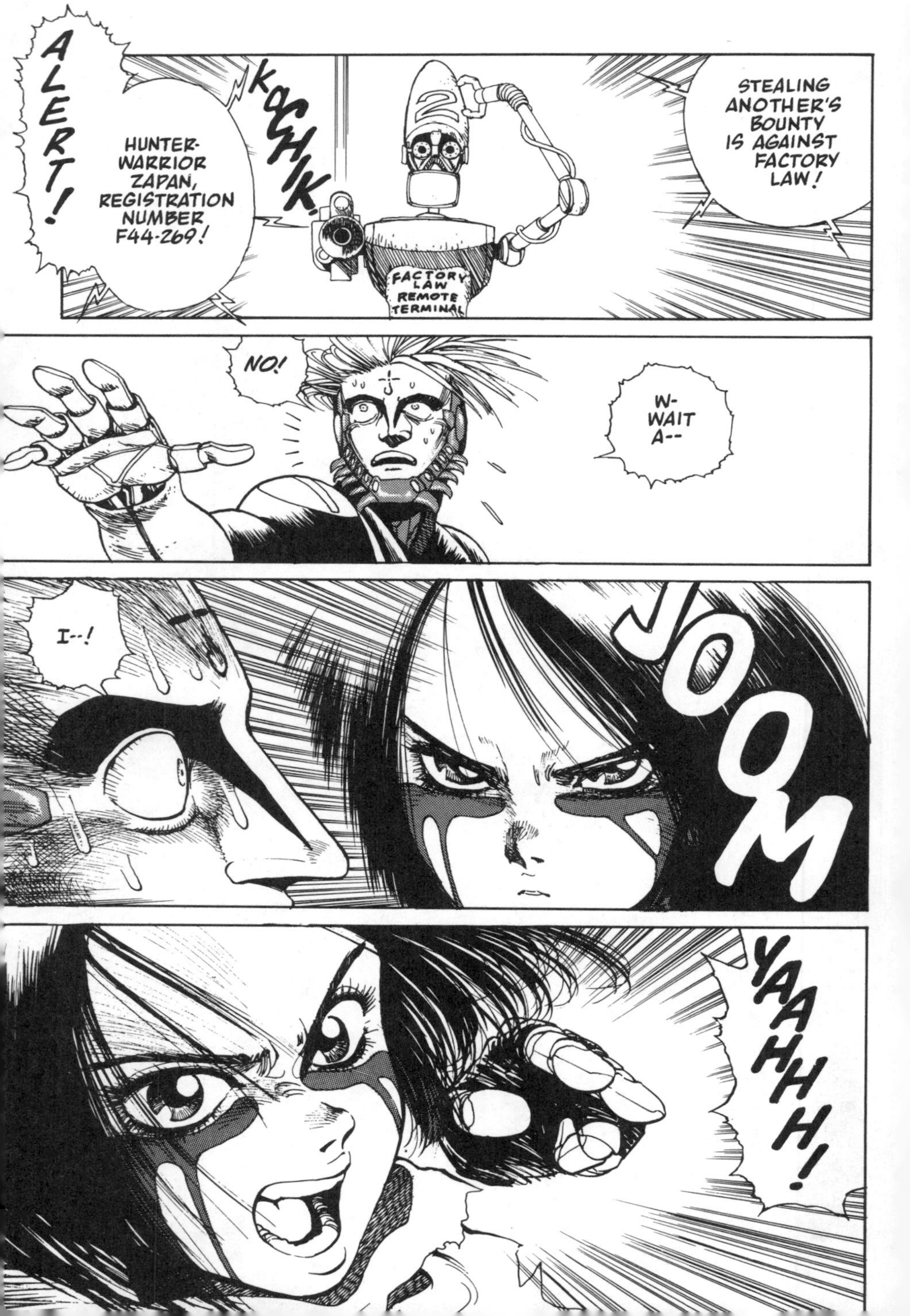
ALERT!
HUNTER-WARRIOR ZAPAN, REGISTRATION NUMBER F44-269!
KACHIK!
FACTORY LAW REMOTE TERMINAL
STEALING ANOTHER'S BOUNTY IS AGAINST FACTORY LAW!
NO!
W-WAIT A--
I--!
JOOM
YAAHHH!

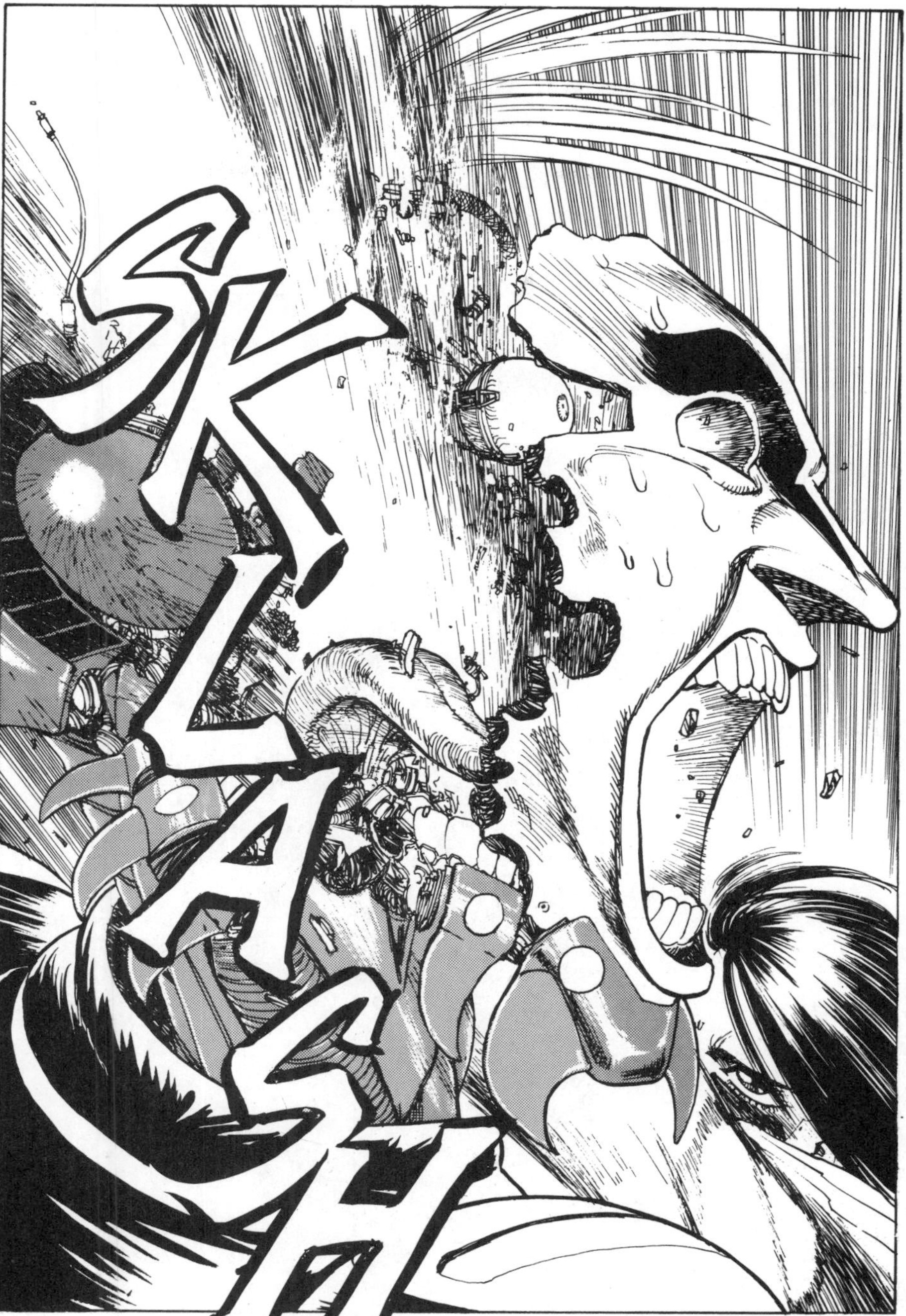
SKLASH

BITTER DREAMS
Struggle 4: Broken Hearts

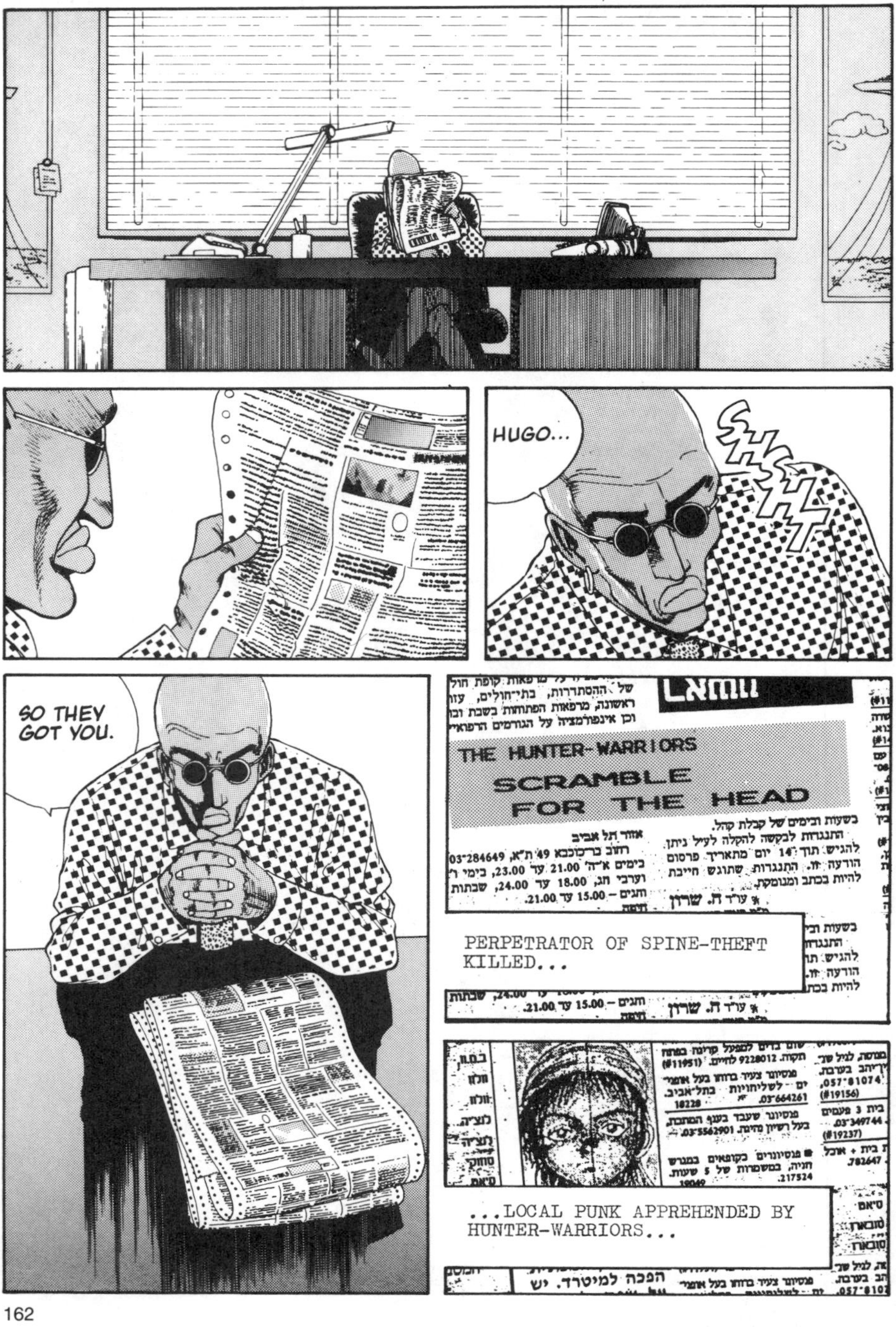
HUGO...
SO THEY GOT YOU.
THE HUNTER-WARRIORS
SCRAMBLE FOR THE HEAD
PERPETRATOR OF SPINE-THEFT KILLED...
...LOCAL PUNK APPREHENDED BY HUNTER-WARRIORS...

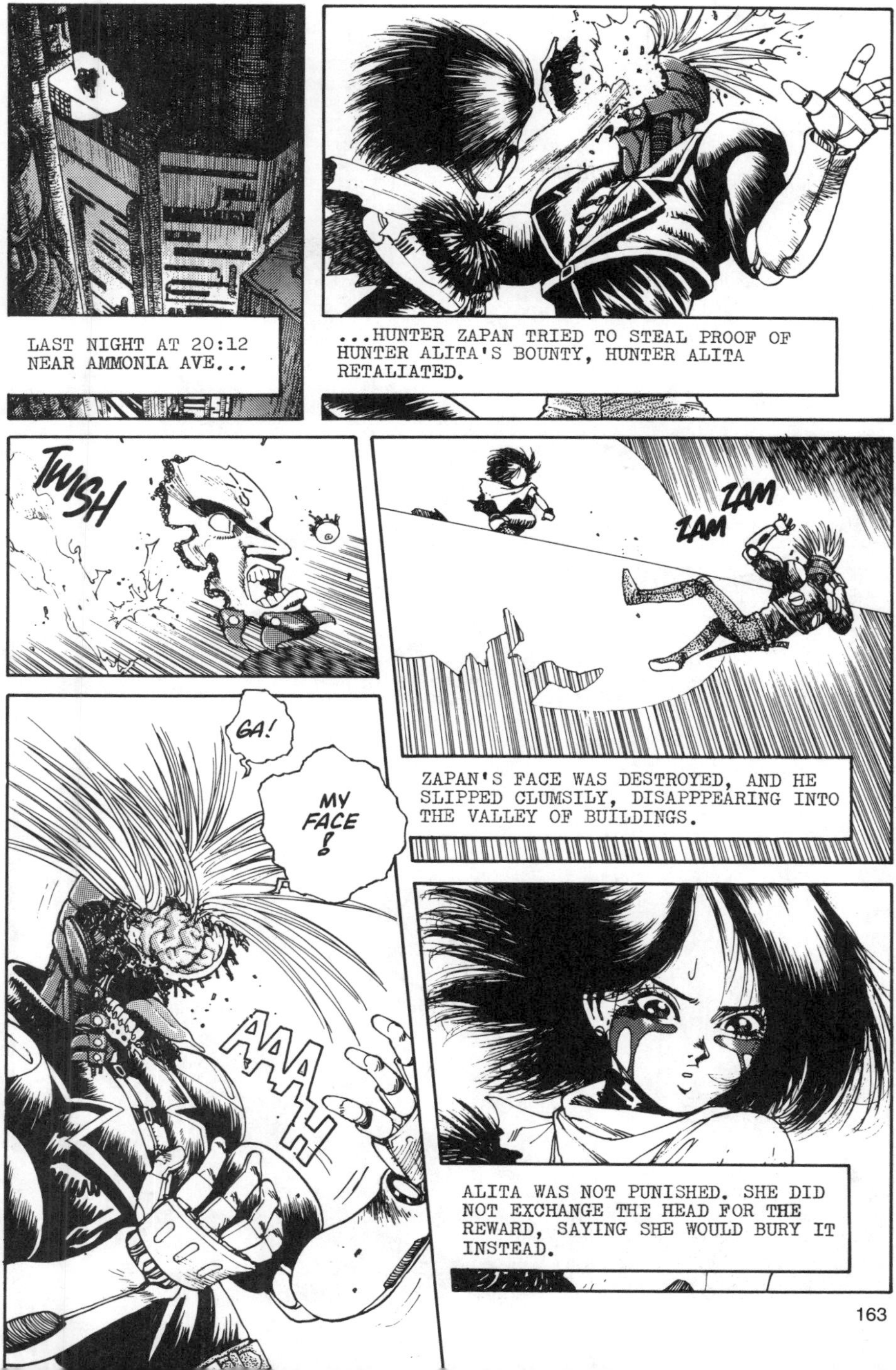
LAST NIGHT AT 20:12
NEAR AMMONIA AVE...
...HUNTER ZAPAN TRIED TO STEAL PROOF OF HUNTER ALITA'S BOUNTY, HUNTER ALITA RETALIATED.
TWISH
ZAM
ZAM
ZAPAN'S FACE WAS DESTROYED, AND HE SLIPPED CLUMSILY, DISAPPPEARING INTO THE VALLEY OF BUILDINGS.
GA!
MY FACE!
AAAH
ALITA WAS NOT PUNISHED. SHE DID NOT EXCHANGE THE HEAD FOR THE REWARD, SAYING SHE WOULD BURY IT INSTEAD.

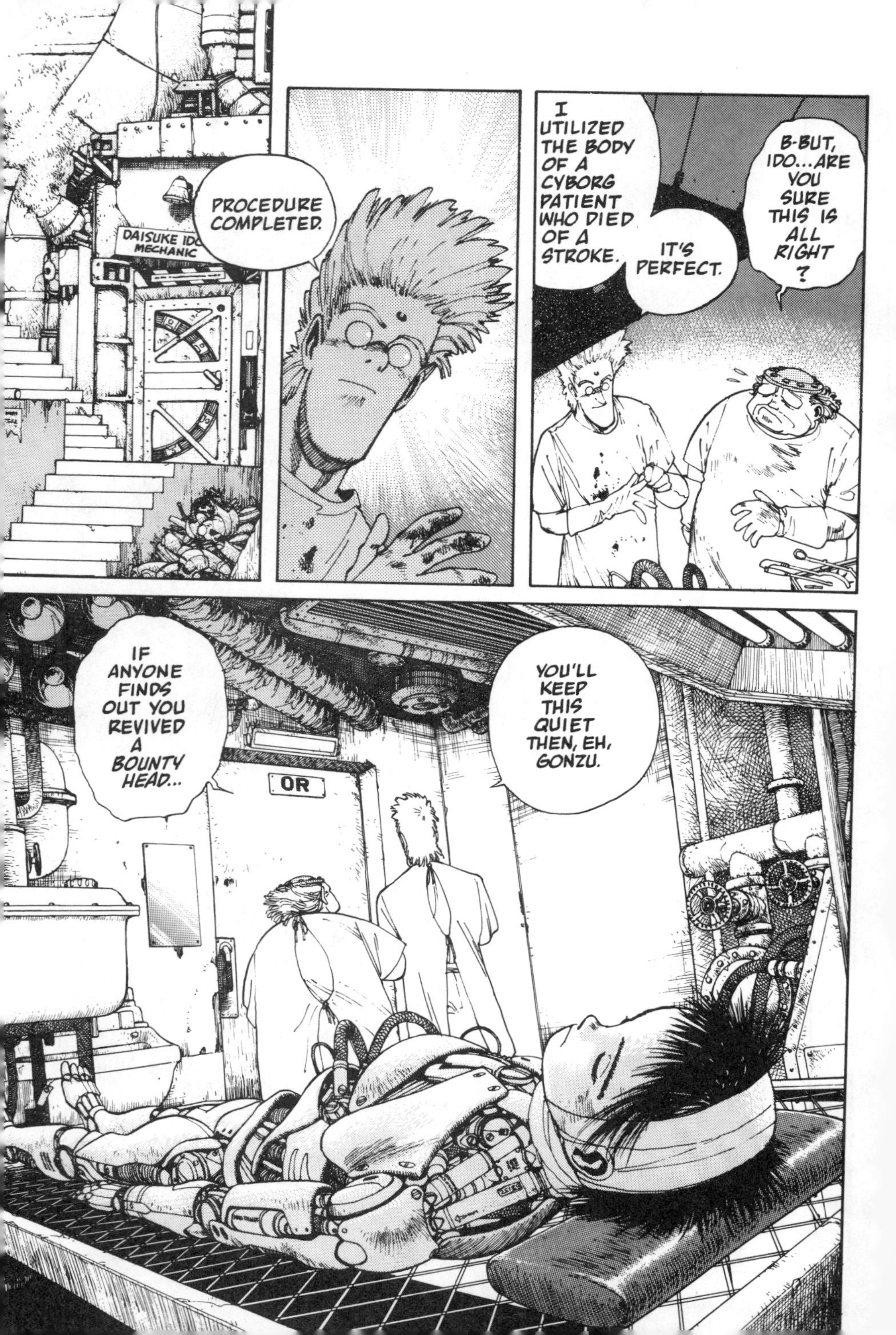
DAISUKE IDO
MECHANIC
PROCEDURE COMPLETED.
I UTILIZED THE BODY OF A CYBORG PATIENT WHO DIED OF A STROKE.
IT'S PERFECT.
B-BUT, IDO...ARE YOU SURE THIS IS ALL RIGHT?
IF ANYONE FINDS OUT YOU REVIVED A BOUNTY HEAD...
OR
YOU'LL KEEP THIS QUIET THEN, EH, GONZU.

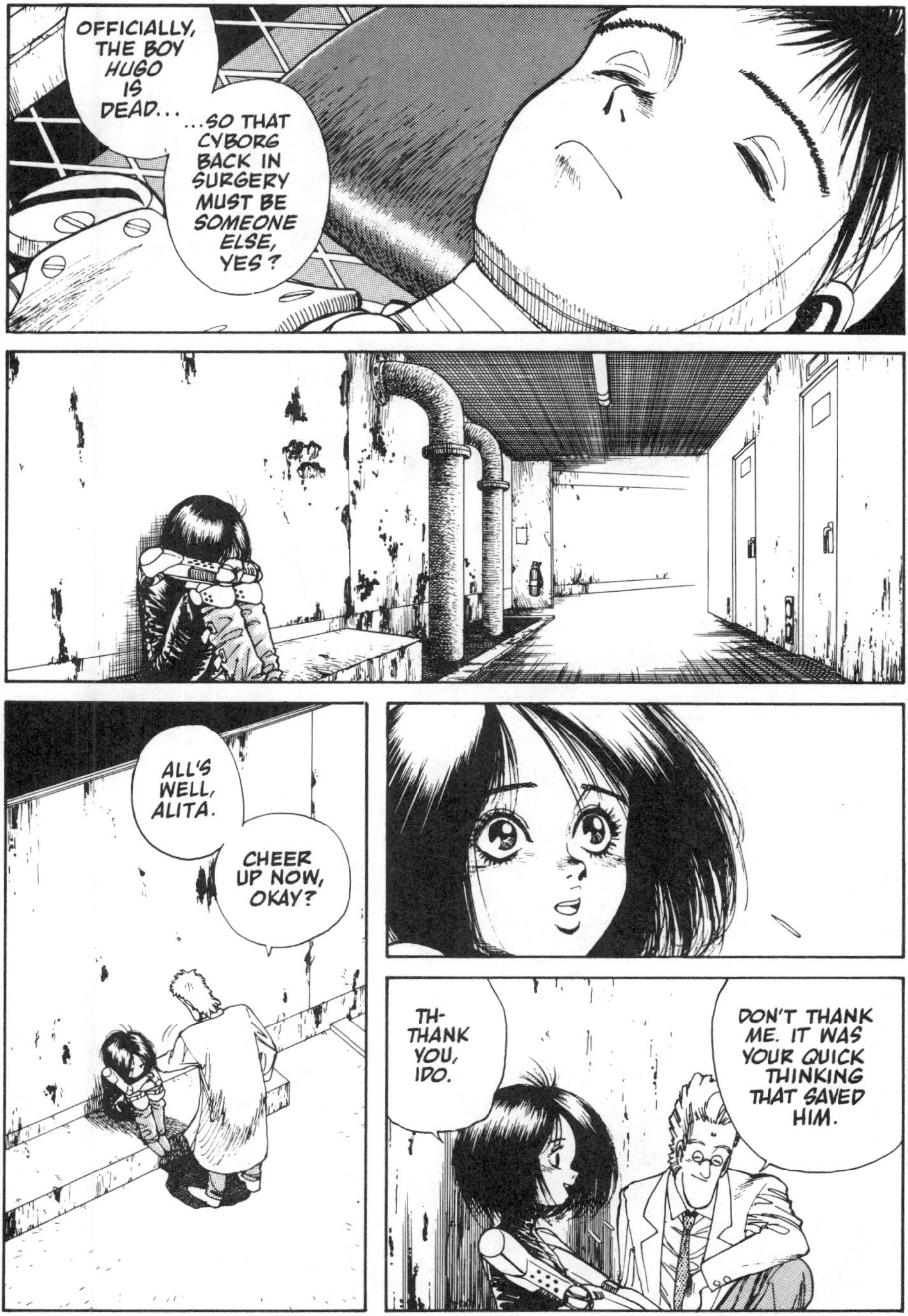
OFFICIALLY, THE BOY HUGO IS DEAD...
...SO THAT CYBORG BACK IN SURGERY MUST BE SOMEONE ELSE, YES?
ALL'S WELL, ALITA.
CHEER UP NOW, OKAY?
TH- THANK YOU, IDO.
DON'T THANK ME. IT WAS YOUR QUICK THINKING THAT SAVED HIM.

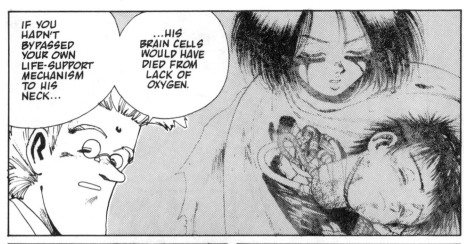

IF YOU HADN'T BYPASSED YOUR OWN LIFE-SUPPORT MECHANISM TO HIS NECK...

...HIS BRAIN CELLS WOULD HAVE DIED FROM LACK OF OXYGEN.

BUT IT WAS MY RECKLESSNESS THAT PUT HUGO IN JEOPARDY...

NO--HIS MISTAKE WAS IN BELIEVING HE COULD GET TO TIPHARES.

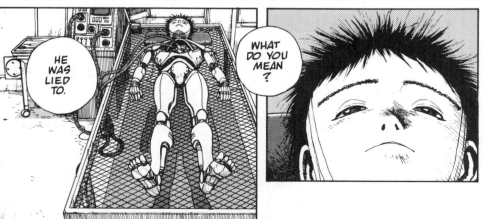

HE WAS LIED TO.

WHAT DO YOU MEAN ?

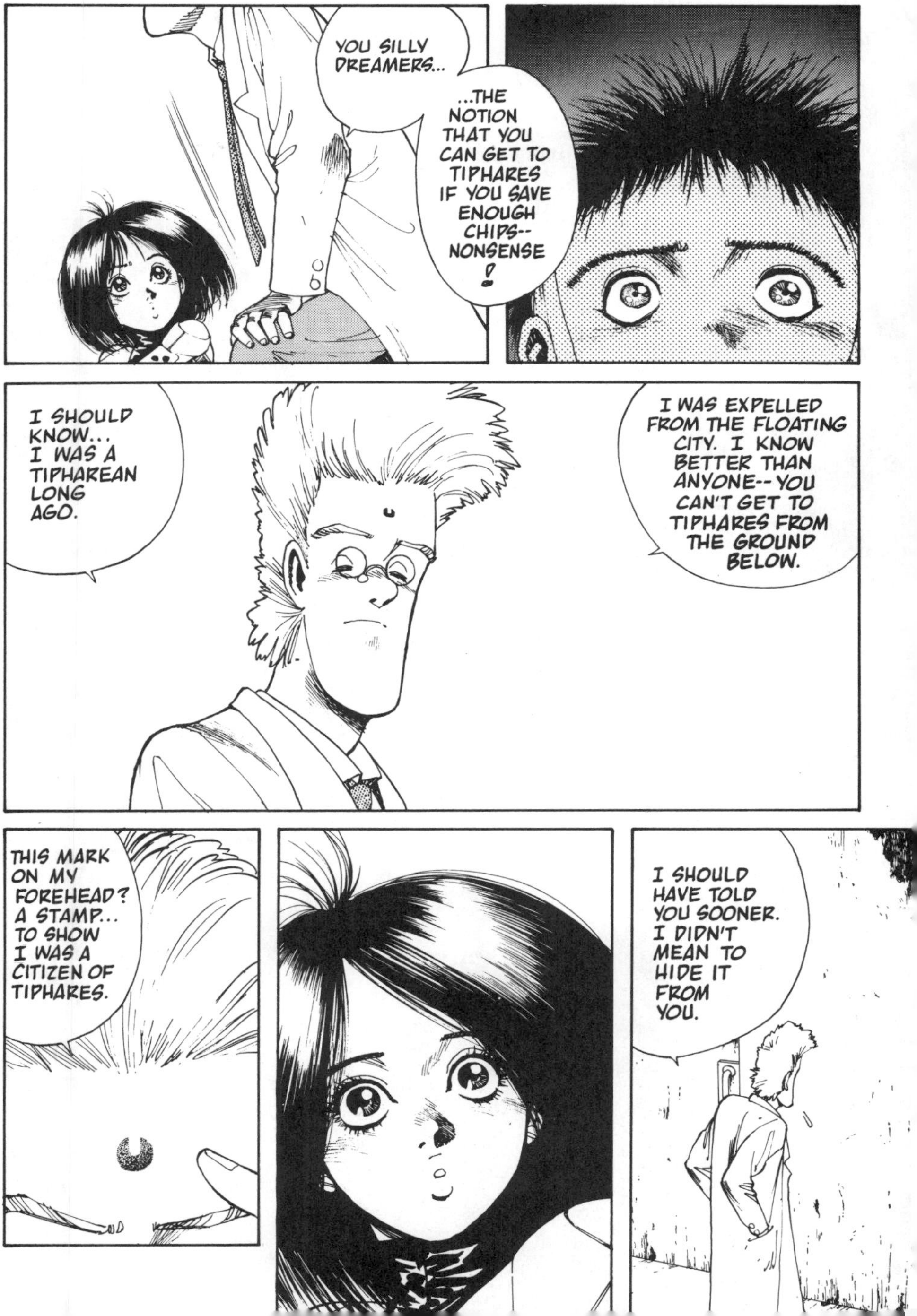
YOU SILLY DREAMERS...
...THE NOTION THAT YOU CAN GET TO TIPHARES IF YOU SAVE ENOUGH CHIPS--NONSENSE!
I SHOULD KNOW... I WAS A TIPHAREAN LONG AGO.
I WAS EXPELLED FROM THE FLOATING CITY. I KNOW BETTER THAN ANYONE--YOU CAN'T GET TO TIPHARES FROM THE GROUND BELOW.
THIS MARK ON MY FOREHEAD? A STAMP... TO SHOW I WAS A CITIZEN OF TIPHARES.
I SHOULD HAVE TOLD YOU SOONER. I DIDN'T MEAN TO HIDE IT FROM YOU.

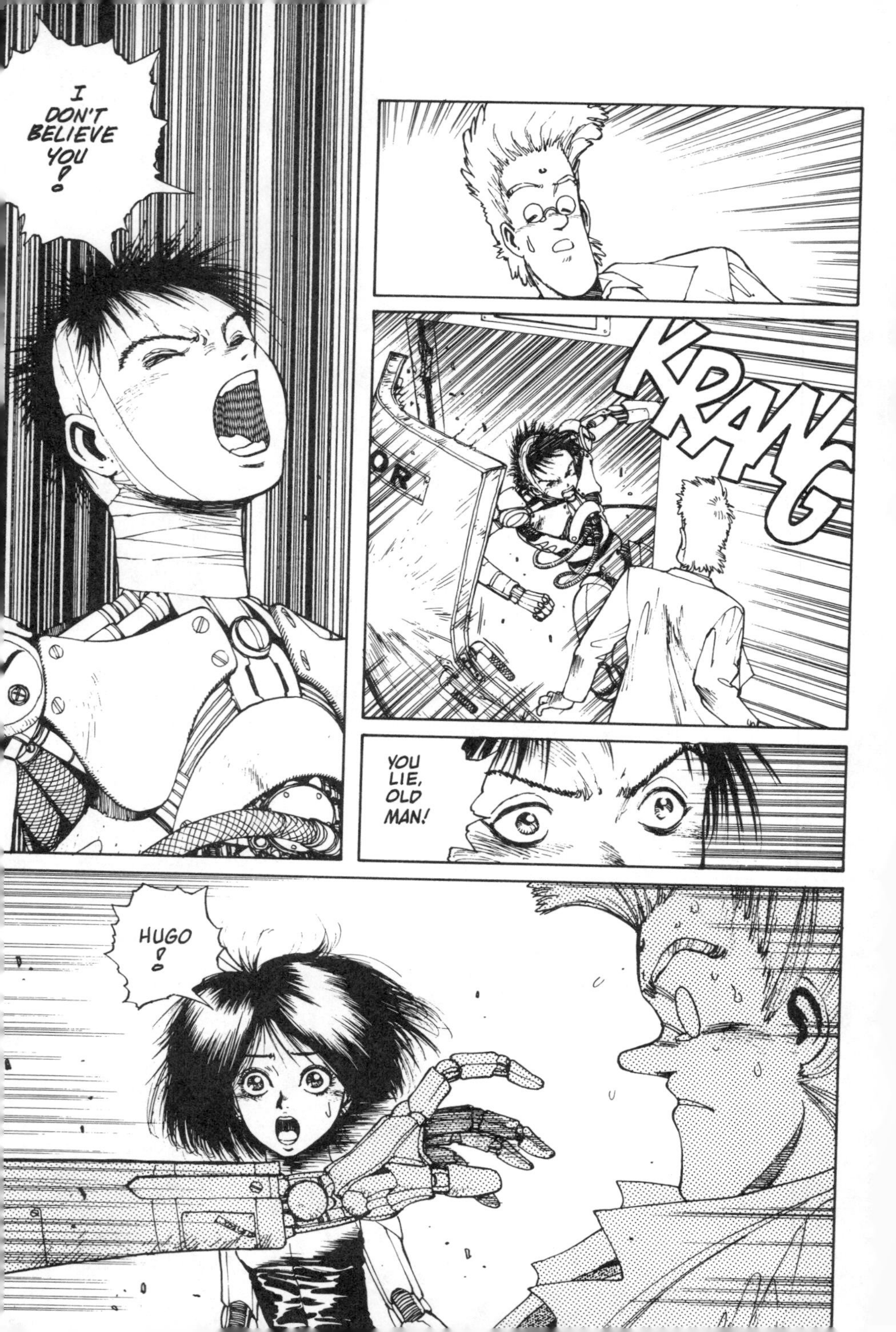
I DON'T BELIEVE YOU!
KRANG
YOU LIE, OLD MAN!
HUGO!

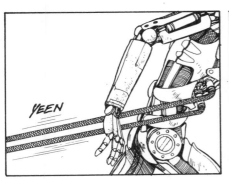

YEEN

KAPOP

KAPOP

!?

ⵌONG

MY BODY...

ungh

...CAN'T MOVE...

KRANG

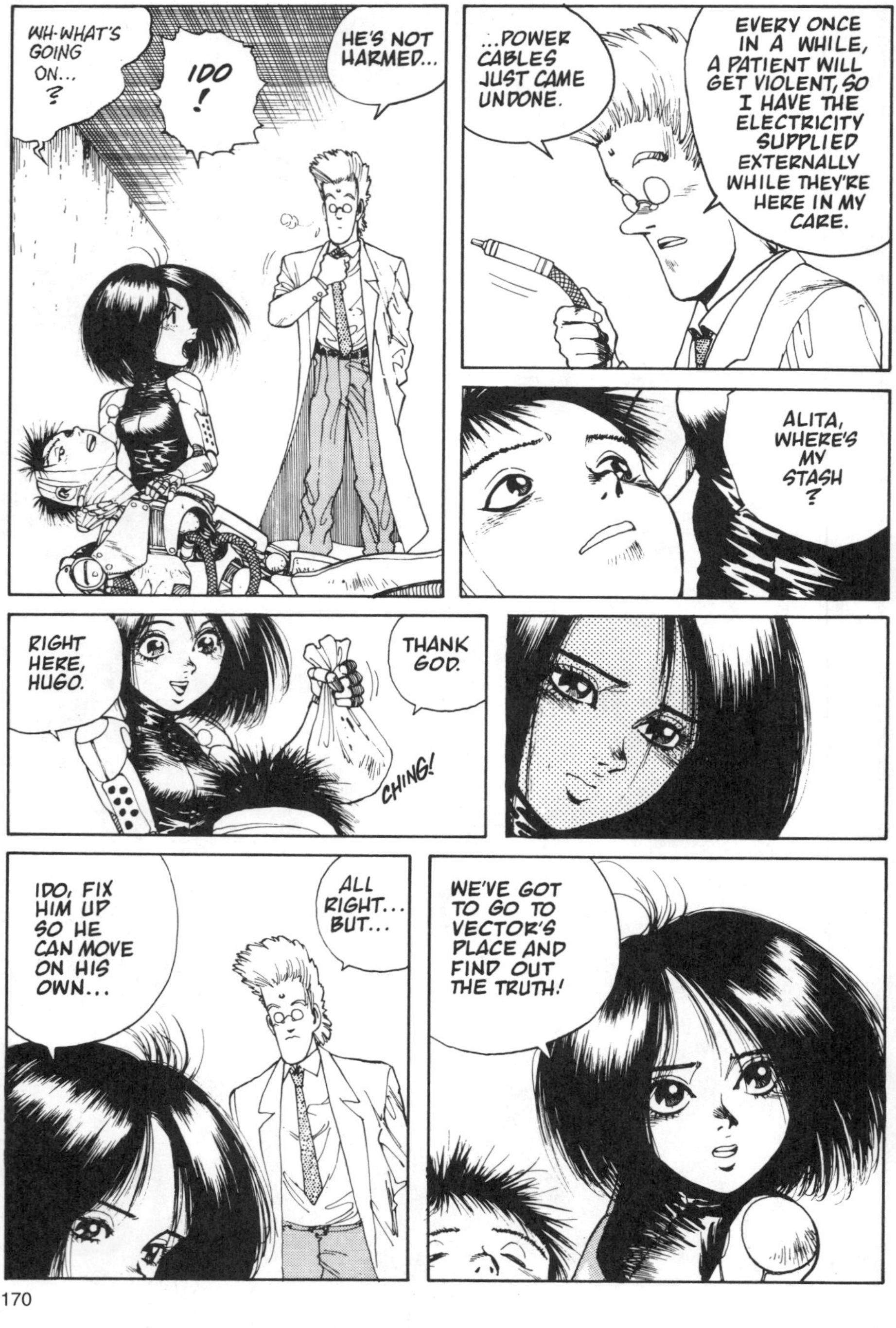
WH-WHAT'S GOING ON...?
IDO!
HE'S NOT HARMED...
...POWER CABLES JUST CAME UNDONE.
EVERY ONCE IN A WHILE, A PATIENT WILL GET VIOLENT, SO I HAVE THE ELECTRICITY SUPPLIED EXTERNALLY WHILE THEY'RE HERE IN MY CARE.
ALITA, WHERE'S MY STASH?
RIGHT HERE, HUGO.
THANK GOD.
CHING!
IDO, FIX HIM UP SO HE CAN MOVE ON HIS OWN...
ALL RIGHT... BUT...
WE'VE GOT TO GO TO VECTOR'S PLACE AND FIND OUT THE TRUTH!

AND IF IT TURNS OUT HE WAS LYING TO HUGO...!

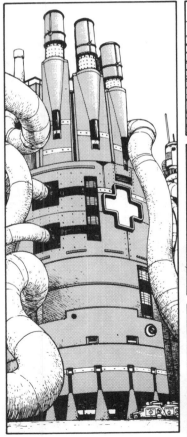

MR. VECTOR! TWO STRANGE KIDS--THEY *INSIST* ON SEEING YOU!

I'M WORKING. GET RID OF THEM.

WHUD

!?

THOMP

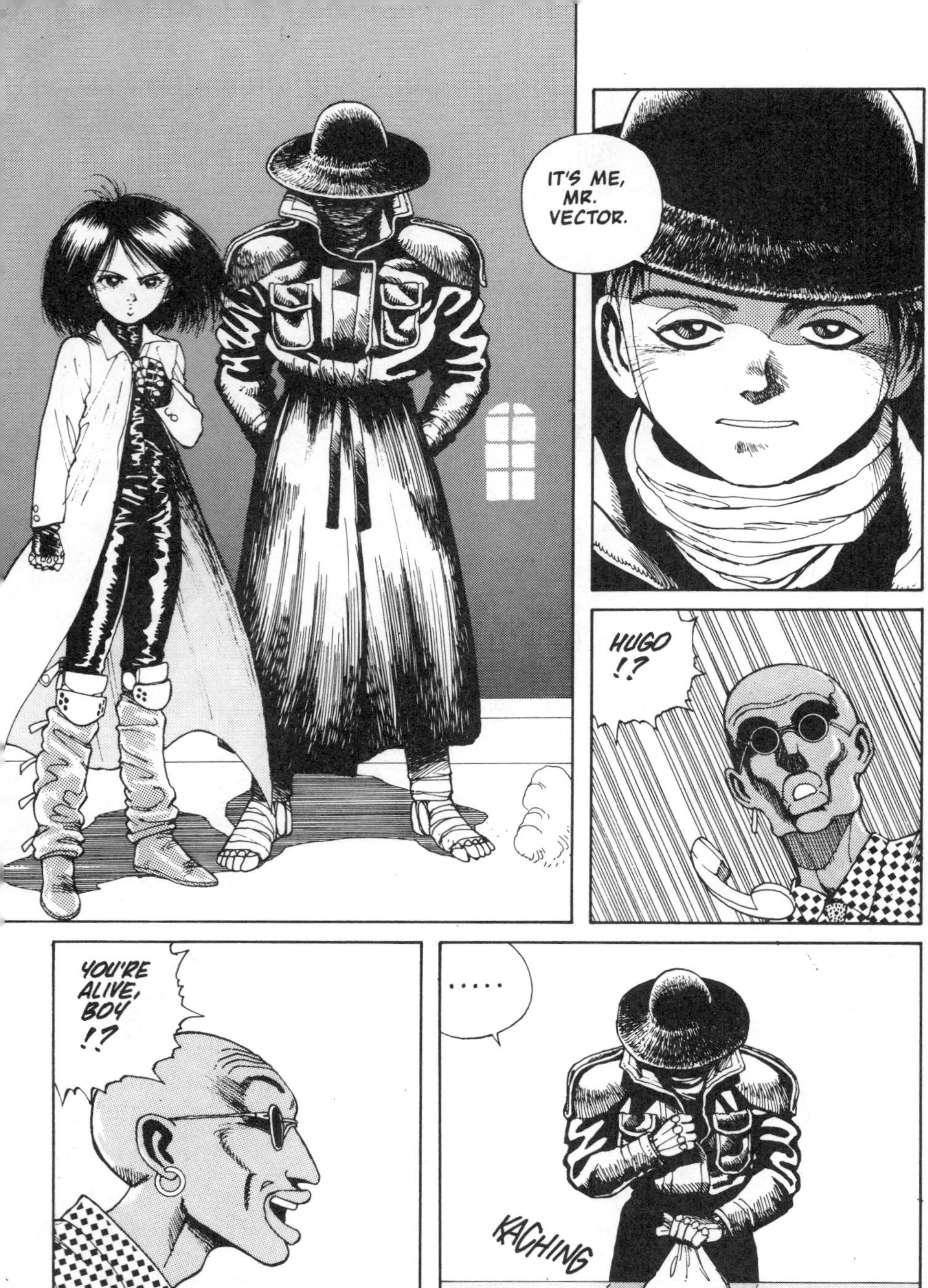
IT'S ME, MR. VECTOR.
HUGO !?
YOU'RE ALIVE, BOY !?
.....
KACHING

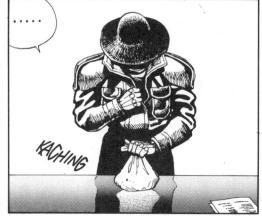

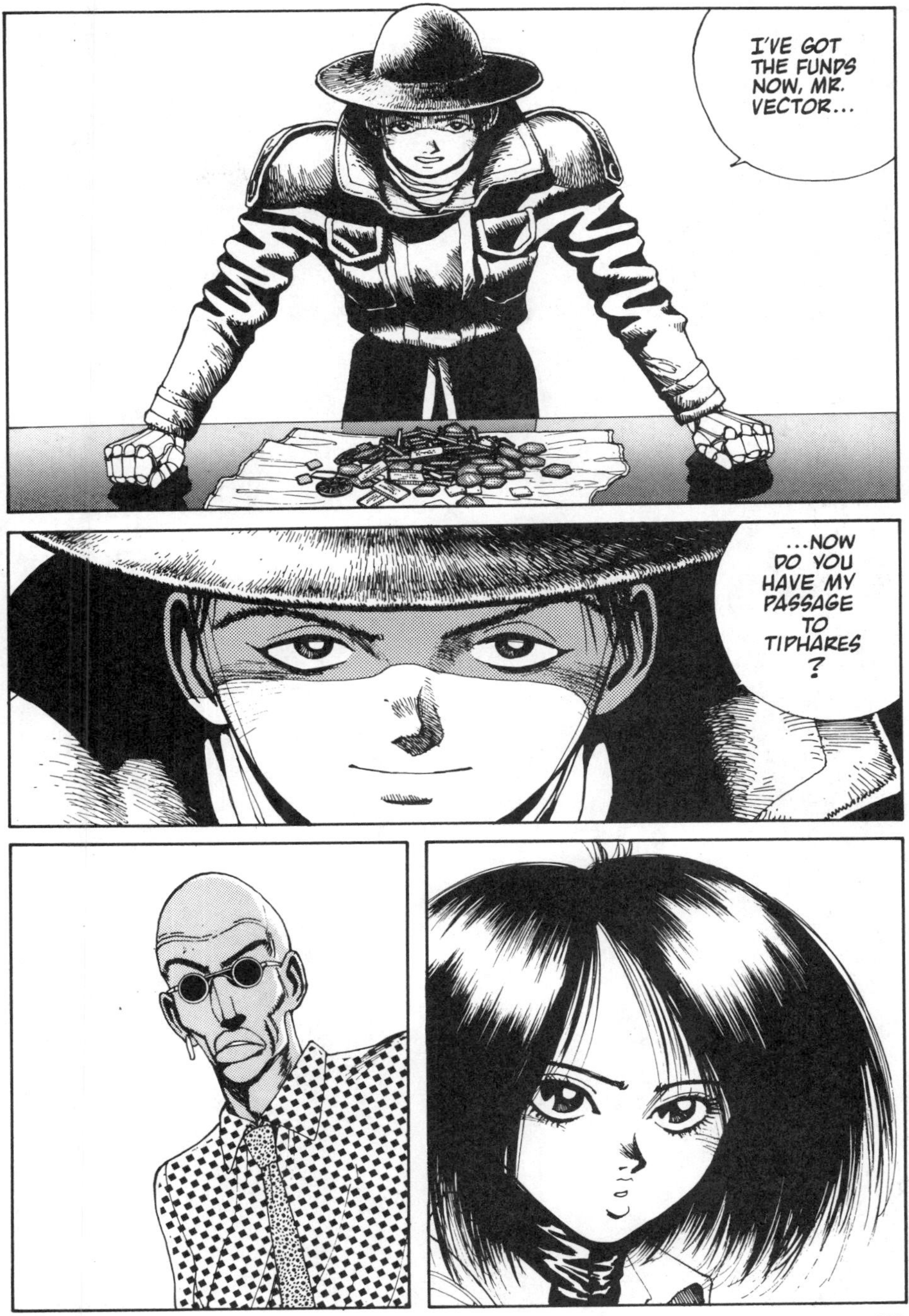
I'VE GOT THE FUNDS NOW, MR. VECTOR...
...NOW DO YOU HAVE MY PASSAGE TO TIPHARES ?

HEY, HEY-- HOLD UP, BOY...

...YOU GOT A PLAN ONCE YOU GET THERE?

I'LL BECOME A BEGGAR.

NOW THINK ABOUT IT, BOY! I'M OFFERING YOU A FACTORY RELAY ROUTE--

MY MIND IS MADE UP!

HMPH! HOPELESS...

ALL RIGHT, THEN. I CAN SHIP YOU UP TO TIPHARES--

--BUT ONLY LIKE THIS!

SHAASH

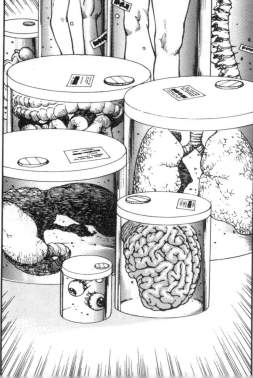

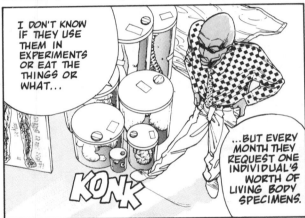

I DON'T KNOW IF THEY USE THEM IN EXPERIMENTS OR EAT THE THINGS OR WHAT...

...BUT EVERY MONTH THEY REQUEST ONE INDIVIDUAL'S WORTH OF LIVING BODY SPECIMENS.

KONK

SO YOU WERE PLANNING TO TAKE MY TEN MILLION CHIPS AND CUT ME INTO TINY PIECES?

OF COURSE NOT, HUGO!

I JUST THOUGHT YOU'D GIVE UP IF I ASKED FOR SOME OUTRAGEOUS SUM.

AND THE STORY THAT YOU'VE BEEN TO TIPHARES?

HYPERBOLE. STRETCHING THE TRUTH. A LITTLE EXAGGERATION... YOU UNDERSTAND-- IT'S GOOD FOR BUSINESS!

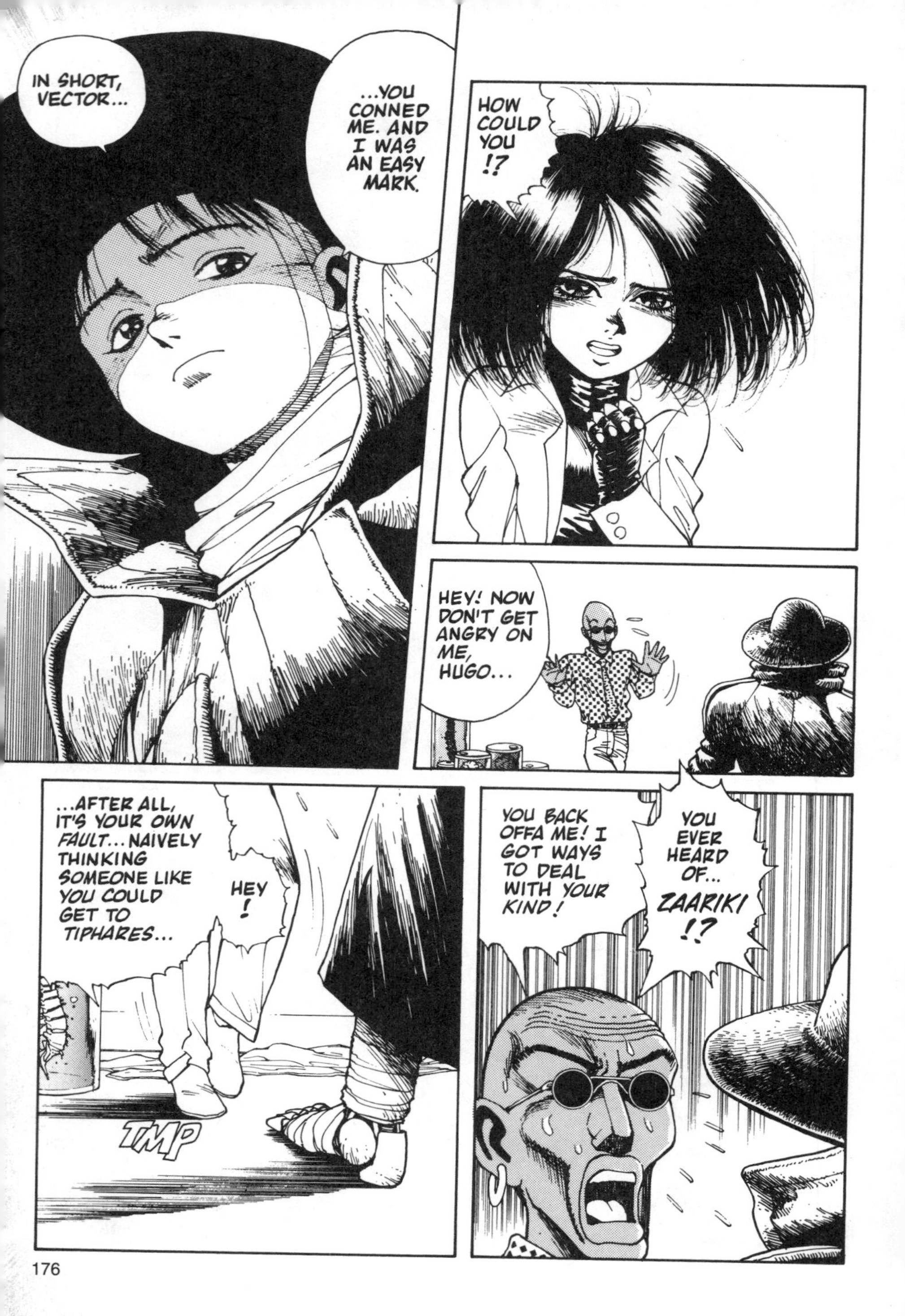
IN SHORT, VECTOR...
...YOU CONNED ME. AND I WAS AN EASY MARK.
HOW COULD YOU !?
HEY! NOW DON'T GET ANGRY ON ME, HUGO...
...AFTER ALL, IT'S YOUR OWN FAULT...NAIVELY THINKING SOMEONE LIKE YOU COULD GET TO TIPHARES...
HEY!
TMP
YOU BACK OFFA ME! I GOT WAYS TO DEAL WITH YOUR KIND!
YOU EVER HEARD OF... ZAARIKI !?

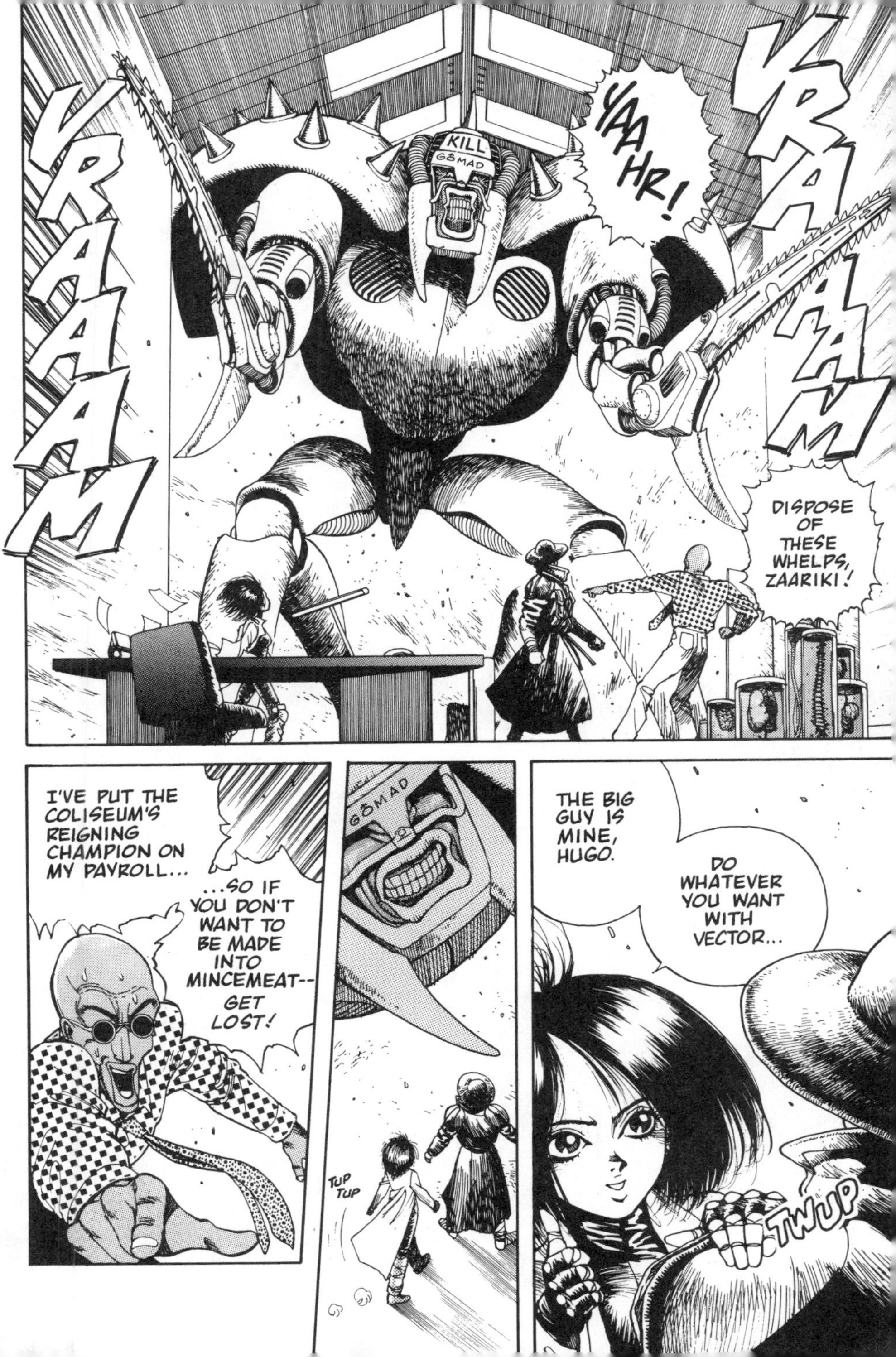
VRAAAAM
KILL
G8MAD
YAAAHR!
VRAAAM
DISPOSE OF THESE WHELPS, ZAARIKI!
I'VE PUT THE COLISEUM'S REIGNING CHAMPION ON MY PAYROLL...
...SO IF YOU DON'T WANT TO BE MADE INTO MINCEMEAT-- GET LOST!
G8MAD
TUP TUP
THE BIG GUY IS MINE, HUGO.
DO WHATEVER YOU WANT WITH VECTOR...
TWUP

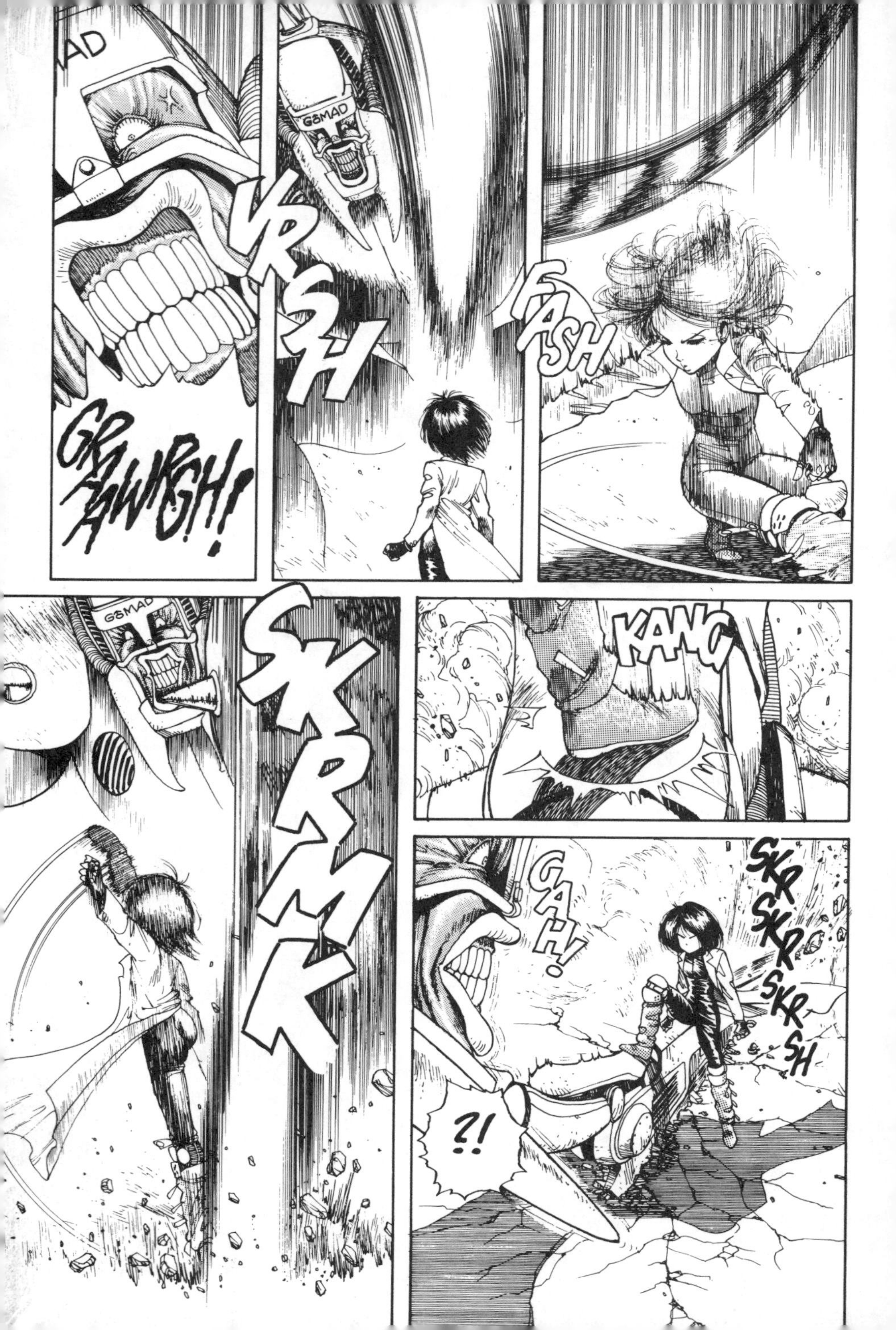
AD
GōMAD
VRSH
GRAWRGH!!
FASH
GōMAD
SKRMK
KANG
GAH!
SKR SKR SKR SKR-SH
?!

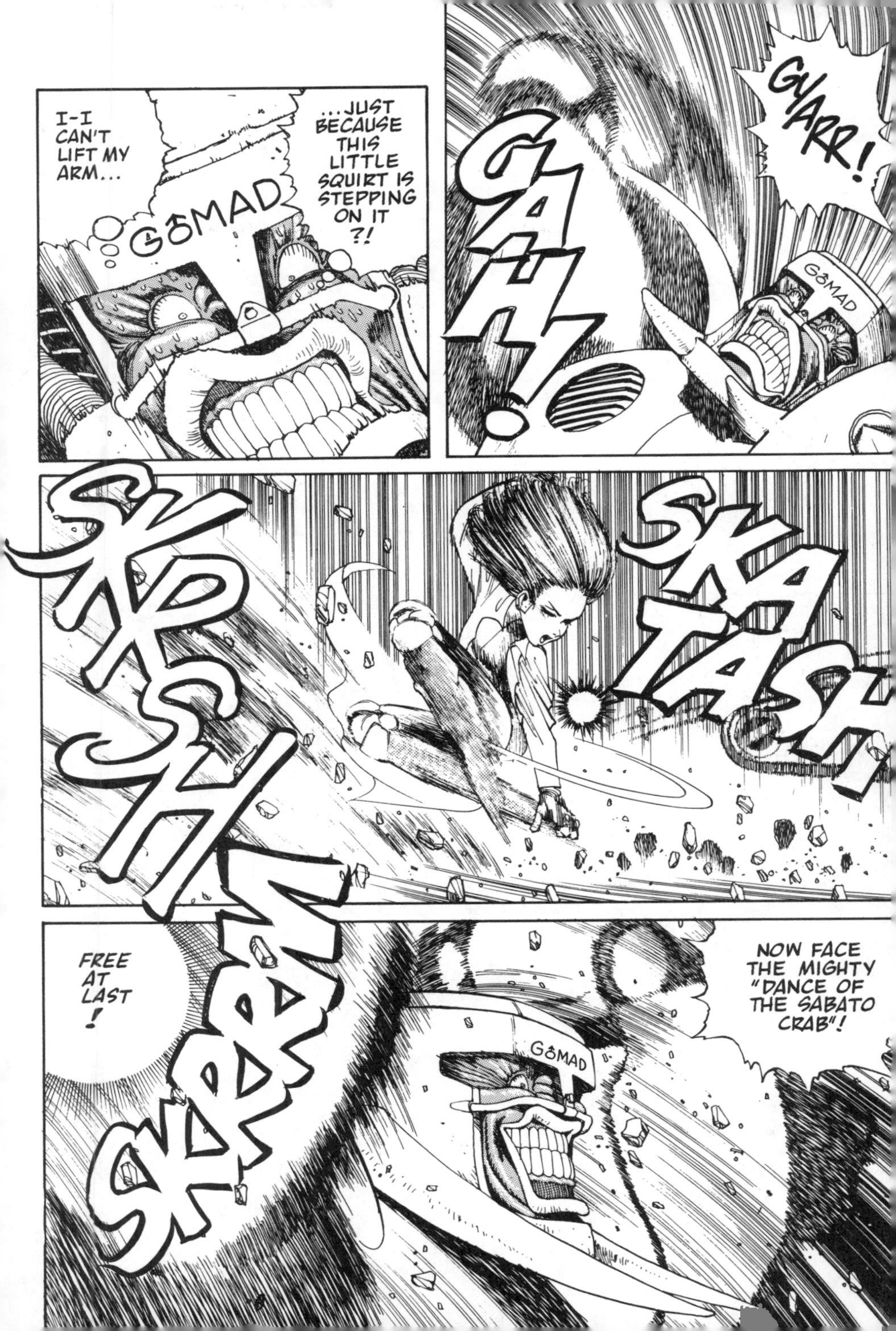
I-I CAN'T LIFT MY ARM...
...JUST BECAUSE THIS LITTLE SQUIRT IS STEPPING ON IT ?!
GÔMAD
GÔMAD
GAHH!
GYARR!
SKRASHH
SKA TASH!
FREE AT LAST!
SKREEN
NOW FACE THE MIGHTY "DANCE OF THE SABATO CRAB"!
GÔMAD

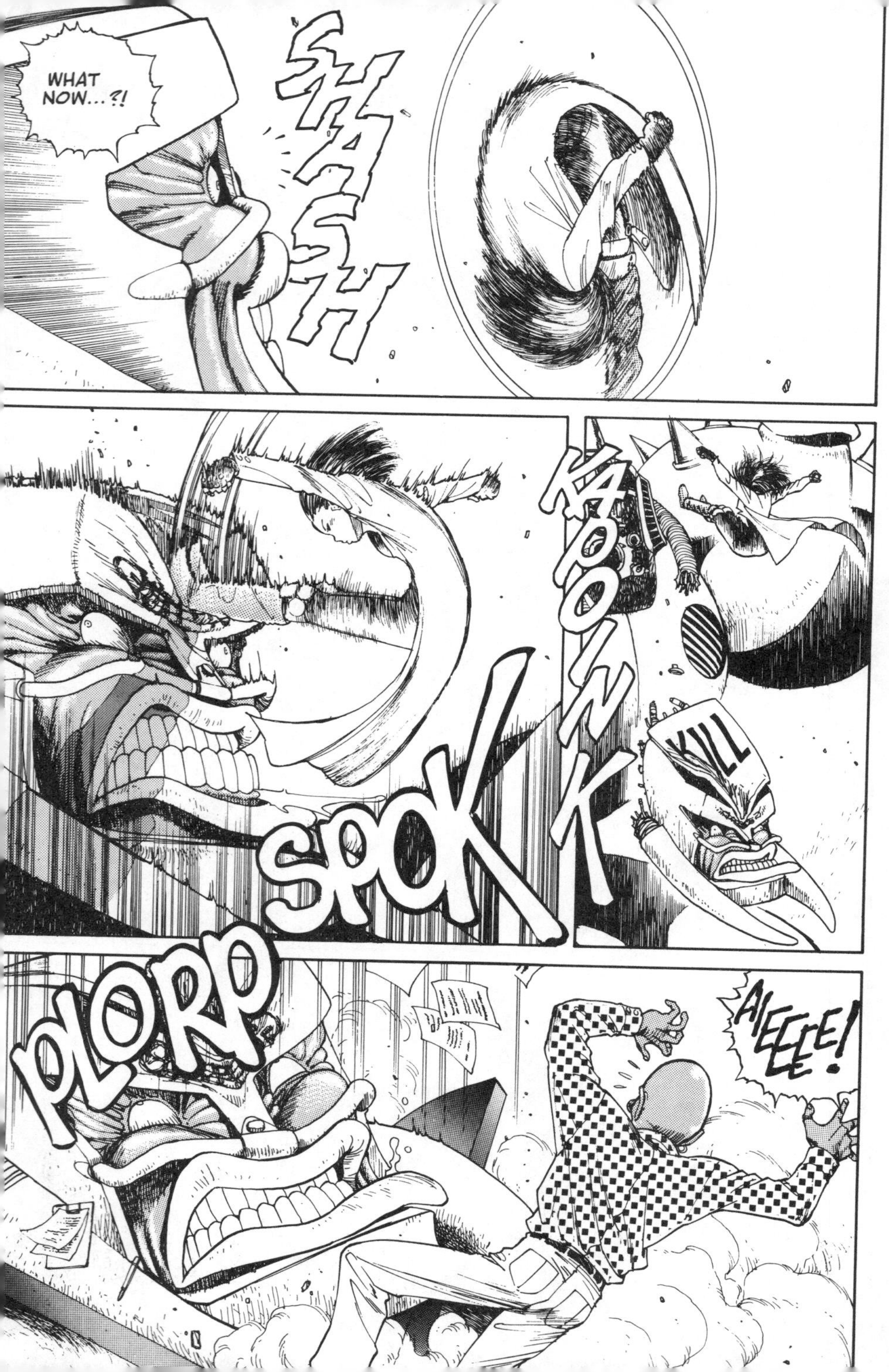
WHAT NOW...?!
SHASHH
KAPOOINK
SPOK
KILL
PLORP
AIEEEEE!

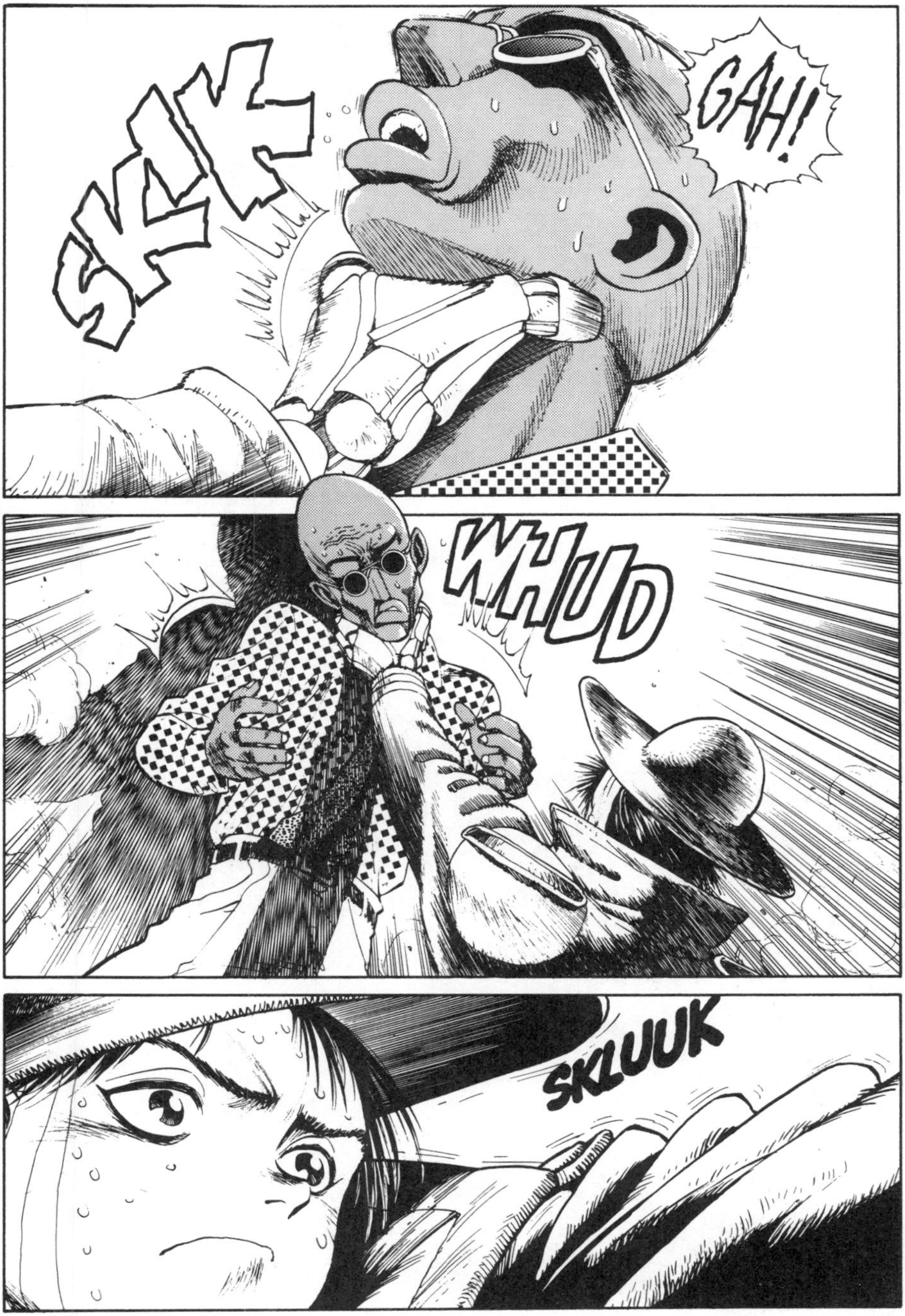
SKAK
GAH!
WHUD
SKLUUK

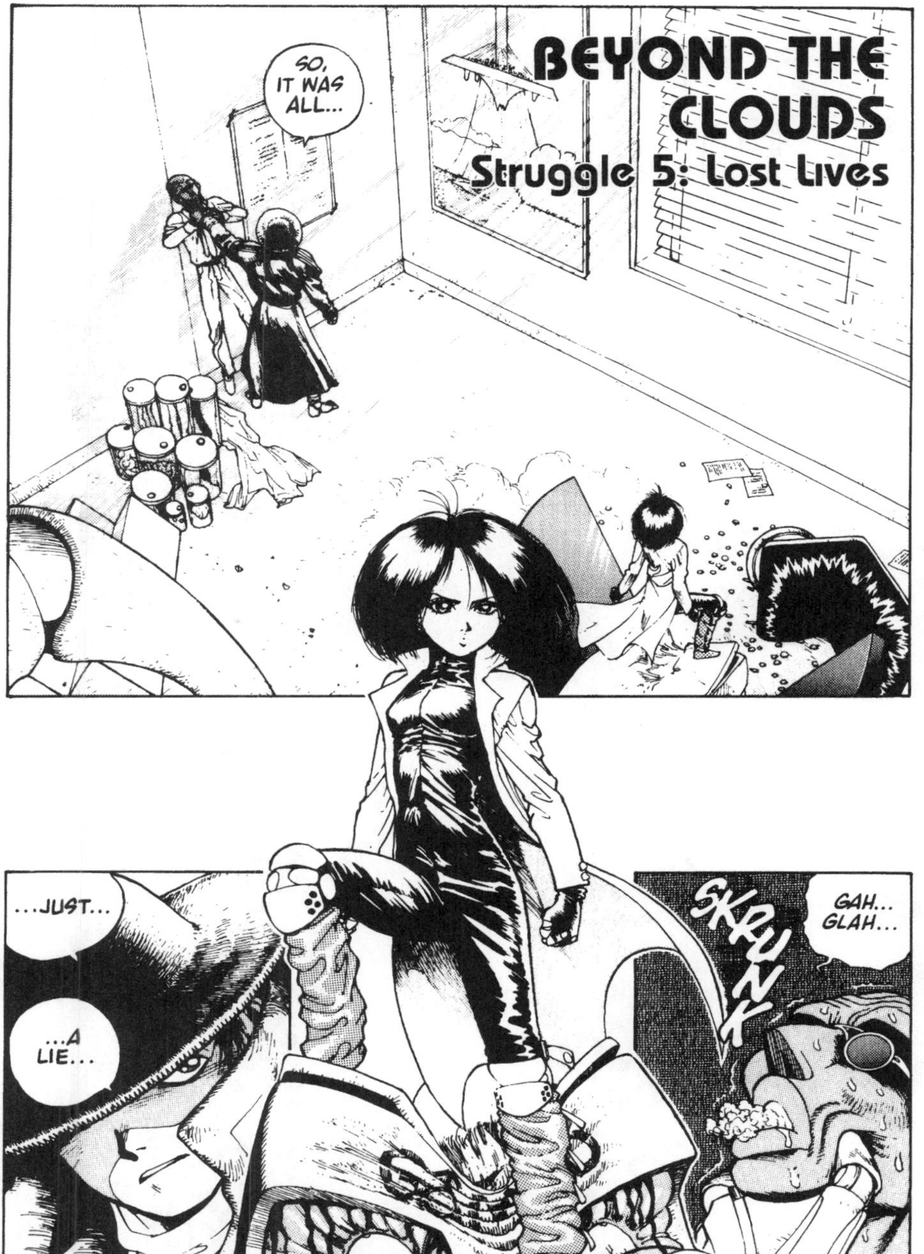
BEYOND THE CLOUDS
Struggle 5: Lost Lives
SO, IT WAS ALL...
...JUST...
...A LIE...
SKRUNK
GAH... GLAH...

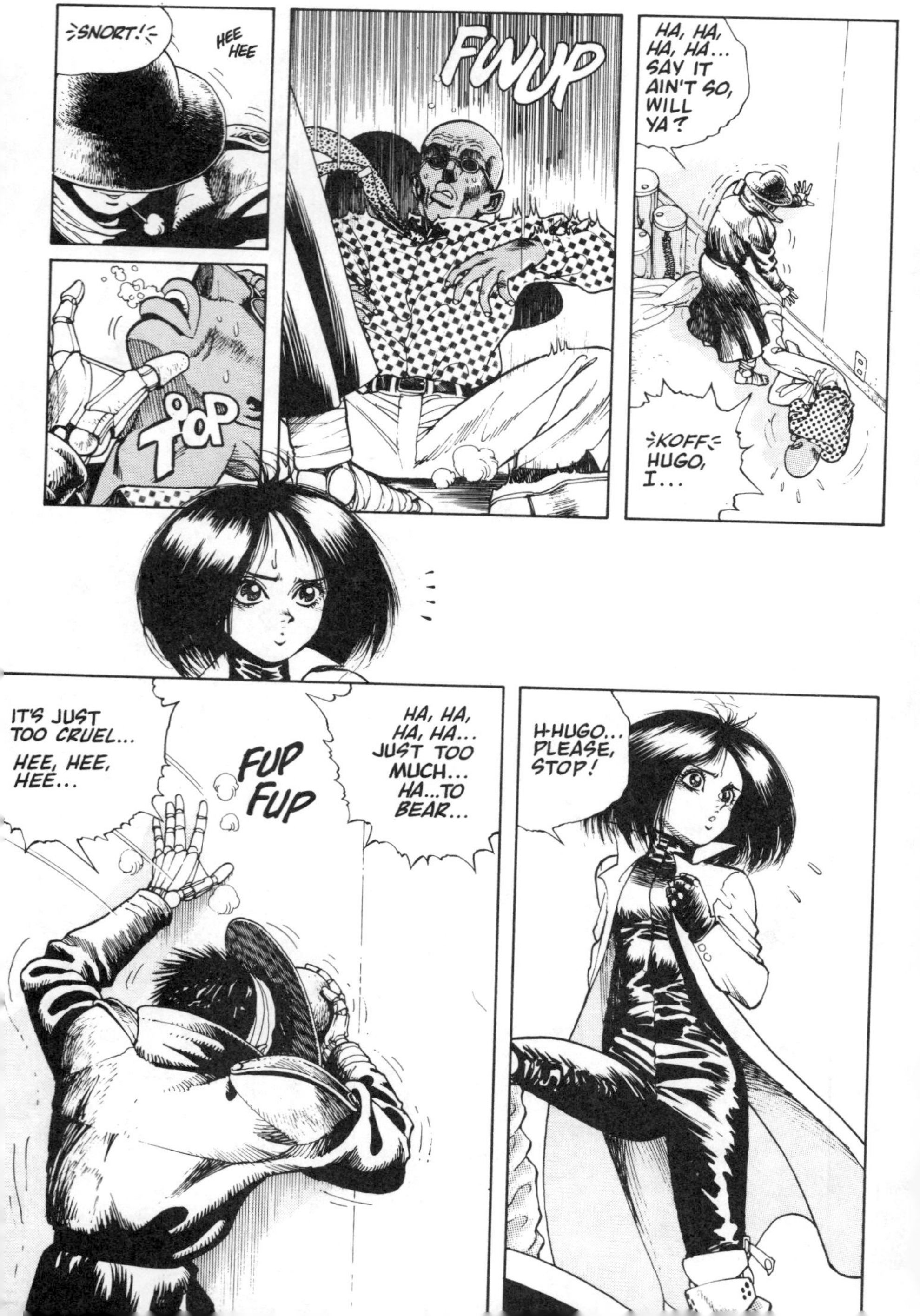

SNORT!
HEE HEE
TOP
FWUP
HA, HA, HA, HA... SAY IT AIN'T SO, WILL YA?
KOFF
HUGO, I...
IT'S JUST TOO CRUEL...
HEE, HEE, HEE...
FUP FUP
HA, HA, HA, HA... JUST TOO MUCH... HA...TO BEAR...
H-HUGO... PLEASE, STOP!

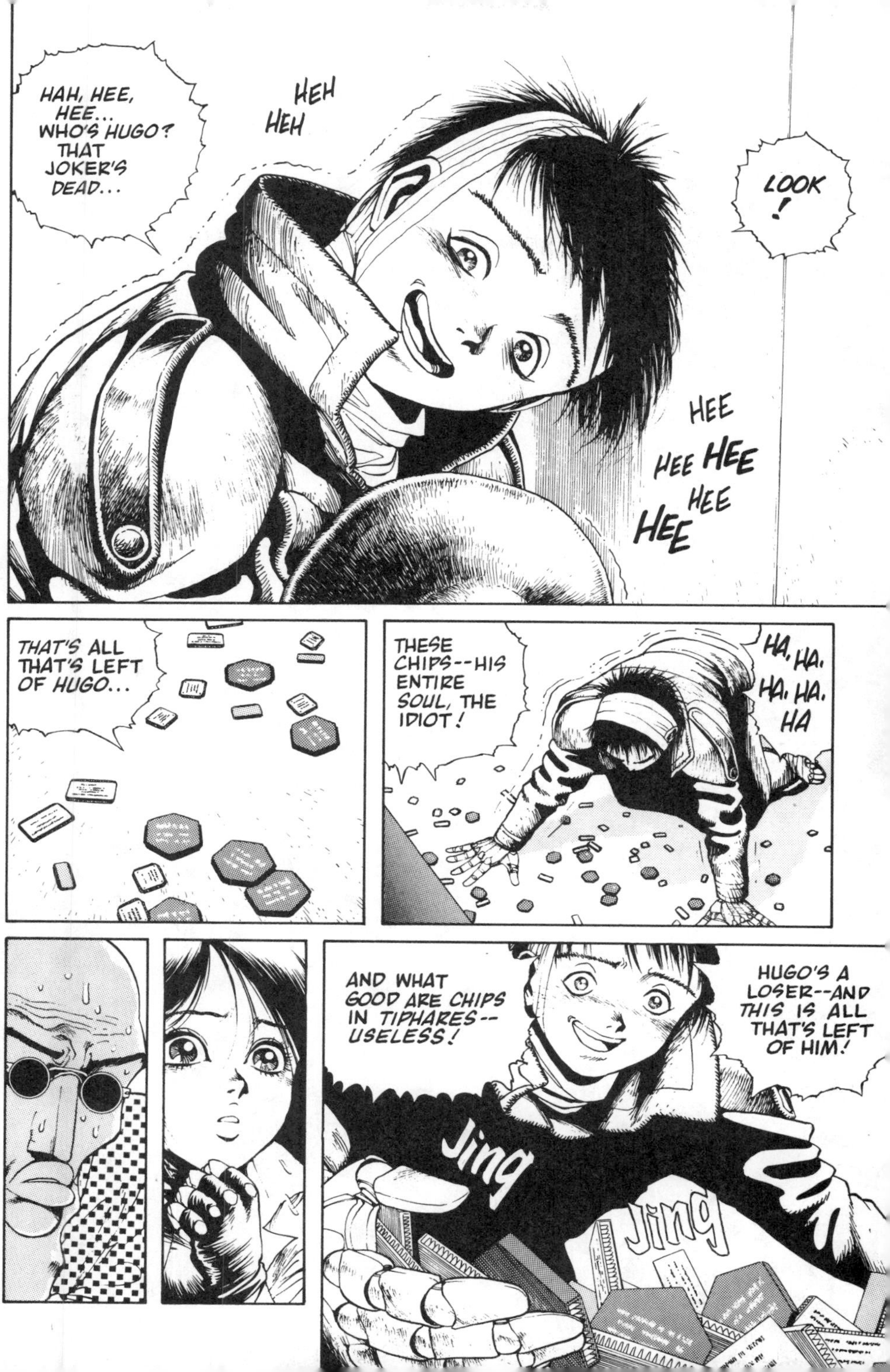
HAH, HEE, HEE... WHO'S HUGO? THAT JOKER'S DEAD...
HEH HEH
LOOK!
HEE HEE HEE HEE HEE
THAT'S ALL THAT'S LEFT OF HUGO...
THESE CHIPS--HIS ENTIRE SOUL, THE IDIOT!
HA, HA. HA, HA. HA
AND WHAT GOOD ARE CHIPS IN TIPHARES--USELESS!
HUGO'S A LOSER--AND THIS IS ALL THAT'S LEFT OF HIM!
Jing
Jing

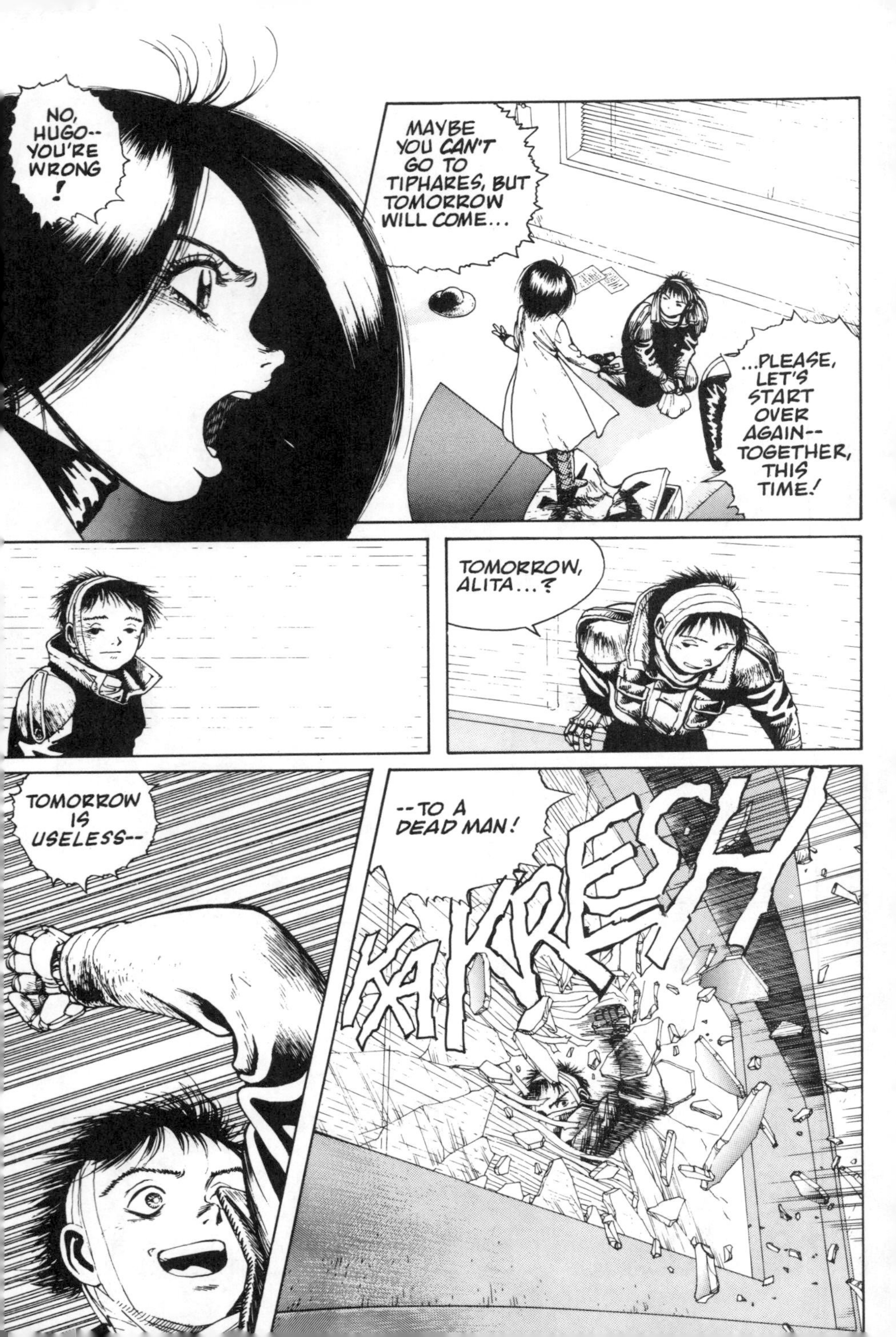
NO, HUGO-- YOU'RE WRONG!
MAYBE YOU CAN'T GO TO TIPHARES, BUT TOMORROW WILL COME...
...PLEASE, LET'S START OVER AGAIN-- TOGETHER, THIS TIME!
TOMORROW, ALITA...?
TOMORROW IS USELESS--
--TO A DEAD MAN!
KAKRESH

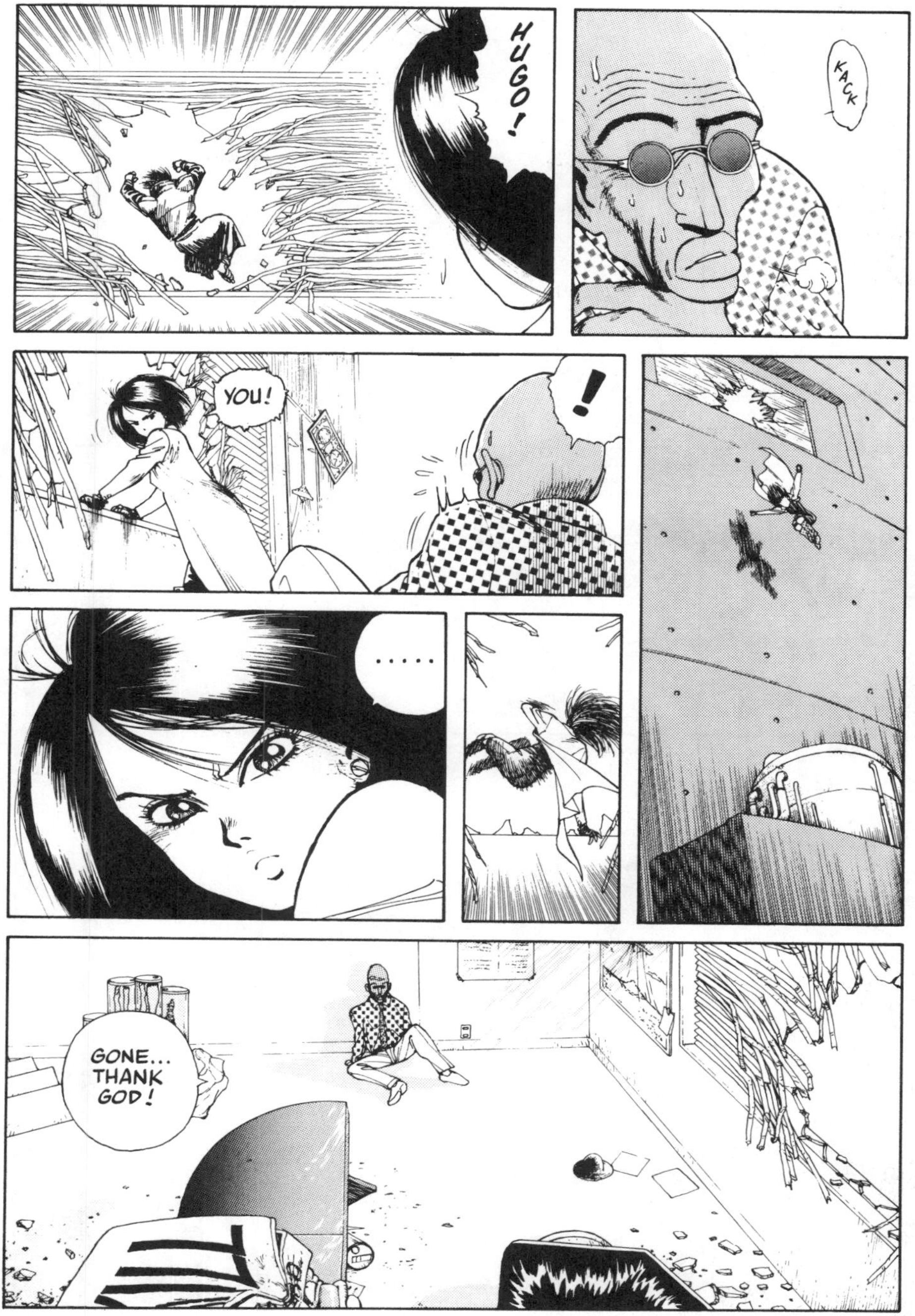
HUGO!
KACK
YOU!
!
......
GONE... THANK GOD!

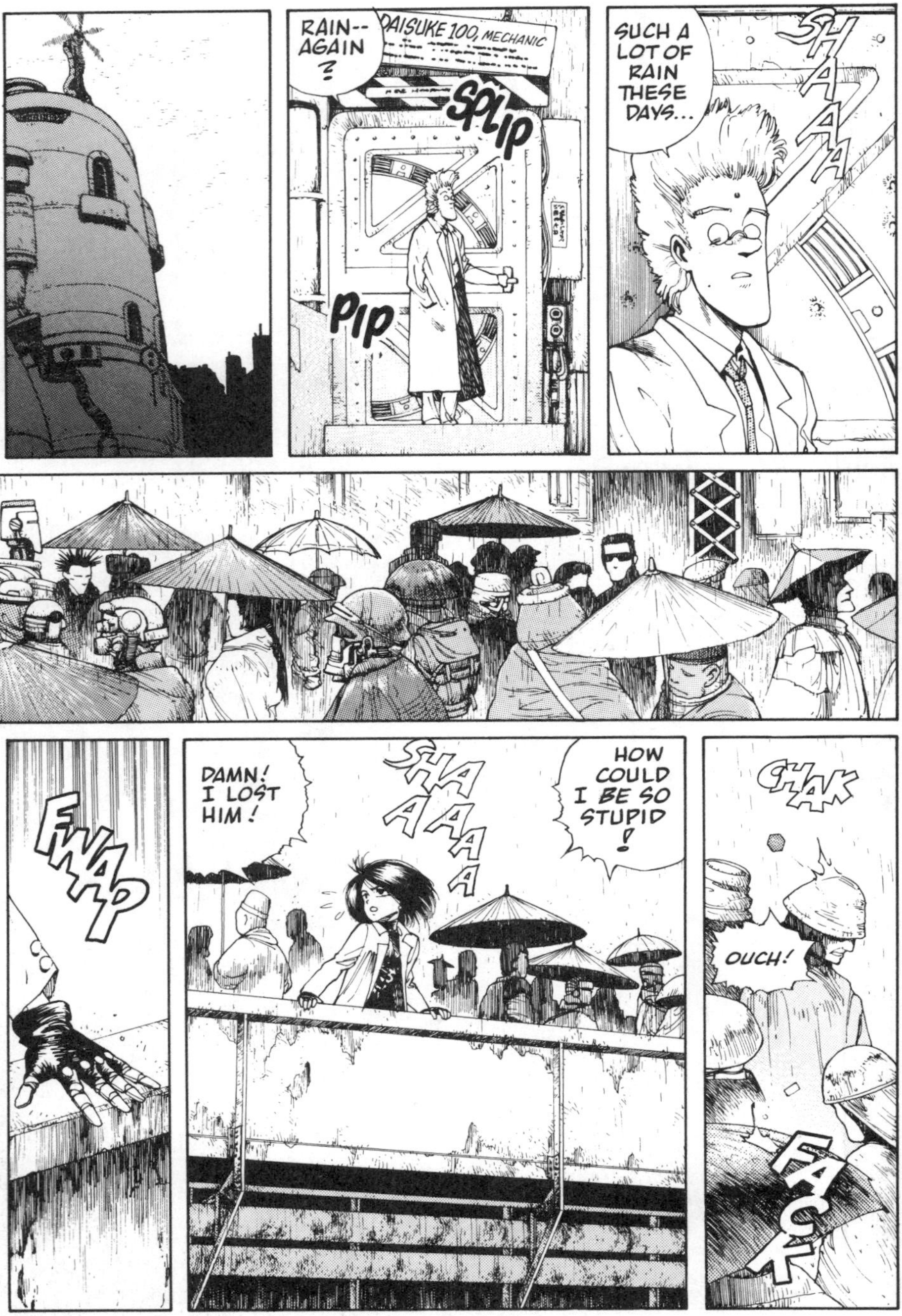
RAIN-- AGAIN ?
DAISUKE 100, MECHANIC
SPLIP
PIP
SUCH A LOT OF RAIN THESE DAYS...
SHAAA
FWAP
DAMN! I LOST HIM!
SHAAAAAA
HOW COULD I BE SO STUPID !
CHAK
OUCH!
FACK

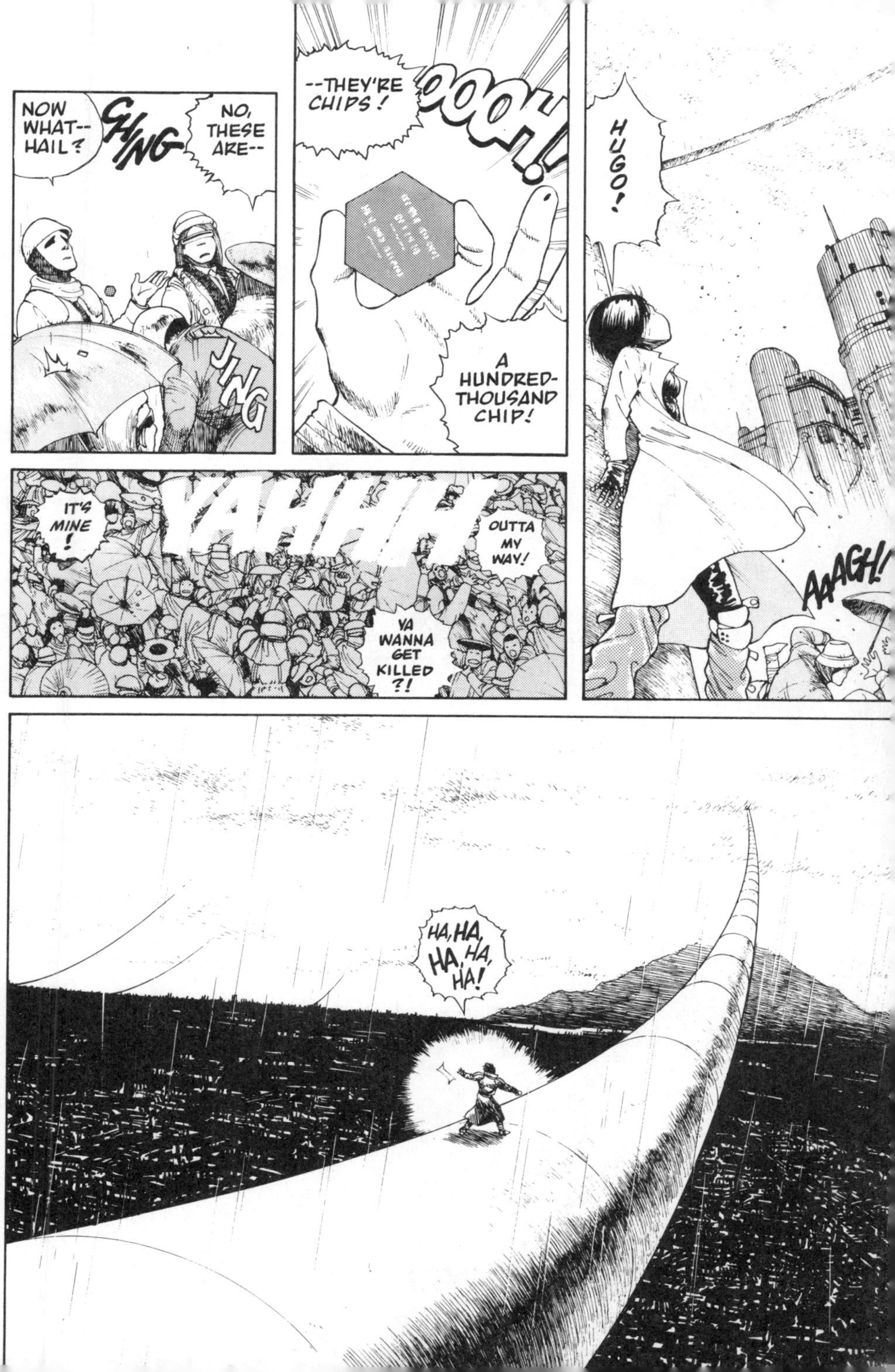
NOW WHAT-- HAIL?
CHING
NO, THESE ARE--
JING
--THEY'RE CHIPS!
OOOH!!
A HUNDRED-THOUSAND CHIP!
HUGO!
IT'S MINE!
YAHHH
OUTTA MY WAY!
YA WANNA GET KILLED?!
AAAGH!
HA, HA, HA, HA, HA!

I'M COMING FOR YOU, TIPHARES!

THERE'S NO STOPPING ME--YOU HEAR?

WHSHSH

WHA--?!

FWMMM

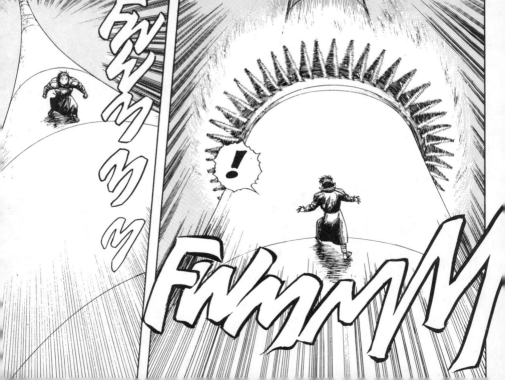

FWMMM

!

FWMMM

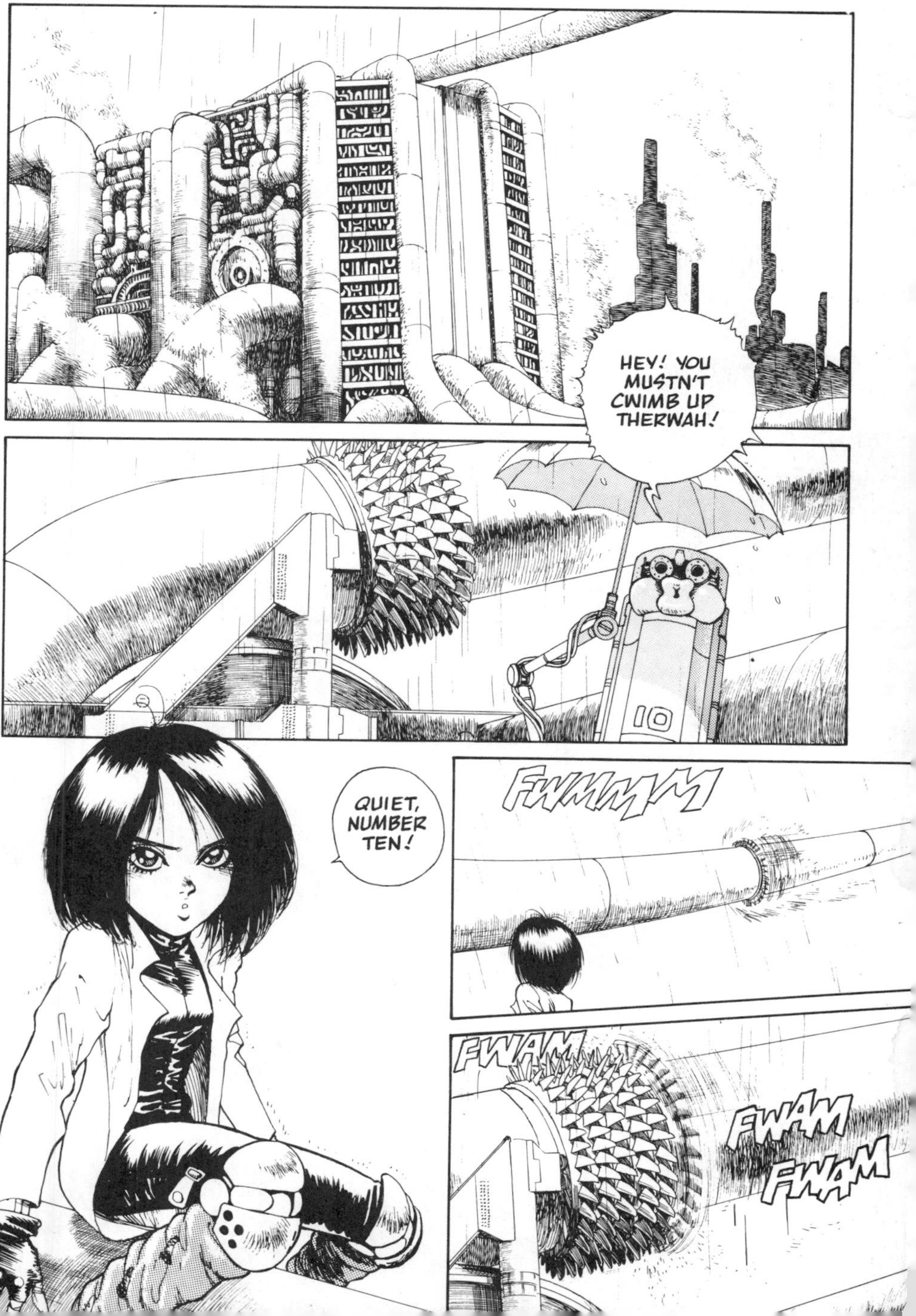
HEY! YOU MUSTN'T CWIMB UP THERWAH!
QUIET, NUMBER TEN!
FWMMMM
FWAM
FWAM
FWAM

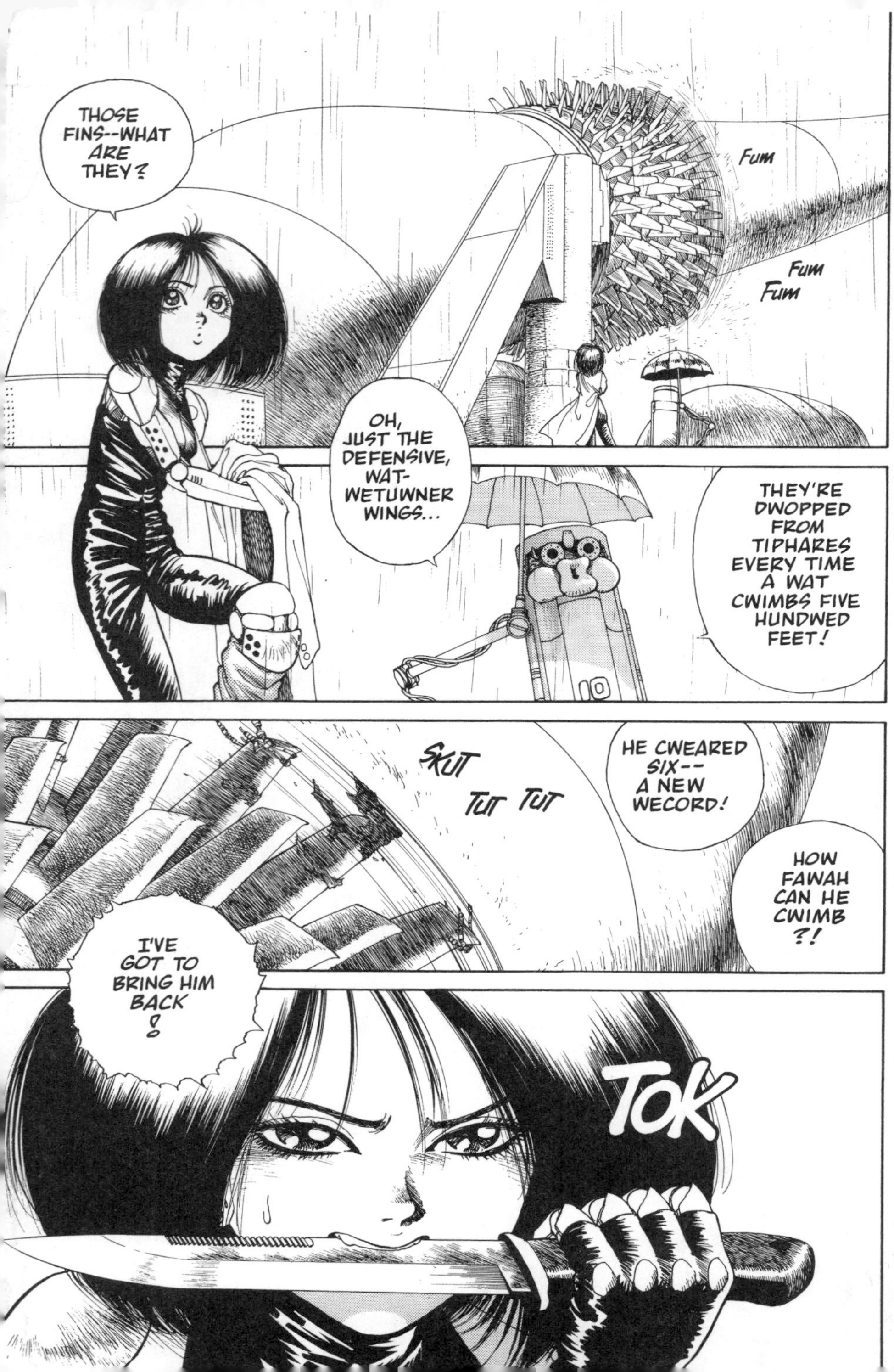

THOSE FINS--WHAT ARE THEY?
Fum
Fum
Fum
OH, JUST THE DEFENSIVE, WAT-WETUWNER WINGS...
THEY'RE DWOPPED FROM TIPHARES EVERY TIME A WAT CWIMBS FIVE HUNDWED FEET!
SKUT
TUT TUT
HE CWEARED SIX-- A NEW WECORD!
HOW FAWAH CAN HE CWIMB?!
I'VE GOT TO BRING HIM BACK!
TOK

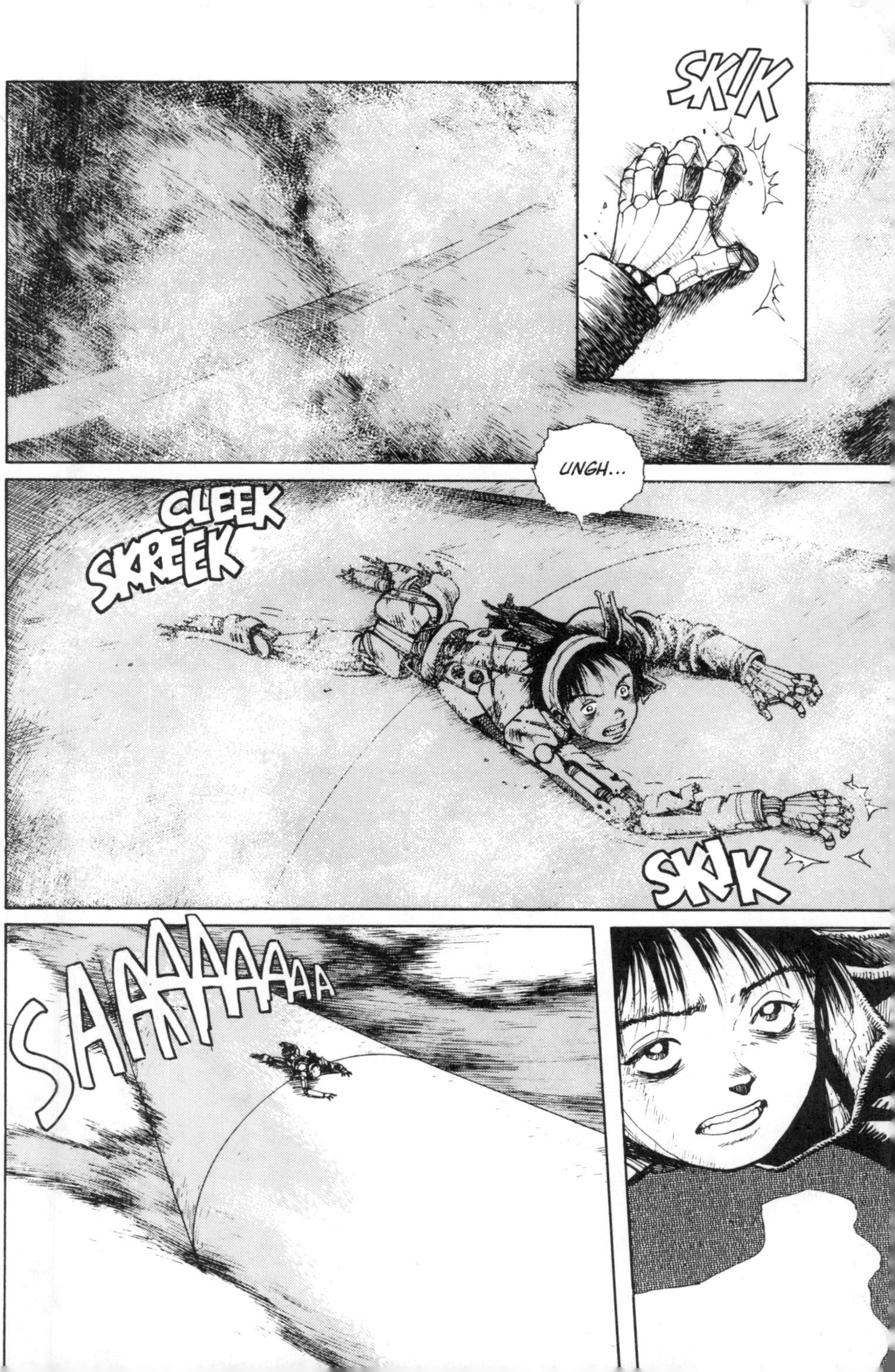
SKIK
UNGH...
CLEEK
SKREEK
SKIK
SAAAAAAAA

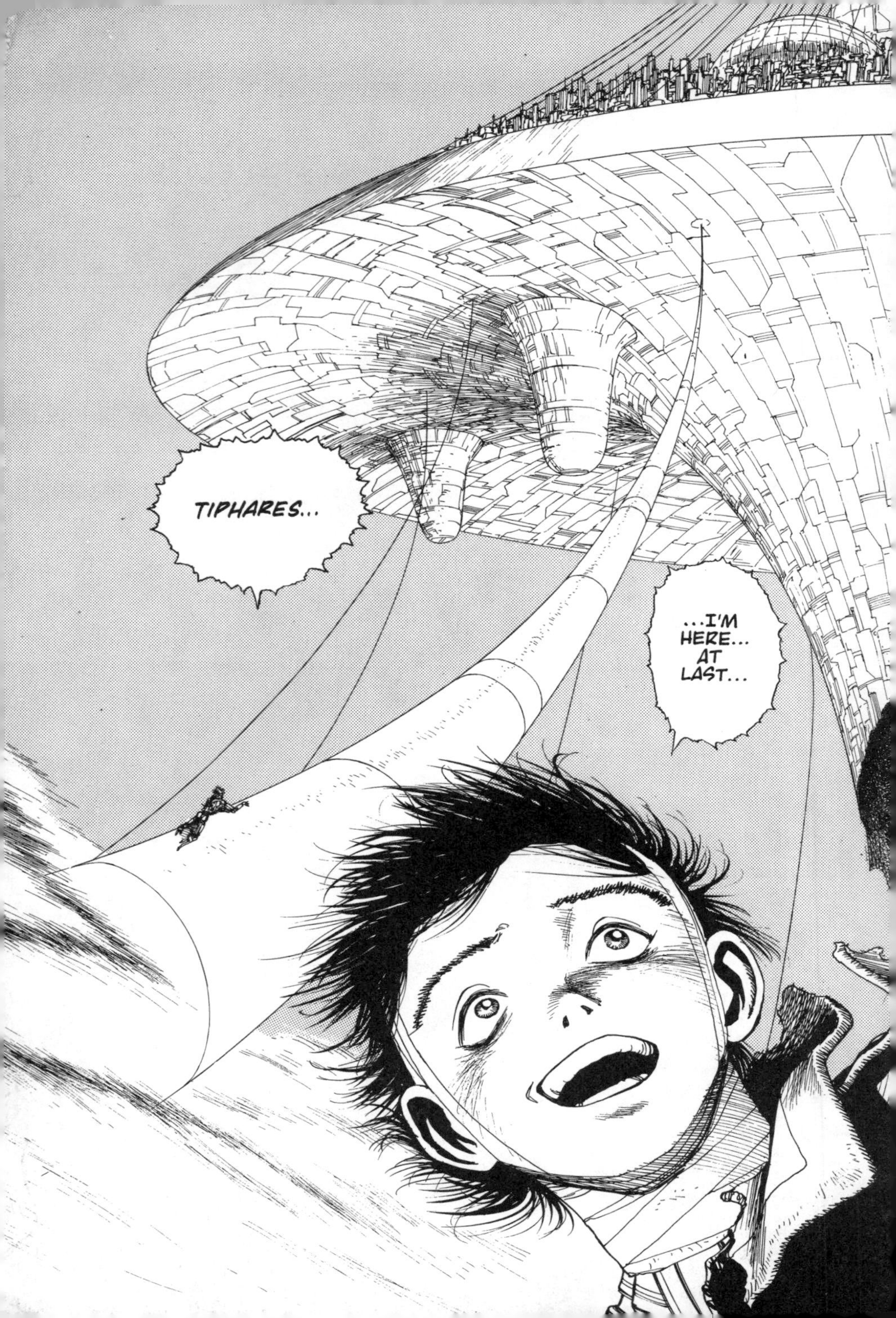
TIPHARES...
...I'M HERE... AT LAST...

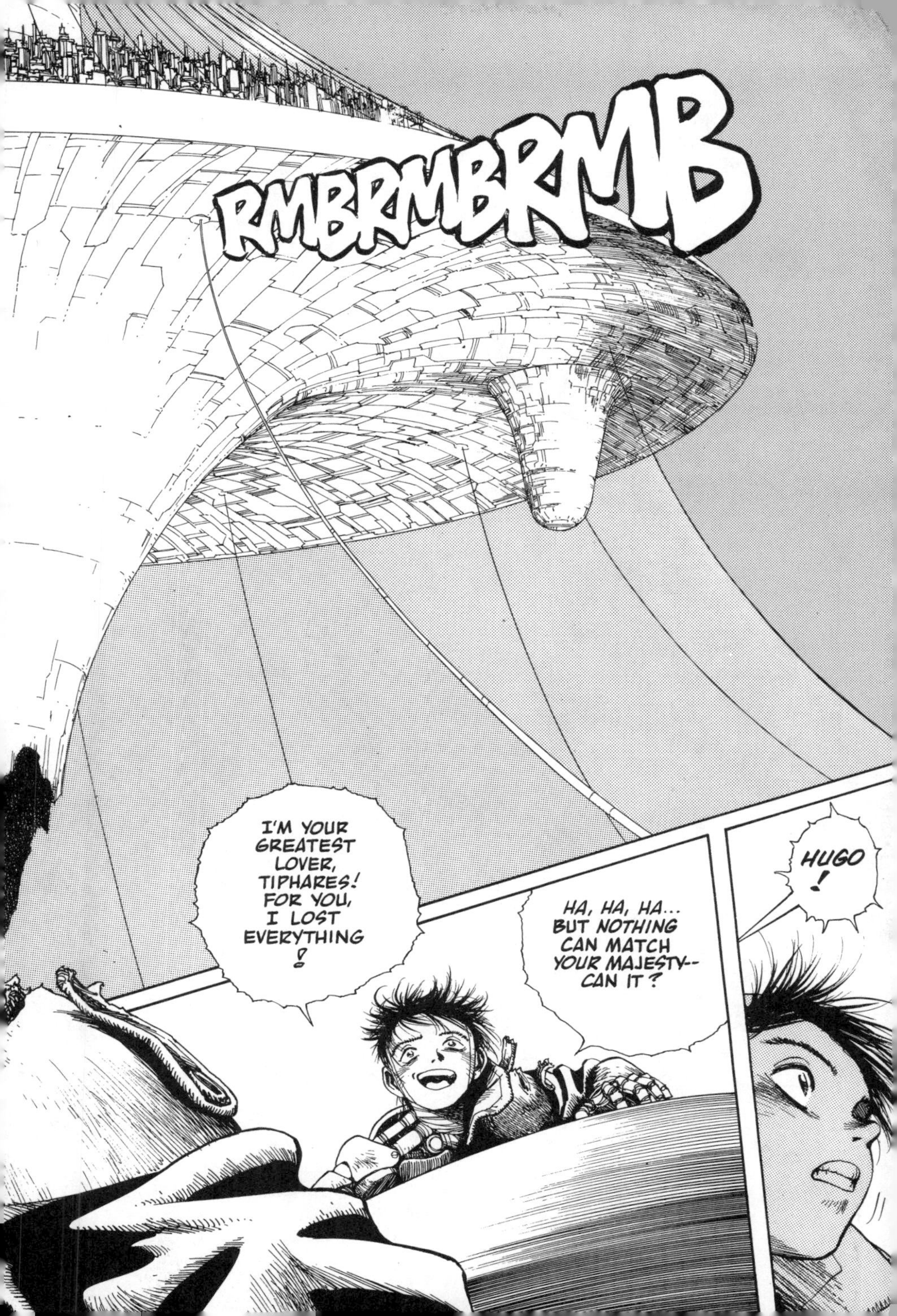
RMBRMBRMB
I'M YOUR GREATEST LOVER, TIPHARES! FOR YOU, I LOST EVERYTHING!
HA, HA, HA... BUT NOTHING CAN MATCH YOUR MAJESTY-- CAN IT?
HUGO!

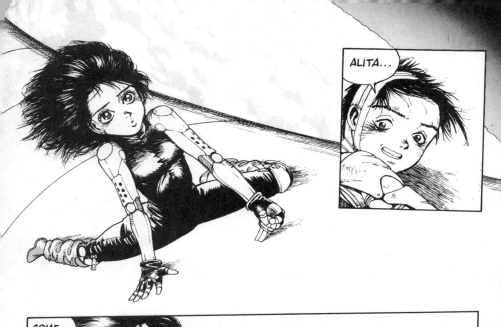

ALITA...

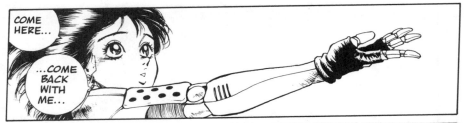

COME HERE...

...COME BACK WITH ME...

BACK DOWN?

NEVER!

THAT SCRAPYARD ALMOST KILLED ME, ALITA!

TIPHARES IS WHERE I BELONG NOW!

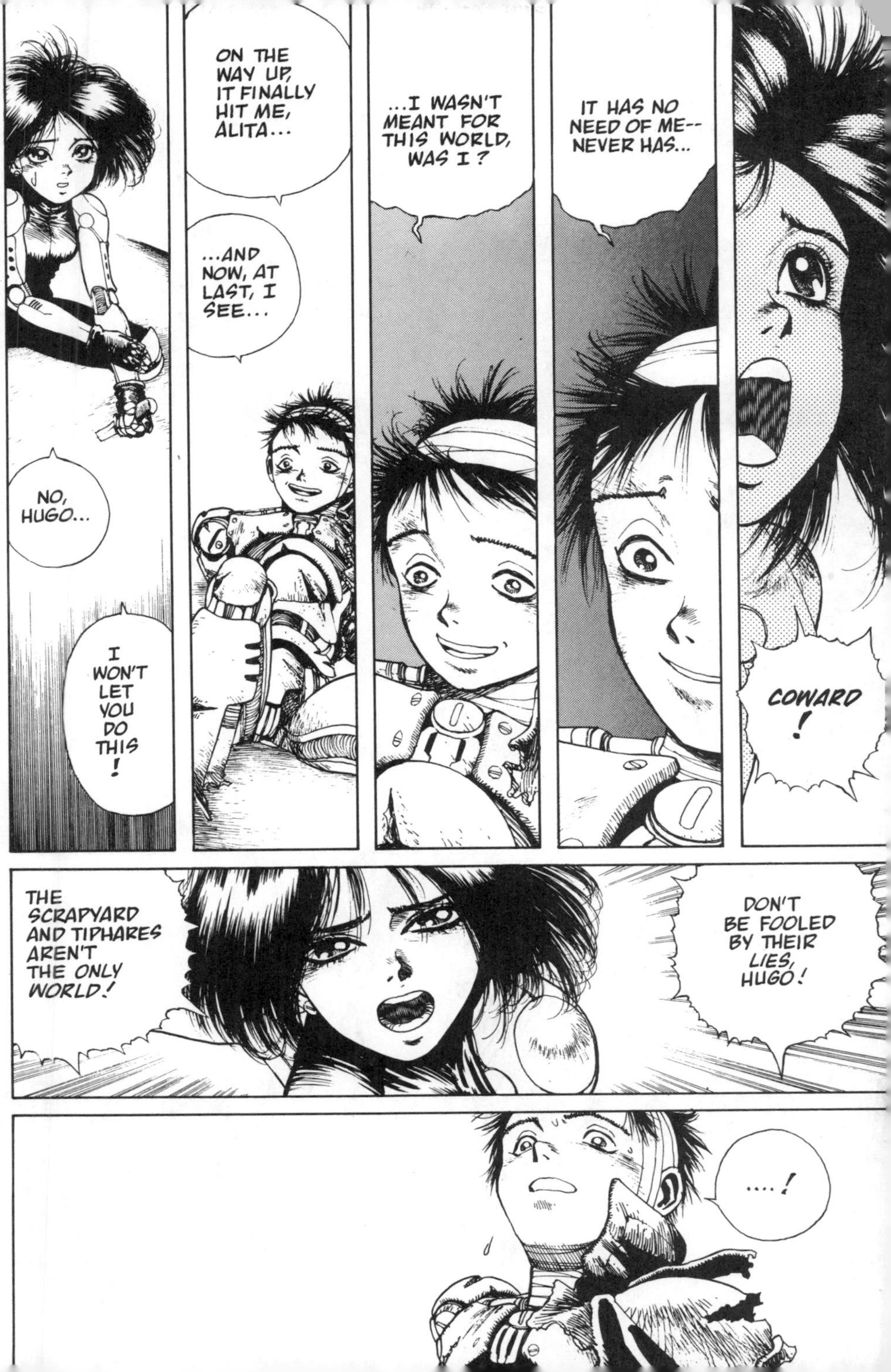
NO, HUGO...
I WON'T LET YOU DO THIS!
ON THE WAY UP, IT FINALLY HIT ME, ALITA...
...AND NOW, AT LAST, I SEE...
...I WASN'T MEANT FOR THIS WORLD, WAS I?
IT HAS NO NEED OF ME-- NEVER HAS...
COWARD!
THE SCRAPYARD AND TIPHARES AREN'T THE ONLY WORLD!
DON'T BE FOOLED BY THEIR LIES, HUGO!
....!

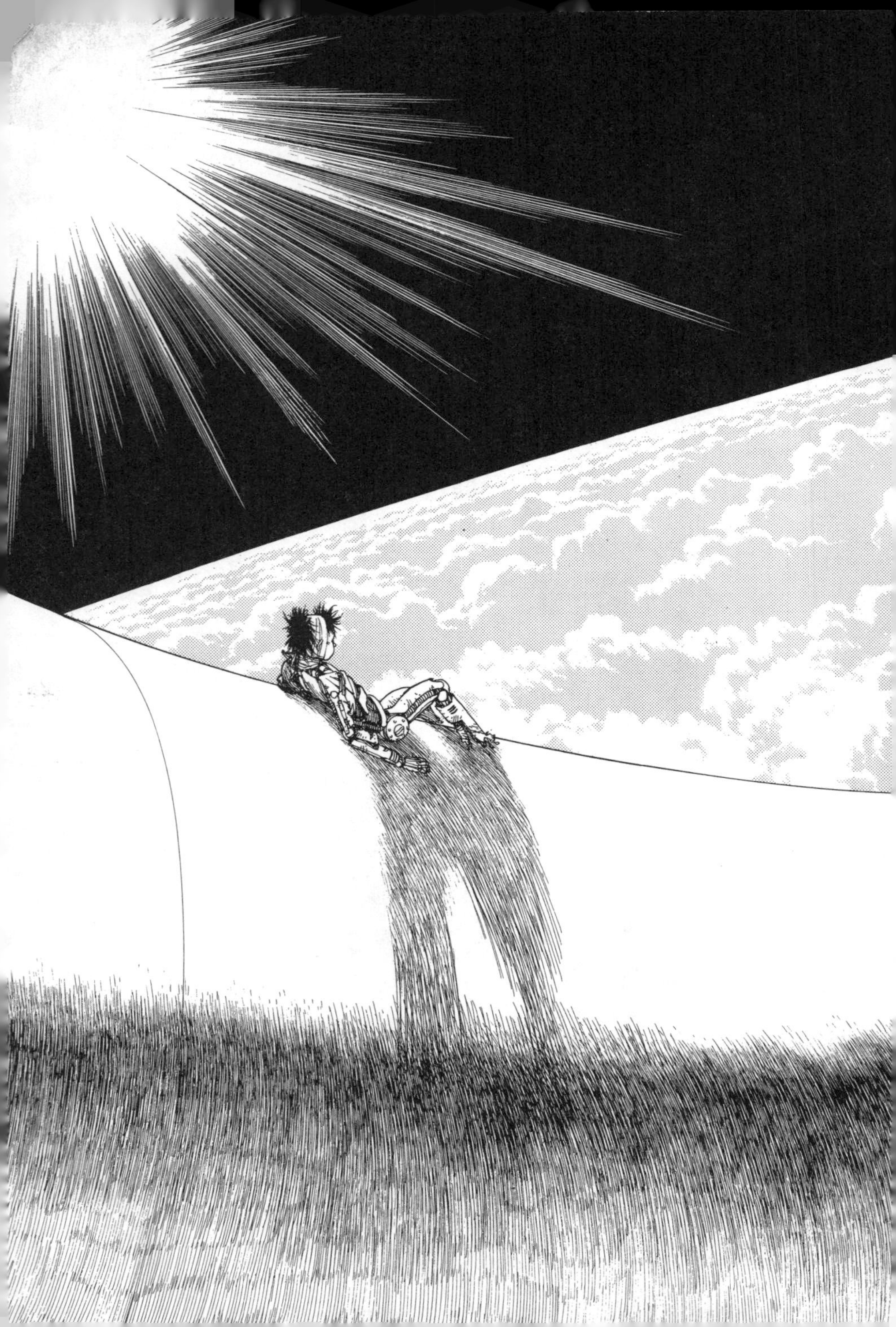

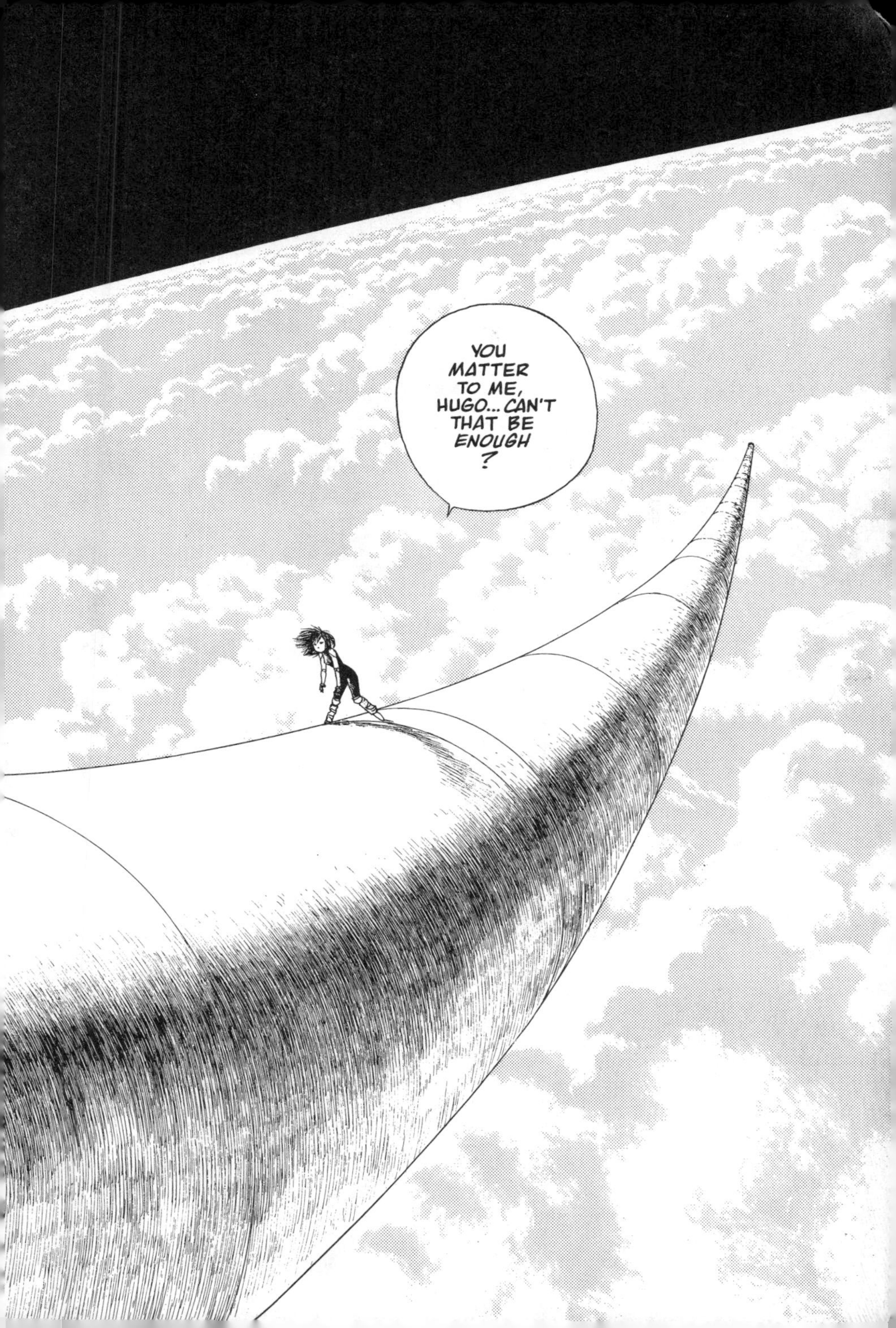
YOU MATTER TO ME, HUGO... CAN'T THAT BE ENOUGH ?

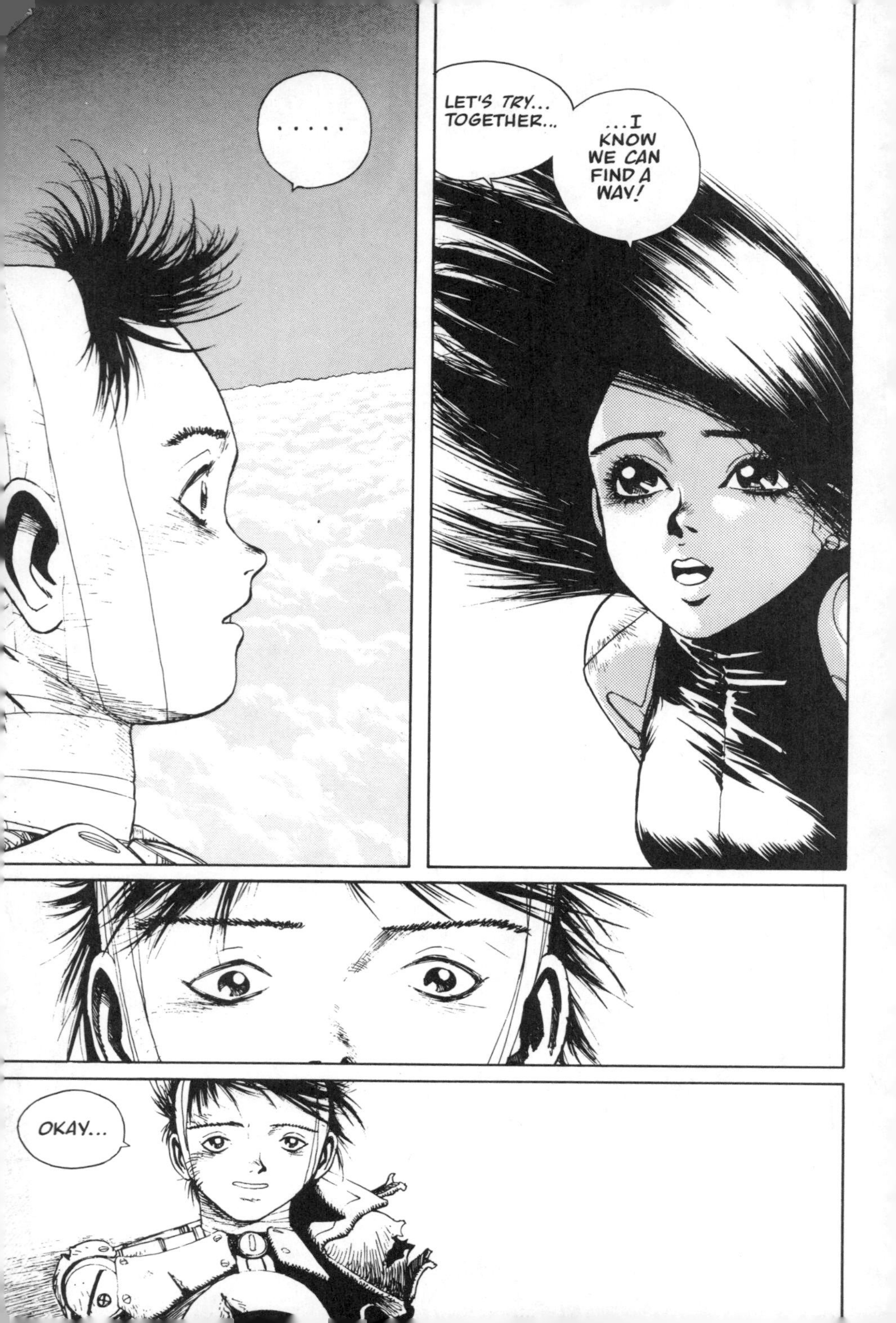
. . . . .
LET'S TRY... TOGETHER...
...I KNOW WE CAN FIND A WAY!
OKAY...

I'VE DONE IT--

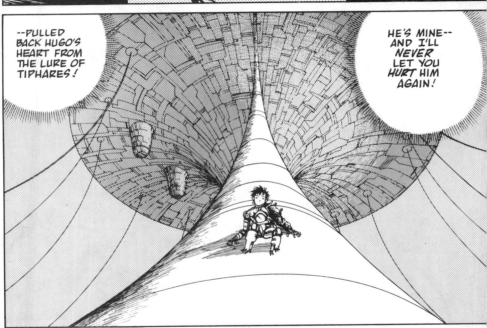

--PULLED BACK HUGO'S HEART FROM THE LURE OF TIPHARES!

HE'S MINE-- AND I'LL *NEVER* LET YOU *HURT* HIM AGAIN!

FWMMM

OH!

HUGO-- LOOK OUT!

FWM

MMV

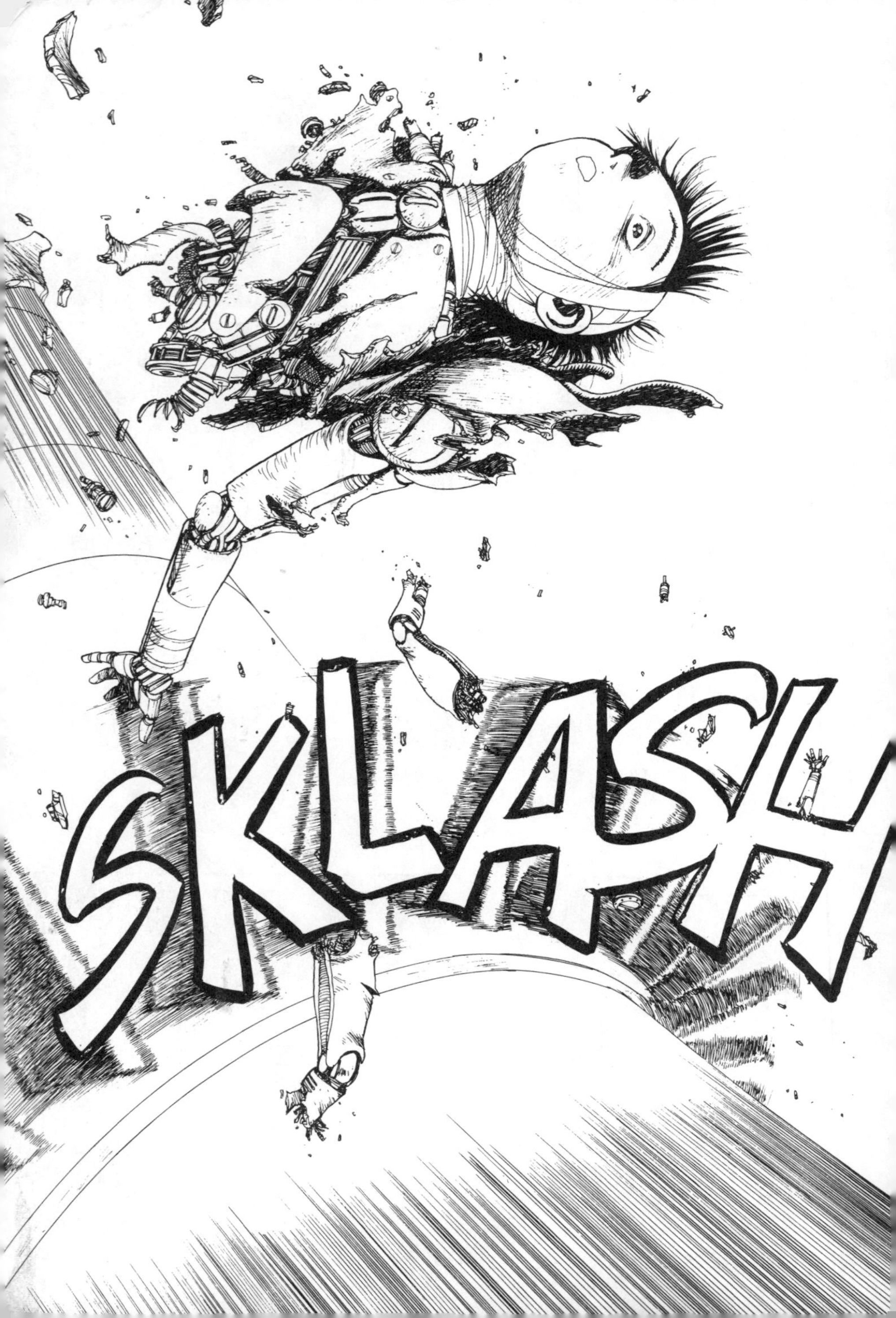
SKLASH

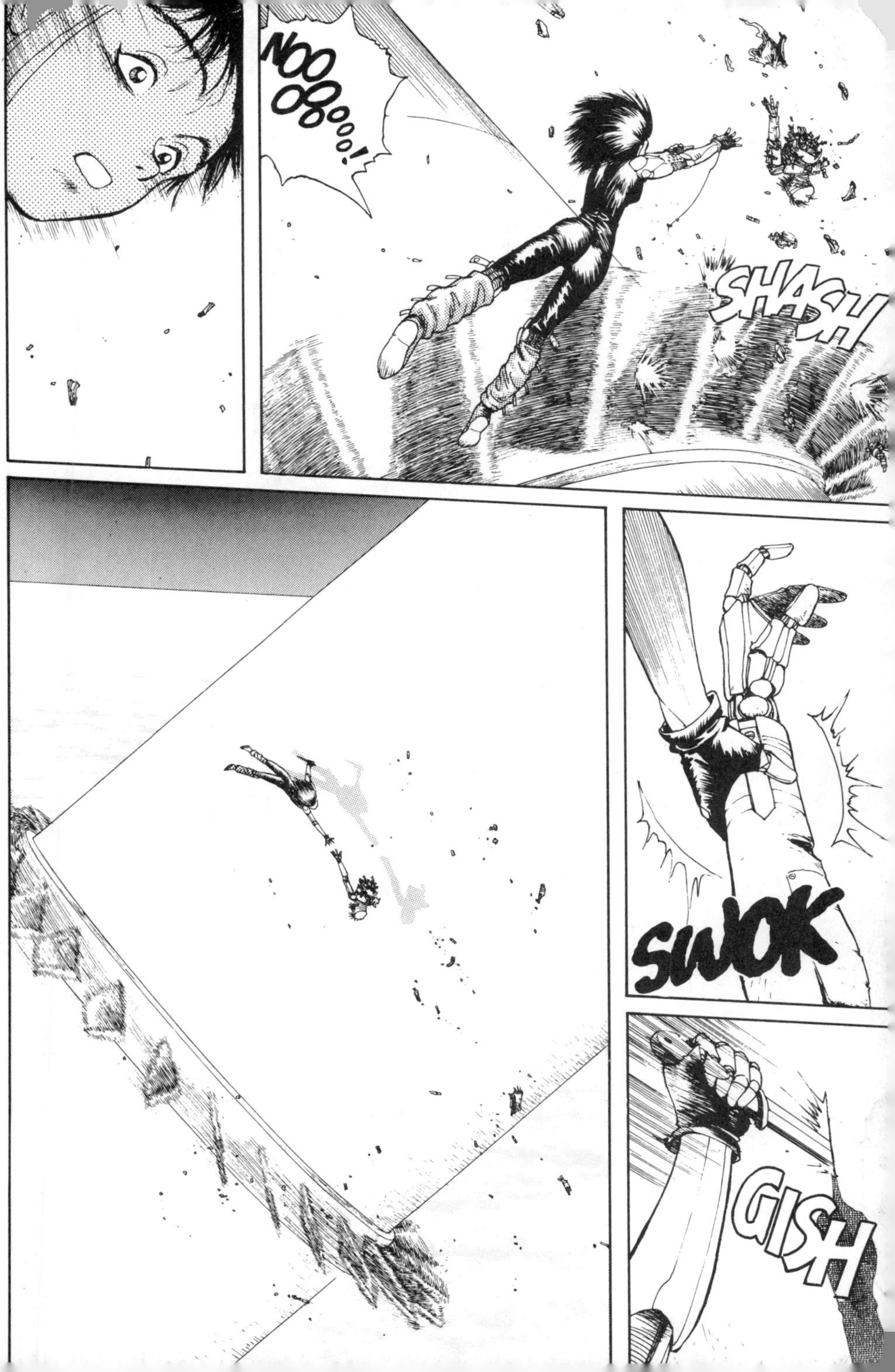

NOOOOOooo!!
SHASH
SWOK
GISH

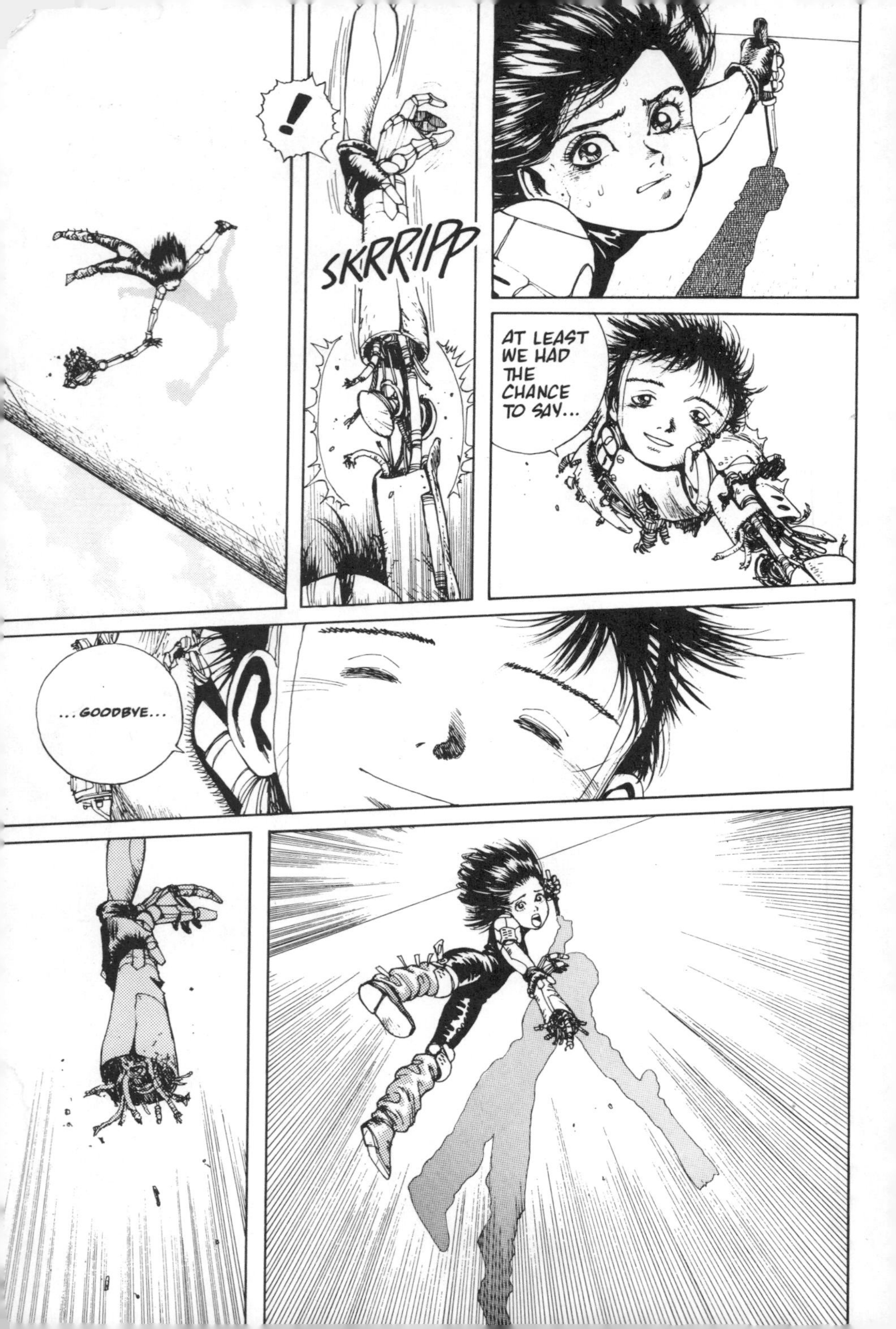
!
SKRRIPP
AT LEAST WE HAD THE CHANCE TO SAY...
...GOODBYE...

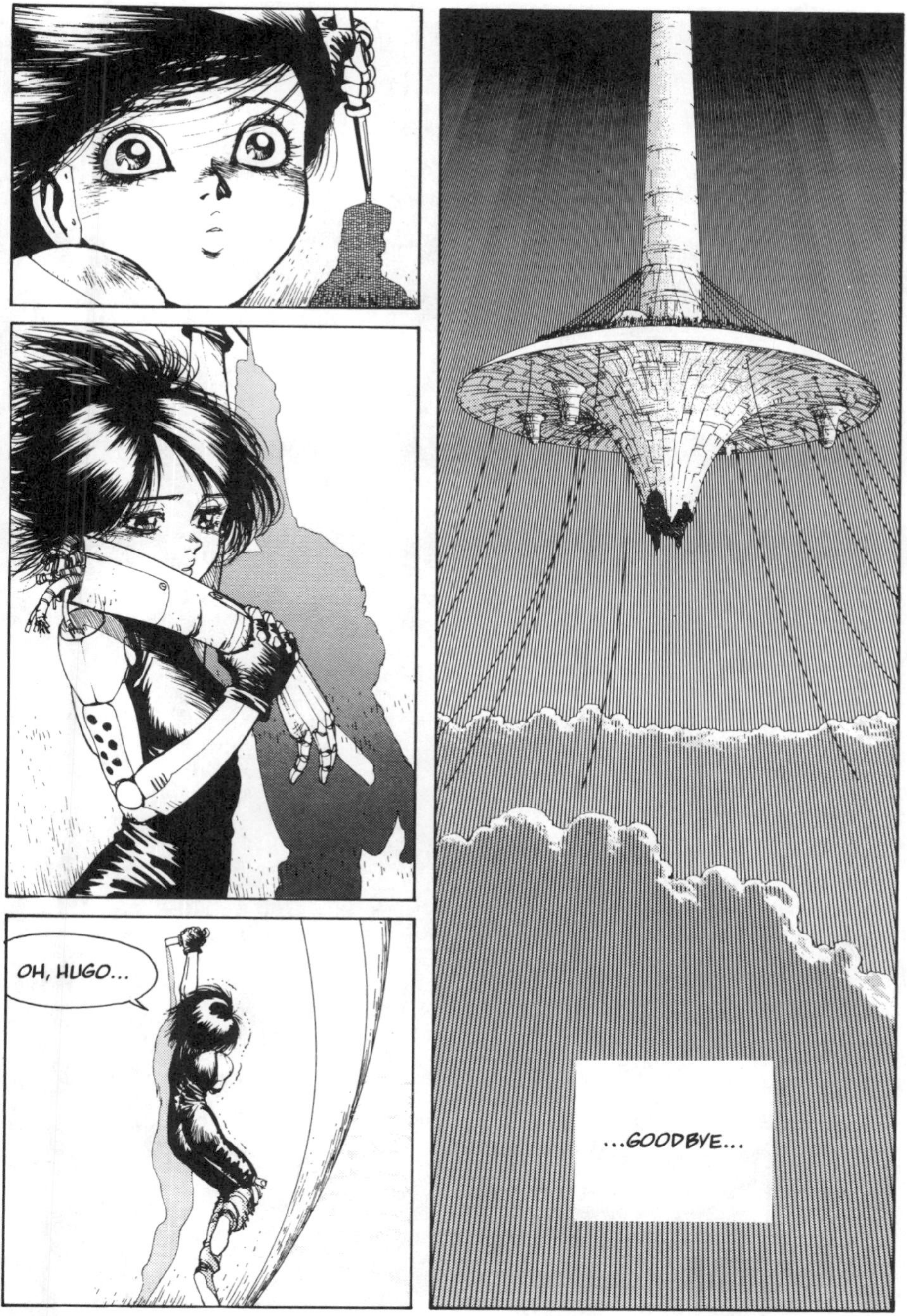
OH, HUGO...
...GOODBYE...

END

NEON GENESIS EVANGELION

ARMAGEDDON FILLS THE CRUMBLING SKY

On the threshold of the new millennium, private armies scour the Earth for super-advanced ancient technologies and artifacts. The powers of these artifacts could usher humanity into a new golden age. . . .or destroy it utterly.

▼

One teenager is all that stands between us and the apocalypse. How does he feel about it?

▼

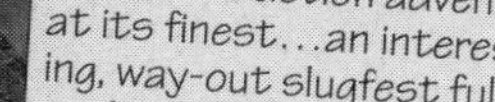

PERSONNEL FILE

NAME: Yu Ominae

CODE NAME: Striker

EMPLOYER: Arcam Foundation

SPECIAL ABILITIES: Outfitted with Arcam's Omihalcon armored muscle suit, this high school student's strength is multiplied thirty-fold. Arcam's top operative, Striker has proved his mettle in battle repeatedly.

ARCAM'S MISSION STATEMENT: To find and destroy or seal away extremely dangerous ancient technology and artifacts to keep them out of the wrong hands.

MISSION REPORTS:
Striker: The Armored Warrior
Striker: The Forest Of No Return
Striker vs. The Third Reich

ONLY A MONSTER COULD TAKE ME ON NOW!

STRIKER